EAST ASIA

HISTORY, POLITICS, SOCIOLOGY, CULTURE

Edited by
Edward Beauchamp
University of Hawaii

A ROUTLEDGE SERIES

EAST ASIA: HISTORY, POLITICS, SOCIOLOGY, CULTURE
EDWARD BEAUCHAMP, *General Editor*

BUILDING CULTURAL NATIONALISM IN MALAYSIA

Identity, Representation, and Citizenship

Timothy P. Daniels

Routledge
Taylor & Francis Group

NEW YORK AND LONDON

Published in 2005 by
Routledge

2 Park Square, Milton Park, Abingdon, Oxfordshire OX14 4RN
711 Third Avenue, New York, NY 10017

Routledge is an imprint of the Taylor & Francis Group, an informa business

First issued in paperback 2012

Library of Congress Cataloging-In-Publication Data
Daniels, Timothy P., 1960–
  Building cultural nationalism in Malaysia : identity, representation, and citizenship / Timothy P. Daniels.
    p. cm.—(East Asia : history, politics, sociology, culture)
  Includes bibliographical references and index.
  ISBN: 0-415-94971-8 (hardback : alk. paper)
    1. Malaysia—Politics and government. 2. Nationalism—Malaysia. I. Title. II. Series : East Asia (New York, N.Y.)

  DS.597.2.D29 2005
  306.2'09595--dc22   2005009246

  ISBN 978-0-415-94971-2 (hardback)
  ISBN 978-0-415-64630-7 (paperback)

For my mother, Lillian Baugh Daniels, who always told me to think for myself and not to follow the crowd.

Contents

PART IV

Illustrations

Acknowledgments

At the State University of New York of Buffalo, I would like to thank Dr. David Banks who influenced my interest in Southeast Asian ethnography. During area studies' courses and long personal discussions with Dr. Banks, my interest in Indonesian and Malaysian ethnography began to evolve. He inspired and motivated me to look beyond narrow, parochial concerns with Black Studies, African history, and Black experiences to bridge these ever important concerns with international and comparative perspectives. Dr. David Banks generously shared his field experiences in Malaysia and his fine expertise in the Malay language, and made a non-traditional student who had returned to university student life after many years of being away feel quite at home in an academic environment. His generous insights given after reading versions of this text have been of immense assistance. I owe Dr. Banks my heartfelt appreciation.

Continuing with academia at the Department of Anthropology at the University of Illinois, I found an intellectual atmosphere in which to thrive. I would like to thank my advisor, Dr. F.K. Lehman, and my committee members, Dr. Janet Keller, Dr. Arlene Torres, and Dr. Clark Cunningham for all their support and encouragement over the years. Each of these scholars has inspired my thinking in their own particular ways. My thanks go to Clark Cunningham for sharing his extensive knowledge of the ethnographic literature of insular Southeast Asia and his scholarship on processes of immigration and cultural change. My thanks go to Arlene Torres for her critical insights into analyzing race, ethnicity, and gender and careful attention to theoretical arguments about public representations and citizenship and nationality. I am also indebted to Arlene for her encouragement and practical support in the process of writing up this research. To Janet Keller I owe a great debt for her efforts to mold me into a solid cognitive anthropologist, for her interest in mental representations and ideology, and for her interest in practice and the dynamics of emerging knowledge. Finally, I owe many aspects of my research's theoretical orientation to Kris Lehman who, for many years, has helped to improve my ethnographic description and analyses. As an instructor and advisor, Kris has generously shared his theoretical perspectives and insights into fieldwork methodology. In addition, his ethnographic field notes computer program was an immense organizational aid during my second ten months in Melaka.

I also want to thank my family and friends in the U.S. for their continued support and encouragement. My thanks also go out to my sister and brothers for the attention they paid to me from a very young age up to the present. I also want to extend special thanks to my mother and my aunts and uncles for continued emotional and financial support over the years. Extra special thanks go out to my wife, Farichah Tri Askari, for her support and companionship during my second ten months of research in Melaka and for her patience and encouragement during the writing up process back in the U.S.

Funding for this doctoral research came from several institutions to which I am immensely grateful. My first ten months of research, from August 1998 to June 1999, were partially funded by a fellowship from the Department of Anthropology at the University of Illinois. My second ten months of research, from October 1999 to August 2000, were funded by a fellowship from the Fulbright-Hays, dissertation research abroad program. The Malaysian-American Commission on Educational Exchange (MACEE) was the institution to locally administer this Fulbright-Hays student research fellowship. I would like to extend special thanks to Kala, Andrew, Yati, and Sandra of MACEE for their assistance in getting my wife and I settled during my second period of research in Malaysia and for making our stay enjoyable. Andrew and Kala were immensely supportive in helping me to organize practical matters of travel and to acquire the required immigration documents and a local affiliate university. Kala, Yati, and Sandra also worked tirelessly to see that any problems of everyday life in Malaysia were speedily solved, or avoided. I also thank the Graduate College of the University of Illinois, which provided me with university fellowships in 1994 and 1995.

I would also like to thank the International Islamic University Malaysia (IIUM) for serving as my official Malaysian affiliate institution and the Department of Sociology and Anthropology at IIUM for accepting me as a visiting scholar and researcher. My thanks go out to Prof. Dr. Mohamed Aris Othman and Dr. Jamil Farooqui for making office space available to me in the department and for organizing a seminar for me to present some of my research findings. My thanks go out to Mohamed Aris

Othman for his assistance in getting me settled in Melaka and in helping me to make some of my initial contacts. I also thank Abdul Aziz, a lecturer in the department of sociology and anthropology, for driving me to Melaka and introducing me to some of his friends in the museum offices. My thanks also go out to several international students, including Burhan, Umar, and Koshar, at IIUM who generously shared their familiarity with the university facilities with me. Special thanks go out to Burhan for his assistance with my search for legal and constitutional sources in the IIUM library. In addition, my extensive discussions with Burhan and Umar, who have spent several years in Malaysia as visiting international students has contributed to my research insights.

I would also like to extend special thanks to several other institutions and organizations in Melaka. My thanks go out to the Museums Corporation of Melaka (PERZIM) for kind use of its facilities and their kind assistance in helping me to find temporary and more permanent lodging in the metropolitan area of Melaka. I also want to thank Rosli and Khamis for their information about local cultures and contacts. My thanks also go out to several voluntary associations and their members for welcoming my participation in their group activities and for their information about local cultures. I am exceedingly grateful to Dr. Ramesh for his medical care when I came down with a strain of typhoid fever. My thanks also go out to the Moidu family for their kindness and support. I would like to acknowledge the friendly reception and assistance I received from committee members, priests and devotees at the Sri Muthu Mariamman Temple, the Sri Poyatha Venayagar Moorthi Temple, the Cheng Hoon Teng Temple, the Yong Chuan Tian Temple, and the Siong Tay Kong Temple.

I also thank Dr. Bambang Purwanto and Dr. Catur Sugiyanto for their kind assistance during the stage of final revisions of this manuscript for publication while I was in Indonesia conducting research affiliated with the Center for Southeast Asian Social Studies, Gadjah Mada University.

My final and unending debt is to all of the local residents of Melaka who related to me in various ways during my almost two-year period of research. I am afraid that I cannot recount and name all of the people who I have interacted with in Melaka to whom I owe a debt of gratitude. I spent some time in most communities of Melaka and I would like to thank them all for their kindness and friendship. I would also like to thank personally a few of my important and close friends, hosts, and teachers. My special thanks go out to Cik Mat Azmi, Cik Mat Noor, Nor Arushah, and my "elder sister," Rosnah, for their kind support, assistance, and companionship. Long hours of conversation over Malaysian style tea and fried bread with

Azmi, Arushah, and Cik Mat Noor made my stay in Malaysia highly enjoyable and enlightening. Rosnah was an unending source of information, advice, and emotional support. I also want to thank Azmi and Noor for the kind transport they provided for me and my wife around Melaka and nearby towns and from Melaka to the airport. I also want to thank Kang Teck Ho for welcoming me into his home and for taking me to some ancient graves that are not easily accessible. My thanks also go to Jo Chua, Vanitha, Shanti, Firman, and Lok Yan for their kind support and assistance.

Preface

On Sunday, August 30, 1998, I sat with hundreds of local residents of Melaka huddled under tarpaulin and umbrellas watching the "Countdown to National Independence Day" program. This program occurred at night in between persistent bouts of rain on a stage, decorated with nationalist symbols and slogans, set up in front of the Declaration of Independence Memorial. A ruin of a colonial Portuguese fort and several old colonial buildings that government officials have turned into museums and marketed as tourist attractions, in a city billed as the "historic city," lie down the road in an area marked for "development." A recently built multistory hotel and large shopping center, and rows of small businesses are located in this area on land "reclaimed" from the sea. Melaka, formerly colonized by a succession of European regimes, Portuguese, Dutch and British, is now the capital city of a state of the same name, located in the southwestern portion of Peninsular Malaysia (see Map). The most recent census of Malaysia in 2000 records the Melaka state population as 635,791, (2.7% of the national population of 23.27 million) 63.8% *Bumiputera* ('sons of the soil'; Malays and other indigenous peoples), 29.1% Chinese, 6.5% Indians, and 0.6% "others." Melaka is also highly diverse in terms of religion, with 64.2% Muslims, 24.1% Buddhists, 5.6% Hindus, 3.9% Christians, and 1.5% Confucians/Taoists and followers of other traditional Chinese religion (Department of Statistics, Malaysia). Over half of the state population— 67.2% of the state population is urban, according to the 2000 Census—resides in the central district that includes the city of Melaka. On this occasion, the eve of the forty-first Malaysian Independence Day, a sample of this diverse population packed into seats and raised stands braving the intermittent gusts of wind and rain that followed them.

A Malay director of a development corporation and his wife and a Malay civil servant sat next to me on some cushioned seats that organizers had saved from earlier downpours by some tarpaulin laid over them. Before

organizers started the program, we spoke to each other and became acquainted. After the opening speech of the countdown program, the master of
ceremonies introduced a group of dancers who mounted the stage and performed to thundering applause. The dancers, four men and ten women, were
wearing various styles of dress. Rosli[1], the director of a local development
corporation, told me that the large red and blue headdress with flaps in the
back, worn by one of the female dancers, was a *"Minang"* style hat. Saiful,
the civil servant, added that these dancers represent all of the peoples in
Malaysia. He pointed out the attire that represented local Malay customs and
the customary Malay dress from other states. Then Saiful pointed out the
outfits that represented Chinese, Indians, and Portuguese. I asked if some of
these dancers were of these cultural categories, and Saiful, clarifying matters
for me, stated that all of the dancers were local Malays but their dress represented these various cultural categories. This Malay dance troupe performed
several dances, using a combination of dance styles, including Buddhist and
Hindu-style hand movements, and Portuguese, Hindu, and Malay footwork;
it was a "collage" of various categories of people and cultures in the state of
Melaka, and Malaysia as a whole, on a "Malay background." Malay performers were enacting diversity. Later in the evening, several Malay singers
and a few Chinese singers performed on stage. One of the Chinese performers sang in the Malay language and the other in Mandarin.

Some youngsters sang a song on two nationalist themes and campaigns: buying and supporting *buatan Malaysia* (Malaysian-made products)
and *Malaysia Boleh* (Malaysia Can Do It). Around 11PM, after a few hours
of performances, a male coordinator initiated a question and answer event
on stage shouting the question, *"Negara Kita Tanggung Jawab siapa?"*
("Our country is whose responsibility?"), several times, and the flag-waving
audience, shouted back the answer, *"Kita, Kita, Kita"* ("Ours, Ours,
Ours"). The coordinator asked Malay and Chinese youth, under the age of
eighteen, questions on nationalist themes, and other civil servants awarded
them prizes after they properly answered these questions.

This countdown program reached its climax when a Malay leader of a
white uniformed military outfit marched in front of the stage and saluted the
Chief Minister of the state of Melaka who handed him a large, folded
Malaysian flag. After receiving the flag, the uniformed man returned to his
troops, and led them to the flag post and raised the colors. As they raised the
Malaysian flag, the master of ceremonies announced that there were two
minutes remaining before midnight. After they raised the flag, the Chief
Minister of Melaka called out *"Merdeka"* (Freedom) three times and the
crowd answered with *"Merdeka"* three times. *"Merdeka"* continued to ring

through the large crowd and flags were waving in the hot and humid tropical air. These intense expressions of patriotism struck me as rather peculiar as people began to disperse out of the area in cars, on motorcycles, or on foot. I have rarely witnessed this sort of spirited display of national pride in local communities in the United States.

Developing a strong sense of national unity and identity has been a major concern of the recently independent Malaysian government. Events like the one described above and the National Independence Day celebrations the next day (see chapter five) took place in urban areas all over Malaysia. The ruling political elite use these events to explicitly promulgate nationalist ideals and to instill feelings of loyalty, attachment and belonging to the imagined national community (Anderson 1983). Although we should not assume that national governments' must invent cultural commonality in order to attain common political loyalty, the Malaysian government has definitely sought to do so. The subjects of Malaya, a British colony, did not achieve *Merdeka* or formal political independence in 1957 through a bloody struggle, or even a long-standing nationalist movement, that may have forged deep links between the diverse groups that composed colonial Malaya society. A predominantly Chinese communist insurgency did wage war against the colonial government for roughly ten years, from the late 1940s to the late 1950s, but their military campaign failed to attract significant cross-communal support before the government put it down (Andaya and Andaya 1982:257–161; Karl Hack 1999). British colonial rulers negotiated and worked with the leaders of the racially divided communities and eventually brokered an arrangement generally agreeable to the Malays, Chinese, and Indians, the three largest components of colonial Malaya. Perhaps none of the communities was satisfied totally with the compromise that resulted in *Merdeka* but at least it facilitated the hand-over of the formal reins of political power from Britain to local leaders. The resulting postcolonial situation I encountered in the late Twentieth Century defies simple description in terms of some popular pluralist and multicultural models.

Post-independence Malaysia has undergone many changes that distance it from the plural society models of J.S. Furnivall (1956 [1948]) and M.G. Smith (1965). Although discourses and institutionalized practices have perpetuated the "racially"[2] segmented society of colonial Malaya, in many respects, nowadays, more than in earlier periods, social groups in Malaysia, meet and interact in sites other than the marketplace (see Abdul Rahman Embong 2001). They visit each other's homes and go to public schools together where teachers conduct classes in the Malay language. They interact in social cliques engaging in recreational activities together and participate in voluntary associations with members of various racial groups and believers of different faiths (Ackerman and Lee 1988; Embong 2001; Armstrong 1988). It is common to find people of different racial groups worshipping in the same sacred places and taking part in the religious activities of other religions. The racial division of labor has begun to break down with members of social groups filling economic positions formerly occupied almost exclusively by other groups. In addition, diverse categories of persons increasingly inhabit many old neighborhoods and new residential estates—designated as "high, middle, and low income"—built within the last few decades.

On the other hand, many separate institutions that cater primarily to particular social segments are still prominent features of the social structure. There are Chinese and Indian schools in which the medium of education is Mandarin and Tamil respectively. Yet, these schools have to adhere to the criteria set by the government. Racial groups still maintain different kinship systems and religious institutions that are strongly associated with these particular groups. Recreational activities are often an extension of racially segmented associations and neighborhood groups. In Melaka, most Malays still reside in outlying villages and neighborhoods, Indians on or around agricultural estates, and Chinese in urban neighborhoods not far from the business district. Malays fill most of the civil service positions, Indians most plantation labor positions, and Chinese own most of the private businesses. There is a two-tiered legal and juridical system consisting of a national civil law system for all criminal cases and a dual state level system for personal and family law, one civil law system for non-Muslims and an Islamic law system only for Muslims. Amidst cultural diversity, there are many areas of shared values and standards. Even a "common will" is evident on many issues, while on others there remain deep-seated divisions. Although many aspects of a formerly plural colonial society exist, it is clear that "citizens" of post-independence Malaysia mix *and* combine.

In addition to deviating from the model of a plural society in terms of significant social, cultural, and institutional integration, Malaysian society also deviates in terms of the distinctive feature according to Smith, political domination by a cultural minority (cf. Mandal 2001:141–164; Siddique 2001:165–182). The Malay majority is the politically dominant group as they control the official reins of government. Ever since independence, the Malay component in the ruling alliance has been the dominant component. Yet, unlike many other societies with plural features, such as the US, Canada, and Brazil, the politically dominant group is not the economically dominant group. In Malaysia, the Malay majority finds itself at an economic disadvantage vis-à-vis a significantly large Chinese "minority" that has dominated the private economic sphere since independence despite numerous efforts by the Malay-dominated government to change this situation. In fact, this feature of political domination by an economically dominated majority distinguishes contemporary Malaysia from all *colonized* Southeast Asian and Caribbean plural societies discussed by Furnivall and Smith. However, Malaysia is not unique amongst other post-colonial Southeast Asian countries in this regard. This discontinuity in political and economic domination has been a source of continued tension in Malaysia and other post-colonial Southeast Asian countries such as Indonesia, Thailand, and the Philippines. This tension has taken different forms in these countries due to a number factors including demographics and varying patterns of assimilation, differentiation, and stratification. Nevertheless, the disproportionate control of wealth by Chinese "minorities" in these countries has led to official and intermittent suppression of overseas Chinese communities (see Skinner 1957, 1960; Lim 1983; Ong and Nonini 1997; Nonini 1997; Blanc 1997). It has also had an impact on overseas Indian integration and marginalization in Southeast Asia (see Mani 1993a, 1993b; Bachtiar 1993; Chandra Muzaffar 1993).

Contemporary Malaysian society does not fit into the model of an "egalitarian or democratic multicultural" (Rex 1996:2) society either. Rex argues that the distinctive feature of an ideal, multicultural society rests upon the distinction between the public and the private domain. "One might envisage a society which is unitary in the public domain but which encourages diversity in what are thought of as private or communal matters" (Rex 1996:15). Rex's model insists upon the sharing of a single political culture in the public domain, a "new abstract moral system" like the ones that emerged in European history with the development of "civil society." In contemporary Malaysian society there is no "unitary public domain" in the sense of political, economic, and legal rights that extend to all Malaysians. "Special rights" for the *Bumiputera* or natives of Malaysia are recognized in the Malaysian Constitution and in many subsequent laws such as the New Economic Policy. These laws extend special rights to land and other economic and educational benefits to the Malay majority and other members of the *Bumiputera* category. This complex of differential rights in the public domain are conventionally thought of as an effort to create a condition of equality, bringing the Malay majority "on par" with the other large segments of the Malaysian population, especially with the relatively prosperous Chinese segment. Thus, they are interpreted as a set of affirmative action programs discriminating in a positive sense to correct patterns of inequality rooted in the colonial era. Differential rights, with positive or negative motives, do not, and should not, exist in the public domain in Rex's ideal multicultural society.

In addition, separate legal institutions for personal and family law for Muslims and non-Muslims precludes the application of the multicultural model to Malaysian society. For Rex, and other "liberal" multiculturalists, separate legal institutions and laws for Muslims amount to the improper extension of a "folk" value system into the public domain as well as an unequal application of law: law in a properly "abstract" system would apply to all "citizens" in the same manner. On the other hand, cultural diversity in the private and communal arenas is recognized by the larger Malaysian society and viewed as a shining example of 'multiculturalism' for other nations to emulate, a form of state 'multiculturalism' (Bennett 1998; Sarkissian 2000:12).

The diverse social groups in Melaka are interconnected in a complex pattern of social relations that encompass economic, political, religious, organizational, and social-familial ties that defy explanation from a pluralist or multiculturalist perspective. These pluralist and multicultural "models," are at best descriptive typologies that are unable to account for widespread patterns of integration on the one hand and differential rights in the public sphere on the other. Although pluralist or multiculturalist models fail to adequately describe contemporary Malaysian society, versions of these notions and issues they traverse are part of competing local and national discourses. I will maintain an ambivalent position on top-down and bottom-up forms of multicultural ideology that are characteristic of competing discursive fields in Malaysia (see Bennett 1998:3–4), and argue that several key conceptions are embedded within these discourses, conceptions which impinge on the quality of belonging to Malaysian society. My task will be to move beyond failed typologies and the level of societal classification to cognitively describe and analyze belonging in contemporary Malaysian society.

TOWARDS A COGNITIVE DESCRIPTION AND ANALYSIS OF BELONGING

In Melaka, I observed several public celebrations and exhibitions, such as the "Countdown to National Independence Day" celebrations described above, that tend to include diverse social groups, or at least cultural markers associated with them, while simultaneously laying stress upon one social group, the Malay majority, and their cultural markers. Many ethnographers of contemporary Malaysian society have made similar observations (Sarkissian 1997, 1998, 2000; Nonini 1997). Sarkissian (1997, 1998) describes how

Melaka's regional culture shows include Malay, Chinese, Indian, and Eurasian dance performances, but are biased towards Malays. Chinese, Indian, and Eurasian dances are staged but they lack the multiplicity of Malay dance forms. Nonini (1997:206–8) notes that many contested cultural issues revolve around state imposed policies that assume a "Malaysian national culture" based upon Malay culture. This pattern of state cultural politics—of state 'pluralist multiculturalism'or 'multiculturalist pluralism'—tends to express and reproduce a hierarchical sense of belonging. Everyone belongs to the "national community" but not as much or in the same way. I will argue that social groups have their sense of belonging and qualitative citizenship shaped by state policies as well as their own efforts at being fully incorporated into the larger society (see Rosaldo 1994a, 1994b, 1997; Ong 1993, 1999; Ong and Nonini 1997; Mitchell 1997; Flores and Benmayor 1997).

Similarly, social relations in households and families, religious sites, and voluntary associations and cliques tend to span diverse social groups but not in the same ways. All social groups tend to interact in these varied settings, but they include Malays and non-Malays in different fashions. People often expressed contrasting and ambivalent ideas and feelings about their incorporation in Malaysian society; on the one hand, everyone is an equal member of Malaysia's multiracial society, but on the other hand, some members are second and third class "citizens." I will focus upon how local people in Melaka make sense of these seemingly contradictory ideas and practices and how their negotiations and resolutions relate to their qualitative citizenship in Malaysian society. I argue that there are two deep-seated and diffuse, seemingly opposed and contradictory notions, and alternative models, in Malaysian society constraining processes of inclusion and exclusion and contributing substantially to senses of belonging of local people in Melaka. These two key notions and alternative models pertain to hopeful and legal connections between diverse groups and Malay privilege and entitlement. Negotiations of these notions also underlie and are partially productive of patterns of cultural representation and social relations.

FIELDWORK IN MELAKA

This study is based upon research I conducted the research during two ten-month stays in Melaka, from August 1998 to June 1999 and from October 1999 to August 2000. When I first arrived in Melaka, Malaysia was in the midst of an economic crisis, after a few decades of steady economic growth, its economy was on a downward spiral like the economies in most Southeast Asian countries. A few months after my arrival, Malaysia fell into a political crisis as well, following the arrest and imprisonment of the highly popular Deputy Prime Minister, Anwar Ibrahim. These turn of events made some of the concerns of my study even more significant. After a few short stints of research in Indonesia, I was wondering how Malaysia was staving off mass riots while racial and religious violence swept across the Indonesian archipelago. I figured that the multicultural policies of the Malaysian government had a lot to do with it, and I still do but not in the same way. Thus, it was with this research question that I set out to analyze the relationship between representations of regional identity, public festivals, and the formation of social cliques and voluntary associations. Melaka, a city with a long cosmopolitan history and relatively diverse population (see chapters 2 and 3) compared to other parts of Peninsular Malaysia was a perfect site for such a study. My aim was to discern to what extent multicultural representations and practices contribute to the emergence of interracial social cliques and associations. I hypothesized that I would find interracial social cliques and voluntary associations in Melaka, in contrast to their general absence in Palembang, Indonesia due to the way regional culture shows and inter-religious open house visiting structure feeling (R. Williams 1977; B. Williams 1988) and contribute to a sense of belonging.

My methodology included participant-observation, collecting surveys, public and organizational records, and hundreds of open-ended and structured interviews and discussions with friends and contacts. My most important survey involved presenting local residents of Melaka with an empty map of the city and asking them to fill it in with the kinds of people who inhabit these spaces. This survey provided data on the local categories of persons and their associations with particular urban spaces (see chapters three and seven). In addition, I used non-leading prompts to elicit assumptions and meanings that constrain the ways local people draw these maps. After I have developed contacts in each locally constructed "racial" community and made some initial observations of public celebrations and social interactions, I began to conduct open-ended semi-structured interviews. In these interviews, I gathered data on the class and status backgrounds of clique and association members. I used Davis, Gardner and Gardner's (1988 [1941]) and Drake and Cayton's (1993 [1945]) method of combining local perceptions of status with occupational, educational or income data. These data allowed me to analyze the social scope of these social organizations. Following the first round of open-ended interviews and recorded verbal behaviors during performance, I conducted a preliminary discourse analysis in the field using cognitive methods of micro-analyzing a segment of discourse in order to develop explicit models of tacit cultural knowledge (Agar and

Hobbs' 1985; Holland and Eisenhart 1990; Strauss 1992; Witherspoon 1977; Quinn 1985, 1987; Hutchins 1980; Lehman CSRN).

Although my analytic methods take note of linguistic cues and consider the significance of language in local communities, I attempt to make a consistent distinction of linguistic cues, semantic and syntactic, and cognition (see Lehman 1995). The fact that my respondents spoke a number of languages, including Malay, English, Tamil, and Mandarin, and I was only competent to conduct interviews in Malay and English, complicated my task. My respondents had at least one of these two languages in their linguistic repertoire and some of them spoke all four. I conducted a microanalysis of discourse recorded in Malay before translation into English, using the same standards of data analysis that I used with discourse recorded in English or with combinations of Malay and English. In many cases, my respondents used Malay terms in otherwise English language contexts and I attempt to take account of the meanings of these words in this context as well as the meaning of language shifts. More importantly, in my analytic methods, I strive to take into account of the possibility of a variety of underlying models and schemata respondents' expressed in the same language or across languages as well as the possibility of their expressing the same or similar models and schemata across languages. For instance, Quinn (1985) found that speakers of English using the same lexical item "commitment" held three different underlying models. My analytic methods, stemming from an intensionalist approach to meaning rather than an objectivist approach, allow for variability and similarity of underlying cognition in Malay and English discourse (see Lehman 1995).

From this preliminary discourse analysis, I formulated more specific and structured interviews. These focused upon eliciting specific responses as well as employing native intuitions to test the validity of my explicit constructions. I then returned to make more independent observations and repeated cycles of discourse analysis and interviews and participation in order to further refine these models (Holland and Quinn 1987; Keller and Keller 1996; Lehman 1997).

In the process of making contacts for admission and acceptance into social and religious activities and for later discussions and interviews, I had to negotiate many negative attitudes about Muslims and Americans. In the Chinese, Indian, and *Melaka Portugis* non-Muslim communities, people initially suspected me, as a Muslim, of being similar in worldview and values to Malay Muslims, who members of these communities were often in conflict with over a range of political, economic, and cultural issues. Over time, many members of these communities came to make a distinction between me, as an

American Muslim, and local *Malay* Muslims. Despite the fact that I was not a reflection of their prototypical *American,* seeing that I am "Black" and not "White," they still associated cosmopolitan and "modern" perspectives and values with me in contrast to the narrow and parochial views they frequently associated with Malays. On the other hand, in the Malay and Indian Muslim communities, while I was welcomed as a fellow Muslim, I was occasionally not trusted or criticized because I am an *American.* Some Malays felt that I may be a spy in the service of anti-Muslim American interests or that I share "liberal" perspectives frequently expressed in criticism of Muslim societies. Over time, many Malay and Indian Muslims came to see me as distinct from some American politicians and leaders who express these perspectives. Sometimes these issues arose early in my negotiation of relationships with members of these communities, and sometimes they arose later or not at all, but they were always a concern of mine after coming up earlier in my field-work experience. For instance, when the U.S. was engaged in hostile relations with some predominantly Muslim countries, Malay Muslims often queried me about the rationale behind U.S. international policy and the often adversarial stance to Muslims around the world. Moreover, following the controversial and much publicized statements of U.S. Vice President Al Gore, who was in Malaysia representing President Clinton at the APEC Business Summit in November of 1998, members of Malay and non-Malay communities questioned me and hurled verbal attacks at me as the resident-American. Vice President Gore reportedly applauded the "brave Malaysian people" for demanding *"reformasi"* in the streets of Kuala Lumpur, what was interpreted in the national media as gross intervention in the affairs of Malaysia. I had to negotiate these and other issues carefully as I built and developed relationships in Melaka's diverse society.

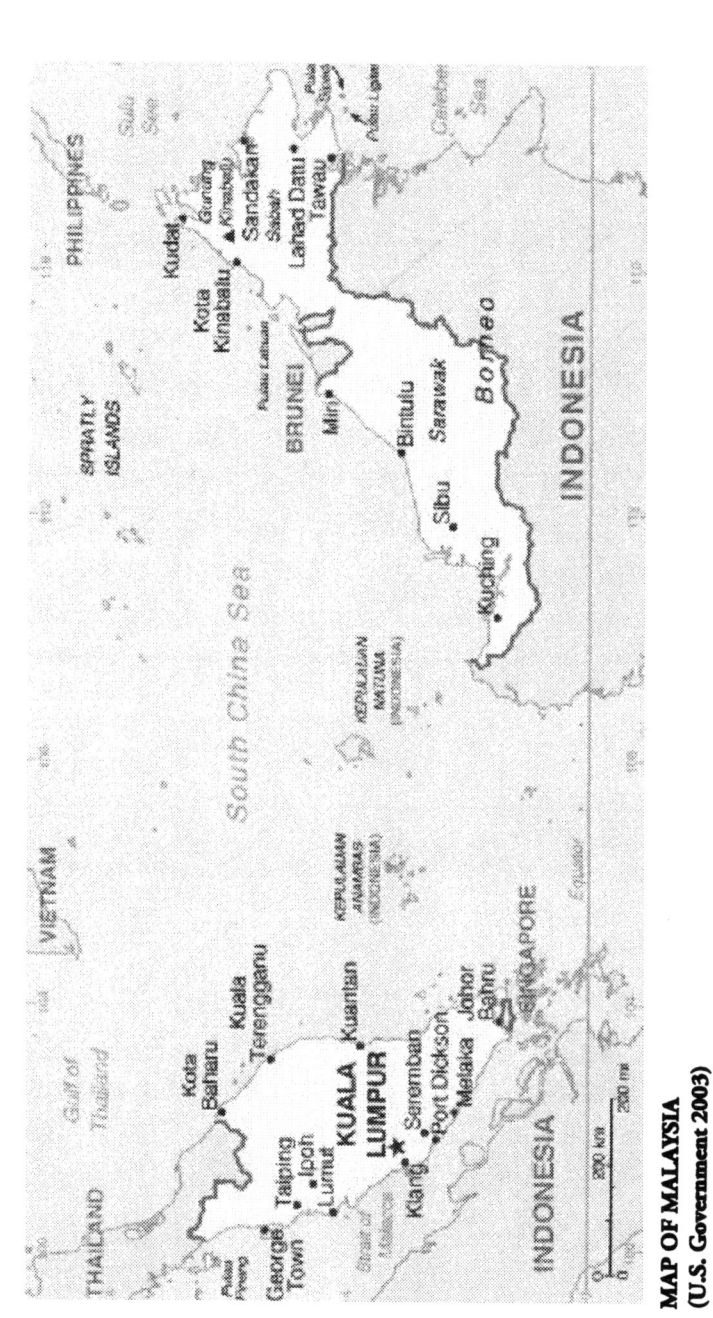

MAP OF MALAYSIA
(U.S. Government 2003)

Part I

Chapter One
Nation, Citizens, and Theorizing Belonging

NATIONS, CITIZENS, AND BELONGING

After over forty years of political independence, Malaysians are still aflame with nationalist sentiments and yearnings, which were not even dampened by the heavy rain punctuating the "Countdown to National Independence Day" program. Most Malaysians I have spoken with, evoking a conventional sense of togetherness, were convinced that their unity would withstand the scorching effect of economic and political crises. The apparent contradiction between their intense outpouring of patriotism and expressions of hopeful togetherness, and the Malay-bias of such public celebrations, not to speak of tensions over Malay privileges bestowed upon the political and cultural majority, struck me early in my research period in Melaka. Could these public expressions just be a hopeful facade masking a fire below? Could these politically orchestrated displays actually resonate with people in local communities in Melaka?

I set out to understand the views and interpretations of diverse members of Malaysian society about their situation and relationships to each other. I also tried to comprehend how they conceive of these apparent contradictions, in public events and social relations, and possibly resolve them. In my efforts to analyze the views of Malaysians of various backgrounds, I became disappointed with popular pluralist and multiculturalist perspectives, which failed to adequately describe and provide a framework for understanding social structures and local knowledge of people in Melaka. Thus, I turned to refining some new ideas about citizenship and belonging, and combining them with a cognitive perspective, which strives to understand the knowledge and practices of everyday people in contexts such as public celebrations.

3

This study examines processes of qualified or cultural citizenship and belonging in Melaka, Malaysia. It focuses upon diverse residents of this southwestern state of Peninsular Malaysia (see Map) and their negotiations of belonging and incorporation in Malaysian society. I take public celebrations and exhibitions, religious festivals and open house visiting, and interracial and inter-religious voluntary associations and cliques and intermarriages as sites through which to describe and analyze these processes of negotiation. I argue residents of Melaka and local and national leaders use several representations, schemata and models, of Malaysian society to create dominant and alternative senses of belonging and qualitative citizenship. In this chapter, I will discuss some theoretical issues surrounding conceptions of "nation" and "citizenship" and present the cognitive approach I will use to examine negotiations of qualified citizenship and belonging.

Many contemporary scholars have interrogated the taken-for-granted notions of "nation" and "citizenship" from a constructionist perspective and pointed out how these mental objects are discursive formulations (Anderson 1983; Jackson and Penrose 1993; Manzo 1996; Dominquez 1989; Yuval-Davis 1991; Gilroy 1987, 1991; Maurer 1997). As is the case with many related social and cultural constructs such as race, ethnicity, and gender, "nation" and "citizenship" are an integral part of social relations and are constitutive of structures of inequality (see Maurer 1997; Chavez 1998 [1992]). Jackson and Penrose (1993:7–8) historicize the notion of "nation" and note that discourses of "nation" have been, and are underlain with four distinct, but often overlapping senses: "nation" as "racial group," "nation" as cultural entity, "nation" as political entity, and "nation" as synonymous with "country," a territorial unit. The "liberal" notion of "nation" as a political entity emerged in eighteenth century Europe out of struggles against religious and dynastic empires. This notion congealed out of a surfeit of cultural materials from numerous interactions and diffusion of ideas of peoples inside and outside of Europe (cf. Anderson 1983; Maurer 1997; Wallerstein 1974). It is not of purely European origin, but it took shape in Europe in a particular fashion before Europeans exported it back around the world. An abstract notion of "the people," defined as "citizens" who had a rightful claim to power, developed in opposition to traditional modes of legitimizing and resting power in the hands of the Church and royal families.

After congealing in Europe from a long history of interactions among diverse peoples, this liberal notion of "nation" was intertwined in the European world system (cf. Wallerstein 1974) and implanted into colonies and former colonies (Anderson 1983; Bennett 1996; Flores et al. 1999). These liberal notions of "nation" and "citizenship" are part of present day discourses in places around the world where governments profess to be democracies, republics, as well as monarchies and theocracies. They are nearly global phenomena and need to be studied from a cross-cultural perspective analyzing their particular forms and histories in particular societies (see Yuval-Davis 1991; Ong 1999; Manzo 1996).

It is not surprising, though it is important to mention, that these widely exported liberal notions appeared to have entailed inherent contradictions from the very start. The political rulers had to deal with, on the one hand, pre-existing structures of inequality, those between the rising capitalist ruling classes and the peasants for instance, and on the other hand, new problems of membership in these new national "communities." Mauer (1997:124–127) argues that Hobbes' dictum, "nature hath made men equall," exemplifies a critical shift in Enlightenment thought towards separating the "laws of nature" and the "laws of men," two things previously held to be one and the same in Renaissance thought. According to Maurer, "Nature" rather than God would now explain structures of inequality that persist despite the regulating and equalizing influences of liberal law. Similarly, Anderson (1983) assumes that a loosening of the mental grip of theological thinking is part of the cultural roots of modern nations and nationalism.

Although there is a strong tendency in liberal thought to make an ideological break from religion we should not be to so quick to take liberal prescriptions as factual and assume that religion does not continue to play a role in the explanation of structures of inequality in liberal nations. Manzo (1996) argues that "modern" nations are hybrids of old and new ideologies, including racial theory and biblical theology, and that overlapping Christian narratives of race and religion have been disseminated around the world. Similarly, Drake (1993 [1945]:263–286) demonstrates how Christian and democratic values were intertwined in the process of explaining the racial hierarchies of the American plantation system (see Daniels 2000:34, 39–40). Moreover, as we study nations, nationalism, and citizenship cross-culturally, we should not discount the influence of other religions, Islam and Buddhism for instance, upon local understandings of social stratification.

In whatever manner scholars have viewed the role of religious thought in relation to liberal nations, they have often noted the contradiction between social stratification and notions of equality. Benedict Anderson (1983:7) rests his very definition of the "nation" as an imagined political *community* upon its ability to transcend whatever structures of inequality that may exist. He states that the "nation" is "imagined as a *community*, because, regardless of the actual inequality and exploitation that may prevail in each, the nation is always conceived as a deep, horizontal comradeship."

From Anderson's perspective, it is this image of belonging to a community of equals that has motivated its members to great lengths, even to kill and to be killed. This "deep, horizontal comradeship" fulfills the need to create a mental realm in which its citizen-members, divided in status and interests, can unite in common identity and common will—possessing an abstract "homogeneous citizenship" and collective motives—as belongers in a limited collectivity of fundamentally similar persons (cf. Maurer 1996–17–18). Yet we must consider the *means* of limiting membership in these imagined communities and the ways in which structures of inequality are also imagined and linked to, and potentially constitutive of, images of the nation. In this regard, I will contribute to this literature on the contradictions of liberal nations by considering how in the case of contemporary Malaysia, citizen-members hold and negotiate horizontal, relatively egalitarian, as well as vertical, hierarchically arranged, images of the nation.

St. Clair Drake (1993[1945]:263–286) argues that the apparent contradiction between liberal democratic and Christian ideals and patterns of social hierarchy and exclusion is resolved by the realization that liberal democratic and Christian ideals are not the "beliefs people live by." The beliefs people live by are the various notions people use to draw distinctions between people and to evaluate human worth, notions that naturalize difference and constitute structures of inequality. Drake argues that evaluative ideas that congealed around "blood"—the innate essence assumed to differentiate races—served to erect racial hierarchies and direct the practice of racial discrimination in the US. Maurer (1996) argues that "Nature" is implicated both in the principles designed to determine membership in the liberal nation as well as in the construction of social hierarchies.

He notes that the two primary criteria historically used to determine nationality and citizenship are the "law of blood"—that follows the principle of inheritance of citizenship from parent to child—and the "law of soil"—that follows the principle of basing citizenship upon the place of birth. Both of these criteria are mutually constitutive, to some degree, and serve to naturalize one's legal membership in liberal nations. Maurer (ibid:123–136) shows how the legal shift, following the 1981 British Nationality Act, from the "law of soil" to the "law of blood" created a new group of "outsiders" and "nonbelongers," turning many immigrants who were "born in" the British Virgin Islands into "aliens." Legal citizenship was a basis of social inequality resting on essentialized distinctions between citizens and "nonbelongers." Yet, many of these immigrants who were excluded from legal citizenship contested the basis of their exclusion and formulated a sense of "cultural citizenship."

LEGAL AND CULTURAL CITIZENSHIP

Out of this contemporary literature about "citizenship" and the growing awareness of the inequality embedded in the notions of "citizen" and "nation" and constructions of national identities, has emerged an important analytic distinction between legal and cultural citizenship. Contemporary analysts have noted how the "concept of the citizen as a purely formal, culturally 'empty,' exchangeable identity—unmarked by regional, ethnic or cultural differences" has this "emptiness" filled in practice "by the naturalised or 'invisible' properties of the socially dominant (or 'national') group" (Bennett 1998:8). Paul Gilroy (1987, 1991) notes how the categories "black" and "British," or "black" and "European" tend to be mutually exclusive. Flores and Benmayor (1997) state the same goes for "nonwhite" and "American" in the US. Similarly, Yuval-Davis (1991) and Renato Rosaldo (1994a, 1994b) note that women are marginal citizens in European and American national communities typically imagined as fraternities of equal white males. White males are the generic citizen-members of national identities such as "British" and "American," and other categories of persons defined by various intersections of racial, ethnic, and gender difference are conditional citizen-members. This conditional status persists even though these citizen-members fulfill the requirements of legal citizenship.

The concept of cultural citizenship includes the processes and histories of legal citizenship but goes beyond them "to encompass a range of gradations in the qualities of citizenship" (Rosaldo 1994a:57). Legal citizenship here should not be considered as being static or in any way given simply by the possession or fulfillment of legal requirements or the lack thereof, but should be considered as constructed through historical and political processes as well. The legal opinions and criteria in regard to citizenship change over time and are imbued with cultural meanings, aspirations and values. On the other hand, many people who do not have the documents required to satisfy the requirements of legal citizenship, may still develop a sense of belonging, and become partially incorporated within society (see Chavez 1998 [1992]; Flores 1997:255–277). Rosaldo (ibid: 57) states that,

> "cultural citizenship refers to the right to be different (in terms of race, ethnicity, or native language) with respect to the norms of the dominant national community, without compromising one's right to belong, in the sense of participating in the nation-state's democratic processes."

For Rosaldo, "cultural citizenship" is a sense of belonging or qualitative citizenship for subordinate social identities—distinct in some fashion from the dominant majority—and the processes in which they claim rights. His conception does not include the qualitative citizenship of dominant majorities such as the "natives" of Fiji and Malaysia who often feel left out "in their own countries" or the whites of the United States who occasionally express similar sentiments. It appears to me that much of this sort of "nativist" discourse includes qualitative citizenship and belonging and should be encompassed within the concept of cultural citizenship. Although members of such groups are conventionally thought to be the default citizen-members of national communities, they may also develop a sense of second-class citizenship or marginalized first class citizenship due to particular social and political policies or processes.

In addition, Rosaldo (1994a, 1994b, 1997), and Flores and Benmayor (1997) lay stress upon the agency of subordinate, non-majority, groups in their collective quests to attain full citizenship rights and inclusion in the general society. Flores and Benmayor (1997:15) state that "cultural citizenship can be thought of as a broad range of activities of everyday life through which Latinos and other groups claim space in society and eventually claim rights." Aihwa Ong (1999:264) criticizes this conception of cultural citizenship as being one-sided, with its emphasis upon the agency of subordinate groups, and adoptive of the "liberal principle of universal equality" it seeks to critique. In contrast, Ong (1999:264) proposes a conception of cultural citizenship that takes both sides of unequal power relationships into account, the agency of subordinates and the domination of the state and civil institutions:

> "In contrast, I use 'cultural citizenship' to refer to the cultural practices and beliefs produced out of negotiating the often ambivalent and contested relations with the state and its hegemonic forms that establish the criteria of belonging within a national population and territory. Cultural citizenship is a dual process of self-making and being-made within webs of power linked to the nation-state and civil society."

Ong (1999) and Mitchell (1997) apply this conception of cultural citizenship to wealthy Chinese immigrants who negotiate their incorporation in American and Canadian societies. In both cases, dominant notions of what it means to be citizen-members of national and local communities discipline them, and their agency is largely limited to appropriating dominant Orientalist discourses to negotiate inclusion in these societies (see also Ong 1993). Lacking the capital and status of these wealthy Chinese immigrants, Cambodian immigrants appear to be almost completely passive recipients of subject-making processes administered by the state and church institutions (see Ong 1999). Similarly, Ong and Nonini (1997) and Nonini (1997) tend to stress state domination in the same manner and exhibit a highly restricted notion of agency consonant with their adoption of Foucault's notion of hegemony. In contrast, I will attempt to correct this flaw by utilizing a less rigid notion of hegemony, one in which citizen-members, disciplined by dominant subject-making processes, are able to produce cultural forms and practices that are not just the "effects" of domination and technologies of power (see Daniels 2000a:38).

This more fluid approach to hegemony and "self-making" is essential for explicating the roles of voluntary associations, participation in festivals and celebrations, interpretations of museum exhibits, and so on, in relation to the growth of a more "civil" society in which diverse "citizen-members" are included as full participants (see Hefner 2001:10). As Hefner points out, voluntary associations, potentially important "social capital" for civil society, may foster *or* hinder the development of a political culture conducive to inclusive, participatory social relations. A flexible approach allows us to take more careful note of the agency of social actors and its significance for qualitative citizenship. Moreover, as Hefner (ibid:43) argues, it is the "synergy of state and society," the interplay between state and society and the growth of an inclusive political culture, "scaled-up" to the state and "scaled-down" to the populace, that is important for the continued development of civil society. The fluid approach that I adopt here enables us to examine not only the flows of political discourse and practice down through society but also upwards from members of society to the state.

BELONGING, CULTURAL CITIZENSHIP, AND A UNIFIED THEORY OF PRACTICE

The notions of "citizen" and "nation" and related ideas can be studied from an interpretative/symbolic or cognitive anthropological perspective. Social scientists formed both of these approaches out of the need to correct the shortcomings of earlier behaviorist approaches which relied heavily upon stimulus-response perspectives to explain behavior (see Hutchins 1980; Dougherty 1985; D'Andrade 1995). Although many anthropologists shared a concern for considering mediating systems of knowledge, there were significant differences about how to characterize such mediations. Some anthropologists focused upon symbols, loosely defined as public units of meaning or codes, and stressed that the main task of anthropology was to discern local meanings (Geertz 1960, 1973; Turner 1969). They argued that people respond to the same stimuli in different ways due to varied public symbols and modes of interpretation. These studies produced some important culturally sensitive analyses of symbolic forms and social processes in behavioral context (see Colby, Fernandez, and Kronenfield 1981). Unfortunately this interpretive, symbolic anthropological, and symbolic interactionist turn towards mediating symbols and interpretations was hampered by its chief proponent's, Clifford Geertz's and Victor Turner's, overt attempts to avoid cognitive anthropologists' concerns with the human mind (see Bradd Shore 1996:32–35). Thus, their theories relied upon observable public displays of symbols and paradigms and lacked a firm stance on acquisition, internalization, and distribution of knowledge. They produced some important insights about local commentaries on social structure, multiple meanings of symbols, and rites of passage, yet the lack of a developed approach to knowledge internalized in human minds weakened the power of their theories.

Most contemporary work on "nation," "citizen," identity and related notions adopt a symbolic and interpretative position, at times coupling this perspective with Marxist and neo-Marxist views. While this work has brought some important insights, it has the same flaw as the work of the early proponents of symbolic and interpretative anthropology. Like Geertz, these researchers tend to imply that the meanings of these notions are "out there" somewhere in public, shared in a public mind. Furthermore, some researchers suggest, in the absence of a theory of mind and internalization, social actors totally redefine and give new meaning anew to these notions in social processes. This tendency often leads to a form of neo-reductionism in which cultural constructs, such as race, ethnicity and nationality, are considered to be the "effects" of macro-economic and political processes, often global ones, and technologies of power (see Gilroy 1991; Ong 1997:25; Maurer 1997:34). While this perspective captures the dynamism of cultural forms, it gives a false impression of wholesale change when actually only particular aspects of cultural notions and social identities are changing. Moreover, it elides the creative capacity of the human mind to produce meanings and frames of interpretation, which are not reducible to broader forces.

I will attempt to avoid shortcomings of symbolic/interpretative perspectives by aligning myself with cognitive anthropological approaches, infusing them with more dynamism than they have often exhibited. In contrast to symbolic/interpretative anthropologists, early cognitive anthropologists of the 50s and 60s, well equipped with a powerful theory of mind, Chomsky's competence model, proceeded to analyze classificatory schemes people need to know in order to identify instances of biological kinds, kinfolk, colors and so forth. These "semantic ethnographers" used several analogies from linguistics to analyze several other domains of human social life (Dougherty 1985). For example, they used the notion of distinctive features, used to analyze phonology in the domain of language, to construct models of "emic" distinctions made by cultural actors in semantic usage, such as, kinship terminologies and folk taxonomies (Goodenough 1970; Lounsbury 1964; Conklin 1954). Extensions of the feature model and work on folk taxonomies eventually gave way to a focus upon more abstract knowledge structures, such as, schemata, models, and theories (D'Andrade 1995). Cognitive anthropology, like Chomsky's linguistic methods, tends to focus upon the formal analysis of knowledge—such as taxonomic structures, semantic features, and lexical sets—abstracted out of the behavioral context (see Colby, Fernandez, and Kronenfield 1981). I attempt to overcome this weakness in cognitive anthropology through paying close attention to social context and the circumstances of cultural performances.

In this study, I will apply schema and model theory to my description and analysis of social identities and some higher-level knowledge structures in which they embed and in part constitute. Schemata are "packets" or "bundles of knowledge" (Strauss 1997:197; Agar 1980:223–238) stored in memory as "conceptual abstractions that mediate between stimuli received by the sense organs and behavioral responses" (Strauss 1997:197). Schemata are detail-rich and foundational representations in contrast to models that characteristically lack rich detail and that people often use as heuristic devices and components in ideological doctrines (F.K. Lehman 1994, 2000). It is also important to distinguish between "personal" and "conventional" models and schemata in order to account for a range of idiosyncratic to widely distributed representations (Shore 1996:46). There is another useful distinction to make between "instituted" models and schemata, that are institutionalized in a publicly available and observable form, and "mental" models and schemata, that are "cognitive representations of these instituted models but are not simply direct mental mappings of social institutions" (ibid:68). "Mental" is used here to refer to the fact that these models and schemata are internalized in some fashion in mind, rather than embodied in artifacts or public events, without entailing any assumptions of how deeply they are internalized.

I will extend schema theory to innovative work done by Ward Goodenough, Roger Keesing, and F.K. Lehman on social identity. Goodenough (1951) and Keesing (1970) argue that "status" and "role" are elements in a cultural system and aspects of knowledge people must have to engage in social relationships. Robert R. Sands and F.K. Lehman (1995) make a further refinement by drawing a clearer distinction between identities and persons and identities and lower-level knowledge, behavioral expectations or role-function and status or evaluative regard, which constitutes them. Researchers may use the elements of this model to pinpoint the particular aspects undergoing change. Moreover, Sands and Lehman (ibid) make an important theoretical distinction between "maximal identities"—broad constructions of one's total social persona such as race, ethnicity and nationality—and "particular functional identities"—more limited and specific social positions such as nurse, pharmacist, and receptionist (see Daniels 1999:40). Maximal identities tend to inflect the behavioral expectations and status of particular social identities. That is, people may expect different behaviors from a doctor and assign different evaluations of this particular functional identity based upon whether the person filling the position is categorized as black or white, Malay or Chinese, male or female. I extend upon this theory by adding the notion of "sub-maximal" identities for social identities less broad as maximal identities but broader than particular functional identities. For instance, I will consider Tamils, Bengalis, and Gujeratis, as sub-maximal identities embedded within the overarching maximal category "Indian." These categories will allow me to explore the differential embedding of sub-maximal categories within maximal identities as well as the differential embedding of maximal identities within the national identity. There may be a graded sense of belonging or "cultural citizenship" in maximal identities as well as in national communities.

In addition, I will use schema theory to describe the bundling together of identity schemata with various notions pertinent to the domain of social relations. People often used these notions in close proximity with combinations of schemata of social identity in local and national discourse. I infer from an analysis of discourse and practice that these notions and constructions are tied together in bundles of knowledge (cf. Agar 1980, 1995). The knowledge that these schemata represent are interpreted as being socially distributed but internalized to variable extents in individual minds.

I consider these schemata to be part of the conceptual component of a unified theory of practice that considers three sets of phenomena: the conceptual, the behavioral, and the contextual (Keller and Keller 1996). Each of these sets of phenomena interpenetrates each other but no set is reducible to any other. The conceptual component governs or partially directs but does not determine practice (ibid: 17). Intervening social and environmental factors, aspects of the contextual component, may preclude the enactment of particular rule-governed behaviors or contribute to their performance (see Lehman 1996:43–47; Goodenough 1970:103). Yet many cognitive anthropologists have noted that knowledge structures entail and incorporate motivating goals (D'Andrade and Strauss 1992; D'Andrade 1995; Keller and Keller 1996; Lehman and Sands 1995).

As D'Andrade (ibid), and Lehman and Sands (1995) observe, knowledge functions socially making social action possible. Keller and Keller (1996:22) assert as one of their primary hypotheses that "knowledge is organized for doing rather than abstracted into various formal arrangements on purely logical or typological grounds." Similarly, Holland and Eisenhart (1990) found that young women in their studies had well-formed schema for schoolwork and romance that entailed motives directing the behavior and life histories of these young college students along different courses. Agar (1985) found that a well-formed arrest schema underlain the discourse of drug addicts or "junkies" he interviewed and motivated many of their actions to avoid arrest and imprisonment. Hutchins (1980) demonstrates that schemata, involving relations between propositions, underlie Trobriand land litigation discourse. These schemata involve goals of land use and allocation, and so, these schemata are cultural models of past transactions and models for future ones, as well as, interpretive frameworks for deciding who has use and allocation rights resulting from past acts. Likewise, Keller and Keller (1996) demonstrate how the well-formed schemata and principles that organize the domain of artist blacksmithing facilitate goals. They found that these schemata entail procedural goals for action (ibid: 119). I will apply the insight that schemata and models entail goals for social practice in my description and analysis of conceptual knowledge local residents have internalized about Malaysian society and interactions amongst its diverse citizenry. This careful attention to embedded goals can help to move a cognitive approach away from the static focus upon idealized knowledge structures towards social dynamics.

Furthermore, D'Andrade (1995) and Strauss (1992) note that schemata vary in their motivational force. D'Andrade (1995) argues that this hierarchy can give us a better way to approach situational variability in regards to behavior by allowing us to relate sub-goals to higher-level goals. Thus, "schemas are context-dependent interpretive devices, connected together in hierarchical networks" (ibid: 233). I will apply this insight to my description and analysis to various goals, and their interconnections, embedded in schemata and models of Malaysian society and the interrelations between groups. Moreover, Strauss demonstrates that schemata may be internalized in different ways and these different "ways of knowing" may directly influence the way they motivate behavior. Her interviews with blue-collar workers in Rhode Island indicate that these workers internalize the standard American success schema in a compact fashion, whereas the breadwinner schema is internalized in a more diffuse fashion and is more motivating in terms of these worker's work-related decisions and actions. She inferred that the more diffusely internalized breadwinner schema was broadly interwoven with individual semantic networks. Similarly, the manner in which the resident's of Melaka internalize representations of "Malaysia's diverse society" and "Malay privilege" influences the motivational force they entail. However, the manner of internalization and the negotiation of these mental representations are dynamic processes subject to change over time. I will attempt to discern how their internalization and motivational force change in relation to practice and accumulated experiences.

Knowledge and embedded motives clearly direct behavior, but practice can also alter knowledge. Ortner (1984) discusses how "the system shapes practice" and how "practice shapes the system." Likewise, Keller and Keller (1996) utilize a practice theory that sidesteps structuralist reductionism, as they note the dialectical relationship between knowledge and practice. People can reproduce and alter knowledge in practice, in a sense putting it at risk in performance (see Sahlins 1981).

> Our emphasis throughout will be both conceptual, concerned with the representation of information, and situated, concerned with the interface of prior knowledge and a present situation . . . It is the emergent and synergistic character of human behavior that becomes apparent as we proceed. By emergence we refer in this work to a person's ability to conceive, act, assess, and reconceive in the process of making something" (Keller and Keller 1996:18).

Yet, one must not assume that just because knowledge is at risk, or even transformed, in particular practices, that these transformations or subversions are socially distributed elsewhere in society. Researchers must look at these instances of situated-knowledge in relation to knowledge under different circumstances. For instance, when I consider the subversion of cultural knowledge in particular sites of celebrations and cultural performances, I do not assume that people subvert this knowledge in other contexts.

Indeed, the contextual component is a very significant aspect of a unified theory of practice. The contextual component refers on macro-level to the political economic structures of society and hierarchical structures of social differentiation, and on a micro-level to the particular situation of social interaction and the social identity relationships entailed. To avoid the "duality of structure" problem in which one assumes that social structure is constituted by practice and also the medium for practice, I will consider the context, taken broadly or narrowly, as always *given* and current practice as reproducing or transforming a particular set of circumstances (Yelvington 1995:4–5). I will attempt to discern relations between particular ethnographic contexts and macro-structural conditions (ibid: 5) that impinge upon practices, knowledge, and motives.

Keller and Keller (1996:28) note the importance of context: "The circumstances are as essential a component of the ideal as are the governing principles. Alternatives will emerge as circumstances change. Both ideal and alternative strategies are equally real, each enacted as deemed appropriate in context." This unified theory of practice directs researchers to concentrate upon how different circumstances shape the emergence and application of knowledge. Furthermore, Ortner (1984:149) argues for the "centrality of domination" in the study of practice and asserts that the "most significant forms of practice are those with intentional or unintentional political implications. Thus, practice for her is the "study of all forms of human action, but from a particular—political—angle." I will consider power relations and domination as an important aspect of the contextual component that shapes the content of knowledge and the parameters of practice. Lave and Wenger (1991) situated knowledge in its social context and attempted to show the social process that shapes knowledge, but they almost lost sight of conceptual phenomena. On the other hand, as Keller and Keller (1996) note, many contemporary cognitive anthropologists falter in the other direction by focusing upon mental objects to the exclusion of social contexts. Keller and Keller (1996), and Holland and Eisenhart (1990) give all three phenomena, context, knowledge and behavior, consideration without reducing any to any other. Holland and Eisenhart find that in the context of peer groups, young college women "become educated in romance" and this acquisition schema shapes their practice in regards to schoolwork and careers. Moreover, "it is only through relating the knowledge and practices of production that we are able to begin to account for this unity of experience" (Keller and Keller 1996). Relating situated knowledge to practice can allow us to approach human behavior, experience and subjectivity in a rigorous fashion.

In this chapter of Part I, I placed my study within some relevant literature and discussed my theoretical concerns and perspectives. Moving beyond largely descriptive pluralist and multiculturalist perspectives, I considered contemporary literature on constructions of "nation" and "citizen" which makes important observations about the inherent contradictions of liberal nations. Building upon the work of many researchers on legal and cultural citizenship, I outlined my broadened approach to legal and cultural citizenship. This broadened approach considers the history and cultural construction of both legal and cultural citizenship and applies to subordinate minorities as well as "natives" and dominant majorities. Moreover, it strives to consider the influence of the state and civic institutions without liquidating the agency of subordinate people of various social identities. I adopt a cognitive anthropological approach to highlight the embedding of social identities within other social identities and within broader, horizontal and vertical, conceptions of the national community. In particular, I use model and schemata theory to describe and analyze social identities and high-level representations of Malaysian society. I also use cognitive methods to infer knowledge structures from natural language discourse and interview and survey data (see preface).

Chapter two of Part I outlines a general historical overview of Melaka, and to some extent of Malaysia, with a view towards legal and cultural citizenship and processes of cultural category and social identity formation. I present the emergence of new cultural categories and underlying meanings in cosmopolitan pre-colonial and colonial society drawing a distinction between the different approaches of Portuguese, Dutch, and British colonialists in relation to the intermixing of people from different cultural categories. In addition, I discuss the construction of the plural society of British Malaya and its impact on local social identities as large numbers of Chinese and Indians immigrated to Melaka. Later, in this chapter I give a detailed description of processes of legal and cultural citizenship in Malaysia, focusing upon the failed Malayan Union plan and the subsequent negotiation of the Federation of Malaysia and the Malaysian Constitution. At the end of this chapter, I develop a brief social history of Melaka in the post-1969 era focusing upon the changing patterns of social structure and context of social relations.

Chapter three of Part II describes the constructions of diverse social identities and their interconnections in the social relational system. In this chapter, I develop and demonstrate the strength and dynamism of combining a cognitive approach with the contemporary view of social constructionism. I demonstrate how this approach can help us to pinpoint particular aspects of social identities that people are transforming in dynamic social processes while noting the reproduction of other aspects. In the following chapter of this section, chapter four, I demonstrate how the identity schemata of the previous chapter are tied together with other notions to construct cultural frameworks of Malaysian society. These notions embed opposing images of the national community and what it means to belong to and possess this "common citizenship."

In Part III, I move on to describe and analyze public celebrations and representations organized and sponsored by the government and private sectors and religious festivals in sacred spaces. Chapter five discusses state-organized celebrations and re-presentations that exemplify the dominant top-down form of "multiculturalism." Here we can note the dominant image of the national community with its ranked hierarchy as we consider National Independence celebrations, Melaka Historic Day celebrations, and several government-managed museums. The following chapter, chapter six, describes how people negotiated and/or subverted this dominant image in celebrations in public, sacred, and personal sites. The dominant ranked image of belonging is "at risk" as local groups negotiate cultural citizenship. Marginalized Indians and economically dominant Chinese parley for position and status in the hierarchy of social identities through staging events in the shopping malls and participating or scoffing participation in government promoted open house practices.

Chapter seven of Part IV discusses the negotiation of qualitative citizenship in regard to patterns of social relations, including cases of intermarriage and resulting distribution of identity and economic benefits, multiracial and multi-religious voluntary associations and cliques. This chapter underscores negotiations of seemingly contradictory notions of belonging in matters of domestic and relational import and some of the tensions involved in border crossings. In this chapter, I consider my original research problem of discerning the effects of local people's understandings of cultural shows and public celebrations upon the emergence of multiracial and multi-religious forms of social organization. Similar to the mixed interpretations of cultural shows, public celebrations and exhibitions, and festivities, patterns of intermarriage and inter-group involvement in voluntary associations and cliques are also mixed, displaying broad interracial and inter-religious involvement while being skewed towards non-Malay membership.

Part VI, Chapter eight, analyzes contested discourses of belonging and resolution of the tensions posed by the internalization of contradictory notions of the national community. Applying Festinger's theory of cognitive dissonance, I describe and analyze the cognitive processes, for Malays and non-Malays, through which the lack of fit between notions of equality and inequality are reduced. I will consider how this resolution is contingent and relational by examining the influence of people's experiences in connection with these notions. At the end of this section, in chapter nine, I conclude my description and analysis of the negotiation of representations of society and cultural citizenship in contemporary Malaysia and assess the contribution of my study to Malaysian ethnography and beyond and to anthropological theory.

Chapter Two
Melaka Past and Present, Cultural Citizenship, and Race-Making

FROM MARITIME EMPIRE TO STRAITS SETTLEMENT

The Melaka Sultanate

The Melaka Sultanate (c. 1400–1511 A.D.) was an integral part of the cycle of Malay maritime empires that controlled and prospered from the trade passing through the Straits of Melaka for several centuries. A Palembang-born prince, Parameswara, of the South Sumatran-based kingdom, Sriwijaya, was the founder of the Melaka kingdom around the end of the fourteenth century. Sriwijaya, a Buddhist kingdom, that had seen its peak in the South China Sea trade cycles, was now in decline. It was caught in between two strong regional powers, Majapahit in Java and Ayudhya in Siam, now known as Thailand. Parameswara, escaping from an assault from Java-based Majapahit, fled first to Singapore, and then to Muar and Melaka. It was the site of a fishing village at the time, but it was soon to become a flourishing entrepot that brought in trade, traders, and cultures from around the world.

In order to hold off strong threats from the north, Siam, and from the southeast, Java, Parameswara established ties with China, becoming one of its vassals. It was at an opportune time, because the Ming rulers were beginning to emphasize external trade again. In 1405, the Ming Emperor recognized Parameswara as the vassal-ruler of Melaka, and, in 1409, he sent a large fleet of ships, led by the Chinese Muslim admiral, Cheng Ho, to stop at Melaka on its way around a large part of the world. Parameswara visited the Imperial court of China in 1411. Ties with China were important for trade and for protection from Siam and Java who both claimed to control the Straits and the peninsular of Malaya.[1]

Melaka grew and trade prospered in Melaka, at the northern side of the Straits, as it had previously on the southern side of the Straits, during the heyday of the Sriwijaya Empire. Traders would stop in Melaka, where they found the facilities suitable, on the cycle of southwest and northeast monsoons and conduct commerce. Melaka provided a relatively safe port, with piracy largely under control, secure storehouses, and an organized system of taxation. Melaka became a famous and legendary coastal Malay empire, one to which the Malays often look back to today as a shining example of Malay pre-colonial glory.

Parameswara and his descendants, who ruled Melaka for a little over a century, developed a mode of statecraft and courtly etiquette, partially based on ideas brought from South Sumatra that provided a cultural model for later Malay Sultanates that grew on the peninsula (Khoo 1996). They developed a hierarchical pattern of ranked nobility and royal subjects. At the top of this traditional hierarchy was the king, carrying the title of sultan or maharaja, who subjects viewed as a quasi-divine ruler who possessed the *daulat* or "forces of power" (see Andaya and Andaya 1982:331). The highest ranked minister was the *Bendahara* who dealt with foreign traders and arbitrated disputes amongst locals and between locals and foreigners (ibid:46). Next in rank was the *Penghulu Bendahari* who was the administrator in charge of the *Syahbandars*—harbor-masters—and all state revenues. The Chief Magistrate and leader of the police and army was third-ranking official or *Temenggung* and the military and royal bodyguard leader, the *Laksamana,* was next in line. The negotiation of the rank of these four most prominent positions was somewhat open, and at times one assumed a higher position than others conventionally assumed to be of higher rank (see ibid:47). Below these high-ranking nobles were lower-ranking nobles and local chiefs or *penghulu.* Malay nobles considered all of the common people, including *orang laut* (seafaring people) and *orang asli* (original inhabitants), to be *hamba melayu* or "Malay slaves and servants." All of the ruler's subjects were expected to give their undivided loyalty and devotion to him regardless of whether he was fair or not, and the crime of treason or *derhaka* was considered to be the most heinous crime one could commit. The ruler in turn was expected not to put his subjects to shame, but if he does, he is only punishable by a higher spiritual power. If any of the subjects, nobles or common people were to turn against their ruler, even though he was a cruel despot, it would amount to *derhaka* and their actions would be interpreted as unjustified and immoral.

Such is the case with the story revolving around two of the five legendary warriors of Melaka, Hang Tuah and Hang Jebat, and its conventional interpretation. Hang Tuah, unfairly accused by the ruler and sentenced to death, was barely able to escape the court with his life. He hid on the outskirts of the kingdom. One of his four sworn brothers, Hang Jebat, could not accept this injustice and plotted against the ruler. A noble who helped Hang Tuah escape, and knew of his whereabouts, asked him to come back to defend their ruler against the feared threats of Hang Jebat. Hang Tuah comes back, loyal as ever to his ruler and kills his sworn brother who stood up on his behalf in the name of justice. Hang Jebat is conventionally remembered as one of the great warriors of Melaka, but one who was a traitor, while Hang Tuah is seen as the hero, who placed loyalty to his ruler above all else. This conventional interpretation is still popular in present day Melaka, but alternative interpretations that view Hang Jebat as the hero, fighting for justice, has gained ground. Since the end of 1998 when Anwar Ibrahim, the former Deputy Prime Minister, was "sacked" (thrown out) from his government position, some Malay residents of Melaka began to compare him to Hang Jebat. From this perspective, Anwar, like Hang Jebat, dared to stand up to a powerful, unjust ruler and suffered the consequences. Notwithstanding such re-interpretations of the Hang Tuah and Hang Jebat saga, a strong sense of identification between the *rakyat* (common people) and their leaders has persisted into the contemporary period.

Parameswara and his heirs maintained and fostered relationships with inland foragers and seagoing folks, as did former coastal Malay empires, and these ties facilitated trade of forest products and relative security from the threat of piracy. Some leaders amongst *orang asli* and *orang laut* peoples received titles from Malay rulers as they became incorporated within the orbit of cosmopolitan rule centered in the Melaka capital. "Malayness" during this and earlier periods became associated with the prestigious culture and customs of maritime kingdoms in the region that were believed to have an ancestry originating in a region of *Tanah Melayu* (land of the Malays)[2] located in southeastern Sumatra (see Andaya and Andaya 1982:45). The "Malay" *bahasa*, language and a constellation of ideals, values, and mannerisms, spread into inland and upriver areas as the "coastal Malays" incorporated these peoples into economic and political relations with the coastal center (cf. Andaya and Andaya 1982:54,119). This association of Malayness with participation in the maritime empires seems to have been widespread in the Malayo-Indonesian world at this time.

During the Melaka period, this 'Malayness' developed a new dimension, which would become more dominant over time, namely, the association with Islam. Although Islam already had a presence in the Malayo-Indonesian world, it was during the 15th Century that the spread of Islam gained greater momentum with the increased influx of Indian Muslim traders and Islamic teachers, and the subsequent conversion of many "Malay" elite from Hindu-Buddhism to Islam. Only a few years after founding the kingdom of Melaka, Parameswara converted to Islam and changed his name to "Megat Iskandar Shah." The conversion of Melaka to Islam served to cement ties with north Sumatran sultanates and Indian and Arab traders. As Melaka grew and became a regional power that incorporated much of the Malayo-Indonesian world, Melaka became a center for proselytizing Islam throughout the region as vassal states were encouraged to adopt Islam. Melaka even affected the conversion of Java from Hindu-Buddhism to Islam (Gullick 1963:24). In the context in which Melaka, and other Malay maritime empires were embracing and spreading Islam, Malay culture—still with vestiges of Hinduism and Buddhism—and identity became intertwined with Islam and Muslim identity.

> Though Islam had been promoted earlier by Samudra-Pasai, the new religion became so closely identified with Malay society in Melaka that to become Moslem, it was said, was to *masuk Melayu,* 'to enter [the fold of the] Melayu' (Andaya and Andaya 1982:55).

Local elites and commoners still considered "Malayness" as intimately tied into maritime culture and Malay *bahasa,* language and mannerisms,[3] but now, Islam was becoming a fundamental feature of this prestigious culture. Many Indian and Arab Muslims were no doubt absorbed into Malay society at this early stage of Melakan history as well as at later stages. These migrant Muslims were active in missionary activities, and their significance to the presence of Islam in Melaka lives on in contemporary Malay oral history as well as worship at ancient graves considered *keramat* or in possession of special spiritual powers (see chapter six). Indian Muslims, mainly Gujarati, Malayali, and Tamil merchants, participated in the trade of Indian textiles and spices, for which there was a high demand. Moreover, some Indian Muslims played important roles in the administration of the port, as harbormasters, and even became involved in the politics of royal succession (see Gullick 1963:23–24). Similarly, many *orang laut* and *orang asli* who adopted Islam and other aspects of coastal Malay "high culture" became incorporated in Malay society and categorized as Malay.

    In addition to Indian and Arab Muslims, there were many other migrant groups, such as Indian Hindus, Persians, Javanese and Chinese, that came to Melaka to engage in trade and many of them also took up residence in Melaka and contributed to the diverse composition of this wealthy cosmopolitan port-city. Indian Hindus, primarily Tamil Hindus from the south-

ern part of the Indian subcontinent, were also, like their Muslim counterparts, key players in trade and court politics. The revenue accrued from taxation of the substantial volume of Indian trade contributed greatly to the
growth of the Melaka Sultanate. By the end of the 15th Century, it had expanded to include several areas of Peninsular "Malaya," islands south and
west of Singapore, and much of the eastern coast of Sumatra (see Mearns
1995:27; Andaya and Andaya 1982:51). Before the beginning of the colonial period in 1511, an Indian Hindu settlement or *kampong kling* was
formed in the northern outskirts of town. A wealthy, Tamil-speaking member of the Chettiar caste of traders and financiers, by the name of Nainu
Chetty, assisted the Portuguese in their invasion of Melaka. In so doing, he
became the first person to be referred to as "*Chetty*" (or "*Chitty*") in the historical record, terms used, at this point in history as shortened forms of
Chettiar, or to refer to any Indian trader (Mearns 1995:28, 53). Later, during the colonial period, a new meaning of "*Chitty*" was to emerge.

Chinese also were an important component of pre-colonial Melakan
society. Many Chinese members of Admiral Cheng Ho's overseas missions,
from 1404 to 1433, probably stayed on in Melaka. According to Malay
sources and oral history, Hang Li Po, a Chinese princess sent to marry one
of the Malay sultans, was a member of one of these missions. She and her
entourage stayed on in Melaka. The fact that she received the title *Hang,* the
same as the five legendary Malay warriors—Hang Tuah, Hang Jebat, Hang
Lekir, Hang Kasturi, and Hang Lekiu—suggests that she was afforded high
status in Malay society. A well named after her, the Hang Li Po Well, located
at the foot of *Bukit Cina* today, was reportedly built in the fifteenth century
by Chinese artisans (Hoyt 1993:22). A Chinese Muslim, Fei-Hsin, reported
that in 1436 Chinese people were living amongst the peoples of Melaka
(ibid: 22). As was the case with Indian trade, a harbormaster was assigned
to coordinate trade from China and its neighbors, indicating that trade in
Chinese products, such as porcelain and tea, was highly valued.

For Malays, the period of the Melaka Sultanate has been, and still is,
an important symbol of a glorious, Malay past in which Malays, indigenous
to the region, held power and forged a prestigious culture with Islam at its
very core. Local and national, Malay-dominated governments are currently
running a tourism campaign under the slogan, "Visit Melaka is to Visit
Malaysia"; Melaka is where "it all began." Moreover, hegemonic claims for
Malay special rights often find their justification in this glorious Malay past.
On the other hand, contemporary Indian and Chinese residents of Melaka,
and Malaysia in general, find a lot of meaning in the early history of Melaka.
They also had an important economic and political presence and made great

contributions to the Melaka Sultanate. The presence of Indians and Chinese in the Straits of Melaka did not begin with the Melaka Sultanate, nor were their numbers as large as they were to become during the colonial period. Yet, many people, on a local and national level, view their presence on the Peninsula during this golden age of Malay history as a basis for their inclusion in the Malaysian nation-state. They were here "when it all started." The roots of the contemporary "Straits-born Chinese and Indian" communities are generally viewed as being planted during the Melaka Sultanate. Moreover, "Straits-born Chinese and Indian" discursive challenges to Malay special rights and claims to exclusive *Bumiputera* (sons of the soil; indigenous) status also rests in assertions about the presence of their ancestors in Melaka at this early date.

The Settler Colonial Period

Portuguese conquerors were the first in a series of European colonialists to gain control of Melaka and to monopolize the trade passing through its harbors. Portuguese expansionists were motivated by a combination of different aims, including a search for riches and the mythical priest-king Prester John, control of Asian spices trade routes, and an anti-Muslim crusading spirit (Andaya and Andaya 1982:55; Hoyt 1993:30). Portuguese conquerors, with the goal of gaining control of the Muslim trading network through which Asian spices passed en route to Europe, attacked and captured the city of Melaka in 1511. Malay rulers, caught up in internal power struggles and with inferior weaponry, were defeated and fled inland, and then to other places in the Malay world where they had bases of support.[4] This defeat marked the end of the Melaka Sultanate. However, as was the case with Srivijaya, Malay rulers found ways to reconstitute their kingdoms in other places such as Johor and Perak, and launched counterattacks on the Portuguese settlers for over one hundred years (see Andaya and Andaya 1982:57–62; Hoyt 1993:34). Nevertheless, European power and culture were here to stay and would have a lasting impact on the course of history in the region.

Soon after seizing control of the city of Melaka, the Portuguese constructed a fortress, called "A Famosa," using stones from Muslim graves, mosques, and other buildings, together with laterite blocks and bricks (Hoyt ibid: 35). Under the Portuguese, a governor's place and bishop's palace, and a number of churches, convents, and several administrative buildings were built. Melaka took on a medieval Catholic and military character during Portuguese colonial times, but the only remainder of this proud architectural legacy is a small portion of the old fort, "A Famosa" (ibid: 37).

The Portuguese successfully gained control of the valuable spice trade with the assistance of Nainu Chetty, the wealthy Tamil Hindu merchant. Portuguese rulers rewarded him with appointments to positions of political leadership, *bendahara,* and harbormaster for the Tamil community. The Indian settlement continued to exist and trade with India was still of importance for some time, but the political influence of the Indian community decreased under Portuguese rule and was never to return to its level during the pre-colonial period. Nainu Chetty, who was moved out of power to appease the Malay community, committed suicide soon thereafter. Portuguese policies of relatively higher taxes on Chinese goods and restrictions on Chinese ownership of lands did little to encourage Chinese migrants to venture to Melaka (see Hoyt 1993:23). Besides many ships steered clear of Melaka due to renewed threats of piracy on the high seas. The high administrative costs of patrolling the seas and constantly combating Malays and *orang laut* along with the corruption and inefficiency of colonial officials gradually led to a weakening of the Portuguese position in Southeast Asia. Portuguese settler colonialists were never able to monopolize trade the way Melaka and Srivijaya were able to in previous periods.

Yet, the Portuguese have left a lasting legacy in the Straits. The King of Portugal and his governor and conqueror in Asia, Alfonso Albuquerque, encouraged intermarriage between Portuguese men and local women with offers of gifts and monetary and employment rewards (Joseph Sta. Maria 1994:3). They viewed miscegenation as a way to populate territories under royal jurisdiction with loyal Catholic subjects. "Evangelization was thus not only one of the main Portuguese motives for overseas expansion, it was also the vehicle for a kind of cultural assimilation not found amongst the other colonizing powers" (Clammer 1986:52). It is important to note here is that the Portuguese settlers did not construct a racial barrier between themselves and the colonized in the same way that the Dutch and British colonizers were to do after them. Portuguese policies, unlike their successors, promoted the creation of a "mixed" Christian population of their descendants. "As a result of these intermarriages a new breed of people with eastern customs and habits evolved. The offsprings [sic] of those marriages were called 'Mesticos' or *Topazes.* Today, they are known as the Malacca Portuguese community" (ibid). *Mesticos* was a Portuguese term used to refer to all "Portuguese half-breeds," and *Topazes* or *Topazese* was a Portuguese term used to refer to *Mesticos* in Melaka, embedding an analogy between their skin color and the yellowish brown color of the precious 'topaz' stone (Bernard Sta. Maria 1982:24). However, Boxer (1947), Schulte Nordholt (1971), and Gunn (1999) note that the term *topasses* was used for people of mixed Portuguese and Asian descent in India, Malacca, Flores, and Timor and other areas where Portuguese took up residence. Boxer (1947:1) identifies the Hindustani word for hat, *topi,* and the Dravidian word for interpreter, *tuppasi,* as potential origins for the term *topasses.* Boxer and Schulte Nordholdt suggest that there is much to commend the Hindustani origin of this term because of the reference to "hats" in many languages, including the Indian *Topee Walas* or "Hat-men," to designate these Portuguese-local hybrids. Many of them wore old-fashioned Portuguese narrow-rimmed hats. However, Gunn (1999:92) suggests that the Dravidian term for "two languages" or "interpreter" was a more likely origin of the term *topasse.* In any case, many descendants of these "mixed marriages" remained in Melaka after the Portuguese lost control of this port-city to the Dutch and then through the British colonial years into the present. They have undergone many changes in identity (Bernard Sta. Maria 1982; Sarkissian 1997) and government officials have recently awarded, unofficially, some of the benefits reserved for *Bumiputera,* making them "honorary" *Bumiputera.* To what extent they perceive themselves as being fully incorporated in Melaka society and accorded full rights of citizenship will be explored later.

The Dutch, like the Portuguese, set sail from Holland on an expansionist mission motivated by several aims. Although religion figured into their motives, they were not swept away with anti-Muslim zeal and the evangelical spirit as were the Portuguese upon their entry into the Straits. The main Dutch rivals in trade and religion were Catholics and not Muslims. Dutch mercantilist empire-builders were competing with their Portuguese and Spanish counterparts who had denied them entry into their ports after 1580. This cut them out of the lucrative trade in spices going on in northern Europe, so they decided to break the Portuguese monopoly. The Dutch mercantilist firm, the United East Indies Company, formed an alliance with two Muslim Sultanates in the Straits, Aceh in northern Sumatra and Johor, just south of Melaka who shared their interests in putting an end to Portuguese restrictive measures on trade in the Straits. After several months of fierce and costly fighting, the Dutch stormed the Portuguese fort and took control of Melaka in 1641. Wealthy Portuguese fled on ship with their riches heading to Portuguese Ceylon (Hoyt 1993:47).

Many wealthy Indian traders, who had developed close ties to the Portuguese, also left Melaka taking their lucrative trade networks with them to other places in the region. Yet, a significant Indian presence remained in Melaka under Dutch rule. Dutch maps and "Chitty" oral histories indicate that it was during this period that the main Indian settlement was moved further inland and east of its former location (Mearns 1995:29). Many

Indians had cut formal ties with trade and were now cultivating the land. "Chitty" Hindus, the leaders of the Indian community in pre-British times, received several land grants from the Dutch, in the second half of the Eighteenth Century, which they used to build several of the oldest functioning temples in Melaka and in Malaysia overall. It appears that the underlying meaning of "Chitty" had changed during this period in the direction of some aspects of contemporary usage; in particular, it now referred to a culturally and physiologically mixed group of Hindus (see Mearns ibid:29). The descendants of early Indian migrants—"Chitties"—formerly known as traders and financiers, have come to be known as the products of intermarriage and acculturation. In this situation of long-term separation from their Indian homeland and intimate social interactions with local "Malays," a new sense of "Chitty" began to emerge.

In contrast to the dwindling Indian numbers in Melaka, the Chinese population grew substantially during the Dutch period. Chinese migrants had considerably more motivation to migrate to Melaka under the Dutch than they did under the Portuguese. Soon after gaining control of Melaka, the United East Indies Company brought some Chinese workers from Batavia, the Dutch colonial center in Java, to rebuild the vegetable gardens that had been destroyed during their long siege of Melaka (Hoyt 1993:24). In addition, Chinese from the southern provinces of Fukien, Kwangtung, and Kwansi fled from the difficult conditions taking hold of China following the Manchu destruction of the Ming dynasty. Many of these Chinese migrants wound up in Melaka looking for a better life, and Dutch administrators who saw something of the Protestant work ethic in them welcomed them. These two waves of Chinese migrants, from within Southeast Asia, and from China, began to merge with the older Chinese community in Melaka, and the "Straits-born Chinese" or *Baba* (male) and *Nyonya* (female) culture and identity began to take shape. Many of the members of the older Chinese communities in Melaka and Batavia, had already acculturated with the Malay and Javanese populations, and the newcomers adopted many of these assimilated patterns and married "local" or "Malay" women, from the peninsula and archipelago.

Chinese migrants began to expand spatially, as existing communities grew larger, and occupationally, moving into some areas of the economy formerly dominated by Malays. Chinese, formerly mostly traders and shopkeepers, began to fill new occupational niches, such as miners and planters. Their communities, lying just on the outskirts of the colonial town, were led by Dutch-appointed leaders, called *Kapitan Cina*, revolved around temples as did the Indian community. The oldest functioning temple in Melaka,

Cheng Hoon Teng Temple, was built in 1645 founded by the second *Kapitan Cina*, Lei Wee King, who also bought the Bukit China Cemetery and donated it to the Chinese community (Hoyt 1993:24).

In the center of the town area, the Dutch built several administrative buildings, fine town houses and some churches. A Dutch Reformed Church, St. Paul's, was built at the site of a Catholic Church wrecked during the Dutch onslaught. The Dutch governor ordered Portuguese Catholics to give up their faith and to convert to Protestant Christianity but they refused. After several decades of persecution, Dutch administrators adopted principles of religious freedom and Catholics were able to build new churches, such as St. Peter's Church, built in 1710.

In contrast to the Portuguese settler colonialists, the Dutch rulers did not encourage intermarriage with local women. By means of puritanical values combined with notions of racial superiority, Dutch officials set out to construct a sense of "whiteness" that set them apart from, and above, the local natives. Unlike the Portuguese, they did not see racial miscegenation or the creation of a new "hybrid" race as the means for leading heathen locals to Christianity. Nevertheless, due to the small population of European women, many Dutch officials and soldiers married Portuguese-Asian "hybrids" or took them as servants or mistresses (ibid:47–48). Along with several colonial buildings remaining in the middle of town, a few descendants of these "Dutch-Eurasians" still live in Melaka today, carrying Dutch surnames, a legacy of the Dutch period in Melaka.

The British gained control of Melaka without the use of military force. Due to the French defeat of the Dutch in the Napoleonic Wars (1795–1815) raging in Europe and the threat of the French taking hold of Dutch possessions in Asia, Dutch officials negotiated the temporary hand over of power to the British in 1795. In any event, British ascendancy in Malaya seemed imminent, given the strong position of British planters in many areas on the peninsula and British control of India-based production of opium, a much sought after commodity in Malaya as in other places in Asia. In 1786, the British claimed possession of Penang, an island in the Straits north of Melaka, after negotiations by an English planter with the Sultan of Kedah. With control of Penang and Melaka, the British completed their domination of trade in the Straits with the founding of Singapore in 1819. The Dutch returned to Southeast Asia after the wars in Europe and the British returned control of Melaka to them, but only temporarily. In 1824, the Anglo-Dutch Treaty turned Melaka back over to the British in return for British possessions in the Indonesian Archipelago, thus consolidating their mutual spheres of influence in the region. This arbitrary colonial partition, dividing the cultural and historical unity of the Malayo-Indonesian world, laid the foundation for later formation of three nation-states: Malaysia, Indonesia, and Singapore.

The British consolidated their control of the Straits and gradually extended its control over the rest of Peninsular Malaya. In 1826, the British organized Melaka, Singapore, Penang, and Wellesley Province (located on the mainland across from the island of Penang) into a single administrative unit called the Straits Settlements. Singapore became the capital of this British colony and Melaka, as a port-city, began to fall in significance. Over the course of around fifty more years, British settler colonialists constructed "British Malaya" in which they exercised direct rule in the Straits Settlements and parts of Borneo and indirect rule over all of the Malay states on the peninsula. After several decades of sending colonial officials to "advise" Malay rulers, the British organized another political unit called the Federated Malay States (FMS), in 1896, with its capital in the tin-rich Kuala Lumpur. The four states in the FMS, Perak, Selangor, Negri Sembilan, and Pahang, were placed under the administrative control of British officials in Kuala Lumpur and Singapore. The other five states of Peninsular Malaysia, Johor, Kedah, Perlis, Kelantan and Terengganu, called the Unfederated Malay States (UMS), gradually came under the control of British officials as well, but never to the same degree as the Straits Settlements and the FMS (see Andaya and Andaya 1982:205–264).

In the context of this gradually expanding colonial structure, the British encouraged a great influx of migrants, primarily Chinese and Indians, and constructed one of the "classic" plural societies in which they organized these two groups along with Malays into a largely segregated system. From 1827 to 1931, the Chinese population in Melaka grew from 4,000 to 85,342 persons, about 40 per cent of the total population (Hayes-Hoyt 1993:25). Many Chinese migrants were recruited to work on British and Chinese owned tapioca plantations and tin mines. In Melaka, many Chinese-owned pepper, gambier, and tapioca plantations were organized under *kongsi,* dialect associations (see Andaya and Andaya 1982:211). Chinese merchants and shopkeepers began to fill middlemen roles in the colonial distribution networks, dominating local wholesale and retail trade and serving as tax collectors for the Straits government. In the nineteenth century, wealthy Straits-born Chinese acquired terrace houses on Heeren and Jonker Streets, two historic Dutch roads in town, and other Chinese lived in houses and over their shops. The concentration of the Chinese population in urban areas, close to their means of livelihood, came to be the characteristic residential pattern in the Straits Settlements and most parts of Malaya.

Although many Straits-born Chinese remained successful in business, Chinese migrants eventually overtook them in terms of economics and prestige. New arrivals that were less culturally assimilated to Malay culture and closer to British culture, for instance, English-speaking rather than Malay-speaking, acquired more prestige. Chinese migrants organized *kongsi* or dialect group associations, clan associations, and secret societies to maintain group cohesion and to serve Chinese interests.

Similarly, the migration of Indians into Melaka increased drastically during the late nineteenth and early twentieth century. The British who sought to fill the growing needs for plantation labor with low caste, illiterate, and destitute Indians from South India carefully planned and coordinated this migration. Initially, the British brought prisoners from India to labor on the plantations and in urban infrastructure projects, but they altered this to rely upon recruited forms of labor (Mearns 1995:32). South Indian Muslims, Chettiar, and Gujaratis were still active in trade, while British planters used many Ceylonese and Malayali Indians as supervisors. Nevertheless, it was the great influx of dark-skinned Tamil Hindus tied into the agricultural estates during this period that gave rise to the category "Indian" as a docile, menial laborer or "coolie." In addition, as was the case with the Straits-born Chinese and more recent Chinese immigrants, higher caste and higher-class "Indians," who gained prestige through interactions with the British, began to overshadow the "Chitty."

In this period, the meaning of "Malayness" made a clear shift in the direction of an indigenous person of the Islamic faith that may possess a wide range of regional variants in culture and custom. These regional variants tended to encompass southern Thailand and areas to the south and west of the peninsula (cf. Andaya and Andaya 1982:112). Islam was an important unifying vehicle for Malays to oppose the encroachment of foreign interests in their territory; some movements and rebellions entailed calling together all Muslims, from whatever background, local "Malay" groups, including Bugis, Achenese, and Minangkabau, as well as *Jawi Peranakan* or Indian-Malay Muslim hybrids. "*Jawi Peranakan*" was a term that differentiated Muslims of mixed Indian, and at times Arab, and Malay parentage from "pure blooded" Malays whose ancestry is from this region. "*Peranakan*" means local-born, a term used for other groups that were *born here*, in *Tanah Melayu* but are not totally of the soil, as original inhabitants. "*Jawi*" refers to a Muslim or someone or something Islamic, and is the name of the Arabic script for the Malay language.[5] Thus, this term is a polite way, without negative stigmas necessarily, to note that the person so categorized is a Muslim, with some Malay "blood" but not "pure" Malay blood. Many

Arab-Malays had already, or would in time, become more greatly sub-merged into the Malay category than the Indian hybrids were to, due to the higher prestige accorded to Arabs, as the "race" of the holy Prophet Muhammad. The emphasis Malays lay upon the Islamic feature of "Malayness" coincided with the British colonial categorization of all Muslims from the region as "Malay."

The British settler colonialists used three generalized categories, "Malay," "Chinese," and "Indian," along with a sense of "whiteness," that was to be held as the epitome of prestige and "civilization," to organize a plural society in service of the colonial economy (see also Lee 1986:30; and Andaya and Andaya 1982:263–264). They exploited "Indians" in rural and urban structures of capitalist production and stereotyped them as loyal and trustworthy but docile and servile in nature. British colonials exploited "Malays" as food producers, rural-dwelling farmers and fisherman, stereo-typed as witty and lively but unreliable, uncivilized and unsophisticated. They admitted some children of Malay rulers to English schools and used them in colonial administration, but overall, they excluded Malays from English schools. "Chinese" were middlemen traders, tax collectors, and rival capitalists who the British stereotyped as industrious and ingenious but also as cruel, immoral, and wicked (see Hoyt 1993:26). Chinese and Indians attended English schools, more than Malays did, but they both also attended Chinese and Indian language medium schools. Likewise, Malays attended Malay-medium schools and Islamic schools. "Whites" were the chief admin-istrators and traders who stereotyped themselves as civilized, industrious, and moral. "Whiteness" was the principal model of prestige and status as-piration and "white" officials protected this image by censoring any films that portrayed "white" men in a negative light and deporting any "white" women engaged in prostitution (Lee 1986:31). The British, like the Dutch before them, separated themselves from non-white segments of colonial so-ciety and largely separated each of the segments from each other. They met in the marketplace and interacted with each other primarily through the British who maintained law and order. It was through these essentialized cat-egories, each considered as a distinct mix of racial and cultural attributes and as a class of persons, that the British perceived and governed colonial society. In the earlier part of the nineteenth century, British colonial cate-gories tended to be more fluid, allowing for shifts in categorization, and less biologically based (Milner 1998:159–161). However, later in the nineteenth century, with the beginning of decennial census taking in 1871 and eco-nomic and political legal codes based upon these census reports, British con-ceptions of local peoples became more fixed and increasingly more biological (see Shamsul A.B. 1998, Milner 1998, and Reid 2001). Although local individuals and groups have given new meanings and uses to social categories over time, the emphasis British colonial categories eventually placed upon "descent" and "blood" and distinct cultural attributes has had a lasting impact on local constructions of social categories and identities.

British perceptions and policies largely disregarded or were suspicious of the hybrid categories of *Jawi Peranakan,* or Indian-Malays and Arab-Malays, and Eurasians in favor of the four generalized overarching categories (Andaya and Andaya 1982:180). It appears that at some point in the early twentieth century, in the wake of the large influx of Indian Hindu laborers and the rise of Malay nationalism, Malays and other locals replaced the category of *Jawi Peranakan* with the more stigmatizing category *"Mamak." "Mamak,"* a term originally used to refer to Indian converts to Islam, began to take on the additional senses of Indian-Malay hybrids and any Indian who was a Muslim thereby distinguishing Indian Muslims from the much larger Indian Hindu and Malay Muslim populations. To some extent, Indian and Malay suspicion of Indian Muslims may reflect British attitudes toward such cultural and racial mixtures. Chinese and Indian *Peranakan*—the Straits-born Chinese and Indians—were only significant to British concerns to the extent that they were part of the "Chinese" and "Indian" categories. Descendants of mixed marriages between Malays and Indians or Arabs were not trusted and British rulers excluded them from the upper levels of the administration and social prestige. Eurasians received a land grant for a settlement in Melaka and were employed as lower level clerks, engineers, and supervisors, but overall they were marginalized in the British scheme of things.

It should be noted here that although the British did not incorporate these categories of persons into a notion of legal citizenship or nationality, they were viewed as "subjects," to varying degrees, of the British Empire, and as such, they were to adhere to British values and dictates. It was not that they had to assimilate British culture and customs, but rather that they had to comply with a British standard of civility and propriety. Thus, the British "civilizing mission" in Malaya was not striving to create a "civil society" in which all of her subjects would share a particular "collective will" of shared values embedded and reproduced in a set of shared public institutions. Each group, to a large extent had its own public institutions that reproduced its own set of shared values, but British standards were to serve as a guide to interactions between the groups. When the groups met in the marketplace, or other public places, they were to adhere to British standards.

Slavery, especially as practiced by the Malay elite, but also by wealthy segments of the Chinese and Indian populations, and land tenure arrangements was a target of British reform-minded individuals. They also sought to contain and nullify what they perceived as the "wicked" and "cruel" edge of Chinese capitalists. Separate local courts were set up to administer Islamic and customary law of the Malays and other groups, but each group had to adhere to British Civil Law which was made into a federal system in the Straits Settlements and the FMS. The fact that "traditional" values and beliefs, particular to each group, were not to direct practice in public spaces where British standards were the epitome of prestige and civilization is exemplified by the Tengku Kudin's skirting of Islamic principles in order to impress the British. "His desire to foster a 'civilized' reputation in the Straits Settlements is suggested by his ostentatious sherry drinking and the pack of dogs he maintained in defiance of Islamic prohibitions" (Andaya and Andaya 1982:151). Nonetheless, it was the "Chinese" and not the "Malays" or "Indians" who were viewed by the British as coming closest to fulfilling the model of civilization. As industrious reflections of the Puritan work ethic, as lighter-skinned in physical appearance, and as educated in the English language and culture, Chinese were considered to be superior to other groups in the plural society. It was unthinkable from this perspective for Chinese to be governed by Malays; one British official, Pickering, imagined the situation of Malays governing Chinese as being "like the white settlers of America submitting to the rule of Indian chiefs" (quoted in Andaya and Andaya 1982:178).

Yet, it would be just this political arrangement, and its concomitant social and cultural complications, which was to come about following the British return to Malaya in the wake of the Second World War and the Japanese Occupation. During the brief but brutal period of Japanese occupation of the Malayo-Indonesian world, from 1942 to 1945, Malay nationalism, stirring since early in the twentieth century, found encouragement from the Japanese, as did Indian nationalism. Japanese invaders, after having delivered the harshest and most brutal treatment of the Chinese over any other group in Malaya, finally organized Chinese into some political clubs near the end of the occupation. It must be noted here that feelings of racial animosity between the Malays and Chinese were aggravated by the fact that the Japanese used Malay forces to fight against Chinese resistance groups, and in the immediate post-war years, many Malay "collaborators" were attacked by Chinese resistance organizations that had taken over regional governments (ibid:252–253).[6] This inter-racial violence and British perceptions of the lack of Malay loyalty was to have some influence on the process of negotiations leading up to the granting of political independence and to matters of legal and cultural citizenship.

CONSTRUCTION OF MALAYSIAN NATIONALITY AND LEGAL AND CULTURAL CITIZENSHIP

In this context, in which the three broad "races" of British Malayan colonial society were mobilized as nationalist and resistance organizations, the British returned after World War II with a plan to create two centralized colonies on the road to political independence. This plan would form Melaka and Penang, and the FMS and UMS into a Malayan Union, while Singapore would become a separate British colony. The British, as a signatory to the Atlantic Charter and as allies of post-war American champions of the principle of self-determination, were openly committed to a process of turning political power over to an independent Malayan nation. The Malayan Union plan sought to centralize power as a precursor of the turning over of power. A common Malaysian nationality and legal and cultural citizenship were constructed and negotiated in this situation of mobilized Malay, Chinese, and Indian segments (Andaya and Andaya 1982:252–3; Hashim 1983:34–36), and a colonial administration dedicated to turning over political power.

According to the proposals of the Malayan Union, for the first time in Malaya, there would be one single citizenship status providing a common set of civic and political rights to all residents of Malaya.

> *Malayan Union citizenship* was to be conferred automatically on all persons born and still ordinarily resident in Malaya (including Singapore) and on all persons who, although not born in Malaya, had been ordinarily resident there for not less than 10 or 15 years preceding 15 February 1942. In addition application for citizenship might be made by any person who had resided in Malaya for 5 out of the 8 years preceding his application (including the immediately preceding year). (Gullick 1963:224).

This unitary citizenship would be tied to several nationalities, since citizens of the Union could still maintain their British, Chinese, and Indian nationalities (Gullick 1963:89, 223). Many residents of Melaka, and other Straits Settlements, who were British subjects according to *jus soli* or the law of the soil, as they or their fathers' were born in British territory, found the fact that they could maintain their British nationality as an important advantage of the Malayan Union. Although some non-Malay people disagreed with some provisions of the Malayan Union, most of them found it acceptable, especially its extension of equal citizenship rights and the elimination of Malay privileges (see Hashim 1983:47–48; Koon 1998:56–57; Andaya and Andaya 1982:255–256).

Due to the perception that the Malay population had been generally disloyal to Britain during the Japanese invasion and occupation, in contrast to the Indian and Chinese populations, the Malayan Union scheme eliminated the favored position typically bestowed upon Malays in British prewar policies. It proposed to discontinue the sovereignty of the Malay Sultans, autonomy of Malay states under British protection, and special Malay privileges such as predominance in the administrative civil service. As Andaya and Andaya (1982:255) point out: "the pretense that the British were merely assisting the Malay rulers to govern their lands was finally removed." It was the widespread perception amongst Malays that the Malayan Union plan meant they would be totally colonized that galvanized a Malay mass movement (Mohamad 1999:17; A. Ibrahim 1992:508). From the Malay perspective, it entailed the denial of their status as a "nation" and deprived them of their birthright as natives of the region and this they felt was unacceptable (Hashim 1983:47).

Before the inauguration of the Malayan Union scheme in 1946, delegates representing forty-one Malay associations from all over Malaya and Singapore convened in Kuala Lumpur to protest the Malayan Union plan and formed UMNO, the United Malays National Organization, to fight for Malay rights. UMNO issued statements condemning the Malayan Union plan and initiated a strategy to oppose and frustrate its implementation (ibid: 47). Although the Malayan Union plan was inaugurated on 1 April 1946, due to the strength and effectiveness of the opposition it was never brought into effect. It was eventually revoked in 1948 with the formation of the Federation of Malaya.

The British, Malay rulers, and UMNO, carrying over the basic idea of a common citizenship, negotiated the plan for a Federation of Malaya which was acceptable to the Malay population. In the Federation, power was centralized in British administrative structures, but the sovereignty of the Sultans, individuality of the states, and Malay special privileges were upheld (Andaya and Andaya 1982:256). A much more restricted form of citizenship with narrower eligibility rules was applied in the Federation. Federal citizenship was conferred by operation of law upon any subject of a Malay ruler of a State, any British subject *born in* Penang and Melaka who fulfilled a fifteen-year residence requirement, any British subject *born anywhere in* the Federation of Malaya whose *father or both parents* had been born there or fulfilled a fifteen-year requirement, any person *born in* the Federation of Malaya who spoke the Malay language and conformed to Malay custom, and any person born to a *father* who is a federal citizen (Gullick 1963:224–225). In addition, an application for citizenship could be made by persons *born in* the Federation who had been *resident therein* for 8 of 12 preceding years, and any person who had *resided in* the Federation for 15 of the 20 immediately preceding years. These applicants for citizenship would also have to pass tests of good character and possess an adequate level of linguistic competence in Malay or English language and make a declaration of permanent residency and an oath of loyalty to the Federation (ibid:225).

These citizenship requirements entailed a combination of the "law of soil" and the "law of blood." The "subject of a Malay ruler" was defined in such a way so as to include practically all persons of "Malay blood" in the Malay States but it did include some others as well. Many Malays who were born in Melaka or Penang and did not qualify on the basis of "blood" relationships to a Malay ruler, could qualify for citizenship based upon "the law of soil" and cultural characteristics associated with Malays. Those who were "British subjects" had additional "law of soil" and "law of blood" requirements on top of those that qualified them as "British subjects." They had to be "born in" particular places and in some specified cases, they could "inherit" eligibility through at least the *paternal line* if the father or both parents fulfilled requirements in relation to particular places. If people were not federal citizens based upon the *naturalizing* operation of liberal law, they could also be *naturalized* through additional means given that they fulfill particular "law of place" requirements. They had to pass tests and perform rites that would certify that they possess the right *nature* to be accepted as citizen-members.

> In addition to the entire Malay population about 350,000 Chinese and 225,000 Indians qualified as citizens by operation of law. In the period 1949–52 an additional 307,000 Chinese and 33,000 Indians successfully applied for registration as federal citizens. In effect all Malays, perhaps a third of the Chinese and half the Indian population qualified in time under the 1948 citizenship rules (Gullick 1963:225).

In 1952 the concept of state nationality was refined, linking federal citizenship with either British nationality in Melaka and Penang or nationality of one of the nine Malay States, and some of the 1948 citizenship rules were relaxed slightly to admit many more non-Malays to the Federation (ibid:226). There was added significance to being a citizen at this time because political elections were being introduced for the first time and thus the category of citizen now entailed a hierarchy of electors and non-electors. Malays wanted this hierarchy to be skewed in their favor, a condition that the restrictive citizenship rules created for them, so that they would be assured political domination in the Federation heading towards independence.

On the other hand, the non-Malays, who had been arguing for a broader application of the "law of soil" and political and economic equality, were disappointed with the 1948 and 1952 rulings. Almost immediately following the implementation of the 1948 Federation of Malaya plan, some discontented Chinese staged an insurrection against the government led by the Malaysian Communist Party.

Meanwhile, less radical segments of the Chinese and Indian communities participated in other organizations, the Malaysian Chinese Association (MCA), and the Malaysian Indian Congress (MIC), that formed a political alliance with their Malay counterpart, UMNO. Even though the MIC continued to agitate against the ideas of giving Islam priority, Malay special rights in the public sector, and the pre-eminence of Malays in Malayan politics, they finally joined the coalition in 1954 after the earlier successful coalition of UMNO and MCA in 1952 (Kim 1993:276–277). The British were somewhat disappointed with the fact that these organizations were communally based, parties representing particular racial segments of Malayan society. On the other hand, they found consolation in the fact that these parties represented the three largest racial segments of Malayan society and that they were working together in an Alliance with some shared goals. Following the overwhelming victory of the Alliance in the federal elections of 1955, the Reid Constitutional Commission gave consideration to the views represented by the Alliance Party (Andaya and Andaya 1982:261).

The Reid Constitutional Commission, consisting of members from the United Kingdom, Australia, Indian, and Pakistan, drafted a constitution, which was submitted to detailed examination by a party appointed by the British Government, the Conference of Rulers, and the Government of the Federation (A. Ibrahim 1992:508). This commission modeled the Malaysian Constitution upon the American and Indian constitutions (ibid: 510). Upon the basis of recommendations from this review party, the Constitution of an independent Federation of Malaya was promulgated on "*Merdeka* Day," August 31, 1957 in Melaka. The historic city of Melaka was chosen as a symbolic gesture of declaring political independence in a place where the long history of colonization had begun. The "*Merdeka*" Constitution embodied the compromise between the Malay, Chinese, and Indian segments of the population, the three major races of British Malaya and now of the Federation of Malaya or Malaysia. MCA, and other non-Malay organizations, focused upon obtaining citizenship rights based on the "law of soil" or "jus soli" and a more liberal provision for citizenship, so that they could be included in the political processes of post-independence Malaya. In addition, the MCA negotiated and insisted upon the inclusion of article 153, which protects Chinese economic interests from the potential threat of Malay special privileges, and obtained a verbal commitment from the President of UMNO, Tunku Abdul Rahman, to review and eventually terminate Malay special rights (Koon 1998:58). In turn, MCA conceded to UMNO, the special position of Malay rulers, Islam as the state religion and safeguards on Islam as the religion of the Malays, Malay as the national language of the Federation, and special rights treatment for Malays as natives of the "country" (see Hashim 1983:54).

Non-Malays conceded a great deal of inequality to attain the best possible form of citizenship they could obtain. Citizenship under the Independence Constitution was made more simple and inclusive; nationality, now unified throughout the Federation of Malaya, and citizenship extended by operation of law to:

(a) any person who was already a federal citizen under the previous rules at the date of independence (31 August 1957);

(b) any person born in the Federation on or after the date of independence. The Chinese demand for *ius soli* was at last conceded but not retrospectively;

(c) any person whose father was at the date of his birth a federal citizen (subject to certain safeguards).

In addition application for citizenship could be made by:

(d) any person born in the Federation before independence who had been resident therein for 5 years of the preceding 7 years;

(e) any person who had been resident in the Federation for 8 out of the preceding 12 years. (Gullick 1963:227)

The good character and linguistic tests and rites of naturalization applied to these latter categories of applicants. In the Constitutional Amendments of 1962 and 1963 an additional requirement was imposed on (b) that at least one parent had to be a citizen or a permanent resident at the time of the child's birth. This further restricted application of the "law of the soil" as a basis for citizenship. The combination of "law of blood" and "law of soil" was continued from the 1948 Constitution, but the "law of soil" was made broader in its application. Although this is a narrower application of the "law of soil" as compared to the American Constitution, many more people *born in* the Federation of Malaya were granted citizenship under the 1957 Constitution who would have been excluded under the terms of citizenship in 1948 and 1952. The criteria for applicants or naturalization were only a little more stringent than the much-criticized Malayan Union rules (ibid).

Moreover, the "law of soil" and "law of blood" citizenship stipulations entail gender inequality, as Malaysian women are not accorded the same rights as their male counterparts. In particular, the 1957 Constitution and current citizenship laws continued the male-bias of the earlier laws with its emphasis on the *paternal line*. A Malaysian woman married to a foreign male can only confer her Malaysian nationality and citizenship upon her child if the child is *born in* Malaysia. Whereas the "law of blood" holds for Malaysian men married to foreign women, given that the laws allow them to confer their Malaysian nationality and citizenship upon their offspring whether or not their offspring were *born in* Malaysia. Malaysian women must rely upon the "law of soil" in these cases, because their children cannot inherit these rights via the *maternal line*. In addition, the Malaysian Federal Constitution allows Malaysian husbands to bring their foreign wives into Malaysia and to acquire permanent residency for them, whereas Malaysian wives are not accorded the same rights. Their husbands, if they are going to stay in Malaysia, must constantly renew temporary visit permits to stay with their Malaysian wives. This bias towards the *paternal line* is a widespread principle in Malaysian society, referred to popularly as the principle of *following the father,* and the state and local people have institutionalized it in connection with marriage and the official categorization of children in general (see chapter seven).

Similarly, constitutional guarantees of fundamental liberties, equal protection, and religious freedom are more restricted than in the amended American Constitution. The rights to freedom of speech, assembly, and to form associations, and even the right to move freely and to reside throughout the Federation are qualified and may be diminished in the Malaysian Constitution (A. Ibrahim 1992:512–513). These limitations on fundamental liberties construct a strong centralized state and limits democratic and civil rights in order to insulate the state from the deleterious effects of the exercise of such freedoms by any and all of its citizen-members, Malays and non-Malays alike. In terms of equal protection, the negotiated compromise between Malays and non-Malays is again inscribed in the Malaysian Constitution. Article 8(1) declares that all persons are equal before the law and entitled to equal protection of the law and that discrimination on the basis of religion, race, descent or place of birth has been outlawed; whereas Article 8(2) qualifies this declaration of equality by legitimizing exceptions authorized in other clauses of the Constitution. Namely, it legitimizes the inequality inscribed in Article 153 that provides that it shall be the responsibility of the *Yang de Peruan Agong* to safeguard the special position of the Malays and natives of any of the States of Sabah and Sarawak and the legitimate interests of other communities in accordance with the provisions of the Article. It expressly provides for reservation of quotas in respect of services, permits and education for the Malays and natives of Sabah and Sarawak (ibid: 513–514).

According to a constitutional law expert, the legal right of equality has not served any useful purpose and remains to be fully explored in Malaysia (Jain 1992:546). The principle of religious freedom is also upheld in general terms but qualified in a crucial manner. Article 11(1) guarantees the right of every person to profess and practice his or her religion, "subject to any law relating to public order, public health or morality" (ibid: 558). Besides the latter qualification, the right to propagate religious doctrine or beliefs amongst Muslims is subject to "any restrictions which a State law may impose" (ibid). Such a state law exists in Melaka and I will discuss it later. These constitutional qualifications laid on legal citizenship and some fundamental rights inscribe and embody the conditional nature of the position of non-Malays in Malaysia.

On the other hand, Malays were victorious in their efforts to inscribe their political dominance and position as the privileged natives into the Constitution.

It is in Article 153 of the constitution that the notion of the necessity of protecting the "special position" of the Malays, or the **bumiputra**, is elaborated and given the force of legal sanction. Amongst other things, Article 153 provides for a quota system of opportunities in three main areas; the public service, the general economic field, and in education. The object is to advance Malays to the levels supposedly enjoyed by other ethnic categories, locally referred to as 'races.' It is this Article above all others which requires for its application the identification of each citizen's 'race,' and results in that race—Malay, Chinese, Indian or Other—being a permanent feature of one's identity, through the medium of the identity card which all citizens and residents over twelve must carry (Mearns 1986:76).

In the Constitution, Malays are included in the category of "natives of the soil" or *Bumiputera,* a broad racialized conception of groups assumed to have been the original native peoples of the region. Malays and other *Bumiputera,* as the natives, had a special historic and *natural* relationship with the land of the region that the colonizers and immigrants do not have. In addition, the Constitution distinguishes Malays in cultural terms from other *Bumiputera*. Malays are defined as Muslims, habitual speakers of the Malay language, and followers of Malay custom or *adat*. As no other groups are defined in racial or cultural terms in the Constitution, this selective inscription of race and culture facilitates the opposition of Malays and non-Malays and *Bumiputera* and non-*Bumiputera* for political and economic purposes. Being included in, or excluded from, these categories, Malay and *Bumiputera*, has a definite and strong effect upon whether or not one will receive a series of political, economic and social benefits. Although this explicit definition of "Malay" formalizes boundaries of Malay identity and provides legal means for regulating membership in the Malay category, these boundaries can be and are negotiated and persons in some respects considered outside of the Malay category find a way to be included (cf. Lee 1986:33). In any event, being included in this category is clearly beneficial in terms of receiving access to material benefits in the public sector.

In addition, the political and symbolic hegemony of Malays is inscribed in the Constitution in regards to the position of Malay Rulers and Ministers, Islam and the Malay language. The sovereignty, prerogatives, powers and jurisdiction of the nine Malay Rulers are protected in the Constitution. It provides for a Council of Rulers that elects one amongst their numbers every five years to serve as the King or *Yang di Pertuan Agong* ("The One Who Has Been Made the Great Lord"). These nine Malay Rulers are constitutional monarchs after the Westminster model in which the King and other Rulers "shall act in accordance with the advice of the Cabinet or a Minister acting under the authority of the Cabinet" (A. Ibrahim 1992:518). Thus, the effective political power is vested in the Prime Minister and Chief Minister or Grand Minister who advises the King and Ruler of each state respectively. This generally rests political and symbolic power in the hands of Malays, but Penang is an exception. In Penang, a Chinese Chief Minister holds political power owing to the overwhelming majority of the Chinese population in the state; however, the Malay Governor still holds symbolic power. The Constitution declares Islam as the official state religion, although there is freedom to practice and profess other religions. In effect, similar to India, Malaysia appears by all other characteristics to be a "secular" society, and this has been a point of contention for the Islamic opposition party, PAS, that argues that under the Alliance coalition, nowadays called *Barisan Nasional*, the Malaysian government does not uphold Islamic principles. Nevertheless, the symbolic advantage bestowed on Malays with Islam, a definitive marker of their cultural identity, singled out as the national state religion and with state-level Islamic courts is significant. Likewise, the adoption of the Malay language as the national language used for all official purposes bestows symbolic advantages on Malays, but it also provides them with practical advantages of taking educational courses in their native language.

From this brief look into postwar negotiations of Malaysian nationality and citizenship, we can note that processes of legal citizenship are dynamic and ongoing. Malay opposition to the Malayan Union plan and non-Malay and Malay compromise over the principle of *jus soli* and Malay privileges and American and Indian constitutional models all contributed to the social construction of Malaysian legal citizenship. This legal citizenship evokes an imagined community in which all Malaysians are horizontally aligned as equal members of the nation. Indeed, the fact that such a community is still imagined despite explicit inscriptions of inequality speaks to the discursive power of modern liberal nationalism. The compromise or contract between Malays and non-Malays was embodied in the recurrent pattern of coupling principles of equality with bias towards Malays. Malay "blood" which connects Malay subjects to Rulers and native "blood" connecting them to the soil, *Tanah Melayu,* was incorporated into the construction of legal citizenship. Furthermore, cultural markers such as Islam and Malay language and custom assumed to have a natural connection to Malayness were prominent in the Constitution. Malaysian legal citizenship is still open to negotiation through constitutional amendments, court cases and decisions, and legislation of new laws and new interpretations of existing laws.

Moreover, negotiations over legal citizenship entail and constrain cultural citizenship. Political contests over the union and federation plans expressed conflicting notions about what it meant to be a citizen-member of the Malaysian nation. Malays felt left out of a union plan that did not preserve their special position as natives and threatened by the prospect of losing political and economic control to immigrants. On the other hand, Chinese and Indians felt disappointed by the defeat of the union plan that promised them equal political and economic rights with the Malay population. Social and cultural tensions over these images of belonging to the Malaysian nation continue into the present period. In fact, the outcome of previous negotiations inscribed in the Constitution and other legal documents constitute a hegemonic form of cultural citizenship, making Malaysian subjects. Malaysians of all racial and religious backgrounds are supposed to respect and uphold the national constitution and its emphasis upon Malay culture. The Malay-dominated government and civic institutions routinely construct and project national culture and identity with a Malay foundation (Lee 1986:36–40; Nonini 1997:206–207). On the other hand, Chinese, Indians, and other non-Malay groups actively strive to incorporate themselves more fully within Malaysian society, despite of, and in response to the bias inscribed and re-enacted in public policies. Chinese and Indians often contest the disciplining influences of the Malaysian government and civic institutions and formulate a sense of community and belonging in various contexts not under the direct control of Malay civil servants and administrators.

Malay, Chinese, and Indian contests over symbolic issues and the allocation of prestige and status are an integral part of processes of cultural citizenship (cf. Lee 1986). Malays, the inheritors of political power in post-independence Malaysia, do not command the same level of control and prestige that the British colonizers were able to muster over all segments of the colonial plural society. Hence, after the removal of the British prestige-giver and model of status allocation, there is no clear consensus on the relative position of social groups and an ambiguous status order has been the result (ibid:35). Several factors contribute to this ambiguous status order, not least of which is the fact that Malays are only dominant politically while Chinese are dominant economically. This is clearly in contrast to the joint economic and political domination of the British and of the "creole" nationalists who seized the reins of power in the newly independent states of the Western Hemisphere, for instance in the U.S. and in most Latin American nations. In addition, there are the lingering effects of racial stereotypes (see Teik 1989) constructed during the colonial era in which it was almost an aberration as noted earlier for Malay natives to rule the more "advanced and superior" Chinese population. Finally, there are also the effects of economic globalization and the prominent role that Chinese capitalists play within global and regional networks and government development projects. Given these factors, despite Malay political power and symbolic advantages embedded in the Constitution, Chinese, and to some extent Indians and other groups, vie for relative position in the status hierarchy. Although these symbolic negotiations and contests do not transform the established power arrangements in society overall, they do contest, transform, and potentially subvert the enactment of these arrangements in particular contexts and in so doing are part of self-making processes of cultural citizenship.

These issues of power arrangements and relative position of the social groups were a central matter of dispute in the 1960s, especially with the more radical segment of the Chinese community. The Chinese-led Communist insurrection had been put down, but many of the issues surrounding the official status of Mandarin, Chinese-medium schools and universities, and Malay special privileges were still hotly contested. Such issues dominated the elections of this period and culminated in the May 1969 riots.

This racial riot was immediately precipitated by the enormous victory of non-Malay opposition parties in the general election and their public victory celebrations. Malays took offense to these celebrations and fierce violence erupted, especially in Kuala Lumpur but the violence spread to other places as well. Malay armed forces retaliated against Chinese and an Emergency government was formed to take control of the country. In the wake of this bloody incident, new Malay leaders rose to the fore dedicated to implement the mandate more fully for Malay special rights.

> This is evident in the launching of the New Economic Policy (NEP) in the early 1970s, which introduced on a large scale economic concessions to the Malays in the form of scholarships, housing preferences, employment and business opportunities. The implementation of this policy has obviously alienated many non-Malays who now perceive their power base as being gradually eclipsed by the activities of the Malay political establishment (Lee 1986:34).

Another important result of the communal riots of 1969 was the legal restrictions placed upon the questioning of certain sensitive issues. In particular, it was now an offense to question matters relating to citizenship, the national language, the special position of Malays and natives of Sabah and Sarawak and the "legitimate interests of other communities," and saving the sovereignty of the Rulers (A. Ibrahim 1992:523). Furthermore, they decided that a law making an amendment to any of these controversial parts of the Constitution could only be passed with the consent of the Conference of Rulers (ibid). This sent the message that Malay hegemony was here to stay and that the dominant construction of cultural citizenship had to be accepted by immigrant races.

CONTEMPORARY MELAKA AND CULTURAL CITIZENSHIP

Local people generally think the communal riots of 1969, referred to popularly as simply "May 13th," were less severe and ferocious in Melaka than in Kuala Lumpur. Residents of Melaka tend to avoid talking about this tragic historic incident as a topic of conversation, although they often noted it in passing as a vivid example of what could happen if the current government policies, touted for promoting racial harmony, were disrupted for some reason. Nevertheless, some residents have related to me pieces of their memories about "May 13th." A middle-aged Indian Catholic man told me that everything seemed to have stopped in Melaka, because most of the businesses in town which were, and still are, practically almost all Chinese-owned shut down. Chinese closed their stores all across town. A younger

Chinese Buddhist-Taoist man informed me that many Chinese still harbor resentment towards Malays due to the loss of Chinese lives and property when the Malay armed forces intervened in the mass disturbances. From his perspective, these sorts of racial conflicts hurt Malays more than they do Chinese, because Chinese will stop going to Malay restaurants which would hurt them economically whereas Malays already do not go to Chinese restaurants due to Islamic food prohibitions. A Malay teenager, a high school student, informed me that one of his neighbors lost his mother during the riots. She was outside of their home during the riots and has been amongst the "disappeared" ever since. They believe that Chinese gangs murdered his friend's mother. A Malay urban professional, a man in his thirties, informed me that the news of just how brutal these riots were has not been exposed to the world and he gave me some examples of stories he has heard. The Malaysian government put a lid on detailed information about just how bloody and brutal these riots were but these events live on in the memories of the residents of Melaka and other places in Malaysia.

In post-May 13th Melaka of the 1970s, the broad divisions of social segments formed under colonial rule were still reflected in the highly segregated residential patterns and infrequent social interactions between members of these social segments. The urban area was still a "Chinese town" overwhelmingly inhabited by Chinese residents who lived above or not far from their places of work and business and worship. Not far from the old colonial center of town where several old, Dutch and British buildings still stand, were several streets filled with Chinese shop houses and workshops and clan and dialect group houses and temples, including the most prominent Cheng Hoon Teng Temple. Malays, the majority in the state of Melaka, were a small minority in town and were rarely seen in large numbers except over the weekends when they would come to town from outlying villages in order to shop and to socialize with friends and relatives (Clammer 1986:53). There were a few Malay neighborhoods in town, like *Kampung Morten* and a few others located off of the main roads, and some Malays were in town working as civil servants, Malay and Islamic book sellers, and street hawkers and food stall operators. Some Chettiar and Gujerati Indians lived in town close to a small set of businesses they owned and operated or in marginal communities, like the Chitty Hindu community in Gajah Berang, but most Indians lived outside of town on, or near, palm oil and rubber estates. Eurasians resided in the Portuguese settlement, a neighborhood established with British assistance in the 1930s on land along the coast where many found their livelihood fishing, and near an old Catholic Church in Bandar Hilir, two areas in walking distance from each other lying south of the

Melaka River. Interactions between these segregated social segments were largely restricted to functional relations, economic and political relations, but some members of these communities interacted at religious sites that held sacred meanings spanning many of these communities.

During this time period, at least in the early 1970s, there was a government cultural policy that restrained public displays of non-Malay culture and non-Islamic religions. In 1971, the Malaysian government formulated a national cultural policy based upon the stated principles of emphasizing indigenous cultures, Islam, and elements of other cultures it judged to be suitable for incorporation into Malaysia's national culture (see Kahn and Loh 1992:13; Beng 1992:283). To some extent, Buddhist-Taoist and Hindu festivals and cultural performances such as lion and dragon dances, and public processions had restrictions placed upon them. Chinese-medium and Tamil-medium television programming was restricted, especially programs exhibiting classical Chinese costumes and Mainland Chinese dynasties. Remember it was the *public* celebration of non-Malay groups that sparked the May 13th incident. Many Malays interpreted these public cultural shows as expressions of Chinese and Indian chauvinism and lack of loyalty and as potential opposition to the dominant model of cultural citizenship predicated upon emphasizing Malay culture in *public* spaces. The state gradually removed some of these restrictions and granted police permits for religious festivals and Chinese and Indian communities staged religious processions and cultural shows centered in their respective communities, urban spaces associated with their social identities, and were allowed to pass through public streets.

By the end of the 1970s, the old patterns of residential and social separation began to change under the concerted effort of government agencies dedicated to implementing the New Economic Policy (NEP). The Malacca State Development Corporation (MSDC), established in 1971, worked to create economic opportunities for *Bumiputera*, encouraged tourism and developed housing and commercial facilities. MSDC formed the Bumiputera Business Community and Development Programme that helped many *Bumiputera* establish small and medium-sized industries in several areas around the state of Melaka. This was an expression of the Malay desire for a greater share of the economic resources. "Targets were set so that by 1990, Malay corporate ownership would be 30 per cent, non-Malay 40 per cent, and foreign 30 per cent in contrast to 1.9 per cent, 37.4 per cent, and 60.7 per cent respectively in 1970" (Jesudson 1989:1–2). The MSDC and other state agencies also provided spaces for Malay food stalls and helped to develop some new commercial buildings across from the old center of town on land reclaimed from the sea (Mearns 1995:60). Some industrial estates and free trade zones were developed to attract foreign capital investment and joint ventures between Malay entrepreneurs or state officials and foreign capital was encouraged (ibid).

As an integral part of UMNO plans, Malays were moved from rural to urban areas to fill jobs in the expanding commercial and manufacturing sectors and to attend educational institutions. The UMNO "movement" sought to alleviate rural poverty and to breakdown old colonial barriers by facilitating the entry of Malays into urban employment and education. Private companies were compelled to hire a high percentage of Malays in keeping with special Malay rights and the NEP. Large numbers of unskilled, young Malay women were recruited to work in factories in the free trade zones (Ong 1987; Mearns 1995:78–79). The state and municipal governments also intervened in the housing industry to secure a percentage of this sector for Malay contractors and entrepreneurs and to develop housing for a growing Malay presence in town. In the late 1970s, the state government sponsored several multistory blocks of low-cost, municipally owned apartment buildings (Mearns 1995:66). Moreover, some housing estates began to crop up on the edges of town, some of them on Malay land. These processes of using Malay customary lands, lands reserved for Malays, for development purposes, agribusiness and housing for instance, contributed to the decline in Malay agricultural pursuits and the concomitant growth of the Malay working class. Mostly Chinese and a few Indians lived in these new housing estates, but some Malays profited from their construction. Stemming from these development projects and other NEP programs, a small but established Malay upper class and budding working class became visible in Melaka.

In the 1980s the pace of these economic and demographic changes rose drastically altering the appearance of old historic Melaka. The old colonial buildings in Melaka were joined by almost constant construction of new commercial buildings and industrial and housing estates. Several new free trade zones and industrial parks were created bringing a large quantity of foreign capital into Melaka. Numerous electronics companies owned by American, European, East Asian, and Malaysian Chinese interests were dominant in these new industrial estates located in several areas outside of the center of town. A curious reproduction and adaptation of colonial racial hierarchies came to characterize the division of labor in these factories. Europeans and Chinese filled the top and middle management positions and some Indians filled the lower management and skilled labor roles such as engineers and mechanics. Malays, mandated by NEP quotas to fill a certain percentage of positions, predominated in the low wage, unskilled positions of line operators, part inspectors, and machine operators. Malays who entered the lower management were typically used to supervise overwhelmingly Malay production line workers. Some Indians and a few Chinese were hired in these unskilled positions as well. Large numbers of Malay women were still represented in the lowest rung of the factory production, but numbers of young Malay men, hired to perform more physically demanding labor, were on the rise too. Malay workers were shuttled back and forth on factory buses from outlying *kampungs* and urban apartment buildings to factories for each work shift. More apartment complexes and low income housing was built to accommodate their housing needs. In this process of economic transformation, outlying predominantly Malay *kampungs,* rural communities or villages, were turned into suburban satellites of the commercial and industrial center for which they supplied the bulk of low wage, unskilled workers. It gradually became rarer to observe Malay villagers engaged in agricultural pursuits, although some continued to combine agricultural and urban labor for some time.

In addition, an expanding Malay civil service worked to enhance the tourist industry in Melaka. Malay civil servants developed museums in several old colonial buildings and a new tourist attraction, and had the Cultural Museum or Sultan's Palace, constructed nearby. The state placed these museums under the control of Malay municipal and state civil servants who used these museums and their environs for enacting and reproducing the dominant model of cultural citizenship, laying stress on the Malay component of a multiracial society. However, cultural restrictions placed on public displays of non-Malay cultures and religions were eased and new cultural policies formed that emphasized representing Malaysia as a culturally diverse society, a mix of all Asian cultures. This state-down multiculturalism grew into a major theme of the tourist industry. To support growth in the tourist industry, Chinese businessmen constructed several Chinese-owned hotels opening up new employment opportunities for Malay workers in the hospitality and service industry.

Malays, Chinese, and Indians began living in the same neighborhoods in increasing numbers. Many Malay workers, living in town, resided in apartment buildings with Chinese and Indian neighbors. In addition, an increasing segment of the Malay middle class took up residence, beside their Chinese and Indian counterparts, in some of the housing estates springing up all over Melaka by the end of the 1980s. More Malay children attended urban public schools, some of them formerly Catholic convent schools, with Chinese and Indian children. These economic, residential, and education-related changes were bringing members of racial groups formerly separate plural segments into more frequent contact and social interaction.

In this context of increasing social interactions between Malays and non-Malays, the Malay elite strove to maintain the distinctiveness and separateness of Malay *Bumiputera* from all other groups. This distinction, inscribed in the Constitution, is the basis for Malay special rights and consequentially for the differential distribution of resources and access to power and prestige. Malay political and religious leaders used two of the key markers of Malay identity, Islam and Malay customs, to tighten the boundaries between Malays and non-Malays. In contrast to the Administration of Muslim Law Enactment of 1959, the Islamic Family Enactment, 1983, explicitly restricts marriage between Muslims and non-Muslims stating that no Muslim woman shall marry a non-Muslim and that no Muslim man shall marry a non-Muslim except a *kitabiyah*. "*Kitabiya*" was defined in this enactment as a "woman whose ancestors were from the Bani Ya'qub" or "a Christian woman whose ancestors were Christians before the prophethood of the Prophet Muhammad" or "a Jewess [sic] whose ancestors were Jews before the prophethood of the Prophet 'Isa." Before the state passed this law, locals conventionally understood in Melaka society that a non-Muslim, regardless of gender, had to convert to Islam before marrying a Muslim. Many non-Muslims resented, and continue to resent, the fact that conversion to Islam is a legal requirement to marry a Muslim. This explicit codification in law serves to ground these conventional understandings of Malay customs, merging Islam and *adat,* in particular interpretations of the Quran and Sunnah (traditions of the Prophet Muhammad). Since a non-Muslim woman, who is a Jew or Christian, would have to trace her ancestry back several centuries to demonstrate descent from the early community of Christians or Jews, for all practical purposes, this totally restricts marriage between Muslims and non-Muslims. Accompanying, this enactment was a development and expansion of Islamic institutions and agencies geared towards facilitating the conversion of non-Muslims interested in marrying Muslims to Islam and in the process to the culture of most Muslims in Malaysia, Malay culture.

In addition, the Control and Restriction of the Propagation of Non-Islamic Religions Enactment of 1988 exemplifies this pattern of race making and policing of boundaries. Consistent with Article 11(4) of the Federal Constitution, which provides for such restrictions by states, the state government of Melaka passed this enactment, which formally makes "propagation" of non-Islamic religions to Muslims a legal offense. According to this enactment a person commits a crime if he or she influences a Muslim to follow or to take part in any non-Islamic religion, including any ceremonies, acts of worship and other religious activities or to forsake or disfavor the religion of Islam. In addition, particular words and expressions associated with Islam, such as *"Ibadah," "Salat," "Rasul," "Nabi,"* "Imam," *"Dakwah,"* and *"Assalamualaikum," "Alhamdulillah," "Allahu Akbar,"* *"Subhanallah"* and so forth, were listed and restricted from being associated with non-Islamic religions or from being spoken by non-Muslims.[7] Dialogues between Malays and other Muslims and non-Muslims on the subject of religion were discouraged and the unrestrained social interactions between Malays and non-Malays became highly strained.

Similarly, state intervention disrupted interactions between Malays and other Muslims and non-Muslims at sites where some sectors of each of the main racial groups of Melaka had developed a pattern of religious interaction. Namely, inter-racial and inter-religious interactions and worship at ancient Muslim graves, locals considered as *keramat* or in possession of special spiritual powers, was the target of Malay political and religious leaders. They considered such activities "un-Islamic" and deemed them criminal offenses for Muslims in state interpretations of Islamic law. These legal measures, placing stress upon Islam and Malay distinctiveness, served to reconstruct and fortify racial borders situating Malays as the preferred race, while creating obstacles for the full incorporation and belonging of non-Malays. Many non-Muslims responded to this growing climate of Malay and Islamic exclusiveness by assigning greater significance to their racial and religious identities and by forging greater ties between themselves and other non-Malays and non-*Bumiputera* (cf. Ackerman and Lee 1988).

In the 1990s, tensions between hegemonic and alternative models of cultural citizenship became even more accentuated within the context of continuing patterns of industrialization, commercialization, and rural-urban transformation. Galvanized by Prime Minister Mahathir Mohamad's declaration of "Vision 2020," the state government of Melaka encouraged the proliferation of "development" projects aimed at turning Melaka into a "developed industrial center by 2000" and achieving "fully developed status by 2010." More industrial parks were constructed still dominated by foreign and local Chinese capital and more housing estates and condominiums sprung up around Melaka inhabited by an increasingly multiracial population. More hotels and commercial enterprises were constructed and opened up for business in Melaka bringing even more Malay laborers from the countryside and suburban neighborhoods. In addition, many Malay professionals moved into Melaka filling civil service and development sector positions. Several modern air-conditioned shopping centers were built as part of this commercial growth and were filled up with predominantly Chinese traders and business owners. A few of these shopping centers were equipped with large stages that became important sites for cultural shows and festivities and consequently for constructions and negotiations of cultural citizenship.

CONCLUSION

The Melaka Sultanate was a cosmopolitan center of trade and culture that drew a diverse population from around the region and around the world. "Malay" culture and identity had long been intertwined with these maritime empires and trading entrepots, but in this period it also became strongly associated with Islam. Indian and Chinese traders and officials played an important role in early Melakan society. Some early communities of Indians and Chinese formed during this period and underwent a process of acculturation with the Malay community whereby they adopted many aspects of Malay culture. The Portuguese conquest of Melaka in 1511 initiated a series of colonial intrusions eventually putting an end to the Malay cycle of maritime empires.

In the subsequent period of European settler colonialism, several new cultural categories emerged and old ones took on new meanings. Portuguese rulers encouraged intermarriage with locals and left a "*Melaka Portugis*" community as a living legacy in Melaka after their defeat at the hands of the Dutch. During the Dutch and British periods, there was a significant rise in the immigration of Chinese and Indians and some of these newcomers merged with older communities of "Straits-born" Chinese and Indians. However, others maintained their distinctiveness and eventually overtook the assimilated "Straits-born" communities as the dominant political and economic leaders of the Chinese and Indian communities. The older assimilated communities became somewhat stigmatized minorities within their respective cultural categories for having lost some of their original heritage. "Indians" became associated with menial labor and "Chinese" became associated with business and trade. "Malays" became associated with rural areas and agricultural pursuits and regional "Malay" variants or subgroups emerged.

During the British period, these cultural categories were organized into largely separate social segments constituting the classic plural society. The British promulgated racial stereotypes and ideology to buttress the colonial hierarchies erected for their political and economic benefit. These social and cultural divisions presented major obstacles for the social segments to surmount during and after the independence negotiations. Malays demanded continued recognition of their status as the "natives" of Malaya and perpetuation of Malay special rights. In turn, non-Malay social segments demanded equal citizenship rights based on the principle of *jus soli* and hence enfranchising all persons "born in" Malaya. The outcome was a delicate compromise, between parties representing the three major races that they inscribed into the Federal Constitution of Malaysia. The May 13, 1969 riots nearly shattered this fragile social contract, but a new group of Malay leaders rose to the fore and seized the reins of power.

These new Malay leaders were committed to maintaining the delicate compromise but in contrast to earlier leaders, they felt that Malay sentiments and demands had to be given precedence if there was going to be racial harmony and peace in the country. They formulated the New Economic Policy to broadly institutionalize special benefits for Malays with the expressed purpose of bringing up to par with other wealthier races.

The implementation of this program, and others related to it, brought major changes to Melaka in the last three decades. These programs and policies have transformed a former "Chinatown" into an increasingly multiracial city with large numbers of Malays moving into town to work in new industries and to live in new housing estates and apartment buildings. In many respects, the old colonial divisions of the plural society were beginning to breakdown under the weight of people of different categories having more contact and interaction across social segments. However, Malay officials and civil servants have instituted measures to control and police the unwelcome crossing of racial borders and many old sentiments and tensions have rekindled in all social segments in Melaka.

In this chapter, I described the historical processes in which diverse social groups came to Melaka and in which cultural categories and their meanings emerged. In addition, I described the processes of legal and cultural citizenship and the contemporary context in Melaka. Now, I will turn to a detailed description and analysis of cultural categories and their underlying meanings in contemporary Melakan society.

Part II

Chapter Three
Cultural, Categories, Hybridity, and Identity Schema

St. Clair Drake (1963), F.K. Lehman (1967), and Fredrik Barth (1969) use a theoretical perspective that treats the categorization of humans in society as cultural and social constructions. In the work of these scholars, cultural categories are not interpreted as reflections of natural divisions of humankind or as having any intrinsic foundation in biological or cultural characteristics; instead, they are viewed as human conceptual inventions used for various social and political purposes. This perspective has become an important benchmark of contemporary social scientific description and analysis.

Many social scientists have merged this view with symbolic and interpretive theory (Geertz 1973; Paul Gilroy 1991; Jackson and Penrose 1993; Mauer 1997; Jayne O. Ifekwunigwe 1999; Kahn and Loh 1992; Kahn 1998; Ibrahim 1998). These scholars have focused upon the meanings and understandings attached to constructed social categories. Paul Gilroy (1991), Jackson and Penrose (1993), and Mauer (1997) demonstrate how the meanings attached to cultural categories change over time and are influenced by power struggles. "Examining the way these groups are formed and sometimes reproduce can point to a view of 'race' as a political category. As such, its meanings are unfixed and subject to the outcomes of struggle" (Gilroy 1991:24). Although this merging of the "constructionist" perspective with symbolic and interpretive theory offers a way to highlight social dynamics, it fails to clearly elucidate which aspects of social categorization are being transformed or contested and which ones are being reproduced in social processes.

Furthermore, some explorations of interracial and intercultural "hybridity" tend to assume that persons in these "in between" social spaces are only loosely tied to either, or any, cultural category or social identity implicated in such "admixtures" (Anzaldua 1987: 76; Bhaba 1994:219; Ifekwunigwe 1999:20).

> "That is, narrated across time and space, the testimonies of *bi-racialized metis(se)* identities featured in *Scattered Belongings*, lucidly illustrate the ways in which, acting *metis(se)* subjects can and do negotiate, challenge and subvert *all* of the subject positions—'One' (White) the 'Other' (Black) or 'Neither' (*metis(se)*)" (Ifekwunigwe 1999:21).

Such discussions of "hybridity" present useful ethnographic descriptions of particular racialized contexts and suggest ways to transcend essentialist thinking in social action and analysis. Yet, they contribute little towards a general theory of "hybridity" which requires more rigorous analysis of cultural categories and the components of underlying knowledge that constitute them.[1]

To avoid the limitations of merging the "constructionist" view with symbolic and interpretive theory, I will use cognitive anthropological theory to describe and analyze cultural categories. Similar to symbolic approaches, the cognitive approach does not concern itself with the "truth value" or validity of these categories (Jackendoff 1993:157–176). Whether cultural categories and the understandings they entail are accurate representations of the persons so categorized is not at issue. On the other hand, what convictions people hold as to what meaningful differences exists between collectivities of persons, and how they come to hold such convictions and how these convictions change over time, is of primary concern. Of course, any two members, of the same society, who share a great deal of background knowledge, may disagree about how a person or group of people should be categorized. This fact causes little theoretical angst for a cognitive approach that can highlight the particular aspects of categorization in dispute.

I will use a distinction between high-level categories and low-level knowledge in my description and analysis of social identity in Melaka. High-level categories includes "maximal" cultural categories, such as Malay, Chinese, Indian, Chitty and so on; categories that entail a broad range of knowledge structures and signify "one's total social persona" (Sands and Lehman 1995). These high-level categories are constructed of low-level knowledge: role-function and status-value. Role-function refers to the behavioral expectations and the status-value refers to the ranking and evaluations associated with each category. High-level categories and low-level knowledge are bundled together in detail-rich identity schemata (F.K. Lehman 1997; Strauss 1992).

These components can be utilized to discern which aspects are being transformed and reproduced in social processes. For instance, high-level categories may be changing as in the changes from "Negroes" to "Coloreds" to "Blacks" and to "African American" in the United States of America (see Smitherman 1977:35–42). Aspects of low-level knowledge, behavioral expectations and evaluations were changing in the various social and political periods in which one of these categories was opted for over the previous one. Or in other contexts, the high-level categories may remain the same but the low-level knowledge constructing it and giving it new meaning may be changing. This appears to be the case in Paul Gilroy's discussion of the new ideological uses of "Black" to refer only to "people of African descent" whereas it had been used previously for "Afro-Asian unity" (1991:39).

Similarly, I use these components to underscore the links "hybrids" may have to either category involved in these assumed "mixtures" or to different high-level categories used to name particular "hybrids." I will deploy this cognitive approach to highlight the imagined links of "blood" and/or "culture" that underlie high-level categories. Hence, this approach can transcend the analytic problems involved in subsuming "race" within "ethnicity" or making artificial dichotomies between these "types" of cultural categories (Banton 1983; Torres, Miron, and Inda 1999: 5–6; see Harrison 1995: 47). The essential elements of "blood" and/or "culture" can be usefully described as behavioral expectations or attributes that construct high-level categories. Evaluations, attached to each intermingled element, are contributing aspects of the position categories occupy in a hierarchical system of relations. It is not just the rule of placement, for instance "hypo- or hyper-descent" or paternity, but also the valence attached to these elements that construct superiority or inferiority (cf. Ifekwunigwe 1999: 190) within a relational system.

Thus, the various components of this cognitive approach are well suited to analyzing a complex system of social relations like those in the urban area of Melaka. Many researchers have correctly demonstrated that one must study social groups in relation to other social groups in a system of relations rather than in isolation (see Faye Harrison 1995). Social groups are often defined, at least in part, in opposition or relation to other groups (see W.E.B. DuBois 1899; Allison Davis and Burleigh Gardener and Mary Gardener 1988 [1941]; St. Clair Drake 1993 [1945]). These researchers explicated the meanings of "Blackness" and "Whiteness" by studying them in relation to one another. Similarly, I will attempt to explicate the meanings of "Malay," "Chinese," "Indian," and "Portuguese" cultural categories as they relate to one another in the urban area of Melaka.

In this chapter, I will describe the maximal social identities in Melaka and the ways they mutually contribute to the shifting meanings associated with each other, and how they embed a multiplicity of "sub-maximal" so-cial identities, including several "hybrids" that are tied into overarching maximal categories in a varied manner.

MAXIMAL SOCIAL IDENTITIES IN MELAKA

Upon my first visit to the city of Melaka, I was struck by its social and cul-tural diversity and the multiplicity of categories used for people who interact on a daily basis. One can walk, as thousands of tourists do each year, from an area with "Indian" businesses selling sari, *punjabi* suits, and jasmine flow-ers, to a large "Chinese" commercial district called "Bunga Raya," or to sev-eral museums, housed in former Dutch and British colonial buildings, run by mostly "Malay" civil servants. One can just as easily walk from these areas to an old Catholic convent school turned government secondary school where "Malay," "Chinese," "Indian," and "Portuguese" girls attend classes conducted in the national language, *Bahasa Malaysia* (Malaysian Language), a version of the Malay language. After almost a year of asking questions about these cultural categories and interacting with people in Melaka, I began to understand some of the knowledge underlying these terms. I will at-tempt to explicitly represent some of these notions below.

"Malay" is the high-level category people used to refer to the Muslim majority of Malaysia. People considered Malays to be the "pure" Muslims who were "born as" Muslims, with Muslim parents. Islam, in relation to Malay-ness, is a religion inherited from one's parents and forefathers. Locals conventionally applied the phrase "*keturunan* Islam" for those who inherit Islam from their parents and is used to distinguish Malays, "pure Muslims," from *saudara baru* or converts to the Islamic faith. They also often used "Muslim race" and "*orang Islam*"—Muslim—in everyday discourse to refer to Malays. This major attribute of Malay social identity is evaluated posi-tively in the general society, since Islam is the official religion of Malaysia. "Malays" are one of the "races" of *Bumiputera*—sons of the soil—people assumed to be original inhabitants of the Malay Peninsular. In fact, people often referred to the land in this region as *Tanah Melayu* or "Malay land." As original inhabitants of the land, Malays hold a claim to the special status of people who fully belong, just as Chinese belong in China and Indians be-long in India, Malays belong in Malaysia. They are the "generic" Malaysians, possessing not only legal citizenship, but default cultural citi-zenship as well.

Stemming from their special status as full "belongers," Malays are ex-pected to be the political and military rulers of Malaysia. The nine Malay Sultans, who elect one of themselves to be the "*Yang Dipertuan Agong*"—

King—every five years, and Governors, in the four states without Sultans, are important symbols of sovereignty and political legitimacy. Melaka, Penang, Sabah, and Sarawak, are states with Malay Governors. In addition, the real paramount political power in the country is vested in a Malay Prime Minister and in each state with a Malay majority, which is every state except Penang, political power is vested in a Malay Chief Minister. In addition, Malays are expected to fill most positions in the government, armed forces and civil service. These "Malay" attributes of being the original inhabitants and political rulers and administrators raise the ranking of Malayness.

On the other hand, Malay status is devaluated by their being considered a "brown skinned race." In a context like Malaysia, where "fair" or light-complexioned skin tones, are considered preferable, the "brown" skin tones associated with Malay-ness, carry negative ratings. Several brands of skin bleach are marketed to Malays to lighten their skin color.

In addition, the behavioral expectation for Malays to live on the outskirts of cities and towns in areas called *kampung*—villages or rural communities—stigmatize them as backwards. Most of the local respondents to my map survey associated Malays with *kampung* spaces located primarily outside of the core town area, including the districts of Alor Gajah and Jasin, but a few are located in town off from major streets. *Kampung* residential spaces are associated with traditional values and outdated ways of thinking that people often criticized as being impediments to development and modernization (see Lian, Kwen Fee 2001).

Locals also expected "Malays" to speak the Malay language or *Bahasa Melayu* as their language of preference. The Malay language is widely distributed in Southeast Asia encompassing Indonesia and parts of southern Thailand. *Bahasa Melayu* has been standardized and gradually institutionalized after Independence as the national language, *Bahasa Malaysia,* and as such, all members of Malaysian society are expected to develop competence in it. Official government functions and most primary, secondary and college education are supposed to be conducted in the *Bahasa Malaysia,* simply called "BM" in popular discourse. The fact that government officials and formal decrees have recognized a language associated with Malay cultural heritage as the national language signifies a positive evaluation of this behavioral expectation.

A form of etiquette or mannerisms attributed to Malays is often associated with the Malay language (Andaya and Andaya 1982:119). Locals expected Malays to engage in open and friendly dialogue in which exchanges about one's family, employment, background, and present destination are normal and acceptable. They considered this form of speaking to be an expression of the "Malay" gregarious and "easy-going" disposition, assuming Malays to be oriented towards social life and inheriting a sort of gregarious "nature."

In addition to speaking the Malay language and being gregarious, locals expected Malays to prepare and consume food generously spiced with hot chili peppers. Chili peppers are routinely used as ingredients, added in the process of food preparation, or *sambal,* hot sauce served separately, in cuisine associated with Malays. People also expected Malays to wear *sarong* and *kebaya, baju kurung, baju melayu,*[2] and various styles of headdress associated with "Muslims." They expected Malay women to wear *kerudung* or scarves covering their heads and Malay men are expected to wear *songkok* or *kopiah,* Islamic-style headgear.

"Malays" are assumed to have "Muslim names," personal names associated with the Islamic faith. These "Muslim names" are Malay versions of Arabic names with *"bin"* (son of) or *"binti"* (daughter of)[3] used between the personal name and the person's father's name. For instance, *Mohamad Taib Bin Daud,* in which *Mohamad Taib* is the personal name and *Daud* his father's name. According to Malay naming customs, no family or clan names are inherited from generation to generation. *Mohamad Taib's* son or daughter will not have *Daud* at the end of his or her name, but will have *Mohamad Taib* following their *bin* or *binti,* as in *Nor Arusha Binti Mohamad Taib.* Furthermore, boards with verses of the Holy Quran, written in Arabic script, are often hung over the doorways of Malay homes. Taken together, the high-level category "Malay" and these low-level behavioral expectations and evaluations comprise a widely distributed, or "conventional," identity schema.

Despite recent political divisions in the Malay community, most social fragments still operate with the assumptions that Malays are the "natives" or "earliest rulers" of *Tanah Melayu* and that they should therefore dominate the political, military, and administrative realms of society. However, social actors have expressed major differences in contemporary political contests between UMNO and Malay-based Islamic organizations, such as the Islamic Party of Malaysia, PAS, and *dakwah* and *silat* organizations,[4] in regards to modernization and Islam. UMNO leaders and members tend to emphasize goals of "modernizing Malays," removing the negative evaluation associated with Malay rural existence by integrating them to "mainstream" urban economic life and replacing "backward" rural values with "modern" values (Mahathir Mohamad 1970:170–173, 1999:36–40). In conjunction with this focus, UMNO has promoted a "moderate" approach to Islam emphasizing interpretations that are consistent with scientific and technological advancement and economic "progress." In contrast, PAS, the Islamic party, as well as many *dakwah* and *silat* groups, tends to lay greater stress upon Muslim identity and Islamic values. They strive to extend Islamic principles and way of life throughout Malaysian society. In addition, particular forms of Islamic dress are at times associated with these opposing political ideologies and alternative productions of "Malay" identity. For instance, black *songkok* have increasingly become a marker for supporters of UMNO, while white *kopiah* have become markers for supporters of PAS. Similarly, blue clothing has become associated with UMNO supporters and green clothing with PAS and Darul Arqam (Malay-based *dakwah* organization) supporters and members. Malays, in current political processes, have turned these variations in Islamic dress into physical expressions of differing evaluations of underlying attributes and behavioral expectations that construct the "Malay" cultural category.

Similar to "Malay," the high-level category "Chinese" is underlain with a strong religion-based behavioral expectation; locals assumed persons included in this category to be "Buddhist." "Buddhist" is a convenient label for someone who believes in a complex synthesis of Buddhism, Taoism, and Confucianism. Many local Chinese have asked me if I am Muslim. After I answer the question in the affirmative, I have often asked if they are Muslim too. They generally responded by telling me emphatically that they are "pure Chinese." This means that they are not only racially "pure Chinese," but they are culturally "pure Chinese" too. Instead of adopting a religious identity associated with other "races," they claim the religious identity, in the Malaysian context, associated with the Chinese "race." In Malaysian society where Islam is the national religion, being a category of non-Muslims, "Buddhists" are given a negative ranking.

On the other hand, being "Chinese" is highly ranked because persons in this category are assumed to be "fair skinned" or "white" and having a light skin tone is evaluated positively in general Malaysian society. "Chinese," like the "white" skinned colonizers that ruled Malaysia for several centuries, are considered to be superior to the "brown" and "black" skinned "races" in Malaysia. People conventionally assumed them to be in possession of a naturally superior essence, one transmitted through "blood."

People expected "Chinese" to engage in business activities. They have an inclination for trade and possess the character traits required for success in business; locals considered "Chinese" to be hard working, clever and oriented towards turning a profit. As such, Chinese are assumed to hold economic power and to fill executive positions in the private corporate sector. Furthermore, "Chinese" are expected to live in urban areas, small towns and larger cities, where they own stores and conduct business. Many respondents to my map survey expressed a strong association between "Chinese" and the inner core or "old town" areas where several large businesses areas are located. A few respondents called this area a sort of "China town" section of Melaka. These urban localities and the "Chinese" who inhabit them are associated with economic and social advancement, "modernity" and "development," values given a positive spin by government discourse and policies over the past three decades. Behavioral expectations of business acumen and urban residency lift up the ranking of "Chinese" in Melaka.

Yet, "Chinese" are considered to be one of the groups of "immigrants" whose origins lie elsewhere, outside of *Tanah Melayu*. The underlying behavioral expectation of filling "immigrant" status is contrasted with *Bumiputera* status. Whereas *Bumiputeras* belong to this land, "immigrants" are assumed to have a special relationship with another territory from which their ancestors hailed. In this "discourse of origins," each "race" has an original place that they are *truly* from, although they may live elsewhere, this original place is the place they "belong." For "Chinese" this place is China. As "immigrants," Chinese are not full "belongers" in Malaysian society; they may qualify for "legal citizenship" but full "cultural citizenship" still lies outside of their grasp.

"Chinese" are assumed to be speakers of at least one dialect of Chinese language. They are thought to prefer speaking one of the Chinese dialects in intimate and formal settings. Most "Chinese" residents of Melaka are speakers of a variety of the Hokkien dialect, but there are speakers of several other dialects, including Hakka, Cantonese, Hailam, Teochew, Hainanese, living in Melaka as well. In addition, the Mandarin spoken dialect, considered to be the "standard" Chinese language, is used as the medium of education in the private Chinese schools in Melaka and is often used in other public settings. There are several daily newspapers and television news programs using written and spoken Mandarin and television sitcoms and movies using Mandarin or Cantonese. The behavioral expectation for "Chinese" to prefer speaking a language other than the national language, *Bahasa Malaysia*, lowers their standing in the general society.

Locals expected "Chinese" to be less gregarious and open than their Malay counterparts, and considered "Chinese" to be more private and secretive than are members other cultural categories. Although this more "distant" or "cold" orientation may be viewed as good for business, it is generally devalued as a pattern of overall social relations. The Malay model of etiquette, often associated with "*bahasa,*" is the more highly valued pattern. In this pattern of using language, it is polite to *tanya*—to ask—

about the affairs of people, and they are expected to reciprocate by being open and inquiring into your affairs in turn.

People also assumed "Chinese" to eat pork and to wear "modern" attire. They expected "Chinese" women to wear miniskirts, short blouses, and skin-tight pants, and "Chinese" men are expected to wear shorts or jeans in casual settings. In more formal settings, locals expected "Chinese" women to wear "western" style dresses and gowns, and "Chinese" men to wear "western" style suits and ties. "Chinese" are expected to wear white gowns and tuxedos for their weddings. Associating this style of dress with "developed nations," people often labeled it as "modern." Yet in a setting in which Islamic sensibilities about food and dress are dominant, the behavioral expectations of eating pork and wearing less modest attire are evaluated negatively. "Chinese" are often stigmatized as pork eaters and indecent dressers.

Locals expected "Chinese" to have "Chinese" clan names that they pass down from generation to generation. These names are inherited according to the patrilineal principle, flowing through a long line of men. Boards, with the Chinese characters for these clan names written on them, are often hung over the doorways of Chinese homes. Chinese are also expected to adopt European nicknames, such as "Bobby" or "Molly," which they may even use on business cards and amongst friends in public institutions, whereas these nicknames do on appear on official records. This practice of adopting European nicknames is often an irritant in social relations with Malays who tend to interpret this practice as an expression of Chinese feelings of superiority. Along with the boards displaying clan names, "Chinese" homes are often indexed by the presence of small red altars attached to the outside of their homes with incense and other offerings placed on them.

Similar to "Malays" and "Chinese," people primarily defined "Indians" by religion. The high-level category "Indian" embeds strong assumptions that persons in this category will be Hindus. In everyday discourse, people often use "Indian" and "Hindu" interchangeably; "Indians" are "Hindu" and "Hindus" are "Indian" continuing the intertwining of "race" and religion I described earlier in regard to other categories. "Indian" homes are generally indexed by the presence of framed pictures of Hindu deities hanging over the front doorways. As believers in one of the non-Islamic faiths, Hindus are not accorded positive evaluation in the eyes of the general public.

In addition, "Indians" are expected to be "dark skinned" or "*hitam*"—black skinned—people, a trait accorded negative evaluation in Malaysia.[5] "Indians" are considered to be at the opposite pole of skin tone from that occupied by the "Chinese" and other "*orang putih*"—white people. "Malays" and other categories are considered to be intermediate between these two poles. As a "dark skinned" race, "Indians" are conventionally assumed to be of an inferior nature as compared to the more "fair skinned" races.

Locals considered "Indians" to be another "immigrant" race and expected them to inhabit the estates or plantations outside of the town areas. They are generally considered to be "coolies" who perform strenuous manual labor on palm oil and rubber plantations located in Jasin and Alor Gajah, the two districts of the state of Melaka lying outside of the commercial center of *"Melaka Tengah"* (central district of Melaka). "Indians" are "immigrants" brought to Malaya by the British colonizers to labor in the plantation sector, where they still find themselves today, because they are suited by "nature" to perform this work. "Indians" are expected to be docile and servile in character. Nowadays, after *Merdeka* or national independence, "Indians" work on plantations owned primarily by "Chinese" and a few "Malays." As non-*Bumiputera* immigrants, manual laborers, and residents of estates outside of the city centers, "Indians" are ranked lowly in Malaysian society.

On the other hand, "Indians" are also associated with professional occupations such as medicine and law. They are considered to be very capable doctors and lawyers, professionals with high status in Malaysian society. I have often been told to just take a look at a listing of all the doctors and lawyers in Melaka, and I will see lots of Indian names. Thus, "Indians" are associated with two occupational extremes: lowly ranked "coolie" labor and high status professionals. This two-sided image of "Indians" was also reflected in the map survey in which many respondents associated "Indians" both with outlying agricultural estates and "Indian Street" (Temenggong Street) where several Indian businesses and professional offices are located.

Local people expected "Indians" to speak an Indian language as their preferred language and to have Indian names. Most "Indians" in Melaka speak Tamil, but there are local "Indians" who speak other Indian languages such as Malayalum, Telegu, Gujerati, Hindi, and Punjabi. "Indians" often speak Indian languages at home, amongst friends, and in community events. In addition, there is one "vernacular" public elementary school in Melaka, which uses Tamil as the medium of education. There are newspapers, television news programs and movies that use written or spoken Tamil. Yet, speakers of Tamil or other Indian languages, like speakers of Chinese dialects, receive the same negative evaluation in general Malaysian society for speaking a language other than the official national language.

Indian naming practices, in Melaka, involve the use of Indian names but they have been made to adhere to the "Malay" model. Following Malaysian independence, laws were passed mandating that Indians adopt the "Malay" naming formula for legal documents such as identification cards. Indians were no longer able to use their family names the way they did previously, because in the "Malay" formula the father's name appears at the end. However, instead of using the "*bin*" and "*binti*" before the father's name, Indians were mandated to use "anak lelaki" (son of) or "anak perempuan" (daughter of), abbreviated as A/L and A/P on identification cards. These terms correspond to each other and have the same literal meaning, but the former terms index Muslims and the latter terms index non-Muslims. Local "Indian" names are composed of a personal name and their father's name. For instance, *Kantheeban Annamalai* is a local Indian name in which the first name is the personal name and the last name is the person's father's name. His father, *Annamalai*, carries his grandfather's name as his last name, and so on. This also applies for women until they are married at which time they will use their husband's name in informal settings; for instance, *Mrs. Kantheeban* or *Vanitha Kantheeban,* in which the second name, *Kantheeban,* is her husband's name. Her name before marriage, *Vanitha A/P Dorasamy,* (her father's name), is still used on official documents. Even when the mediating terms, "anak lelaki" or "anak perempuan" are not used, people understand that the name reads as "Vanitha the daugher of Dorasamy" or "Kantheeban the son of Annamalai." If Vanitha and Kantheeban have a son named Arun, his last name will be Kantheeban, his father's personal name, and on his birth certificate, his mother's name will appear with her father's name rather than her husband's name, and "A/L" or "anak lelaki" will appear before his father's name.

In addition to speaking Indian languages and having Indian names, local Melakans expected "Indians" to prepare and eat "Indian" cuisine and to wear "Indian" attire. Some foods associated with "Indians" are various kinds of curry gravies—chicken and fish curry and *dahl* (split pigeon pea gravy)—and mutton and various types of *roti* or breads such as *roti canai,* a form of fried bread, usually eaten by dipping it into gravy. "Indian" cuisine is often served and eaten on banana leaves. These foods, sold by many "Indian" restaurants in Melaka, have become popular and are prepared and eaten by Malaysians of all cultural categories. This tends to produce a positive evaluation for the "Indian" category, especially since people generally do not associate any *haram* (forbidden to Muslims) items with "Indian" cuisine.

Similarly, there is no general condemnation of "Indian" attire. Indian men are expected to wear *dhoti* wraps around their lower bodies and *kurta* shirts, and Indian women are expected to wear sari and *punjabi* suits. People considered these forms of attire to be traditional Indian dress and other "races" seldom wore them. The evaluation of Indian attire tends to be only slightly negative, in the sense that it does represent the attire of a "minority race" and not the "Malay" majority. In contrast, local people generally viewed members of non-Malay races who wear "Malay" style clothing as being or becoming "Malaysianized."

While many Malay-based Islamic movements grew over the last three decades, non-Islamic religious movements sprung up as well (see Ackerman and Lee 1988). These Buddhist-Taoist, Hindu, and Christian movements expressed a heightened sense of racial and religious identity partially in response to the greater emphasis Malay governmental and non-governmental institutions laid upon Malay Muslim identity, often intertwining race and religion. In this context of growing Malay separation and exclusiveness, non-Islamic movements grew, raising the significance of the religious attributes and behavioral expectations of non-Muslims. Many Indians in Melaka, as was the case in Kuala Lumpur (see Ackerman and Lee 1988), became actively involved in the Satya Sai Baba Movement. Many reform-minded Chinese Buddhist-Taoists joined missionary oriented Buddhist-Taoist organizations and opened a new temple that combined many aspects of "modern" or Christian worship with traditional Chinese practices. Similarly, many Catholics, Indians, Chinese and "*Portugis*" in Melaka organized and participated in Charismatic prayer meetings conducted in private homes.

In addition to emphasizing the underlying religious attributes and behavioral expectations of their cultural categories, many non-Malay and non-*Bumiputera* persons and institutions have sought to forge closer ties between themselves and other non-Malay and non-*Bumiputera* persons and organizations. This growing "non" identity has emerged in part from the *Bumi/non-Bumi* distinction inscribed in the Constitution, the New Economic Policy and other hegemonic policies and practices. In response to this dominant mode of race-making, non-*Bumiputera* and "immigrant" attributes and behavioral expectations are used as a common thread tying these various categories together into a shared identity of "non-belongers" seeking to create a sense of solidarity and cultural citizenship.

The three cultural categories described so far, "Malays," "Chinese," and "Indians" are considered the three main "races" of Melaka and of Malaysia in general. A few local residents even told me that these are the only three types of races in Melaka. "Malays" are the "first group" or "majority"; and the Chinese are the "second group" and the Indians are the "third group." The government typically uses the "Malay-Chinese-Indian-Other" formula for official documents. Yet, most local residents have informed me that there are several other types of "races" or *bangsa* living in Melaka and to these I will now turn.

"Serani" is one of these high-level categories, a category associated with Christianity. "Serani" is derived from "nasrani," the word for "Kristian" in Malay. But unlike the case with "Malay," "Chinese," and "Indian" categories, the mere mention of their religious faith, Christianity, does not by default signify the "Serani" category because there are large numbers of Chinese and Indian Christians in Melaka. Yet "Serani" are expected to be Christian, "Katolik" in particular, and are often indexed by the wearing of crosses around their necks and the hanging of framed pictures of Mother Mary, Jesus Christ, or angels over the doorways of their homes. As with Buddhists and Hindus, "Serani" are evaluated negatively as people who embrace a religion other than Islam, the official national religion.

Local Melakans considered "Serani" to be the descendants of European men, Portuguese or Dutch, who intermarried with Asian women. Thus, people often used "Serani" interchangeable with the category "Eurasian." "Serani" or "Eurasians" are expected to use European names, especially surnames. Although locals fundamentally regarded them as the descendants of "immigrants," Malay government officials have given them a sort of honorary *Bumiputera* status within the last two decades. Extension of *Bumiputera* status to "Serani" has allowed them to enjoy some of the special benefits this status affords.[6] Yet, the emphasis upon their European, colonial forefathers, highlights that they are not true "sons of the soil" as their roots lie elsewhere. In addition, people expected "Serani" people to speak English or "Kristang," a Portuguese creole, rather than the national language. This emphasis upon European ancestry and language carries a low ranking in general Malaysian society.

Furthermore, they receive negative evaluations for their expected occupation, place of residence, and skin tone. Locals assumed "Serani" to be fishermen who live off the coast in a "settlement" granted to them by the British colonial government several decades ago. Indeed, most of the respondents to my map survey associated "Serani" or "Eurasian" and "*Portugis*" with this "settlement" which was occasionally called "*kampung Portugis.*" The Malaysian national government has built a "*Portugis* Square" in the coastal settlement to foster tourism in Melaka. "Portugis" sold some of the fish and shrimp caught off the coast, in the Straits of Melaka, in many of the restaurants located both inside and outside of this square. Streets in this settlement bear Portuguese, Dutch, and British surnames, named after famous European personalities.

Although people assumed them to have "*orang putih*" ancestors, "Serani" are expected to be "brown skinned" and many locals find it difficult to distinguish them from "Malays." Other locals find it difficult to associate them with any particular phenotypic characteristics, stating that many of "Serani" look like "Indians" or "Chinese" while others look like "Malays." People often say that they have to refer to cultural traits such as the wearing of crosses, European names or the speaking of English or Kristang, to distinguish them from other cultural categories. Yet, the general expectation that they are of various shades of darker-than-"fair"-complexion leaves them with lower ranking in Malaysian society.

Similarly, "*Baba*" (male) and "*Nyonya*" (female), also called "*Peranakan*" or "Straits-born Chinese," are considered to be less "fair" skinned than "pure" Chinese and are consequently ranked lower in terms of this attribute. People considered them as offspring of Chinese immigrants who intermarried with "local people" or "Malays." Conventionally, people think that it was Chinese men, in particular, who intermarried with local "Malay" women. The "hybrid" offspring of these interracial marriages of the distant past are viewed as being both racially and culturally "mixed" or *campur*. Many of the respondents to my map survey still associate *Baba* and *Nyonya* with several streets in the old part of town where they used to own much of the property and where some *Baba* currently own and operate a museum representing their heritage. However, over the years *Babas* and *Nyonyas* have lost control of most of the property in this area to recent Chinese immigrants of various dialect groups. Map survey respondents also tended to associate *Babas* and *Nyonyas* with several "mixed" or "*campur*" spaces north of the Melaka River, places such as Tengkera and Kelebang, and viewed them as living in several neighborhoods dispersed around the town area.

Local people expected *Baba* and *Nyonya* to have maintained their forefather's belief in "Chinese" religion and practice of "Chinese" customs, although they have adopted "Malay" culture in many other areas of life. Locals assumed Chinese *Peranakan* to be "Buddhists" or followers of Buddhist, Taoist, and Confucian beliefs and practices. They are expected to pray in Buddhist-Taoist temples, to keep ancestral tablets, and to have Chinese names. Small red altars with offerings to the gods often index their homes as with "pure" Chinese. On the other hand, they are expected to speak Malay in their homes rather than any Chinese language. They are assumed to have little proficiency in any Chinese language. *Baba* and *Nyonya* are viewed as being gregarious and open like "Malays." In addition, *Peranakan* are expected to wear "Malay" style clothing such as the *sarong* and *kebaya*, to sing "Malay" style songs such as *dondang sayang*, and to cook hot spicy cuisine like "Malays." *Baba* and *Nyonya* receive negative evaluations for their maintenance of "Chinese" religion, but positive evaluations for "Malay" culture traits that they have adopted over the years.

Local Melakans conventionally described another "hybrid" high-level category, "Chitty," as the Indian version of Chinese *Peranakan* or *Baba* and *Nyonya*. They are the descendants of "Indian" Hindu men who migrated to Melaka centuries ago and intermarried with local "Malay" women. Thus, "Chitties" are expected to be lighter skinned than "Indians" but darker skinned than "Malays." Similar to *Baba* and *Nyonya*, people viewed them as being racially and culturally mixed.

"Chitties" are expected to have maintained the Hindu faith and are therefore considered to be Hindus. Locals expected them to pray in Hindu temples, many of which are located in the neighborhood or *kampung* associated with their category. Many respondents to my map survey associated "Chitty" with this neighborhood, popularly known as "*kampung* Chitty," situated off Gadjah Berang Street. In addition, people expected "Chitties" to have "Indian" names and to have framed pictures of Hindu deities over their doorways like other Hindus. On the other hand, locals expected "Chitties" to speak Malay rather than any Indian language, possessing little proficiency with these languages. Likewise, "Chitties" are expected to perform "Malay" style dance and song and to cook hot spicy foods like "Malays." "Chitties" are viewed as adopting the "Malay" style of social relations and etiquette, characterized by gregariousness, openness and the tendency to *tanya*. "Chitty" women are expected to wear the *sarong* and *kebaya* and "Chitty" men wear a style of headdress and shirt similar to "Malay" styles. Similar to the *Baba* and *Nyonya* high-level category, "Chitties" also are assigned mixed assessments for these mixed cultural attributes. They are assessed negatively for being Hindu worshippers and continuing "Indian" culture, while they are assessed positively for the "Malay" behavioral expectations. Futhermore, *Baba* and *Nyonya* and Chitty, or Chinese and Indian *Peranakan,* are still viewed as the descendants of "immigrants" and have not been extended honorary *Bumiputera* status like "Serani." People thereby ranked them with other "non-belongers" living in, but not fully belonging to, *Tanah Melayu*.

"*Mamak*" is the high-level category used to refer to the "Indian Muslim" minority of Malaysia. They are a minority in both the "Indian" and "Muslim" communities. In the "Indian" community, they are an enigma because they are not Hindu, and in the "Muslim" community, they are an enigma because they are not "Malay." Because they are not "Malay," they are not considered to be "pure" Muslims, and are stigmatized as "Indian" converts to Islam. People considered "*Mamak*" to be one type of *mualaf* or converts to Islam (*saudara baru*); converts with some degree of "Indian" ancestry. Chinese converts, and converts of other "races," do not have a race-specific category and are just labeled with the general category *mualaf*. Local people rarely used the phrase *"keturunan* Islam" in relation to *"Mamak,"* who are not assumed to have Islam in their "blood," but are assumed to have embraced the Islamic faith through marriage to "pure" Muslims or "Malays." Thus, people also applied this category to the "Indian" spouse and offspring of contemporary intermarriages between Indian Hindus and Malays. Conversion to Islam is now a legal requirement for non-Muslims to marry Muslims, unlike intermarriages with "Malays" in the past, as in the case of Indian and Chinese *Peranakan. "Mamak"* are assessed favorably as believers in the official national religion of Malaysia, but they are assessed negatively as less than "pure" or "real" Muslims. Many local respondents to my map survey associated "Indian Muslims" with several areas of Melaka they considered to be "mixed" spaces, or stated that "Indian Muslims" live dispersed throughout Melaka society.

"*Mamak*" are considered to be culturally mixed like the "Chitty," but in this case "Indians" or "Indian" descendants have adopted Islam while maintaining other aspects of "Indian" culture, in contrast to Chitty who maintained Hinduism but adopted other aspects of "Malay" culture. Local people often expected *"Mamak"* people to speak an Indian language, to wear Indian clothing styles and to prepare and consume Indian style cuisine. In addition, people expected them to have "Indian"-style Muslim names without the *bin* or *binti* or "Malay"-style Muslim names with *bin* or *binti Abdullah* at the end of their names, marking them as converts to Islam. New converts to Islam are required to change their names to "Muslim" names and to add *bin* or *binti Abdullah*. Along with the assumption of conversion to Islam, people expected *"Mamak"* to follow "Malay culture" in terms of marriage custom and occasionally in terms of attire.

Local Melakans conventionally thought of *"Mamak"* as non-*Bumiputera,* as they are the descendants of "Indian" immigrants. Many "Mamak" feel that the best they can do to be "belongers" in Malaysian society is to become legal citizens, especially after they or their family members have experienced administrative problems and long delays with becoming permanent residents. But many *"Mamak"* try to negotiate "Malay" identity and achieve at least honorary *"Bumiputera"* status by assimilating into "Malay culture" or as they may prefer to put it, "Malaysian culture." Instead of the *dhoti, Mamak* men may wear *baju melayu* and Islamic headdresses, and instead of sari, Indian Muslim women may don *baju kurung* and *sarong kebaya. "Mamak"* negotiations of "Malay" identity are made easier if they have Muslim parents and therefore can adopt the *"bin"* and *"binti"* preceding their father's names instead of the stigmatizing

"*Abdullah.*" Actual "*Mamak*" converts may find this problematic, but their "*Mamak*" offspring often negotiate "Malay" identity by identifying with the "Malay" parent of either gender. In the Malaysian Constitution, a "Malay" person is one who embraces Islam, speaks Malay, and adopts Malay culture. Some "*Mamak*" argue that they fulfill these conditions.[7]

Finally, "*orang asli*" is the high-level category for the other "race" of *Bumiputera*—or sons of the soil—beside "Malays." Like "Malays," people considered them as original inhabitants of *Tanah Melayu* who supposedly enjoy preferential treatment due to *Bumiputera* status. Yet, in Melaka people assumed they live in a few villages in the undeveloped forest zones and to be "primitive" in culture. Locals expected them to wear little to no clothing and to eat a variety of wild plants and animals. "*Orang asli*" are also expected to speak distinct "*orang asli*" languages rather than *Bahasa Malaysia*. Many local residents of Melaka do not know that there are some "*orang asli*" villages in Melaka, because they rarely interact with "*orang asli*" from Melaka who are a marginalized minority in the state. They do not have political parties representing them in Melaka and they do not own much property.

"*Orang asli*" in Melaka live in approximately twelve villages on the outskirts of "development" where they hunt and gather food and occasionally work on palm oil and rubber plantations. Residents of Melaka more frequently encounter an "*orang asli*" person from Sabah or Sarawak, many of whom have migrated to Melaka for employment purposes. Locals considered "*Orang asli*" to be believers in "primitive" religion or animism, and they are often recipients of Islamic missionary work organized by "Malay" civil servants and non-governmental organizations. Despite being ranked highly as *true Bumiputera,* they are assessed lowly as primitive and powerless non-Muslims who are slowly being brought into "modern civilization."

SUBMAXIMAL SOCIAL IDENTITIES

Many of the maximal identities discussed above, Malay, Chinese, Indian, *Serani,* and *orang asli,* have other categories, "submaximal" categories, embedded within them. Locals view these submaximal categories as types of the more general maximal category. In addition, some of the maximal categories discussed above, despite their distinctiveness, are submerged within other categories, and are, thereby, submaximal categories as well. Namely, locals view the Baba and Nyonya, Chitty, and Mamak as types of more general cultural categories. Submaximal categories are embedded within the more general maximal categories in various ways; that is, they are tied into maximal categories with attributes that are variable. Some may be more "focal" to the overarching category, while others may be more peripheral or marginally included in the category. Thus, some submaximal categories enjoy more "cultural citizenship" within their cultural categories than others. In this section, I will discuss what characterizes these submaximal categories and what ties them into high-level maximal categories; and thus we will have a better view of variations in embedding.

The "Malay" maximal identity has several submaximal categories such as Minangkabau, Javanese, Bugis, Acehnese, and *Temenggong* embedded within it. Locals assumed each of these subgroups to have originated from particular places within *Tanah Melayu*. Minangkabau, Javanese, Bugis and Acehnese can trace their roots to some part of the string of islands now known as Indonesia; the Minangkabau are from West Sumatra, Javanese from Java, Bugis from Riau and Sulawesi, and Acehnese from Northern Sumatra. People thought all of these submerged groups to have come to Malaysia a long time ago and have "mixed" with peninsular Malays. They thought *Temenggong* to be the original Malays of Melaka, the ones who descend from the Malays of the great maritime Sultanate of Melaka. Although Portuguese invaders and colonial rulers destroyed the Sultanate of Melaka, this identity persists attached to the memory of this once vibrant coastal empire.[8]

Local Malays thought each of these submaximal identities had their own *adat,* or customs and traditional patterns of culture, in the past, but the only ones that remain today are the *"adat perpatih"* and *"adat temenggong."* *Adat perpatih* is the corpus of matrilineally oriented customs and laws associated with the *Minangkabau,* or *Minang,* and are viewed in contrast to *adat temenggong* which is seen as being more closely in tune with Islamic principles and laws. While other submaximal identities have shed most of their unique customs following *adat temenggong,* Minang have held steadfastly to their customary principles and laws. Many Temenggong Malays characterize Minang posture via *adat* with the saying *biar mati anak jangan mati adat* (let our children die rather than our adat).

Yet, each of these submaximal categories is tied into the "Malay" category as Muslims whose ancestors were spread across the region, from Philippines to Mainland Southeast Asia, centuries ago. They all speak Malay and local Malays viewed them as the same "race" of people. The "core" submaximal category is *temenggong* and the other categories are construed as having been absorbed into this category, becoming more alike due to the homogenizing influence of Islam.[9] Only the *Minang* stand out as not totally absorbed, because of their continued adherence to *adat perpatih* with its non-Islamic rules of inheritance and descent.

Local people generally accepted, in public, the children of contemporary interracial marriages with one "Malay" parent as "Malay." Many local "Malays" have an Arab, Chinese, Indian, or European ancestor, but choose to identify themselves as "Malay" and are recognized by others as such due to the fact that they and their non-Malay parent are embracing Islam. In fact, local Malays generally viewed these children of mixed marriages as being absorbed into the "core" Malay submaximal category as long as they are not following "adat perpatih." Thus, the children of intermarriages with Malays are less marginal to the Malay category than *Minang,* although they may have problems negotiating *Bumiputera* status if their fathers are not Malay.

On the other hand, Malays generally considered "Malay" Christians with two Malay parents as outside of the Malay category, since they have embraced another religion other than Islam. I have not met a "Malay" Christian, but I have been told they exist, in small numbers, despite laws prohibiting the propagation of other religions to Muslims. Several controversial issues surround the matter of this oxymoron, "Malay Christian," including questions of whether they have been coerced into leaving the Islamic faith and whether they should be prosecuted or not under the law.

In addition, local people considered recent Indonesian immigrants as outside of the maximal "Malay" identity due to the fact they do not possess legal citizenship in Malaysia; they are Indonesian nationals. Unlike the Minang, Bugis, Acehnese, and Javanese who have been absorbed into the "Malay" category in the past, these contemporary immigrants have to cross the border of legal documentation. Hundreds of thousands of Indonesian workers come to Malaysia legally and illegally and fill positions in the plantation, construction, and service sectors of the economy. Local people and newspaper journalists labeled these immigrant workers as "*Indons,*" and stigmatized them as "illegals," and as such, they are frequently targets of immigration officials. In addition, wealthy employers abused and brutalized many female "*Indon*" domestic workers. Malaysian government officials arrested thousands of "undocumented" Indonesian workers during the recent economic crisis in 1998 and 1999 and sent them back to Indonesia via jetties departing from Melaka. Yet, when "*Indons*" acquire legal citizenship in Malaysia, they are absorbed into the "Malay" maximal category and become *Bumiputera* as well.

Similarly, the "Chinese" maximal category embeds several submaximal categories such as Hokkien, Cantonese, Hailam, Teochew, Hainanese and others. Local Chinese characterize these subgroups as speakers of different dialects of Chinese who have come from different regions of China.

In the past, Chinese considered them to have specialized in different occupations, but these distinctions have gradually been erased over the years.

All of these dialect groups are tightly tied into the "Chinese" category, because they are of the same racial and historical origins, immigrants from China, and share an ancient heritage of Buddhist-Taoist-Confucian religion and customs. Although they speak different dialects, they all share the Mandarin written language that ties them all together as Chinese. Hence, the core Chinese are members of one of these dialect groups who are Buddhist-Taoists and are "pure" culturally and racially. Local Chinese viewed "Chinese" Christians, of whom there are many in Melaka, as still being "Chinese" due their being racially "pure" and their continued adherence to Chinese customs. They still attend the Chinese New Year activities and participate in the family feasts and gatherings on the eve of the New Year and many maintain their ancestral tablets. Chinese viewed them as "pure Chinese" who just pray differently because they are Christians. However, they viewed "Chinese Muslims" as outside of the Chinese category; local Chinese said they have *sudah masuk melayu* (already become Malay). Local people conventionally used this phrase to refer to conversion to Islam, conflating the embracing of Islam with the embracing of "Malay" identity. Chinese often use this phrase to express their view that a Chinese person who has converted to Islam has already left behind his or her identity and culture. "Chinese" often note the change of name upon conversion and their new religious obligations as evidence that they are no longer "Chinese" (cf. Lian, Kwen Fee 2001:874). In addition, "Chinese Muslims" may find it difficult to still attend the family gatherings, highly valued by most Chinese, where family members often serve pork.

The "Indian" maximal identity has Tamil, Telegu, Malayali, Gujerati, Sikh, Punjabi, Bengali and other submaximal categories embedded within it. Local Indians characterized these submaximal categories by language, place of origin and background in India. They often grouped and spoke of them in terms of "North" and "South" Indians or "Aryans" and "Dravidians." Local Indians generally considered Tamils, Telegu, and Malayali to be the "South" Indians or "Dravidians," since they originated from the southern provinces of India and speak structurally related Dravidian languages. Likewise, they considered Gujerati, Bengali, Punjabi and Sikhs to be "North" Indians and "Aryans" as they come from the northern provinces of India and speak Aryan languages. Local people often viewed racialized distinctions to be underlying these distinctions as well, with the South Indians being viewed as darker skinned and the northern Indians as lighter skinned.

Yet, they are all tied into the "Indian" categories as subgroups that share Indian historical and cultural origins and the Hindu faith. Core Indians are the Tamil Hindus who are the majority in the Indian category and enjoy the privilege of having Tamil institutionalized in "Indian" vernacular schools and in news programs on television. Other Indians who speak one of the Indian languages and practice Hinduism are also solidly embedded within the Indian category, although North Indians are occasionally viewed as having some different Hindu practices and observances. Of the "North" Indians, Sikhs are the most marginalized because of their perceived religious differences. But they are still viewed as "Indian" since these differences are still seen as practicing a variant of Hinduism and many Sikhs participate in Hindu temple festivals, a key facet of Indian social solidarity. "Indian" Christians are even more marginalized in the "Indian" category, because they are outside of the Hindu faith. They do not come to temple festivals and often do not use Indian names. Yet they often follow many other Indian customs such as the public donning of *pottu* (dots of colored paste or ash on the forehead) and sari in public and the wearing of *maleh* (garland) during wedding ceremonies conducted in church. "Indian" Muslims are the most marginalized and local Indians only minimally viewed them as still being "Indian." They are outside of the Hindu faith and are viewed as having *sudah masuk melayu* (already become Malay). Like their Chinese counterparts, they are assumed to be following Malay culture and customs. Unlike "Indian" Christians, they do not wear *pottu* and often wear clothing styles associated with Malays. Futhermore, "Indian" Muslims are assumed to follow Malay *adat* in regard to wedding ceremonies. On the other hand, local Indians still viewed them as being "Indian," at least nominally, because their ancestors originated from India and they still prepare and consume "Indian" cuisine.

The "Serani," a hybrid category (discussed further below), also has some submaximal categories, such as Portuguese, Dutch, British and Irish embedded within it. These four categories are considered to be the descendants of European settlers who remained in Melaka and intermarried with local women. All these subgroups share the attribute of being Christians and are thus tied into the "Serani" category as *Nasroni*. Yet, over the years Dutch, British and Irish "Serani" have been absorbed into the "*Portugis*" category as a result of intermarriages with this most populous subgroup of "Serani." Other than a few Dutch, British and Irish surnames, these groups have been submerged into the "Portugis" category and many reside in, and participate in the Catholic activities of, the Portuguese Settlement (see Sarkissian 2000:26). In Melaka, "Portugis" is the core submaximal category of "Serani" and is often viewed as being synonymous with the maximal category.

HYBRIDS AND MAXIMAL IDENTITIES

The three "hybrid" submaximal categories, "Portugis," "Baba and Nyonya" and "Chitty" are caught "betwixt and between" maximal categories in peculiar ways. "Portugis" who are mixtures of Portuguese men with Malay, Chinese, or Indian women, are tied to the "Portugis" category through the blood of their forefathers. They are not considered to be "halfies" or equally "Portugis" and one of the Asian maximal categories; the "blood" of "*orang putih*," from centuries ago, takes precedence over Asian "blood." "Portugis" are the descendants of Portuguese settlers. Portuguese racial features are said to still be visible scattered amongst the current community.

Yet, unlike the other hybrid categories of "*Baba* and *Nyonya*" and "Chitty," "Portugis" do not have a large population of "pure Portugis" in Melaka with whom to develop social ties and to replenish their "racial" stock. Although they are not tied into the Asian maximal categories, their inclusion in the "Portuguese" category is incomplete. Portuguese are considered to be "*orang putih*" (white people) and the "Portugis" in Melaka are generally considered to be brown to dark skinned people. To distinguish these hybrids from the Portuguese of Portugal, they are often called "*Melaka Portugis.*" Over recent years, under Malay rule, "Portugis" have tended to give greater recognition to how they are culturally mixed having assimilated many aspects of Malay culture, whereas under British colonial rule, they tended to emphasize British culture and identity, especially upper class Eurasians (see Sarkissian 1998, 2000:32–34).

They frequently marry "Indian" and "Chinese" Catholics who adopt "Portugis" identity and are absorbed into the "*Melaka Portugis*" community. Many of the "Indian" and "Chinese" Catholics opt to identify as "*Portugis,*" a community tied together through Catholicism, rather than to continue their awkward marginality in the mostly Hindu, "Indian" category and the mostly Buddhist, "Chinese" category. If the Chinese or Indians are not already Catholics, Catholic priests recommend conversion or seek to at least reach an agreement that the children of the marriage will be baptized and brought up as Catholics. Thus, the "*Portugis*" category continues to absorb Asian "blood" expanding its community linked together through Catholicism and continued recognition of their Portuguese ancestors.

In contrast, the "*Baba* and *Nyonya*" have a large population of "pure" Chinese to relate with socially and into which to be re-absorbed. Yet, these *Peranakan* or "Straits-born Chinese" are only marginally embedded within the "Chinese" category, tied in only because they still practice Chinese religion and follow Chinese customs. They are on the outskirts of the "Chinese" category due to the widespread conception that they are mixed racially and culturally; they are not "pure" Chinese in either fashion. Locals think they are intermixed with Malay "blood" and culture. In fact, other than Chinese religion, many "core" Chinese view them as following only "10% of Chinese culture and 90% of Malay culture." They speak Malay rather than any Chinese dialect or the "standard" Mandarin that helps to connect all Chinese. These perceptions marginalize *Peranakan* more than Chinese Christians within the "Chinese" maximal identity but of course, less than "Chinese" Muslims. Many "*Baba* and *Nyonya*" challenge their weak embedding in the "Chinese" category by arguing that many of them did not intermarry with Malays and assimilated into Malay culture through other means. Likewise, they argue that they are "more Chinese" than the "pure Chinese" because they follow the traditions for Chinese weddings and other rituals more strictly than supposed "pure" Chinese do.

Similarly, Chitties are embedded within a relatively large Indian population. They are tied into the "Indian" maximal category like other submaximal categories through Hinduism. Although Chitties do not speak any Indian languages proficiently and have adopted many aspects of Malay culture, they are still considered to be "Indian." In fact, they are viewed as more "Indian" than "Indian" Christians, because they are still staunch Hindus and not only do they participate in Hindu temple festivals, but they also have several of the oldest Hindu temples in Melaka under their community's management. "Indian" Christians, despite being "pure" racially and possessing proficiency in Indian languages, are absent from Hindu temple activities, which are central to Indian social solidarity and identity. Furthermore, unlike Mandarin for Chinese, Indians do not have a language that ties them all together. That is, they do not give the connection of language the same weight as with Chinese. Yet many "core" Tamil Indians do chide "Chitty" for being Hindu and not speaking Tamil. Recently some classes have been set up in area temples to develop Chitty proficiency in Tamil, tying them more closely to the core of the Indian maximal category.

CONCLUSION

These categories are social and cultural constructions undergoing change and negotiation in dynamic historical and political contexts. By focusing upon how low-level knowledge constructs these categories and how a variety of sub-maximal categories are embedded in maximal categories, I have sought to highlight the significance of merging constructionist perspectives with a cognitive approach. I have demonstrated that with a cognitive approach we can more rigorously and accurately discern the elements that are being transformed or contested in social processes and those that are being reproduced. For instance, I noted that the Muslim and "backward" attributes of the Malay category are being negotiated and contested in the current political crisis in the Malay community. Meanwhile, non-Malays have been appropriating and re-evaluating their religious and non-*Bumiputera* and "immigrant" attributes. Some of these attributes or their valences are changing while others are being reproduced under current conditions.

In addition, I have demonstrated the variable manner in which "hybrid" categories in Melaka are tied into various maximal categories. Despite the long physical separation from the Portuguese community and continuing patterns of intermarriage with local Asians, "*Melaka Portugis*" are considered to be Portuguese descendants. Connections with various Asian identities are not valued in the same way; the blood of their fore*fathers* takes precedence. Similarly, Chinese and Indian *Peranakan*, the *Babas* and *Nyonyas* and Chitties, are embedded in the "Chinese" and "Indian" categories, the presumed categories of their *male ancestors*, and not in the "Malay" category. The attributes of religion and customs connect them into the "Chinese" and "Indian" categories while precluding their link to the "Malay" category. Yet Chinese *Peranakan* tend to be more marginalized within the "Chinese" category than Chitty are within the "Indian" category due to the greater stress laid upon racial purity and standard unifying language amongst local Chinese. Locals negotiated and reproduced the positioning of "core" and "marginal" submaximal categories in social processes.

These maximal and submaximal identity schemata are well-formed mental representations, widely distributed in Melaka society. These identity schemata embed motives for social action as members of these diverse cultural categories interact with each other. Moreover, these maximal identity schemata are embedded in other schemata, and models, that bunch together these representations along with various notions. These models and schemata pertaining to notions of Malaysia's diverse society and the special position of Malays will be the focus of the next chapter. Just as the manner of embedding of submaximal categories into maximal categories indicate a sense of "cultural citizenship" or inclusion on this level, the manner in which models and schemata of Malaysia's society are negotiated indicates how members of cultural categories are incorporated within Malaysian society on a broader level.

Chapter Four

Discourse and Schemta of Malaysian Society

The Malaysian-Malaysia concept is no longer relevant as we approach the new millennium, Malaysian Youth Council (MYC) president Saifuddin Abdullah said . . . 'We Malaysians have a certain contract among us whereby we understand and appreciate each other's status as citizens and at the same time allow the Malays the privilege of being the natives of the country. The Malaysian-Malaysia notion will only jeopardise this contract which has long been accepted by all of us . . .' (*The Sun,* Friday May 14, 1999).

Maximal and submaximal identities not only constitute representations of Melaka's, and Malaysia's, diverse social fabric, but they also are components in higher-level models and schemata that people use to understand Malaysian society. People not only considered these cultural categories to be representative of social groups that exist in Melaka and Malaysia, but they also understood them as having particular kinds of interrelations amongst themselves. They conventionally understood certain notions to define the nature of social interaction and interconnection between these maximal and submaximal identities. Taken together, multiple cultural categories and several mediating notions, form higher-level models and schemata that local residents in Melaka use to construe what it means to be a member of Melakan and Malaysian society.

In order to underscore the difference between ideological doctrines and more fundamental knowledge people use to organize their lives, I make an analytic distinction between models and schemata in relation to higher-level knowledge in the social relational domain (see Lehman 2000). Models and schemata are both, with a varying degree of detail, bundles of interrelated elements used to represent something and are often, but not always, stored somewhere in long term memory (cf. D'Andrade 1995:151–2; Wilson and

Keil 1999:729–30) and are basic units of discourse (cf. Hutchins 1980). Whereas models are representations typically contained within ideological formulations, schemata are more fundamental mental representations that have a closer relationship to the generative mechanisms within the domain of social relations. I make this distinction without assuming schemata are more widely distributed in society, more diffusely internalized or directive of behavior; these matters are to be discerned by rigorous ethnographic research. In fact, it may be that models, propagated and institutionalized by political leaders, can become quite widely distributed, diffusely internalized and can provide motives for people in their daily interactions (cf. Strauss 1992b).

In this chapter, I will infer and make second-order representations of models and schemata from an analysis of a variety of written and spoken sources, including newspapers, books, speeches, and taped interviews and discussions with local residents. Contiguity of terms and topics and abstract relations between propositions are used as evidence to infer underlying models and schemata (see Strauss 1992b; Hutchins 1980; Agar and Hobbs 1985). Through applying these methods, I infer that several alternative models and schemata are embedded in discourse and are used to make sense of Malaysian society and to direct social relations. These models and schemata embed goals and are motivating to varying degrees. I argue that two key schemata, that I will label as "Malaysia's diverse society" and "Malay privilege," underlie national and local discourse and form a sort of widely agreed upon "contract," a seemingly contradictory and flexible social pact. These two schemata are more fundamental, in a cognitive sense, as they are closer to the computational mechanisms in the domain of social relations, whereas the models are particular ideological productions, generated by higher-level cultural theories and shaped by political interests, much more limited in their generative capabilities.

MODELS AND SCHEMA OF MALAYSIA'S DIVERSE SOCIETY

Politicians, national and local officials, use Malaysia's numerous public holidays as prime opportunities to propagate their political ideologies. Speeches are staged in local and national venues, especially for the four major public holidays—Deepavali, Christmas, Hari Raya Aidilfitri, and Chinese New Year—and are often broadcast to the masses via television and newspaper media. In particular, the three national television stations and the national pro-ruling alliance government press routinely feature newspaper articles containing segments of speeches and statements made by national officials. These nationally-distributed Malay, English, Mandarin, and Tamil language daily newspapers provide *Barisan Nasional* political leaders and the Malay sultans with a national medium in which to consistently broadcast their messages to a national audience. For instance, beneath a color photo of ruling alliance members of the three major races amassed around a cake that they were collectively cutting, an article titled "Malaysians Celebrate Deepavali in Unity" read:

> Deepavali, the Festival of Lights, was today celebrated by all Malaysians with unity as its resounding theme . . . Many including diplomats who were met at the open house circuit were impressed by the multi-ethnic crowd at these places . . . At the Gerakan open house, Dr Lim said . . . 'In a multi-racial society like ours, the open house concept is one way to bring Malaysians together. We must remain united and support efforts initiated by Prime Minister Datuk Seri Mahathir Mohamad in reviving the economy.' Emphasizing the adage 'united we stand, divided we fall,' Dr Lim, who is also Primary Industries Minister, said unity would help the nation recover faster . . . Malaysians of other races joined their Indian friends in celebrating Deepavali despite the uncompromising weather (New Straits Times, October 20, 1998).

Deepavali, a popular Indian festival in Malaysia, occurring on the new moon day of the month of *Aippasi* on the Tamil Hindu lunar calendar usually falls in the October-November time span. This year Deepavali was the first of the four major public celebrations to take place providing a key opportunity for the ruling party leaders to connect their ideological doctrine to current political and economic concerns.

Looking at this segment of the article, we can readily notice that there is a repetition of references to the diverse make-up of Malaysian society: "all Malaysians," "multi-ethnic crowd," "multi-racial society," "Malaysians of other races." In addition, these terms and phrases are stated together with terms and notions that define the nature of connections as projected between these diverse groups, terms such as "united" and "friends." Taken together, these propositions construct an abstract image of Malaysians of all racial and ethnic backgrounds tied together in bonds of friendship and unity, an abstract image not only embedded in the discourse but also given a physical form as it is embodied in the color photo. The significance of this abstract image is magnified in the perceptions of an outsider, a foreign diplomat, who consequently acquires a positive impression of Malaysian society, given its "unity in diversity." This also expresses the goal of presenting a united image of "our" national selves to outsiders. Multiracial open houses in which members of each race and religion visit members of all others on their respective festive occasions is projected as a model of unity and a model for unity, "one way to bring Malaysians together."[1]

Not only is there a contiguity of topics relating to festival, celebrations, and open houses and friendly and unified relations between diverse groups, but there is also contiguity between the topic of friendly and unified relations between diverse groups and the topic of facing the economic crisis. Malaysia, a country that had been experiencing consistent economic growth over the last three decades, was thrown into a state of shock and uncertainty following the July 1997 collapse of the Thai *baht* and subsequent spread of this economic crisis across Southeast Asia. By the end of 1998, Malaysia had witnessed racial and religious violence and mass demonstrations spreading across Indonesia and eventually facilitating the downfall of its longtime military strongman, President Suharto. The Malaysian stock market took a dive and Malaysian currency began to spiral out of control like the Thai and Indonesia currencies before it. Mahathir, not only prime minister, but also finance minister, acting in concert with others in his Cabinet, devised some aggressive monetary measures to control the flow of investment capital moving out of Malaysia and fixed the rate of exchange of the Malaysian *ringgit* at 3.8 to the U.S. dollar. In this context, the newspaper article cited above connects the abstract image of Malaysia's diverse population working together in unity and friendship with the goals of supporting government efforts at facing this economic crisis and achieving economic recovery. In the following newspaper excerpt, on the occasion of Christmas, we will find some similar patterns.

> In a message wishing Malaysian Christians a 'Merry Christmas' . . . the prime minister said Malaysians are fortunate and should be thankful that the spirit of tolerance they practise has reinforced unity among them and that the economic difficulties and attempts to spark off riots failed to create disharmony among the masses. 'We should learn from events in other countries whose economic problems has led to clashes between followers of different religions' . . . Malaysia's multi-racial, multi-religious and multi-cultural citizens are able to visit their Christian friends as they had done during Christmas celebrations of past years, he said . . . 'Visiting one another during the festive celebrations can forge closer relations between multi-racial and multi-religious Malaysians and help preserve peace in the country,' said Mahathir (The Sun, December 25, 1998).

Again, we can note that references to "Malaysia's multi-racial, multi-religious, and multi-cultural citizens" are used in conjunction with the terms "unity" and "friends." Yet, this time the term "citizens" was used explicitly to refer to these diverse members of society in contrast to the more general terms "society" and "crowd" used in the previous passage. This is not to say that a well-formed concept of citizenship does not underlie both of these passages, regardless of whether the term was used explicitly or not. In fact, the use of the category "Malaysian" implies a notion of citizenship and nationality. I will pursue this matter in more detail later, but let it be sufficient to note at this point that this may indicate the presence of an even lower-level knowledge structure.

It is again evident that the representation of Malaysia's diverse population tied together in bonds of friendship and unity embeds several goals. Thanks to the "spirit of tolerance" and "visiting one another during festive celebrations" Malaysians "reinforced unity" and "forge closer relations" and "preserve peace in the country" and protect themselves from "riots" and "disharmony" being sparked by economic difficulties and political discontents. The relations between diverse social categories are not only projected as unified and friendly, but also tolerant, close, peaceful, and harmonious. These notions that mediate social relations not only project characteristics of these relations, but they also are goals for the shape these relations should take and for how people of various backgrounds should interrelate with one another.

In the current context of the article, at the end of the 1998, this representation and the motives it embedded within it took on added and special significance. Not only were economic woes continuing with no end in sight, but there was also a growing political crisis following the discharging and subsequent arrest and imprisonment of the Deputy Prime Minister, Datuk Seri Anwar Ibrahim. Anwar Ibrahim, eventually charged with sodomy and corruption, was a very popular political figure in the Malay community and was generally expected to become the next Prime Minister. He is known as an eloquent speaker and charismatic leader, often remembered for his days as a student activist and organizer of ABIM (Malaysian Islamic Youth Front), and a product of post-independence Malay-language education, unlike the older generation of Malay nationalists many of whom are English-educated. Following Anwar Ibrahim's arrest, many protesters, mostly Malays, took to the streets organizing and staging demonstrations and demanding "*reformasi*" (reformation) despite strong repression from the government. The abstract image of Malaysians of all races and religions working together in unity and peace was a central component of the government's discursive attempts to maintain hegemony. Motives of maintaining and promoting racial and religious harmony, peace, and tolerance were highlighted through contrast with waves of violence and economic collapse spreading through other countries, especially Indonesia.[2] Thus, from this dominant perspective, a movement for *reformasi* and *keadilan* (justice) could disturb the harmony and peace between the races and religions and lead to chaos. Consequently, discourse embedding this abstract image and goals was also repeated, often accompanied with color photos, and broadcast on the occasions of *Hari Raya Aidilfitri,* the celebration at the end of the Muslim fasting month, and Chinese New Year.

This representation is also a major unit of the discourse of local *Barisan Nasional* leaders who repeat these hegemonic ideological doctrines in Melaka. The first speech I want to consider is a keynote speech the Chief Minister of Melaka, Datuk Abu Zahar, delivered on the rainy night of the eve of the 1998 National Day Celebrations.

> "Merdeka! [Audience answers: Merdeka!] Merdeka! [Merdeka!] Merdeka! [Merdeka!] Thank-you . . . In the name of all the people and also the leaders and officers of Melaka, I take this opportunity tonight to welcome you in assembly on the threshold of this Independence Day. I am also very proud that we are still able to come together in large numbers, even though our country is still facing an economic crisis. Not thinking of skin color, cultural differences, or religious and ideological differences, we are capable of coming together to proclaim our gratitude for modern amenities bestowed upon us by God . . . The age of our nation is approaching forty one years and this means that within the span of time of the last four decades we have been given the simultaneous unfurling of our maturing thought and actions, which we have all been in harmony with, our thinking and image in the perceptions of all societies and countries, modern and developed societies that always thirst for advancement and development. We have already been successful within forty-one years of making our small country, Malaysia, known, even if we just look at ourselves as a small nation, yet we can project our success to the world that has long before achieved independence.

> Truly, the success achieved by our country has been the result of the unity of the entire plural society in our country. Because of that our pure aspirations and ideals of the long term have to be advanced by us in order to define that independence we attained together for the goal of building a stable country . . . Merdeka! [Merdeka!] We have already seen how many countries that despite having achieved independence much longer than our country has, have found their countries in a state of disorder. We have to be proud that forty-one years is not long compared to what we have achieved. We also have to be proud of being seen as a country with a unique form; we are of all sorts of colors but without shedding blood like people in other countries. And we also follow feelings and unified understandings, approaching with utmost zeal, strong determination, and sincerity, the struggle for placing the image and prestige of our country in the highest regard amongst the countries of the world.

Whosoever looks at our country must see that we are not always the target of ridicule by other countries because of anything we have done or because of what we lack or our laxness. To the contrary, negative perceptions of our country are caused by persistent feelings of jealousy and envy by countries more advanced than our country. Our success is made evident by our incredible standing amongst other developed countries that have already been open to international society. Our beloved country, beloved Malaysia, will definitely become a principal competitor in the group of sophisticated countries in this world. Although people in our country come from all kinds of races, all sorts of religions, and all sorts of cultures, this does not make us think differently about making our country modern and sophisticated. The solidarity between races already formed by our past leaders such as Tunku Abdul Rahman, Tun Abdul Razak . . . and also in current times by our Prime Minister who we love, Mahathir. In such a fashion, our aim of avoiding all taunts and snarls by foreigners and also in order that together with those who strive to make close, intimate bonds amongst ourselves, between races, and thus making our defenses difficult to break by threats from outside. We have to project to the world that we possess our own basic principles for advancing our people without a lot of outside direction and orientation. We have to protect our interior to the point that we project to the world that we are not easily destabilized or frightened.

Independence! [Independence!] Gentlemen and ladies whom I hold in high esteem . . . Malaysia has to become an example or model to international society, including modernized countries . . . Our unity, resulting from dynamic and progressive leadership, along with the support of mature thinking which invites all people who have a simple attitude and whose solution to the problems of racial tolerance is evident. This is the satisfactory weapon that is capable of being examined by all other countries . . ." [my translation]

Terms and phrases connoting multiple cultural categories are used together with terms and phrases referring to the nature of ties between these groups.[3] Propositions such as "all the people," "skin color, cultural differences, or religious, and ideological differences," "entire plural society," "we are all sorts of colors," and "come from all kinds of races, all sorts of religions, and all sorts of cultures," are used in conjunction with propositions such as "come together in large numbers," "capable of coming together," "all been in harmony with," "result of the unity," "without shedding blood," "solidarity between races," "make close, intimate bonds amongst ourselves," and "solution to the problems of racial tolerance." This merging of propositions entails motives for behavior, goals of acting towards each other in a peaceful, tolerant, close, harmonious, and unified

fashion. Furthermore, these bundles of terms and propositions are projected as facilitating additional goals, national aims, including the goals of
"building a stable country," "making our country modern and sophisticated," becoming a "principal competitor" on the world stage, placing the
"image and prestige of the country in the highest regard," projecting "our
success to the world," and becoming "an example or model to international
society." In other words, unified and harmonious relations between members of diverse cultural categories can serve to create national stability,
modernization, economic and technical advancement, and to promote a
positive image of the nation abroad.

Thus, we can note that this representation is used not only to promote
and justify open house visiting and the intermingling of cultural categories
on festive occasions, it is also used as a self-image of the nation and an image
to be proudly projected to outsiders. Imagining "ourselves" as unique in
"our" diversity and harmony is inspiring and uplifting. Despite "our" racial,
religious, and cultural differences, we share a *common will,* shared sentiments and understandings, as citizen-members of the nation. Moreover, the
gaze of outsiders unites "us" Malaysians in contrast to those outsiders of
other nations and emphasizes what "we" have in common creating an "im-
aged community." These aspects of the discourse once again indicate a
deeper, more fundamental scheme of Malaysian society and the ties between
diverse cultural categories.

Before discussing this matter further, I want to present some more examples of local speeches given by local representatives of the ruling alliance front.
The next example I will present is a speech delivered by Datuk Gan Boon
Leong, local chairman of the Malaysian Chinese Association (MCA), a component party of the ruling alliance front. He was speaking to a multiracial audience in the concourse area of Mahkota Parade, a major shopping complex in
Melaka, on the occasion of one of the featured events on the mall's Hari Raya
schedule, the "P. Ramlee and Saloma Impersonation Contest" on the 16th of
January 1999. Before the beginning of the contest, speaking from the podium
on the stage, Datuk Gan using *Bahasa Malaysia*[4] said:

> "Mahkota Parade is not just a center for buying things that has
> opened in Melaka, but it also plays another central role, yea-lah,[5] for
> us. I want to take this opportunity to say thank-you to the managers
> of Mahkota Parade who always openly present and focus upon all fes-
> tivals of each race. Festival activities are organized with utmost re-
> spect and success, attracting the attention of many people, an
> immediate luxury. Mahkota Parade participates in and wants to fur-
> ther our tourism industry. With a program of cultural rights, the

greatness of each race is presented in our midst. Moreover, this can influence and aid our youth towards comprehending traditional culture more fully at a time in which more and more youth are coming to prefer music and dance from Western custom. There are those who consider tradition to be lost. Truly, traditional culture holds a high artistic value and cannot wind up being lost after coming through such a long period of time because we will defend and protect our culture that has come so far, traditions that we have inherited from the distant past.

Cultural activities are moves towards racial harmony and understanding. For instance, open house culture brings into view Malaysian society and has an indirect relationship to our spirit as a Malaysian people consisting of an assortment of races. We all enlarge our understanding of the culture of all races with the theme of enriching political stability and racial harmony. Our country achieved success and prosperity although the economic situation is less than satisfactory. By working together our people stimulate the growth of our country's prosperity.

Finally, I want to say Happy Hari Raya Aidul Fitri to Muslims and to others I want to say happy gathering and visiting in enjoyment of Hari Raya. Yea-lah. Thank you." [my translation]

Datuk Gan's discourse exhibits the familiar bundling of phrases such as "festivals of each race," "greatness of each race," "culture of all races" with phrases such as "utmost respect and success," "racial harmony and understanding," "spirit as a Malaysian people," "understanding of the culture," "enriching political stability," and "happy gathering and visiting." In accord with the nature of the speech situation, his speech has a greater focus upon the cultural attributes of each race and how their cultural activities can facilitate mutual understanding than the previous speech. Yet we can still note the presence of the same central component of discourse, one used to speak about and to represent the expected relations between various groups in Malaysian society. It is important to note that Datuk Gan, a local Chinese leader speaking at a major Malay cultural event, points out that the officers of Mahkota Parade, who are all Chinese, are organizing events for all races, not just Chinese, at a shopping complex owned and controlled by Chinese capital. This goes to say that members of the Chinese community are practicing the multicultural ideological doctrines promulgated by national and local ruling alliance leaders. Moreover, he states that they are promoting a program of "cultural rights" in which each race is included and within which each race can strive to exhibit their distinctive cultural greatness and preserve their cultural heritage. This notion of "cultural rights" seems to reach deeper into the organizing principles of the domain of social relations than the representation delineated so far.

This notion of "cultural rights" as well as the representation of Malaysians of all backgrounds getting along with each other seems to be embedded within a keynote speech, Datuk Raghovan, the local Malaysian Indian Congress (MIC) chairman, delivered on the same stage in Makhota Parade. Speaking to a very large multiracial audience who came to watch the highly popular "Sari Queen Contest" on the 10th of November 1998, Datuk Raghovan using *Bahasa Malaysia* said:

> "Indians are the third largest race in this country. Like other festivals, Hari Raya and Chinese New Year, Deepavali is also celebrated in this country. Like other festivals participated in by all races, not just by the Indian race, but also by the *Bumiputera* race and the *Tionghua* race. The Indian Chamber of Commerce in Melaka, since many years in the past, has for each year been closely involved with the Deepavali Festival. But this year we have a little change. Initially, we held the festival in Temenggung Street. But this year we have organized Pesta Deepavali in Mahkota Parade and also in Kotamas . . . There are those who say that this change is for the best, and there are those who say that this change is not satisfactory . . . But for me, I see this as more festive than in past years, two years ago, and in former years, because we just had, how do you say it [searching for the word], we just had an *audience* [in English] almost totally consisting of the Indian race. Whereas this year we have an *audience* from all races, not just Indians. There are *Bumiputera* people, Chinese people, and also people from the West. This gives them the opportunity not just to witness dances but also a sample of the culture of Indians who reside in this state.
>
> In addition, for Deepavali Festival we also give assistance to disabled people and to the elderly . . . To the Indian race we request that they organize open days, or open houses, for Deepavali, as usual, giving the opportunity to all of our friends to visit and to enjoy and to celebrate Deepavali together with us. To other races I want to request that they make plans to visit the homes of Indians for Deepavali." [my translation]

The bunching of the elements "participated in by all races," "audience from all races," "to other races," "all of our friends," "together with us," forms the familiar component in these discourses. Although the goal of friendly and harmonious relations is clearly embedded, the additional goals of political stability and economic modernity and development are absent, at least explicitly. These terms and propositions are used so regularly in conjunction that people tend to assume that they are implied even when they are not directly expressed. Yet, we can observe another significant usage of the representation of Malaysians of diverse backgrounds relating with each other in friendly and harmonious relations.

That is, Datuk Raghovan used this abstract image here to justify changes in the public staging of Deepavali festivities and to negotiate the inclusion of Indian culture and the Indian race in the broader society. Local Indians publicly celebrated the Deepavali festival in previous years on Temenggung Street, a street in an area of town where several Indian businesses are located, but this year organizers changed its venue to the stage in Mahkota Parade. This change will facilitate a greater exposure of Indian culture to all of the races that make up Melaka society, especially to the two largest races, *Bumiputera* and *Tionghua* (Chinese). In addition, the fact that local Indian culture provides an additional asset to the state's tourism industry enhances the prestige of "the third largest race in Malaysia" and evokes the self-image of a unique society projected into the gaze of outsiders. Although the notion of "cultural rights" is not mentioned explicitly, an idea of this sort seems to underlie the stress laid upon how Deepavali is like major festivals of other races, especially the two largest groups who hold the most prestige. The size of each group often serves as an index of their ranking. The Indian Datuk implies that the main Indian festival, representing the Indian race, should be celebrated publicly by all of the races just like the main festivals of the larger races. Indians have the "right" to expose the greatness of their culture and distinctiveness to a broad audience.

I have also observed the frequent repetition of the familiar representation of Malaysian multiracial society in the discourse of other local residents of Melaka. These segments are derived from a series of open-ended interviews in which I spoke to local residents about their perceptions of Malaysian and Melakan society. This first segment comes from an interview I conducted with Sue Lin, a *Nyonya* Chinese schoolteacher.[6]

I: But anyway, what do you think about the society in Melaka?

R: You mean the culture?

I: The culture of multiracialism, in terms of Malaysian society.

R: Well, I think Melaka, on the whole, the people here are very close. The different races, if you go around, they are very close as compared with other states. Just say for example in this area, even though, you have a lot of Chinese, the Malays are able to blend themselves in, you know. I think the people in Melaka, especially in Melaka, they can get along very well, as compared with the other states, I think, yeah. All the races are very close. If you go and visit, have you visited the Indian Chitties?

I: Yes, I have visited the Chitties.

R: Yeah, so you see, around that area you even have the Chinese, they are very close, and they all speak in one common language, the Melaka Malay, and it is slightly different from the other states, yeah.

Sue Lin uses the terms "different races" and "all the races" together with "very close" and get along very well," reproducing the bundling of these terms exhibited in the widely broadcast ideological formulations of the ruling front. In this abstract representation, Malays blend in with Chinese and Chinese blend in with Indian Chitties, including the three major races in Malaysian society in a pattern of close social relations. They even share a distinctive way of speaking, "Melaka Malay," despite coming from different racial backgrounds.

Similarly, Puan Josephine, an elderly *Melaka Portugis* woman, uses this representation in her description of social relations in Melaka.

I: What is the meaning of the multiracial society in Malaysia?

R: All of the races I have seen and mixed with are good, from whichever race, Malays, Chinese, Indians; all are good. There is no problems or conflicts. We are all like family . . . All of the people I mix with, my neighbors who live close by, from what I remember are good. What they speak about we understand and what we speak about they understand . . . People have their own races and their races have their own ways to pray or types of food, and some do not eat this or that. It is like, you do not eat this and we do not eat this. These are the things we have to ask and talk about. It is like this: you, you have your ways-lah, and we, we have our ways-lah. There are even those who do not mix when it comes to food. We are all like family, like brothers and sisters. We understand what particular people do not eat. Like Muslims do not eat pork right, so we do not offer them pork; it is just like that-lah. [my translation]

Puan Josephine again combines references to a multiplicity of cultural categories with images of close and intimate relations.[7] She uses words such as "neighbors" and "family" and "brothers and sisters" to characterize the nature of ties between the diverse groups in Malaysian and Melakan society. Here we can also note that this representation is motivating in regard to directing people to socially mix with each other and to have dialogues about their respective cultural preferences and for each group to understand and respect these cultural differences.

In my interview with Haji Rashid, a middle-aged Malay Muslim, we can observe another expression of this representation, placing its construction within the historical context of the early post-independence days.

I: What was changing in Melaka, and in Malaysia in general from the colonial times to independence?

R: OK, that time, I think politically, when we, that time 1957, I was still in Melaka. The movement, the progressiveness is not that fast,

> very slow pace. Because I think Tunku knows, in order to unite the three big nationalities, racial polities, is not easy, to maintain each one's likeness, or this one, satisfaction, very slow, very slow. They do some sort of, like you know, agreement with these three principal races, at a slow pace and with very careful consideration, because they are not like Mahathir now, where everything has been set up, all has been lined out, laid out, simply to help him. At that time everything was very slow.

Here, the bundling of "three big nationalities," "racial polities," and "three principal races," are used in proximity with "in order to unite" and "to maintain each one's likeness" or "satisfaction" forming the abstract image we have noted in previous examples.[8] Yet this example demonstrates how this representation is used to interpret historical processes in modern Malaysia. From this perspective, the unity and harmonious relations between the three major races in Malaysian society may be assumed in the current context, but at the early stages of independence, under the first Prime Minister, Tunku Abdul Rahman, these ties were just being constructed. Haji Rashid notes that this was not an easy process and it was brought into effect through an *agreement*—echoing the excerpt at the beginning of this chapter—between the three principal races.

So far, in this chapter, I have inferred a mental representation of Malaysian society and the relations between diverse cultural categories from a consideration of dominant national and local discourse. Judging from my discussions and interviews with local people, this representation appears to be widely distributed in Melakan society, spanning maximal and submaximal cultural categories. Semantic and propositional cues indicate its presence as a central component in discourse on a variety of topics, especially those connected with festivals, Malaysian cultures and society, and economic and political development. Furthermore, this representation appears to be diffusely internalized in long-term memory and motivating as it resonates with some experiences of local residents and directs social relations to some extent. Nevertheless, in order to put this representation into perspective, I will analyze samples of discourse produced by some of the opposition or alternative parties. This will assist us in distinguishing elements of this abstract image that are mere products of ideological formulations and those that may be indicative of even deeper mental representations, schemata of Malaysian society.

Parti Agama Islam SeMalaysia (PAS), the Islamic Party of Malaysia, except for a short period spent within the ruling alliance, has been an opposition party. PAS, a highly popular party in the eastern states of Peninsular

Malaysia for the last few decades, finally won the state election and has ruled in the state of Kelantan since 1991. Moreover, following strong Malay resentment and anger at the way the government treated the former Deputy Prime Minister, Anwar Ibrahim, PAS has become even stronger and is looking forward to making more political headway in the upcoming election. *Harakah,* the PAS newspaper, has extensive distribution but is officially only to be sold to its membership. Nevertheless, in practice, the paper has become a hot commodity and many non-members get their hands on it. The following excerpt is from an article titled "Kelantan Chinese praise Nik Aziz" (Nik Aziz is the Menteri Besar or head of state in Kelantan) from the 4th of October 1999 issue.

> The Kelantan State Administration under PAS never discriminated between groups in the state in relation to all of their rights and things that they hold to be significant. This condition allows all the people of the state to live with peace and comfort. The PAS government has never taken or block the rights of any of the races in the state, despite having different religious understandings, different customary ways, and different political understandings . . . It is said that as long as the PAS government has ruled in Kelantan, since 1991, the Chinese community has never felt alienated or that their rights were violated; instead, they receive justice and equal treatment in all matters, including in terms of religion and education . . . [my translation]

Once again, we can note the familiar bunching of terms and phrases such as "groups in the state," "any of the races," "different religious, different customary ways, and different political understandings" with terms and phrases such as "live with peace and comfort" and "never felt alienated." This bundling of elements suggests that there is a similar underlying component in this discourse as in the discourse discussed earlier. Yet there are some major differences. There are no references in this discourse to economic modernization, technical development and political stability. In fact, these goals are generally not emphasized in *Harakah,* and to the contrary, these goals, especially the way they have been implemented by the ruling alliance government, are a major point of contention.

PAS leaders and local members often criticize the ruling federal government for their corruption, cronyism, and overly extravagant spending in development and modernization projects. On several occasions when I was driven home by taxi drivers who were members of PAS, they would point out several uncompleted "development" projects along the coast and criticize the government's drive to modernize and to build gigantic structure after gigantic structure even while there is an economic crisis. These large empty structures were an embodiment of the uselessness and futility of the government projects, and what more, of their misplaced values and morals.

In addition, PAS leaders and supporters have recast the beneficent leaders, responsible for constructing racial unity and harmony, of ruling alliance discourse as cruel and oppressive leaders. This depiction of the ruling alliance leaders was given greater impetus following the brutal beating of former Deputy Prime Minister, Anwar Ibrahim while in police custody awaiting trial. Yet instead of abandoning the ideology of racial unity and harmony espoused by the ruling alliance, opposition leaders appropriate this ideology as their own arguing that they will best serve its goals and aspirations. Indeed, in the context in which this article was published, the Islamic Party's usage of this mental representation took on added significance. PAS leaders were constantly combating assertions by the ruling alliance leaders that they would only represent the interests of the Malay and Muslim community and not the interests of other races and religions if they achieved greater political power in Malaysian society. Moreover, as PAS, DAP, KeADILan, and PRM formed an Alternative Front, a multiracial alliance to counter the ruling alliance, and these groups approached the November 1999 election, this sort of rhetoric became even more prevalent.[9]

In any event, what is important for us to note here is that the discourse of PAS and other opposition parties contained the representation of diverse Malaysian cultural categories interconnected through peaceful and harmonious relationships; yet, these groups embedded different goals within this representation. PAS stressed Islamic values and morals and the goals of extending the influence of Islamic principles throughout Malaysian society culminating with the establishment of an Islamic state in which each race and religion would have equal rights as subjects of a state governing with Islamic law. The other opposition parties in the Alternative Front are socialist leaning and reform-minded parties who tend to emphasize improving human rights, social justice, and clean, transparent, and democratic government. This Alternative Front published a joint platform that combined these goals, emphasizing justice, equal rights, and democracy. In effect, these parties constructed alternative *models* of Malaysia's diverse society consistent with their ideological doctrines. These models do not appear to be as widely distributed throughout society in Melaka as the dominant model, but they also appear to embed motives for action for those who have some degree of conviction in them.

Noting that there are alternative models routinely produced according to the ideological doctrines of particular parties and persons, we must continue to look deeper for knowledge that underlies the similarities in these models. I want to turn our attention back to several of the cues that I mentioned in passing might indicate the presence of a deeper mental representation in the domain of social relations. Namely, the notion of "cultural rights," explicitly and implicitly expressed in local Chinese and Indian ruling alliance leaders' speeches, the use of the mental model as a self-image and image projected to outsiders, and explicit and implicit references to Malaysia's diverse citizenry. In addition, the last excerpt from an issue of *Harakah* lays a great deal of stress upon rights, both cultural and political rights. It points out that not only are things peaceful and comfortable for all cultural categories, but that they are not discriminated against and do not have any of their *rights* denied to them on the bases of cultural differences. This article did not use the term *citizen* but the coupling of terms such as *rakyat* (people) and *hak* (rights) indicates some sort of well-formed concept of *citizenship*.

In relation to my discussions and interviews with local residents about their interpretations of social relations between diverse groups in Malaysian society, there was a tendency for many of them to repeat hegemonic ideological formulations and models. When I gave examples of social problems or tensions, they often denied that they existed or sought some way to justify them that would still be consistent with the image they wanted to project to me, a foreigner. For instance, when I mentioned to Sue Lin that I did not see any Malays participate in the festivals in the Indian Chitty community, she told me that perhaps Malays do not know the dates of these festivals because they often change. Some people would not go any further than upholding the hopeful national image to me, but others showed less restraint or went further after they became more acquainted with me. For instance, when I asked Flora Goh, a Chinese businesswoman, which groups form the upper class or *orang kaya* in Melaka, she told me:

> Our Malaysian government, ah, they claim themselves to be the *Bumi*. *Bumi* that means they are the original people. Therefore, they have every right to protect this *Bumi* people, so somehow or other, they sponsor, they sponsor their people, these *Bumiputeras*. So they are considered the first class. So we poor Chinese, our country is China. We only *tompang*, we call it tompang . . . Tompang means to say that, uh, we are just using this place, you know, temporary shelter for us . . . Should anything happen, uh, should anything happen and then we leave this country, let's say, then we have got to go back to our original country, all right. But then we have been born here, so we cannot claim China to be our country now, you know, that kind of thing. So unless the government make it so obvious that Chinese have to go back to their own country, then, I think that would be, I don't know, if, whether that is going to happen . . . This is how we see about it . . . We are citizens.

> But of course our government did not say that we are second class. It
> did not specify it in that manner, but we feel it in that manner.

This response clearly goes beyond and in some ways contradicts the hopeful images and models presented by many other respondents. Not only does this discourse contain an explicit reference to citizenship and the principle of soil or place, being "born here," but it also expresses a qualified and graded sense of citizenship, "first class and second class." According to Flora, Chinese citizens feel that they are only "*tompang*," her pronunciation of the Malay word "tumpang," temporary sojourners or guests in a country in which *Bumis* or *Bumiputeras* are the "original people."[10] She goes on to express a notion of Malay privilege, which I will discuss in more detail in the next section. Nonetheless, I should note, this notion of Malay or *Bumi* special rights clearly combines with a notion of citizenship and contributes to the production of her sense of cultural citizenship.

Some additional evidence of the presence of a schema related to a conception of citizenship—and to qualified citizenship—is supplied by the response of many Malaysians, *Bumi* and non-*Bumi*, to my informing them that I am an "American." After ruling out that I meant to say African or that I am a South "American," many Malaysians went on to tell me that I must have meant to say that I am a "citizen" of America. The default image they have of Americans, persons who are inherently or naturally Americans, consists of persons who are white and not persons who are black. Persons who do not fit into the default image are only Americans because they have American citizenship bestowed upon them. Similarly, they apply this logic to the Malaysian context. *Bumiputera*, Malays and *orang asli*, are recognized as the default members of the category "Malaysian," whereas non-*Bumi* Malaysians are only Malaysian due to the operation of law which has bestowed citizenship upon them.

I infer from these data that a well-formed conception of citizenship forms the core of a schema of Malaysia's diverse society. This schema is a mental representation of Malaysian from diverse backgrounds, and of diverse cultural categories, sharing in a formal citizenship that bestows rights and obligations upon them and entails a common bond with their comrades. As members of such a formal category, they share certain fundamental qualities amongst themselves and have a definite sense of fellowship connecting them as members of an overarching category. It is with such a schema that Malaysians interpret all citizens as having some claim to sharing the space and land considered to be the territory of Malaysia and to have some equal rights before the law. This explicates the first part of the "contract" referred to at the beginning of this chapter, the part that relates to the status of citizenship, and now, I turn to the second part, the part that relates to Malay special rights.

MODELS AND SCHEMA OF MALAY PRIVILEGE

National and local ruling alliance leaders do not speak of Malay privilege as openly or freely as they speak about the unique and diverse Malaysian society. The representation of Malaysian society as a harmonious diverse society is a hopeful and inspiring image, one that can be enthusiastically projected to foreigners, whereas representations of Malay privilege entail references to prejudice, discrimination, and inequality, things that one would rather not talk about, much less project to outsiders. Moreover, following the 1969 May 13th racial riot government officials passed laws restricting discussion of several topics relating to Malay privileges. Yet there have been, and still are, occasions in which national and local leaders speak, directly or indirectly, of Malay privilege. This notion is an important aspect of dominant ideological doctrine. One of the most significant occasions for the promulgation of this notion was in the *Malay Dilemma* (1970), a book written by Mahathir Mohamad after his expulsion from UMNO. In this book, Mahathir Mohamad historicizes the economic condition of Malays vis-à-vis other races and argues for more government intervention to address patterns of racial inequality. Mahathir (1970:74–76) wrote:

> The scholarships which poor Malay children are receiving are morally justifiable and socially necessary. They are the means to progress for a backward community in a progressing nation. They are a means of rectifying racial inequality, and of raising the Malays to the level of the Chinese and Indians . . . The motive behind preferential treatment is not to put the Malays in a superior position, but to bring them up to the level of the non-Malays. Under the British Colonial regime it has already become obvious that not only were the Malays economically backward, but they were also educationally behind . . . True, not all the non-Malays were wealthy and able to acquire a good education. But, because a good number were, the educational standard of the Malays began to fall far behind that of the non-Malays . . . It is therefore not for reasons of Malay superiority that preferential treatment for Malays in scholarship awards was insisted upon. The scholarships are not a manifestation of racial inequality. They are a means of breaking down the superior position of the non-Malays in the field of education. [my emphasis]

In this discourse, we can note the repetitive reference to the dichotomy "Malays" and "non-Malays." This dichotomy is used in conjunction with terms and phrases such as "poor," "backward," "began to fall behind," "economically backward," and "educationally behind." The combinations of these terms arranges an opposition in which the Malays are poor, backwards, and behind, and the non-Malays, especially Chinese and Indians, are rich, advanced, and ahead. This proposition is connected to another proposition that asserts that Malays require help to erase this inequality. Thus, phrases like "means of progress for a backward community," "means of rectifying racial inequality," "raising the Malays to the level of the Chinese and Indians," "bring them up to the level of the non-Malays" and used together with terms like "scholarships" and "preferential treatment." The bundling of terms constructs a mental representation of disadvantaged Malays receiving support to bring them on par with non-Malays. Indeed, the goal of eradicating the socio-economic disparity between Malays and non-Malays is evident in this discourse and it is a major motive embedded within this representation.

This representation is used for numerous interpretative purposes. In the context of Mahathir Mohamad's book, *Malay Dilemma*, it was frequently used to explain the meaning of racial "equality" and to justify preferential provisions for Malays. Racial "equality" is not treating persons of each racial category in the same manner that would only reproduce inequality, but to the contrary, it is the ideal of bringing all races up to approximately the same level. To achieve this aim, drawing parallels with the American context, Mahathir argues that "positive discrimination" or "affirmative action" should be used to combat a history of *de facto* social and economic discrimination against the Malay population (Mahathir 1970, 1999:36). This mental representation is used for some of the same purposes in Mahathir Mohamad's recent book, *A New Deal for Asia* (1999:33–36):

> After the race riots, the government quickly recognised that closing the gap between the Malays and other ethnic groups would be essential for the long-term stability and prosperity of the country. Moving the Malays (or *bumiputeras,* as the indigenous people of Malaysia are called) into the mainstream of economic activity was easier said than done . . . Since the main rift was between the *bumiputeras and other groups,* the main focus of these new policies was to draw the Malays into the mainstream economic life of the nation . . . It was made very easy for Malays to hold shares in government-owned enterprises. Loans, business premises and plenty of other benefits and economic opportunities were made available. It is clearly not true that only a few Malays benefited from the NEP; every *bumiputera* benefited . . . The indigenous people have become more urbanised, entered the mainstream money economy, and gained access to a much larger share of the wealth

of the country. The NEP can be said to have changed the scene of
Malaysia almost completely. No longer are the towns mainly Chinese
and the rural areas populated mainly by Malays and other *bumiputeras* . . . To achieve the targets we had set in the NEP within twenty
years, Malaysia had to implement positive discrimination, or what
Americans would call 'affirmative action.' Some of the other ethnic
groups, first of all the Chinese and Indians, may sometimes have felt
that this preferential treatment was not entirely fair. Without the NEP,
however, Malaysia would never have achieved the level of social stability and economic well-being it enjoyed in the 1990s. In a way, the economic crisis experienced from 1997 onward has been a testimony to the
success of the policy. Had we not had a reasonably equitable and
racially stable Malaysia in times of economic hardship, the situation
could easily have deteriorated and we might have suffered the same fate
as, for example, Indonesia. As twenty years of the NEP drew to a close,
we decided to continue with a ten-year National Development Policy
(NDP) designed to complete the work started in 1971 with the NEP.
The hope was that by the turn of the century, the economic disparities
between the races would have been largely eliminated.

Similarly, the dichotomy between "Malays" or "*bumiputeras*" and non-
Malays (or "other ethnic groups" or "Chinese and Indians") is expressed in
this discourse. This dichotomy is coupled with the opposition of features associated with Malays and non-Malays. Malays and other *bumiputeras* were
more "rural" and outside of the "economic mainstream," while non-Malays
and non-*Bumiputeras* were more "urban" and inside "mainstream economic activities." These terms and oppositions were, once again, used together with, or included within, terms and phrases that refer to leveling
inequality and the institutional tools used to achieve such leveling. In particular, these phrases were used to point out the leveling of inequality: "closing
the gap between Malays and other ethnic groups," "gained access to a much
greater share of the wealth," "draw Malays into the mainstream" and "economic disparities between the races would have been largely eliminated." In
close proximity, these terms and phrases were used to refer to the institutional tools for leveling: "NEP," "NDP," "implement affirmative action,"
"positive discrimination," "preferential treatment," "made very easy for
Malays," and "plenty of other benefits and economic opportunities were
made available."

    In addition to the embedded motives of the order of "closing the gap
between Malays and other ethnic groups," apparent on the surface of this
discourse as well as the previous one, there are some more goals stressed in
this discourse segment. These are the goals of "long-term stability," "social
stability," "prosperity," and "economic well-being" that Mahathir argues

would not exist were it not for the more immediate and fundamental goal of achieving a "reasonably equitable" distribution of the wealth. In fact, these long-term national goals were expressed prominently in the earlier book as well. Moreover, these are the same ideological extensions routinely associated with the dominant model of Malaysia's diverse society that we discussed above. These conditional goals or ideological extensions often serve as a link connecting the propositions contained within dominant models of Malaysia's diverse society and Malay privilege.

For instance, consider the article in the Christmas edition of the newspaper cited above that quoted some of the Malaysian Prime Minister's Christmas message to the nation. First, this article spoke about how the country is recovering from the economic crisis and will celebrate this year's Christmas in peace and harmony amongst friends of all races and religions. Immediately following references to failed attempts to spark riots in Malaysia and religious violence in other countries, the journalist interjected the following short segment before returning to the cheerful image of Malaysia's diverse society. In the midst of this routine holiday message article, Prime Minister Mahathir Mohamad reportedly asserted, "It is obviously clear that efforts to bridge the development gap between races have effectively minimised potential racial tensions when crisis hits a nation" (quoted in *The Sun*, December 25, 1998). This brief statement situated within discourse focusing on harmonious and friendly relations amongst Malaysians embeds a mental representation of Malay special rights. Thus, the proposition that "Malaysians of diverse backgrounds enjoy peaceful and harmonious relations" is contingent upon the proposition that, "Malays must be brought on par with non-Malays through preferential treatment." The former goals are dependent upon the realization of the latter more fundamental goals (cf. D'Andrade 1995:232).

Besides explaining and justifying preferential treatment for Malays, the usage in these discourses demonstrates that this mental representation is also used to neutralize the willingness of Malaysians to oppose ruling alliance policies and to make demands for their own cultural categories and social groups. Politicians and mainstream newspapers frequently reminded people that if it were not for government "affirmative action" programs for Malays the relative peace, prosperity and stability would fall apart and dissipate.

'Datuk Seri Dr Mahathir Mohamad said today Malaysians should remember that they cannot demand everything for their own race as this will not be good for national well-being. He said if every race demanded everything for itself but the country was not peaceful and did not progress, it would end up getting nothing . . . Whenever we do something for one race, we must consider all races. If something is done without considering the sensitivities, there'll be disappointment, and the government cannot develop the country, he said. (New Straits Times, November 5, 1999).

The Prime Minister made these comments in response to requests from Chinese vernacular schools for more financial support from the government. Providing more financial support for Chinese students and schools does not fit the model of bringing Malay students up to par with the Chinese students. He implies that if Chinese were to make these sorts of demands for their own race, it could inflame the sensitivities of the Malay community, which could lead to conflict and put a halt to national progress. The Prime Minister made this address to a group of Chinese school principals at a time, before the 1999 election, in which government officials were targeting many Malay schools for teaching Malay children to dislike national ruling alliance leaders. Government representatives turned down requests for additional funds, but they applauded Chinese teachers for focusing upon imparting knowledge instead of politics. On other occasions, this mental representation has been used in discourse addressed directly to the Malay community. For instance, consider the following newspaper excerpt about the Prime Minister's *Hari Raya Aidilfitri* message that was also aired over Radio Television Malaysia:

> He said there are parties who, purposely and for specific interests, are teaching the people not to be thankful for what they enjoyed or to be grateful to those who made it possible. They are taught not to be grateful to those who gave them the bounty because, ostensibly, they are entitled to the bounty which would have been given by others anyway . . . This change in the meaning of gratitude has serious implications to our society. If we are not appreciative and grateful to those who give us something, then surely no one will want to give us anything . . . If we bite the hand that gives us gifts or assistance or saves us, who will strive, sometimes at great lengths, to give us anything? . . . Saying that the Muslims in Malaysia today are disunited and weak, Mahathir warned that if they are not grateful to their benefactors, there will be no mutual help among their community (*The Sun*, January 8, 2000).

He made this statement not long after the 1999 election in which PAS won the election in two states, Kelantan and Terengganu, and ran close races in many other states. It became clearer during the election campaign that the Malay community was torn into largely two camps, supporters of the ruling alliance and supporters of the opposition alliance. In this discourse, Mahathir uses the mental representation of Malays receiving special benefits to criticize the

Malay opposition and their supporters for not being grateful for such benefits. The institutional tools for leveling, the NEP, NDP, scholarship programs and other special benefits for Malays, "the Muslims of Malaysia," are interpreted as "gifts" or "assistance" or "bounty" and other things that "saves us." Malays must be grateful to the government "benefactors," such as UMNO for instance who have gifted them this preferential treatment. He argues that Malays should not just construe this preferential treatment as a natural entitlement and turn against the Malay Muslim party that has formulated and administered these programs. Nevertheless, it is just this kind of notion of Malay entitlement that I will demonstrate lies deeply in the domain of social cognition, deeper than the alternative models of Malay privilege.

This dominant representation of Malay privilege, embedded in the discourses we have analyzed so far, is widely distributed in Melakan society amongst all of the maximal and submaximal cultural categories. These local residents have not only been bombarded with radio, television, and newspaper broadcasts of discourse embedding this mental representation but they have also had various experiences with the institutionalization of this image in the form of various government programs and policy. Although residents have varying degrees of commitment to this representation, they generally have a well-formed notion of it. Let us consider a segment of an interview with Rajan, an Indian factory worker in his early thirties.

> Like the JPA, police, department, the army, any of the government departments-lah, preferences are given to the Malay. It is stated in the Constitution . . . Preferences pretty much-lah, because of *patah* (feelings of despair). People that came were *atas* (above them). When those Indian immigrants came, Malays were poor. Chinese were very rich. Indians were still living on the estates. That is why it happened-lah. So after the *Dasar Ekonomi Baru* (New Economic Policy), they give privileges to *Bumis*. . . . manufacturing industry, to get government jobs, to get business opportunities. Everything, Malays are given opportunities, privileges. They are given priorities. So many of the Malays came up from this program-lah. Today, many people have big houses . . . But the government says that the Malays are still poor. Cannot be poor. They are very rich now . . . actually the DEB ended up in 1990 but they extended it for another ten years . . . This DEB was because of the 1969 riot . . . Malays were given privileges, given opportunities and advantages, for Malays-lah . . . It is almost enough.

In Rajan's discourse, we can note the familiar dichotomy of Malays and non-Malays, especially Chinese and Indians, and the association of Malays with poverty in contrast to Chinese. This dichotomy is connected to terms and phrases that refer to leveling inequality such as "Malays came up from

this program-lah" and "many people have big houses" and institutional leveling devices such as "New Economic Policy," "DEB," "Malays are given
opportunities," "they are given priorities," "given opportunities and advantages." Although most of this interview was in English, Rajan, who speaks
Malay, English, Tamil and Mandarin, used Malay for a few key words such
as *patah, atas,* and *Dasar Ekonomi Baru. Patah* refers to the anguish and de-
spair Malays felt concerning the way *immigrant* Chinese and Indians were
situated *atas* or above them on a higher socio-economic plane. The *Dasar
Ekonomic Baru* (DEB), the New Economic Policy in Malay, is the means to
address the inequality Malays were distraught over. Rajan goes on to express his views about how such preferential programs are no longer appropriate, if they ever were, because Malays are no longer poor. This indicates
that although he has internalized a well-formed representation of poor
Malays receiving government assistance to bring them on par with other
races, he thinks that this mental representation no longer applies to the current situation and therefore it lacks strong motivational force for him. In
contrast, Haji Rashid, continuing our discussion about the history of
Melaka, appears to have a greater commitment to the status quo:

> Yeah, and Melaka, at that time, was known as the sleepy hollow of
> Malaysia, or Malaya, at that time. We still do not maintain any good
> logs. They had some disagreements about tenure of lands, and you
> know, and division of property between the three major races, Malays,
> Chinese, and Indians . . . you can see that lots of lands belonging to
> Malays was turned over to the Chinese. That was the very, very early
> stage. Now, I think they have settled everything-lah. They have main-
> tained a lot of bills and . . . so now, say a housing project needs to be
> built, then say like thirty per cent must go to a *Bumiputera.* Bumiputera
> consisting of a Malay or *orang asli,* so like that, and the rest can go for
> non-*Bumis,* non-*Bumiputera.*

Haji Rashid uses this representation of Malay privilege to explain how things
have been set straight after the Malaysian government has formulated new
policies. In earlier times, "rich" Chinese were able to acquire lands from
"poor" Malays and this led to a controversial problem around independence
times, but the new leveling devices have solved all of these problems.
Nowadays, the preferential treatment and favorable quotas for Malays, has
settled the problem of how resources should be distributed. Many Malays
disagree with this proposition and some of them have internalized another
model of Malay privilege. In fact, some local members of the Islamic Party of
Malaysia (PAS) were convinced that these land problems in Melaka were still
disputable and not settled. These Malay Muslim activists were in possession

of legal documents that they argued proved that Malays had just leased a large part of the urban land holdings to Chinese businessmen and they were now trying to make a legal claim to return control of this prime urban landscape to Malays.

Let us take a closer look at the alternative model embedded within the discourse of the Islamic Party of Malaysia (PAS) and how it motivates such political efforts. For instance an article entitled, "Give Bumiputera Enterpreneurs the Opportunity to Develop Primula Beach Resort," appearing in the Friday February 11th 2000 issue of *Harakah,* reads:

> The closure of a hotel, Primula Beach Resort, owned by the Terengganu state government is one policy move consistent with the general business principles of making certain that there is no wastefulness in the use of the people's resources . . . In relation to the hotel closure, this is part of the immediate moves to terminate the operation of all corporations owned by the state government that are not productive. It is unimaginable to provide assistance to state-owned corporations that experience financial losses in cases where no hope exists for recovery through continued operation, because this would incur financial losses upon the *rakyat* (people). It is better to figure that the financial resources under consideration be used to support projects that can give positive results to *rakyat* (the people) such as preparing business space for small businesses, supporting projects to wipe out poverty and so forth. There are projects managed by the government that should be managed by private entrepreneurs. Whenever the government is involved within enterprises like this a situation develops in which Bumiputera entrepreneurs within the same line of business compete with the state-owned corporations. What the government is supposed to do is to give guidance, assistance and support that is needed in order for Bumiputera entrepreneurs to become strong in their efforts to compete with non-Bumiputera entrepreneurs. The experience of state government involvement in business demonstrates that state-owned corporations become intense competitors for Bumiputera entrepreneurs to the point that they cause many Bumiputera to be buried. What is odd is that these state-owned businesses in question also experience financial ruin. Those who directly benefit are non-Bumiputera businesses. Hotel enterprises are one example where the government has to play a role to help and guide Bumiputera efforts rather than to compete with them. The move to give the opportunity to Bumiputera entrepreneurs to take over the Hotel Primula Beach Resort business is a prime example. If this is done by the Terengganu state government then it is certainly hoped that Bumiputera entrepreneurs who are established in the hospitality sector will be given the opportunity to manage the business concerned . . . This is because in the final analysis we want to see Bumiputeras advance within all sorts of business fields, not just state-run businesses. We want to see Bumiputera as entrepreneurs, not the government as entrepreneurs. The true role of

government is to be a catalyst forming Bumiputera businesses and industries out of groups in society . . . As of today whenever we visit business centers in big cities it is very sad that we cannot see the presence of
Bumiputera business. [my translation]

This article was written following the 1999 general election in which PAS
won a majority and formed the state government in the eastern peninsular
state of Terengganu. At this time, the PAS led state government of
Terengganu was striving to implement policies that they felt they had a mandate from the *rakyat* to implement. Many elements present in the bundling
of terms and phrases constituting the dominant model of Malay privilege are
also present here. In particular, the dichotomy between Malays or
Bumiputera and non-Malays or non-*Bumiputera* is combined with the contrast between "poor" and "less developed" and "less successful at business"
Malays and "rich" and "developed" and "successful" non-*Bumiputera*
business people. In addition, these sorts of terms and phrases are used in
conjunction with phrases that refer to leveling inequality such as "to wipe
out poverty," "become strong in their efforts to compete with non-
Bumiputera" and "we want to see *Bumiputeras* advance." However, a
major difference can be noted when it comes to the institutional tools of leveling inequality and assisting the Malay or *Bumiputera* population. That is,
the institutional assistance extended to Malays to level the socio-economic
imbalance vis-à-vis the non-*Bumi* population must be moral, just and prin-
cipled. Constant references to poor and common people, small and non-governmental enterprises, and the role of government as serving the common
people, expresses the populist Islamic canon of this party and its newspaper.
Furthermore, the concern expressed about avoiding wastefulness in government programs embodies Islamic values, as wastefulness is highly immoral
in Islamic teachings; it is considered to be an attribute of *Syaitan* (the Devil).
Thus, this article entails the implication that their programs are moral and
upright in contrast to the wasteful mega-projects of the ruling alliance government. In some other articles embedding this alternative model of Malay
privilege, their moral condemnation of the government is expressed more
explicitly. Consider the following article, entitled "Malay Secondary School
Students Increasingly Squeezed," published prior to the election in the 4th
of October 1999 issue of *Harakah:*

> Ustaz Azizan Abd. Razak states that opportunities for Malay children to
> further their higher education is increasingly being pushed to the side de-
> spite the fact that more private schools are being built . . . He says that
> the opportunity offered by this growth of private colleges for Malay

children to study in institutions of higher learning is being increasingly sidelined because many of these Malay children cannot afford to absorb the really high costs of instruction . . ."This is done when the system of education for *rakyat* that is supposed to be free of costs has already been corporatized, resulting in a situation in which although they are smart their fate is unfortunate because there is no money" . . . This require-ment automatically gives more extensive opportunities to the rich even though they are not really smart . . . This development in the end will make orang Melayu (Malays) unable to further their studies on a high level; it will just be suitable for them to become kuli [coolies] whereas orang kaya [rich people] will forever become 'tuan' (their superiors). This consequence has to be borne by Malays; it is caused by this greedy nationalist leadership looking for profits while the system of education has been privatized by them without considering the importance of ed-ucation for rakyat jelata [common people]" (*Harakah,* October 4, 1999). [my translation]

In this excerpt, the immorality of the national leadership is expressed explic-itly side by side with the mental representation of Malay privilege. National ruling alliance leaders are depicted as greedy privatizing, corporate-oriented, profit-seeking elites who are not mindful of the interests of the common peo-ple. Therefore, their programs cannot rectify the inequality between Malays and non-Malays and are depicted not as leveling tools at all but as a means to perpetuate the lower status of Malays, as *kuli* or manual laborers. In con-trast, PAS programs represent not only an effective but also a moral means to lessen the disparity between "poor" Malays and "orang kaya" and "tuan," because they would provide free education for common people and thereby not punish smart Malay children for being poor.

Clearly, the goals embedded within this alternative model contrast with the secondary goals of political and social stability and economic de-velopment attached to the dominant model. In the case of the alternative model, it is important to note that the goal of leveling socio-economic im-balances is itself contingent upon the goal of constructing moral and just in-stitutional devices to effect such leveling. From their ideological perspective, these goals will be best served ultimately by administration under an Islamic state based in Islamic law. The *secular*-based morality, which is embedded in both models, of correcting past patterns of structural inequality and social and economic discrimination is not sufficient. An additional *religious*-based moral onus is placed on the character of the leveling devices themselves. In sum, an alternative model of Malay privilege, expressed regularly in dis-course produced by PAS members and supporters, incorporates some of the same basic elements of the dominant model. However, the dominant model entails an image of uniform leveling devices, whereas the alternative model entails an image of moral and just leveling devices.

The similarity between these alternative models that are embedded in contrasting ideological formulation suggests that there may be some deeper underlying, more fundamental mental representations and knowledge structures that generate them. Indeed, in much of the earlier discourse, another mental representation was embedded implicitly although at times it was indicated by surface references such as the mention of *entitlement* and *Bumiputera*. In fact, in relation to my discussions and interviews with local residents, there was a tendency to use surface terms that have come to connote complex concepts. For instance, many local people would tell me there is such a thing as *Bumiputera* or *Bahasa Malaysia* that the name of the country is *MALAY*-sia with stress laid on the part in capitals. Use of these key words was also a way to avoid talking about sensitive topics directly and besides most Malaysians know what they index. Yet, many people did produce discourse that embedded and expressed a well-formed schema of Malay privilege more explicitly. We can turn back to the beginning of Flora Goh's statement in which she said, "Our Malaysian government, ah, they claim themselves to be the *Bumi*. *Bumi* that means they are the original people. Therefore, they have every right to protect this *Bumi* people, so somehow or other, they sponsor, they sponsor their people, these *Bumiputeras.*" Here the preferential treatment of *Bumiputera* rests upon, and is justified by the notion that they are the *original people*. Angel Hong, a working class Chinese woman, gives similar reasons in her response to my question pertaining to the emphasis laid upon Malay culture in public celebrations.

> Malay culture is the main culture in Malaysia, because *Bahasa Malaysia* is the communication for these three racial groups [Malays, Chinese, and Indians] . . . *Bahasa Malaysia* is the language of association for these races . . . Because here is a Malay country, what. Malaysia is a Malay country, what . . . Malaysia is a multiracial culture, but, um, because *orang Melayu* is the banyak sekali (majority) in Malaysia that is why they are more involved in the *Bahasa Melayu*, you understand . . . Yes, dancing also, because they are more important, uh, more emphasized in the *Bahasa Melayu*, that means that Malay dance is more important what . . . You must understand that because Malaysia, this is a *orang Melayu* country, it is a Malay country. Malaysia is very big isn't it, but most of the people are Malay. Malay is the biggest so they emphasize Malay culture. [my emphasis]

She explains that the Malay language is the national language and Malay dances are emphasized in public celebrations because Malays are the "majority" and Malaysia is a "Malay country." In Angle Hong's response, terms and phrases that describe Malays as being the "majority" or "biggest" group appears to replace or index the notion that Malays are the "original people." Yet in both of these cases we have the dichotomy between Malays and other races and the singling out of Malays as a special group, with a right to special treatment, due to their being the "original people" or the "majority."[11] In similar fashion, Rajan explains that Malay privileges are rooted in the past:

> Because of the sultans, in the past, the Malay states-lah, because Malays in the past were rich, mostly because of this trade. And then Chinese and Indians, they are newcomers, they are immigrants. They came from China and from India. Chinese came since Melaka Sultanate and Indians also came since the Melaka Sultanate. So they [Malays] came, they have this, uh, five hundred years of history-lah, even though there were *orang asli* here before them . . . Even during independence, a big issue was the issue of *hak-hak istimewa*. It was a very big issue. So the British government negotiated *Tanah Melayu* with the Malays, and with the sultans also, so the big issue was the issue of *hak istimewa melayu,* the special privileges to Malays. Because they said Malays own *Tanah Melayu*. Malays own *Tanah Melayu* and they said Chinese and Indians are immigrants. So if Malays don't get their privileges, there will never be, things like that. So we could not get our independence. So Chinese and Indians were looking at the country, uh, independence is more important. So they say OK we give our way. We give our way but later we want the same advantages.

After referring to the fact that Malays compose over half of the Malaysian population, he went on to explain that special rights for this Malay "majority" rests in their past, a past in which they were the "earliest people" to establish political rule in the form of the "Melaka Sultanate." It was decided in the past that Malays are entitled to special rights because they "own *Tanah Melayu*."[12] The non-Malay part of the Malay/non-Malay dichotomy, such as Chinese and Indians, came from other countries and were "newcomers" and "immigrants" and thereby have no *entitlement* to special rights and privileges. Towards the end of this segment, he expresses the qualified commitment Indians and Chinese have to this notion of Malay special rights. They agreed to it in order for the country to achieve independence while holding out the prospect that in the future all races, all *citizens,* would receive the same benefits. Haji Rashid also situates his explanation and justification for Malay special rights in historical perspective:

As you know, the majority population of Malaysia is Malays humh, because not on the 80 or 75 per cent, but it is only around 60 or 65 per
cent. And, then it seems, Malays do not have a country of their own, not
like Chinese who have, they have China, a very mainland there with mil-
lions of people. They came down here during the Malays Sultanate of
Melaka where there was Hok Aloi and the Kuala Lumpur and our Hang
Li Po came to Melaka. So that was when the Chinese came. They are not
actually the aborigines. Because we Malays are also not the original of
Malaysia, but then we came earlier than them [Chinese]. Because at that
time it was . . . Fifteenth Century we were already here . . . Bugis from
Riau, from Majapahit, we were already here in Melaka during the
Melaka Sultanate, so we are the forefathers . . . Maybe we cannot call
ourselves the *asli*, because there, like myself, my great grandfather was
from the Bugis, from Riau, and maybe he came here as pirates, ha, ha,
ha . . . He came here earlier than the Chinese, in 1511, or early Fifteenth
Century, so for the development of us, we respect the Chinese because
they developed most of these . . . They indulged themselves in these
things, tin mines, rubber estates, like this hawking you know that, and
all these imports. But like I said, we still feel, as I said earlier, that we
want something, the independence that we have achieved. We need
something, not at pass, but slightly at par so it is enough-lah you know
because we Malays always have a certain sort of *cukup tidak apa-apa,
cukuplah* (enough it doesn't matter, enough-lah)[13] because we believe
that Allah is Almighty and He knows how to divide all the property. But
still we need to achieve something to work for.

In Haji Rashid's discourse we can note the familiar bundling of the
Malay/non-Malay dichotomy with terms and phrases that refer to the distinctiveness of the Malay or *Bumiputera* population such as "majority
population," "we came earlier than them," "we were already here in
Melaka," "we are the forefathers." Once again these phrases are utilized
along with terms and phrases that express a sense of *entitlement* or special
benefits for Malays such as "we still feel . . . that we want something," "we
need something, not at pass, but slightly at par," and "we need to achieve
something to work for." Haji Rashid, unlike many other Malays, concedes
that Malays are not the "original people." Nevertheless, the fact that they
are the "earliest people," of the three major racial groups, and "the majority" suffices to make them the "forefathers" of Malaysia and to entitle
them to *hak-hak istimewa* or special rights and privileges. Besides, Chinese
and Indians have a country elsewhere to call their own; Malays only have
Tanah Melayu. The "something" that he feels Malays want, and have a
right to, is not clearly defined but he grabs on to an element of the dominant model of Malay privilege, "slightly at par," to express one form this
sense of entitlement can take and has taken.

In sum, the schema of Malay privilege is a mental representation that bundles together the conceptual division between Malays (or *Bumiputeras*) and non-Malays (or non-*Bumiputeras*), and notions about Malays as the original, majority, or "definitive people" (Mahathir Mohamad 1970:124–127), along with a sense of *entitlement* or rightful claim to some class of distinctive benefits. These distinctive benefits have changed, and will continue to change, over time. During the British colonial era, the schema of Malay privilege encompassed recognition of sovereign Malay sultans, autonomy of the Malay states, rights to serve in large numbers in the civil service, special status afforded to Islam as the "religion of the Malays," and reserve lands set aside for Malay usage.[14] Yet the class of distinctive benefits felt to be encompassed by this schema has changed over time and people have various positions on what it should and should not entail. Clearly from the dominant and alternative models of "Malay privilege" I have described and analyzed above, one can note that some of the meanings it has come to take on relates to the governmental programs of preferential treatment for Malays and to the extension of Islamic principles throughout Malaysian society.

CONCLUSION: NEGOTIATIONS AND EXPERIENCE

Social actors embed and reproduce schemata and models of "Malaysia"s diverse society" and of "Malay privilege" in Malaysian discourses and practices. Local residents in Melaka, from various social backgrounds, negotiate these seemingly contradictory representations in their everyday lives and utilize them as a guide to social relations and to understanding diverse social and cultural forms (Goodenough 1970; Keller and Keller 1996; Lehman 1997; Bradd Shore 1996). These representations embed goals of building and maintaining harmonious and peaceful inter-group relations, respecting everyone's status as citizens, providing special benefits for Malay "natives," and building the "nation" of Malaysia even as they reflect tensions in the process of national formation.

The models and schema of "Malaysia's diverse society" bunches together representations of diverse and distinct social categories and their interrelationships (Agar and Hobbs 1985; D'Andrade 1995; Strauss 1992b; Keller and Keller 1996). Relations between "maximal identity" constructs (Sands and Lehman 1995) are conventionally and hopefully projected as peaceful, harmonious, close, and characterized by mutual tolerance of each other's cultural, primarily religious, differences. Any form of discrimination, inequality, and exclusion is inconsistent with such a perspective. Everyone, regardless of race or religion, is included in and belongs to Malaysia's multiracial society. With the schema of "Malaysia's diverse society," this sense of belonging is grounded in a well-formed notion of citizenship, projecting all Malaysians on a horizontal plane as equal citizen-members of the nation.

On the other hand, the models and schema of "Malay privilege" condenses knowledge about the super-ordination of Malays in Malaysian society. This schema reorders Malaysian multiracial society into a hierarchical schema with Malays singled out as the *Bumiputera,* the original inhabitants of Malaysia, who really matter. Other *Bumiputera* groups are only nominal members of this category or are "primitive" non-Muslims who do not count in the same way. Perhaps no group is totally indigenous who makes a difference in the present social and political order. From this perspective, Malays are the generic or unmarked members of the "nation," the only first-class citizens who fully belong. Other groups in this vertical scheme are immigrants, who are assumed to be full "belongers" of other places, and are Malaysians only by virtue of legal entitlement to citizenship.

The social and political "contract," expressed explicitly in the newspaper excerpt quoted at the beginning of this chapter, incorporating both of these schemata emerged in the early years of Malaysian political independence. Immediately following the racial riots and political crises of 1969, the schemata of "Malaysia's diverse society" and "Malay privilege" became two cornerstones of new cultural and economic policies formulated by dominant political forces to restore order and stability. To appease the Malay majority, the government implemented new economic policies with the professed aim of bringing them up to par with other groups, particularly with Chinese. In addition, the government eventually implemented cultural and political policies of integration and inclusion to appease Chinese, Indians, and other non-Malays, and to make them feel that they had a stake in the nation as well. Each of these two goals appealed to one of the opposing schemata.

These models and schemata entail motivating goals (Strauss 1992a, 1992b; D'Andrade 1995, Keller and Keller 1996; Lehman and Sands 1995). They vary in their motivational force according to the manner of internalization and how they are grounded in people's everyday experiences (Strauss 1992b). The manner of internalization of "Malaysia's diverse society" and "Malay privilege" schemata and models and the resolution of cognitive dissonance these schemata entail are altered through practice and lived experience (Ortner 1984; Keller and Keller 1996). Whether or not local residents come to interpret these models and schemata and the knowledge they entail as "mere rhetoric" or as knowledge they have full commitment to, is a matter for later chapters to elucidate. But it is important, I think, not to assume that just because some models and schemata are not held to fit the way things actually work, that it means that they are not highly motivating.

Because these models and schemata may form potent ideals of how things *should* work and direct practice in the direction of making reality conform to these ideals. Furthermore, people reproduce and rework the network and hierarchy of goals these schemata entail (D'Andrade 1995; Strauss 1992b) in practice. *Bumiputera* and non-*Bumiputera* residents of Melaka rework the manner in which schemata and models are internalized as they engage in various practices. They also rework the interconnections between these representations and the goals they entail as they accumulate experiences during festive seasons, public festivals and displays, and in other social institutions, more directly tied to the distribution of material goods and services, such as schools, businesses, and the civil service.

Negotiations of these models and schemata have a close relationship to dominant and subordinate forms of cultural citizenship and senses of belonging. The state and municipal governments of Melaka and Malay-based civil institutions attempt to implement a dominant form of cultural citizenship that entails a particular form of integration and negotiation between these sets of representations. One in which Malays are the definitive race and other groups' citizenship is contingent upon the definition Malays give to it (see Mahathir Mohamad 1970:124–127). On the other hand, there are many other possible ways to integrate and negotiate these ideas and locals institutionalized some of them elsewhere in Melakan society.

Part III

Chapter Five
Public Celebrations
and Representations

History and past experiences shape models and schemata of "Malaysia's diverse society" and "Malay privilege." National leaders and local people have widely disseminated and institutionalized these representations, as we have seen, in Melaka and across Malaysian society. Similar to "habitus" they habituate and incline people and groups to behave in particular ways (see Bourdieu 1977, 1990). However, these representations are embodied *in* practice rather than embodied practice. Surely, the public celebrations and museum exhibitions discussed in this chapter are not only embodied practices, but they are practices embodied with numerous notions, images, and beliefs. If we were to collapse knowledge and behavior into a single descriptive and analytic concept such as "habitus," we would be at a loss to account for the tension between these representations and the negotiation of such cultural knowledge that goes into producing social events.

Indeed, with such a notion we could conclude, upon visiting the Art Gallery Museum described later in this chapter, that Malaysians, or at least the ones responsible for the exhibits in this museum, are disposed towards equality and diversity. Similarly, an observer of the 11th "Melaka Historic City Day," may conclude that Malaysians are disposed to inequality and hierarchy. The fact is that we are often habituated to act one way in certain contexts and an almost contradictory fashion in other contexts. Only a "unified theory of practice" (see Keller and Keller 1996) that distinguishes between knowledge and behavior is equipped to handle this sort of complexity and ambiguity that is characteristic of social practice and not merely peculiar to these events.

Thus, in my consideration of the National Independence Day Celebration, the Melaka Historic City Day Celebration, and several local museums, I will treat models and schemata as distinct from, but directive of and embodied in, practice. Moreover, I will juxtapose a description of these institutionalized representations to people's "mental" representations, both conventional and personal (see Bradd Shore 1996). These public celebrations and exhibitions are organized by and under the control and management of the Malay-dominated municipal and state governments. I will demonstrate that while these public events embody several, at times conflicting, notions, overall a dominant mode of integrating and negotiating these notions is enacted and reproduced. Moreover, this hegemonic synthesis entails a top-down form of multiculturalism and cultural citizenship.

NATIONAL INDEPENDENCE DAY CELEBRATION

The National Independence Day celebrations are organized on the national and state levels. Malaysia's Prime Minister and his cabinet ministers attend the national-level event, which takes place in the federal capital or one of the state capitals changing locations from year to year. This year, 1998, the 41st national-level National Day celebrations took place in Penang for the first time. From the national to state level, all of the National Day celebrations espoused the same central unifying theme: *Negara Kita, Tanggung Jawab Kita (Our Country, Our Responsibility)*.

In Melaka, the 41st state-level celebration took place in the same location as the 'Countdown to National Independence Day' event (see preface), which local civil servants staged on the eve of the major public celebrations. The main stage, situated in front of the Independence Memorial, was still decorated with the national theme and the red, white, blue, and yellow colors of the Malaysian flag, *Jalur Gemilang*. However, early this morning, government employees rearranged the setting removing the covered seating areas and placing large wooden seats on the stage. By 8AM in the morning of August 31 the national independence anniversary, these large seats were full of *orang atasan*, Malay high officials and their wives, awaiting the opening ceremonies. The Governor and Chief Minister of Melaka and their wives were sitting prominently on the stage and thousands of people of all local cultural categories stood across the road and on the sides of the stage trying to catch some shade on this hot sunny day.

This year's National Day celebration in Melaka comprised opening ceremonies, a parade, and a cultural show that took place later in the afternoon. Opening ceremonies, featuring expressions of Malay authority and Islam, consisted of official statements and Islamic prayers, flag raising, nationalist songs and poetry, a Catholic band performance, and a military demonstration and fly-in. Shortly after 8AM, the Chief Minister's speech from the main stage rang out loudly in all directions. He delivered his speech in Malay or *Bahasa Malaysia* like all other public statements in these events. He spoke about the economic situation and the importance of maintaining their *"aman, damai, toleransi, dan harmoni"* (peace, calm, tolerance, and harmony) in the face of these economic woes. This opening statement, echoing his speech from last night, contained the dominant model of "Malaysia's diverse society." He recited some nationalist slogans, and the crowd responded in kind and he closed with some prayers in Malay and Arabic for the *bangsa* (the Malaysian people in this context) and *negara* (their country). Muslims in several uniformed military units and in the general audience held their hands out in front of them in supplication to Almighty Allah. Chinese and Indian non-Muslims did not extend their hands in prayer and stood listening and looking around.

After the Chief Minister's statement and prayers, the honor guard of the 17th Royal Malay regiment approached the stage and received the flag and proceeded to raise the flag at the flag post just a short ways down the road from the main stage. Malaysians of all races[1] and religions turned towards the *Jalur Gemilang* watching intently as guards raised the flag. Then a local Malay Muslim leader made a religious and nationalist statement and prayer mixing Malay and Arabic and a group of non-Muslim high school girls sang *Negaraku* (My Country). They were followed by a group of Muslim high school girls wearing blue scarves and *baju kurung* who sang *Melaka Maju Jaya* (Melaka Move Forward with Success). Next on the opening agenda was the Melaka champion from the state-level National Day poetry contest, Mohamed Mahat, who recited a poem entitled *"Kita Anak Malaysia"* (We Children of Malaysia).

Then, into this predominantly Malay opening program, was interjected a performance by Melaka's Catholic Band composed of mostly Chinese dressed in black pants, white jackets, red and black hats, and red chest pieces. They came out in these uniforms holding their instruments and marching into the open area, between the stage and the audience, and played several songs. The Chinese in the audience seemed excited with this performance and moved up to take pictures and to view this Catholic band. After this band finished and moved back behind the spectators, a Malay military unit dressed in green uniforms and combat helmets marched into the open area and performed a number of marching formation steps. This military unit surprised the audience by shooting their automatic weapons into the air and dropping smoke bombs with nationalist colors. Colored smoke rose into the air giving the appearance of a battlefield, while the soldiers fell to the ground and performed some ground maneuvers before marching off to loud applause from the audience. The Catholic marching band returned and performed a few more songs.

Then there was an overhead "*Merdeka* Fly-In" coordinated by the Department of Civil Aviation in which pilots from several flying clubs flew planes in formations of three. These planes made a couple of passes before releasing twenty parachuting troops who landed in the muddy Padang Pahlawan field behind the audience or on the concrete road in front of the main stage. This awe-inspiring fly-in and parachuting demonstration ended the opening ceremonies and set the mood for the National Independence Day parade.

A marching band led this parade followed by a uniformed military unit carrying a large outstretched Malaysian flag with men on all sides. A group of young Chinese and Indian high school students from the all girls' convent-turned-public school, Melaka Infant Jesus Convent, carried a 100-meter long flag that they had made at school. Around eighty contingents, consisting of government departments and agencies and private and non-governmental institutions, marched pass the high officials on the main stage and continued around the road circling Padang Pahlawan and into several city streets winding up at Stadium Kubu on the other side of town. Spectators stood on the both sides of the road as they passed through the area looking on at this very colorful parade and taking pictures.

Figure 1 Schoolgirls carrying long Malaysian flag in National Day parade. (Photograph by Timothy P. Daniels)

Almost half of the contingents represented government departments and agencies and consisted of mostly Malays dressed up in police, military, and civil service uniforms.

The government departments that did not wear official uniforms, such as the municipal council, department of social development, department of Islamic religion, Melaka state development board, and department of agriculture, wore Malay-style or "Malaysian-style" clothing: *baju melayu* and *black songkok, batik* shirts, *baju kurung* and *sarong* and *kebaya.* Chinese and Indians in government service wore either the official uniforms or Malay attire of their respective contingents. No groups wore Chinese or Indian attire or exhibited Mandarin or Tamil characters. In contrast, an Islamic group carried placards with Arabic words expressing Islamic concepts and principles. The Department of Traditions included a group of Chitty women and men dressed in their traditional attire, *sarong* and *kebaya,* which reflects Malay cultural influence. Although most of the government contingents consisted of Malays, many of these departments were more diverse in their constitution than other departments. For instance, the medical department, female military units, and municipal departments from Alor Gadjah and Jasin (outlying districts of Melaka) included several Chinese and Indians, whereas the police and military units and Melaka municipal council were overwhelmingly Malay.

In contrast, most of the private sector contingents were predominantly composed of Chinese and a few Indians. Large numbers of Chinese and some Indians and a few *Melaka Portugis* were included in contingents of private businesses and colleges, sporting clubs, and marching bands. These

Figure 2 Malay civil servants marching in National Day parade.
(Photograph by Timothy P. Daniels)

groups wore marching band, scouting, martial arts or nursing uniforms or skirts and blouses but there were no traditional Chinese, Indian, or Portuguese attire exhibited in the parade. In the cultural show that occurred later in the afternoon, some traditional markers of various cultural categories were to be exhibited but in the official parade constituting the "nation" only markers of the preferred race, the Malay race, were presented.

Several hours later this area in front of the Independence Memorial filled up with people again for the start of the National Day cultural show. A Malay civil servant serving as the master of ceremonies welcomed people and announced the four groups that were about to perform and where they would be located around the Padang Pahlawan. These four groups constitute some measure of representation for each of the four major cultural categories in Melaka: Malays, Chinese, Indians, and *Melaka Portugis*. One of the most popular *Melaka Portugis* song and dance troupes was stationed in front of the old ruin of the Portuguese fort, A' Famosa, with their guitars and dressed in Portuguese style dresses, suits, and hats. The other three groups stood in front of the main stage where the master of ceremonies was speaking. There was a Chinese group dressed in red, white and blue or red, yellow and black outfits and some of the boys wore sashes tied around their waists. They were equipped with large stationary drums with large yellow Chinese characters on them, smaller drums strapped around some of the boy's shoulders, cymbals, and a lion dance outfit. The red, white, and blue outfits together with the yellow on the drums completed the colors of the Malaysian flag, the national colors. There was a Malay *kompang*, hand-held drum, troupe dressed in yellow *baju melayu* and white slacks and black *songkok* with a yellow stripe. The only woman in the Malay group wore a white scarf wrapped around her head. The fourth group was a predominantly Indian martial arts group dressed in white karate tops and black pants and belts of various colors depending upon their rank. There were a few Chinese boys in this martial arts group as well. Each of these three groups performed once in front of the stage and then they took up different positions, around the Padang Pahlawan, that the master of ceremonies announced to the public. The crowd dispersed in different directions following the various groups to watch additional performances.

I joined a large crowd that formed around the *Melaka Portugis* group in front of the old fort entrance, *Porto de Santiago*. The three singers with guitars stood in front of the opening portal and the dancers, four young men and four young women, stood on the path in front of them waiting for the elder bandleader, Joe Lazaroo[2], to announce the dances they were to perform. The men wore black suits and hats with white shirts and red bow ties,

Figure 3 *Melaka Portugis* dance troupe performing at National Day cultural show. (Photograph by Timothy P. Daniels)

and the women wore red dresses with black linings and black aprons and stockings. These dancers performed festive skipping and spinning movements as the singers sang songs of romance and frivolity in a local Portuguese creole called *Kristang*.

I walked over to the raised stands across from the main stage where the predominantly Indian martial arts group was performing. Many people were sitting in the stands watching the martial artists take turns demonstrating their skills with various weapons, moving in and out of various forms. Each performer received a large round of applause from a large audience in the stands and standing around the square where they performed this martial arts exhibition.

After watching several martial artists, I walked on the other side of the Padang Pahlawan where the Malay *kompang* group and the Chinese stationary drum group were performing for a small audience that gradually got larger after the other performances ended. The Malay hand held drum group stood in four rows of around six drummers and group leader stood in front and chanted and sang in Malay and Arabic as the drummers beat on the drums with their free hands and followed the chants of the leader. Just down the road was the Chinese drum group. The Chinese boys performed various

Figure 4 Malay *kompang* group at National Day cultural show.
(Photography by Timothy P. Daniels)

movements around their large stationary drums, beating on them and their sticks in unison, and ended with an athletic move in which one of the boys jumped up on the drum finishing in a picturesque pose.

In this cultural show, each of the four cultural categories was included and had an opportunity to take center stage before a public audience. Malay, Chinese, and *Melaka Portugis* performances clearly exhibited some cultural forms of music and/or dance associated with their cultural categories. It is not immediately clear as to how the martial arts exhibition relates to the Indian cultural category because martial arts are equally associated with the Chinese and Malay categories as well. Yet, it is kung fu that is associated with Chinese and *silat* that is associated with Malays. *Hindustani* movies[3] are highly popular in Malaysian society and in them Indian men often engage in violent scenes in which the hero possesses some form of martial arts prowess akin to karate. In addition, karate is popular amongst Indian youth and they often compose a large percentage of participants in karate competitions and exhibitions. In any event, they were the overwhelming majority

Figure 5 Chinese drum group at National Day cultural show. (Photograph by Timothy P. Daniels)

in this martial arts group and were, thereby, incorporated in the National Day cultural program.

The model of "Malaysia's diverse society" and the goals it embeds directed the production of this cultural show and was embodied within it. An effort was made to construct a program in which each of the four cultural categories were represented and the shape the event took with these four groups performing in turn and being posted in various parts of the area embodied this model. Furthermore, the notion of "cultural rights" and membership in Malaysia's diverse society of *citizens* was embodied in this cultural show. Many Chinese and Indians I spoke to about cultural shows have told me that regional and national cultural shows must at least include Malays, Chinese, and Indians, the "three largest races," in order to be viewed as "complete." They have also expressed the feeling that Chinese and Indians have a "right" to be involved and recognized along with Malays as members of Malaysian society. Whereas this discourse expresses conventional "mental" representations of these institutionalized representations of "Malaysia's diverse society," some people have expressed more personalized representations in conversations with me. For instance, Joan, a young Chinese woman, with a *Baba* father and *Melaka Portugis* mother, informed me that the type of cultural shows that she would like to see are ones in which Chinese, Malays, and Indians combine their traditional dances into a single performance. If this were not possible, then she would like to see these groups perform in short segments one after another with their accompanying music and attire on display. Similarly, Mr. Bala, a middle age Indian dance choreographer told me that he plans to create a dance in which all of the peoples of Malaysia, along with a Michael Jackson impersonator, would be included in a single performance weaving in diverse dance styles.

On the other hand, if we consider the National Day cultural show together with the opening ceremonies and parade, we can arrive at a fuller picture of institutionalized representations. As noted earlier, the opening ceremonies and parade clearly stressed Malay culture and religious identity enacting and embodying the model and schemata of "Malay privilege." The fact that "Malay privilege" was enacted in a context infused with nationalist symbolism and pomp and ceremony, whereas "Malaysia's diverse society" was enacted later in the afternoon at a cultural show devoid of such symbolism indicates a particular sort of integration of conceptual knowledge. In particular, this integration of models and schemata "Malay privilege" and "Malaysia's diverse society" is such that Malays are enacted as supreme within a social order in which each group is included. Many Chinese and Indians have expressed conventional "mental" representations informing me that they expect only Islamic prayers in opening ceremonies of official events and that they expect Malay culture to be made to "appear larger" in regional and national cultural shows in which other groups are also included. This integration and negotiation of cultural knowledge produces a form of top-down multiculturalism and cultural citizenship in which non-Malay categories are incorporated within an overall framework biased towards Malays.

MELAKA HISTORIC CITY DAY CELEBRATIONS

The Melaka Historic City Day Celebration is an annual commemoration of the occasion in which Datuk Seri Dr. Mahathir Mohamad declared Melaka as the "Historic City" on April 15, 1989 in his speech delivered in front of the municipal government building in Ayer Keroh, Melaka. According to employees in the municipal office building, the former chief minister of Melaka, Rahim Thamby Chik, came up with the idea but the prime minister made the official declaration. So, in effect, the leaders made the declaration on a national and state level. The state government of Melaka organized Melaka Historic City Day events from its inception until 1995 at which point they passed the task of organizing them to the municipal government of Melaka. Cik Mat Ali and Puan Izza, two Malay municipal civil servants, informed me that there have been two general themes of this celebration since its inception: the "local cultures of Melaka" or "cultural heritage" theme and the Gendang Nusantara. Before 1995, the state government used the "cultural heritage" theme to organize these events, but since the municipal government has taken over, they have organized three Gendang Nusantara events, in 1995, 1997, and 2000. In 1996, they organized an international run because of budgetary problems, and in 1998, there were no events due to the economic crisis. The only year in which the municipal government deployed the "cultural heritage" theme was in 1999, again resulting from budgetary constraints. Cik Mat Ali and Puan Izza[4] assured me that if they had the funds to organize a Gendang Nusantara event each year they would. A Gendang Nusantara festival is much more expensive to stage as we shall soon see. I had an opportunity to witness the 1999 "cultural heritage" event and the Gendang Nusantara III in 2000.

I attended the Tenth Melaka Historic City Day Celebration with my friend, Yati, a forty-year old Malay woman, and her young son, Azmi. Yati's nephew dropped us off down the road from Tun Razak Street as the "Cultural Heritage Parade" was beginning to work its way along this road approaching Taman Cempaka Peringgit Melaka where the main launching events would take place. Yati told me that in former years, this parade took place in the old part of town near all the old colonial buildings and this year was the first time for it to use this route and appear at this location. Thousands of people of all local cultural categories packed on both sides of the roads watching the parade. After the front of the parade reached the threshold of the main staging area, the parade stopped moving forward and we were able to observe each of its contingents as we gradually worked our way to the front.

At the rear of the parade were scores of decorated *becaks* or trishaws (bicycle-powered carriages), bullock carts, and a decorated car. The trishaws were decorated with lights and various kinds of flowers whose names they carried on the side in bold cursive letters. Each decorated trishaw and bullock cart was numbered because judges would assess them as part of contests. In past years these *becaks* and bullock carts were owned by individual contestants but nowadays various departments of government own them and will receive the awards if they win. Each bullock cart had the names of various departments of government on them. Along with various government symbols, these bullock carts had several markers of Malay culture such as traditional Malay houses, traditional Malay houses, *rumah bertangga batu* (houses with stone steps), and traditional Malay games such as *congkak*[5] and *permainan ubi* attached to them. Beside one of the bullock carts some Malay youngsters were playing *per-mainan ubi,* pulling each other along the ground on a flat piece of rough material with small wheels attached beneath it. The string these boys pulled to drag their partners along was from the *ubi* or yam plant, explaining why Malays called this *permainan ubi* or the yam game, Yati said. She remembered how it used to burn her buttocks to ride on these things because they did not used to have wheels on them when she was growing up.

Cik Mat Ali informed me that these bullock carts are unique to Melaka because of the particular curved shape of the roof and the large all wooden wheels that do not use rubber. Only a few craftsmen still possess the traditional skill of making these wheels. These bullock carts reminded Yati of the *mandi safar* festival because they were used during these carnival-like events to carry large groups of Malays from their neighborhoods to beaches where they would party and sleep over night. One of the last *mandi safar* festivals she attended was when she was sixteen years old, just prior to the government termination of this festival based on religious grounds.[6] We also passed by a small car decorated with a deer and coat of arms, the state logo of Melaka that appears on the state flag and other official representations. The assemblage of small deer evokes the story of the founding of Melaka in which these deer performed miraculous acts before the Sumatran prince, Parameswara.

After passing the trishaws, bullock carts, and this coat of arms bearing car, we came to several contingents of cultural troupes representing all the cultural categories of Malaysian society. There were several contingents of Malays from Melaka and some other peninsular states and a professional dance troupe from the federal capital well known for their renditions of *orang asli* (aboriginal) dance and culture. A *Chingay* group from Penang was visible from a distance because its members were carrying gigantic national and Melaka state flags. There were also local contingents of Chinese, Indians, Sikhs, Chitty, *Babas* and *Nyonyas,* and *Melaka Portugis* dressed in their customary attire and with props some of them will use during their performances. We passed three high school bands and a group of young children dressed up in colorful outfits.

Soon after we reached the front of the parade, three masters' of ceremonies, two Malays, a man and woman, and one Indian woman began to announce the program in *Bahasa Malaysia.* The Indian woman introduced some of the later acts in English, while her counterparts only spoke in Malay. The Malay woman was dressed in a *baju kurung* and a *tudung* and the Indian woman was dressed in a modern-style *sarong* and *kebaya* without a *tudung,* while the Malay man wore a suit and a baseball cap. They stood on a small stage facing the raised stands where the high officials were sitting.

The Chief Minister accompanied the Governor to a large gong on the raised stands where he struck it three times officially opening the Historic City Day festivities. Thousands of spectators crowded around the edge of the carpet that organizers laid out in the middle of the plaza where the cultural performances were about to begin. Malay policemen were working to keep the middle lane leading to the plaza open so that the "heritage parade" cultural troupes could enter the carpeted plaza to perform. Yati, Azmi and I wove our way through the standing masses and found a place on the ground in the front from which Azmi could see the program and I could take some pictures and write notes.

The masters' of ceremonies introduced several Malay cultural troupes that performed as part of the opening program before the entrance of the "cultural heritage" contingents onto the main stage. A group of Malay singers and musicians, dressed in *baju melayu* and *sarong* and *kebaya,* performed on a large raised stage facing the high officials. A row of seven Malay drummers stood in front of this stage and beat large stationary drums, *rebana ubi,* with drumsticks accompanying the performers on the stage behind them. While these musicians played some rousing Malay rhythms, several groups of Malay dancers, donning customary Malay attire, performed on the carpeted plaza between them and the high officials. One of the groups was composed of around twenty women and twenty men who were dressed in a variety of styles representing Malays from various states of Malaysia. The women wore flowered headdresses. Another Malay group composed of six men and six women came out and danced while *dondang sayang*[7] songs played in the background. The men in this group were wearing red *songket tanjuk*[8] with black pants and the women were wearing black and gold *songket baju kurung* and red sheer scarves. After these performances, brilliant and colorful fireworks were shot in the sky overhead. I stood up with the other spectators around me and watched the awe-inspiring display.

Following this fireworks display, the masters' of ceremonies announced that the "Cultural Heritage Parade" was going to begin. After masters' of ceremonies introduced them, each of the contingents entered the main stage, the carpeted plaza, carrying a sign designating their troupe and they performed in front of the high officials and audience. Several more Malay cultural groups led the cultural parade. Six Malay *kompang* and *silat* groups came out first followed by a *sirih junjung*[9] group. The Malay men in these groups played their hand drums and performed some Malay martial arts movements. After performing *silat,* these groups of men formed a unified formation behind the women carrying the betelnut cases or *tepak sirih,* an exhibition of a Malay tradition of welcoming guests. Then another

Malay dance, a *bunga manggar* dance, was performed with Malay municipal government dancers carrying these festive symbols.[10] Following this
dance, a private Malay cultural group performed another dance featuring
some prominent Malay symbols. Six women dressed in *songket* and *sanggung lentang*[11] headdresses carried *pahar nikah*, trays used to carry wedding
gifts and to decorate the wedding dais in local Malay customary weddings.

After this opening saturated with Malay symbolism and culture, several other cultural categories presented their performances. A Chinese cultural troupe performed the *Bunga Raya* dance, named after the national
flower, as Chinese music played in the background. The men played small
Chinese-style drums and women in the group wore braided hair loops. Then
one of the predominantly Chinese high school marching bands entered the
stage area and played a few tunes. A *Melaka Portugis* group was next up.
They were dressed in Portuguese-style suits and dresses, the same type of
outfits they wore for the local National Independence cultural show. Six
Melaka Portugis, three men and three women performed skipping and
swinging "square dance" type movements across the carpeted plaza.

Young men and women from the "Sikh Cultural and Sports Club"
took the main stage next. I had watched this same group perform earlier
the same day on the Mahkota Parade shopping center stage in a public celebration of *Vaisakhi*, an annual Sikh religious festival. Six men dressed in
blue Sikh-style attire and armed with long swords led the way for their
dancers. These men walked out in a row and stood in the middle of the carpeted plaza in warrior-like poses facing the high officials and then they
moved to the end of the main stage and stood facing the dancers who did
a Sikh dance called the *bangsara* dance.

Then the *Baba* and *Nyonya* cultural troupe came out and danced to
slow Chinese music. The women were dressed in *sarong* and *kebaya* and the
men in silk Chinese-style pants suits and red and black "Mandarin" hats.
The Indian master of ceremony noted that their dress is "similar to
Malaysian dress." They were followed by the Melaka Chitty troupe that the
master of ceremony described as the "Indian counterparts of the *Baba* and
Nyonya." Although the sign they carried designated them as the "Chitty
group," she called them the "*Datok Chachar* group" after the name of the
Hindu deity for whom they hold a well-known annual festival. "Take note
of their unique and colorful uniforms," she said smiling. The Chitty children
wore *sarong* and *kebaya* and Malay-like *baju* tops. These Chitty youth performed a dance in which the girls carried flowers and the boys carried *bunga
manggar*. Chitty adult men, wearing *sarong* and long Malay-like *baju* and
Javanese-style hats, and women, wearing *sarong* and *kebaya*, marched

across the stage following the children. These Chitty, and *Babas* and *Nyonyas,* Indian and Chinese *Peranakan,* may wear "core" Indian and Chinese-style clothing in other contexts to integrate into these maximal cultural categories, but in this context they wear Malay-style clothing in accord with the disciplining influences of the hegemonic discourse of multiculturalism and cultural citizenship.

Following another brass band performance, a series of Malay cultural troupes from other peninsular states took center stage to perform. A cultural troupe from the state of Johor performed a *kuda kepang* performance, a dance associated with the Malay *adat* from that state. Twenty men riding leather horse props followed five women with leather horse props. They moved slowly across the stage as if they were galloping like horses. This group had some other members come out and dance with large head props with faces similar to characters from Hindu epics, while an elder man held a whip and cracked it occasionally. Although this form of performance originated in Java where it is also called *kuda lumping,* or *jathilan,* it is understood locally as Malay culture from the state of Johor. Another Malay group this time from the state of Negeri Sembilan, was next up and came out dressed in customary Malay attire from their state. They performed a dance with the men wearing *songket* and *tanjuk* and the women wearing large headdresses. The next Malay group was from the northern state of Perak and wore Malay-style attire associated with that state. Yati told me that the women were wearing "*selendang Perak*" and the men were wearing "*baju Perak.*" The dancers performed *silat Melayu* (Malay martial arts) while their musicians played *kompang* and larger drums hanging from their necks.

Following this Malay medley, another predominantly Chinese high school brass band marched out and played a few tunes. Then the professional dance troupe from Kuala Lumpur came out and performed some dances and stunts representing the natives from Sabah and Sarawak. The masters' of ceremonies proclaimed that the "integration we are witnessing tonight is extended to Sabah and Sarawak." These Malay men and women impersonating *Bumiputera* from East Malaysia were dressed in very little clothing, marking them as "primitive" people in the popular imagination. They performed dances and stunts like climbing upright poles. They were talented and received some of the loudest applause from the audience.

Then the Chinese group from Penang did a *Chingay* performance with the gigantic flags of Malaysia and Melaka. Several Chinese men performed stunts on the main stage in which they tossed these large flags into the air and then tried to catch them and balance them on their faces when they came down. They stayed in the carpeted area for some time doing this routine and received lots of applause from the audience. They were followed by a large group of children dressed up in the colorful clothing from the closing ceremonies of the Malaysia hosted Commonwealth Games that occurred near the end of the previous year. The masters' of ceremonies reminded the audience that they should be able to recall these outfits from the sporting event in Kuala Lumpur that was a proud moment for the nation. These children performed some dances and got lots of applause.

Finally, the last high school brass band marched through the main stage area playing their songs followed by the last part of the "cultural heritage parade"—the "kereta kancil" or car decorated with the deer coat of arms, and

Figure 6 *Chingay* group from Penang in cultural show.
(Photography by Timothy P. Daniels)

the decorated trishaws and bullock carts. The judges evaluated the trishaws and bullock carts and announced the top finishers to the audience.

Some youngsters still playing *permainan ubi* held up the rear pulling each other on these small carts.

On the following day, a Melaka state holiday in commemoration of the declaration of "historic city" status, there were cultural performances performed around Padang Pahlawan as part of the Tenth Melaka Historic City Day Celebration. Similar to the "cultural heritage parade" last night and the National Day cultural show, these cultural performances entailed representations of each of the major cultural categories in Melaka. There was a "Kompang Festival" and contest in which several large *kompang* groups, hailing from various local Malay communities, performed while Malay civil servants, contest judges, and a mostly Malay audience sat under a shaded seating area or stood around the plaza watching and judging the teams.

While this *kompang* contest show was going on, just out on the road in front of the Independence Memorial, the *Chingay* performers from Penang were doing their act again, tossing and bobbing the large flag, before a mostly Chinese audience assembled around them. After they finished, most of the crowd went over to see the *Portugis* dance and song troupe perform in front of the old ruin of Fort A'Famosa. It was Joe's group, one of the

Figure 7 Sikh women dancing on stage at cultural show.
(Photography by Timothy P. Daniels)

two most popular *Melaka Portugis* cultural troupes, often seen around town and in Kuala Lumpur. They performed in this same location, wearing the same sort of outfits, for the National Day celebration. A Chinese woman, dressed in *sarong* and *kebaya,* served as the master of ceremony, on a small stage down the road from Joe's group, announcing the program and introducing each of the cultural troupes in *Bahasa Malaysia.* She introduced several Indian groups, including the young men and women from the "Sikh Cultural and Sports Club," and some young Tamil Indian girls who performed some classical Indian dances dressed in traditional attire with dance anklets. These performances by members of the Indian community enacted a representation more unambiguously associated with their cultural category than the martial arts demonstration at the National Day event.

These "multicultural" shows which embody the models and schemata of "Malaysia's diverse society" hold meaning for particular cultural categories as an opportunity to express and preserve their cultural heritage. One of the young men from the Sikh club told me that they participate in these sorts of events to remind the young generation, who are "getting away from their language and culture," of their Sikh identity and heritage. Some Chinese told me that they participate in these events because they want to express pride in their heritage and to let the world know that they are here in Melaka and Malaysia. Thus, these events also embody and enact the schemata and embedded goals of particular cultural categories. Yet, once again we must note, that these identity schemata and the models and schemata of "Malaysia's diverse society" that they partially constitute, are synthesized with models and schemata of "Malay privilege" in a fashion indicative of the hegemonic perspective. Diverse cultural categories, even the Sikh submaximal category, Chinese from Penang, and renditions of Sabah and Sarawak natives, were included and represented in a "cultural heritage parade." However, organizers incorporated this diversity into a program that emphasized Malay culture in the form of its extensive presentation of Malay song and dance and symbolism in the opening ceremonies and with several Malay groups from Melaka and other states. Similarly, they incorporated the diversity of the Padang Pahlawan cultural performance into a program in which the *kompang* show and contest was the featured event, highly publicized and centrally staged. In addition, masters' of ceremonies announced these events in *Bahasa Malaysia* dressed in Malay-style attire regardless of their cultural background. Similarly, the process of assimilation of Chitty and *Babas and Nyonyas* is emphasized in the "heritage parade" context in contrast with the process of reclaiming Chinese and Indian heritage that they are undergoing in other contexts. The hegemonic merging of models and schemata of

"Malaysia's diverse society" and "Malay privilege" produces a form of cultural citizenship predicated upon such "Malay-sianization" in particular social identities (masters' of ceremonies and civil servants) and contexts while in others it is acceptable, and expected, to emphasize cultural distinctiveness.

In contrast, the 11th Melaka Historic City Celebration and other years' events in which the municipal government adopted the "gendang nusantara" theme, indicate no significant embodiment of models and schemata of "Malaysia's diverse society" in the practices that constitute these celebrations. Drums play a central role in all forms of Malay traditional music and the *gendang* is the most popular, and often-heard Malay drum (see Kijang Puteh 1972). *Nusantara* refers to the "Malay Archipelago." So "gendang nusantara" refers to drums of the Malay world that stretches across Southeast Asia. In 2000, the Melaka Historic City celebration featured "Gendang Nusantara III" and like previous Gendang Nusantara events, this one brought "Malays" from all nine states of Peninsular Malaysia and from various parts of Indonesia, especially from Sumatra where there is a large "Malay" population. Organizers made plans to bring Malay cultural troupes from Singapore but they were not able to come this year. In the future, Cik Mat Ali informed me that the Chief Minister of Melaka and the municipal government plan to bring Malay Muslims from other places in the region where there are significant Malay populations such as southern Thailand, Cambodia, Vietnam, southern Philippines, and Brunei Darussalam. "Cultural Heritage" programs are less expensive to organize because they mostly draw upon local cultural troupes in contrast to the "gendang nusantara" programs that incur the high expenses of bringing in performers from all over the region.

The "gendang nusantara" theme reconstructs and is motivated by a Malay maximal identity schema that embeds an image of a "pan-Malay" or "transnational Malay" community. For instance, this segment of discourse from Chief Minister Mohamad Ali Rustam's keynote speech during the main event of Gendang Nusantara III contains and connects the Malay identity schemata with the schemata of "Malay privilege":

> As it is imagined-lah, Melaka will hold this festival every year in order to remember the greatness of Melaka as the artistic and cultural center of the Malay race and to, ourselves, view our genuine Melaka Malaysian people in song, dance, and Malay music or even as one family. [my translation]

The "authentic" character of the songs, dances, and music enact the cultural attributes of Malays, and this "authentic" Malay character from all over the Malayo-Indonesian archipelago is of one family or has the same origins. Furthermore, the people who possess this "authentic" culture are the genuine or definitive people of Melaka and Malaysia, Malays, and this festival should be held each year to remind people of the greatness of their heritage and culture.

Malay cultural artists, for four days, from the 12th through 16th of April, performed at Padang Pahlawan and Dataran Sejarah[12] with the posted and popular theme "Serentak-Seirama, Senada-Sebudaya" (One tempo-one rhythm, one key-one culture). Musicians used various kinds of *gendang* or drums, from small hand-held *kompang* to large *rebana umbi,* along with many other instruments to keep the tempo and rhythm as Malay dancers and singers performed. Malay artists and intellectuals considered these drums as a fundamental part of Malay cultural production, both before and after the advent of Islam in the region. Several Malay orchestras, consisting of drums, guitar, accordion and tambourines, from Melaka played "original Malay music" behind singers of *dondang sayang,* a genre considered to be the "original song of the common people of Melaka." Some Malay orchestras from other states as well as Melaka accompanied singers who sang with a style similar to *dondang sayang* but without the poetic structure and call and response features of *dondang sayang.* Malay civil servants considered these genres part of *muzik asli Melayu* or the "original Malay music." There were also *dikir*[13] performances from Terengganu, Kelantan, and Aceh expressing and enacting the strong Islamic thread and attribute which ties together all of these Malay groups in the region. Several groups used some *gamelan* instruments such as tuned bronze bowls and gongs. The groups from the east-coast states of the peninsular, Pahang, Terengganu, and Kelantan, used a small reed wind instrument called a *serunai.* A group from Johor used some *gamelan* bronze bowls and *rebana* in conjunction with a *kulintang*—a large wooden xylophone—and a large instrument, composed of lots of bamboo tubes of various sizes, called an *angklung.*[14] Their inspired use of these amazing sounding instruments thrilled the audience.

Malay dancers, dressed in Malay attire associated with their particular regions, performed a wide variety of dances. A group from Negeri Sembilan performed some *tarian silat* or martial arts movements performed in a flowing and rhythmic fashion. Dancers from Medan, Indonesia performed the exciting and popular *zapin* dance, weaving and skipping at a face pace around the stage. The Johor dancers performed *kuda kepang* and *permainan kuda kepang.* The latter dance form uses the leather horse props but

Figure 8 Johor group performing *kuda kepang* in Gendang Nusantara III. (Photography by Timothy P. Daniels)

it becomes a sort of skit in which some of the dancers go into trance and run amok. Severaldance groups also performed the graceful and popular Malay-style dance movements often broadcast on national television stations.

In the plaza across from the Independence Memorial, where the *kompang* show and contest took place last year, a covered stage was set up for the various musical groups to perform, and a red carpet was rolled out in front of the stage upon which the dancers performed. Malay civil servants, the organizers and coordinators of these "gendang" events, sat under a tarpaulin-covered area where many red plastic seats were arranged. The daily audience for these events, overwhelmingly Malays and a few tourists sat under this shaded area or stood around the edges of the plaza.

On the evening of the 14th and 15th of April, there were two main events staged at the Dataran Sejarah in which all of the cultural groups appeared together in a single program, whereas during the day at Padang Pahlawan only three or four groups would perform per day. On the 14th, the eve of the state holiday, the Chief Minister delivered a keynote speech and the Governor performed the official beating of the gong launching the 11th Melaka Historic City Day celebration. Organizers shot streamers and fireworks into the air this night and staged an incredible show in which all of the groups from Malaysia and Indonesia performed together on stage under the direction of a Malay conductor and composer. Musicians played drums of various types and sizes, and other instruments, in unison and worked themselves up to a thunderous climax that the audience received with enthusiastic applause. Each of the cultural troupes also performed their own solo acts and civil servants gave them souvenirs on stage. On the following night, the program was much the same without the official opening procedures and fireworks. On both of these occasions there were hundreds of spectators sitting in the amphitheater seats, behind the high official seating area, however these spectators were overwhelming Malay. A few Chinese and Indians watched the program, but their numbers were nowhere near the turnout they had for the "cultural heritage parade" of the previous year. Some of my Chinese contacts, that did not attend this event, expressed a lack of interest in events that featured Malay culture and one of them told me that these types of events were "only for Malays." Similarly, a few Indian contacts expressed a sense of exhaustion with the persistent stress Malay officials and institutions place upon public displays of Malay culture.

In sum, the "gendang nusantara" featured Melaka Historic City Celebrations do not embed, in any significant fashion, models and schemata of "Malaysia's diverse society." Nor do they exhibit the dominant mode of synthesizing these models and schemata with models and schemata of "Malay privilege" as we have seen in the case of "cultural heritage" featured events. Local Chinese and Indians, expressing conventional "mental" representations of "Malaysia's diverse society," tend to interpret these events as "incomplete" representations of Melaka and Malaysia because the three main races are not included and recognized. On the other hand, these "gendang nusantara" featured events do embed and enact the maximal Malay identity schemata and the "schemata of Malay privilege." The emphasis on Malay culture and identity is contained throughout the practices of this event and is undiluted by the inclusion of any other cultures or representations of other cultural categories. Furthermore, the schemata of "Malay privilege" directs the production of this event providing the basis and motives for focusing only upon the Malay race, the definitive and genuine race, in a program that highlights the history and cultural foundation of Melaka and thereby the history and cultural foundation of Malaysia. In turn, the concentrated preoccupation with Malay song, dance, music, dress, language, religion and custom and its natural connection to the "Malayo-Indonesian archipelago" indicates the embodiment of the "Malay privilege" schemata and its reproduction.[15]

MELAKA GOVERNMENT MUSEUMS

More like the National Independence Day celebrations and the "cultural heritage theme" than the "gendang nusantara" theme, Melaka's government managed museums embody a combination of models and schemata of "Malaysia's diverse society" and "Malay privilege." Over the last two decades, the state government of Melaka has developed several museums in the old colonial buildings located in the center of town and marketed them as major tourist attractions. Many of these museums attempt to represent the diverse peoples and cultures of Melaka, whereas other local museums only aim to represent a particular cultural category. For instance, the privately owned and operated *Baba* and *Nyonya* Museum, located in the midst of the old Chinese section of town, has become a major tourist attraction within the "heritage trail" promoted by the government. Other such category-specific museums have not been as successful. A *Melaka Portugis* private museum, located slightly outside of the city core, is not well known and is seldom open for public viewing. Many members of the local Chitty community had assembled artifacts of their cultural heritage and planned to exhibit them in a state-sponsored museum but due to the recent economic crisis local leaders decided to put these plans on hold. However, the Chief Minister of Melaka, on June 19th, 2000 visited the Chitty neighborhood, located at Gadjah Berang Street, and announced that this neighborhood has been legally listed as a "cultural and heritage area" and that the state government will allocate the funds to build a Chitty museum. Therefore, for the time being, the ten government-managed museums located within walking distance from each other are the only museums to represent the variety of peoples and cultures in Melaka. All of these museums are under the management of Malay administrators, collectors, and curators except for the Cultural Museum where there are a few Indian civil servants in middle management positions. I will describe the exhibits of six of these museums, ones that most directly relate to representations of cultural categories in Melaka and Malaysia.[16]

The Art Gallery Museum and the Youth Museum are located on the upper and lower level of the old Melaka General Post Office building. I went upstairs to the Art Gallery and as I entered the first large room immediately in front of the staircase, I saw five pictures. Four of them contained images of *wayang kulit* style Hindu epic characters and the other one was a sort of surrealistic painting of some leaning flags and flag posts. There were about seven more rooms of artwork, mostly paintings, of various styles and images, produced by Malaysian artists of various cultural categories. In front of these rooms was one large room with two pictures, one on each side, hanging outside of the doorway. One is of Malay men beating large drums in the street and the other one is a boat scene. Inside this room, the walls are full of pictures, sketches and photocopied snapshots of various people who represent the various cultural categories of Melaka and Malaysia. There was no sign on the door or inside the room titling this display. Each picture had two labels, one beneath the glass part of the frame, in Malay, and one beneath the picture, pasted or glued to the wall, in English. There were several pictures of Indian men and women, including a few with them dressed in "modern" attire and a few with Indian women dressed in "traditional" attire such as a sari and Indian hair decorations. There was also a picture of a middle-aged "Sikh businessman" and two pictures of Sikh males, young and old, wearing Sikh-style turbans described as "traditional religious clothing." Several sketches or photocopied pictures of Chitty women and men appeared in this room. The Malay labels spelled this high level category as "Cheti, Chetty, and Chitty" but museum officials translated all of these written versions as "strait-born Indian" on the English labels. These Chitty images included a bride and groom from the 1930s and pictures of Chitty men and women in "traditional" attire. Similarly, there were pictures of Chinese people, a Chinese businessman and a Buddhist priest dressed in religious robes. Museum organizers posted several pictures of *Babas* and *Nyonyas* on the wall as well; they were dressed in "traditional costumes," including wedding attire, and described as "strait-born" or of "Chinese-Malay Parentage." One picture of a famous Malay journalist and one of a Malay female film star of the 1950s appeared in this gallery. Other images of Malays included one of a "Lelaki Melayu peranakan Arab," translated as "a man of Malay-Arab parentage," one of a Malay boy wearing an Islamic cap, and one of a Malay woman, wearing a "kebaya" which was described as "traditional Malay dress." In addition, there were several pictures of native cultural categories from Sabah and Sarawak including Iban, Kayan, Bajau, Kelabit, Dayak, and Kenyah people exhibiting "traditional" attire and body ornamentation and customary implements.

Except for the absence of any representation of *Melaka Portugis,* this central room of pictures includes all of the maximal categories of people in Melaka. These framed sketches and photocopies embody some of the underlying knowledge that constructs the diverse high-level cultural categories of Melaka and Malaysia. In a stereotypical fashion, Indians, Chinese, Sikhs, *Babas* and *Nyonyas,* Chitty, and Malays are presented in traditional and/or religious attire associated with their cultural categories. Likewise, Chinese and Sikhs are presented as businessmen and Malays as journalists and film stars. This horizontal display of peoples and cultures, similar to the cultural show on National Day, embodies models and schemata of "Malaysia's diverse society" without any skewing towards Malay super-ordination.

However, when we go downstairs and walk around the Youth Museum, this condition changes. On the left side of the entrance, there is a large showcase with dummies dressed in the uniforms of various Malaysian "youth" organizations. "Youth" refers to a broad range of phases in the life cycle, from adolescents to young adults and older adults just below the phase of elders. Youth are a major focus of the ruling alliance parties as they seek to maintain hegemony or political leadership (Gramsci 1971) through reproducing their values and ideas amongst these younger generations. The groups represented in the first section were the Malaysian Youth Council, 48 Youth Movement, Federation of Malaysian Students Union, Young Malaysia Movement, United Malaysian Youth Movement, Sarawak United National Youth Organization, FELDA Youth Council, and the Selangor State Youth Council. Each of these group uniforms consisted of black or white slacks and *batiks* of various designs. Next in this clothing showcase were the uniforms of the Scouts Federation, St. John Ambulance, Girls Brigade, Girls Guides Association, Girls Ranger, all consisting of slacks, skirts, and blouses. Only the National Youth Week and Youth Day uniform consisted of a light blue *baju kurung* with flowers on it. That is, only clothing associated with the Malay cultural category such as *batiks* and *baju kurung* were presented as official organizational uniforms.

In the next section, towards the back, there are exhibits featuring the World Assembly Youth (WAY), Malaysian Youth Council, Commonwealth Youth Program, and the Asian Youth Council with pictures of group activities and awards. The focused upon Malay youth as did the pictures under the "Youth Vocational Training Activities" that depicted Malay youth being trained in various fields, such as electronics, machinery, food processing, and building construction, and receiving Youth awards delivered by Malay officials. On the other side of this area there was an exhibit telling the history and organizational aims of the Committee for ASEAN Youth Cooperation and the World Assembly of Muslim Youth (WAMY).

Not far away was a section titled "Product From Youth Economic Project" containing some photos of Malay men and women making handicrafts and holding chickens and eggs. On the table and wall next to these photos were various types of handicrafts on display, including baskets, purses, fans, and mirrors with carved wooden frames. Then there was a "Scouts Federation of Malaysian" section with several pictures and framed historical statements and certificates. The British founder of this scouting organization, Lord Baden-Powell, appeared in uniform in one of these pictures in front of a showcase of trophies and plaques.

Towards the middle of the museum was a section titled "Youth Unity Activities" which had framed copies of old newspaper articles telling of youth group activities. There were also pictures of youth engaging in activities such as mountain climbing and tree planting in which Chinese youth were visible. Beneath the pictures was a caption that read: "Activities to strengthen the unity of all races in Malaysia." Similarly, in a section titled "Affiliation to MYC," there was a list of religious-based organizations in which each of the four major religions were represented, with Muslim, Christian, Buddhist and Hindu organizations. Other categories of affiliated organizations were uniformed, socioeconomic-based, student, and state youth councils. In the "National Youth Week and Youth Day" section there are pictures of past celebrations in which youth are holding *bunga manggar* and Malay and Chinese men, wearing *batik* shirts, are reading the Pledge for the National Youth Day and Youth Week at the National Stadium. These exhibits express diversity within the dominant framework.

Likewise, in the "Ministry of Youth and Sports" section, which contained several conference pictures, there was one photo of an Indian, one or two of Chinese, and the rest, around thirteen were of Malays. Inside an elaborate exhibit with a wood and leaf roof there were large encased pictures, with lights behind them, of all of the Ministers of Youth & Sport. They were all Malays, including former Deputy Prime Minister, Anwar bin Ibrahim, who held this position from 1983–84. A history of this ministry was presented above the pictures. There were also large elaborate pictures of all of the Presidents of the Malay Youth Council who were also all Malay.

Around the right side of the main entrance, there was a "History of the Museum" section, which had information about this museum being initiated around the end of 1989. It also mentioned the 100,000 and 50,000 *ringgit* grants from the state government and Ministry of Youth and Sport, respectively, to establish this museum. A picture of some of the local board members for this project included one Chinese man and eleven Malays.

Finally, in a section at the front there was the "Islamic Youth and Malay Nationalism" section that presented a historical statement in Malay and English. An excerpt from the English version of this statement read:

> History has shown that Malay nationalism originated during the first three decades of the 20th century and that it is rooted in Islamic teaching and opposition to the shackles of colonialism, promoted the emancipation of women, encouraged Malays to work hard to improve their

economic conditions to the level enjoyed by non-Malays . . . official mouth-piece of struggle was the magazine Al-Iman.

This museum clearly combines models and schemata of "Malaysia's diverse society" with models and schemata of "Malay privilege" in its manner of arranging and constructing the exhibits. Non-Malays are primarily visible when they are being fit into a Malay-dominated framework, disciplined by Malay political hegemony and cultural supremacy. Chinese and Indian youth organizations were not exhibited on their own with their cultural and religious attire the way these categories were upstairs in the art gallery. In the context of the Youth Museum, the history of the Malaysian "nation," political authority and leadership, and subsequently, the relative status of cultural categories are of more significance than they were upstairs where abstract artistic renditions of cultural difference took precedence.

I found a condition of greater emphasis on the Malay element similar to the Youth Museum, in the People's Museum and the other museums I am going to describe. The People's Museum, with the Governor's Gallery on the second floor, is located in another old colonial building near Padang Pahlawan. On the ground level, there are exhibits with large pictures of the Malaysian King and Queen in all of their regalia and formal dress, books about the history of Melaka and Malay culture, smaller pictures of the four Prime Ministers of Malaysia, and a "Classical Heritage of Malay Women Ornamentation" where some hairpins and other ornaments are in a glass display case. There are also a series of pictures of various museums in Melaka, a standup exhibit with four articles from a local journal posted on it including one about the state mosque, a "Craftsmen and His Heritage" display where there are several photos of Malays making various crafts such as mats, bird cages, drums, fish trap, leather puppets, flutes, a traditional Malay stringed instrument, and quail traps. Near these displays is a "Getting Acquainted with States" section that has maps pinpointing the position of each Malaysian state and providing information about each state such as the state anthems, insignias, and so on. In the final exhibit in this room, there are a series of twelve paintings done by locals depicting the traditional Melaka Malay house. They are very colorful paintings and they present the famous *tangga batu* or stone steps of this traditional Malay house in various colors and from various angels. There are also old sketches of the "Mosque on Kubu Road" (mid-nineteenth century drawing), the "Anglo-Chinese College, 1824," and the "Ruined Gate of the Old Fort, 1834." In this room we have seen a combination of images of historic and contemporary Melaka with images of Malay culture—Malay hair ornaments, handicrafts, traditional houses, and religion—and Malay political authority and sovereignty and the "nation."

In the room across the hall, there is an exhibit that highlights the decade from 1982 to 1992 with lots of pictures of industries and new buildings—infrastructural development—and people working in the industrial and agricultural sectors and engaging in sporting activities. There are large exhibits of architectural structures such as low-income housing projects and elite houses with overhead spotlights shining on them. There is also a section of pictures with the headings of "Festivals" and "Culture" that consists of pictures of local groups dancing. These photos have the following categories attached to them in *Bahasa Malaysia:* "Malay Dance, *Portugis* Dance, Chinese Dance, *Baba Nyonya* Dance, Modern Dance, and Gujeratis Dance" [my translation]. In this room, organizers combined images of "development" with images of cultural diversity, an embodiment of the dominant model of "Malaysia's diverse society" and the goals of economic and technological "development" and prosperity that it embeds.

On the other hand, upstairs in the "Governor's Gallery" we return to the images of Malay sovereignty and political authority that we saw in the other room downstairs. In front, as you arrive upstairs are large pictures of five state governors of Melaka; the first one was Chinese and the rest were Malay. This whole gallery has red velvet backgrounds in the cases given them a royal sort of appearance. On the right of the entrance, there are photos of a Malay Governor with several Malays, religious figures and police, and some "Arabian leaders." In one of these pictures, this Malay Governor appears with a group of Chinese at Au Yin Hill, a Chinese-owned hill resort that contains a series of Chinese-style gardens.

Around the corner, in the "State Awards" and "History of the State Governmental Institutions" sections, there are framed speeches, commendations, official costumes and medals. Organizers have connected a series of small paintings and plates with constitutional information to the history section. The first small painting is of "Parameswara, first Malay Ruler of Melaka" receiving "Admiral Cheng Ho, envoy of Ming Emperor of China in 1409." Several more paintings about the history of the Melaka Sultanate culminate in an area with signs about the "Federal Constitution." These paintings and signs depict the continuity of Malay political authority, in the pre-colonial and post-colonial periods, as if in an unbroken chain.

The "Formal Ceremonies and Visits" section has photos of Malay Governors engaging in formal activities and hosting various VIPs. There are several large cases with a Malay Governor's collection of plaques, medals, silverware, china, *kerises*—Malay traditional curve-bladed weapons—and so on. On the outer wall, there is an exhibit of "Her Majesty Social Activities" and pictures of the rulers' wives in meetings and social activities.

There is also a "Conference of Rulers" section with a picture of all the Malay Rajas seated in a row at one of their meetings in Kuala Lumpur in 1994. Then there are a series of exhibits with biographical data of each of the governors and some official photos. The Chinese governor, appearing with four British men in this section, Chinese owners of Au Yin Hill, and Admiral Cheng Ho, are included in a gallery, indicative of the People's Museum overall, that emphasizes and reproduces Malay political power and sovereignty. Occasional references to cultural diversity, such as the "festivals" and "culture" sections and the newspaper article referring to Melaka's "melting pot" are surrounded by numerous representations of Malay culture, high status and power, and historical contributions to the "nation."

Similarly, the Museum of Literature focuses upon Malay culture, history, and literary traditions and contributions. At the entrance of the Museum of Literature, which is located behind the Museum of History and Ethnography, museum officials have placed a colorful mural under a sign that describes it as the "History of Writing." On the left part of this mural is an image of two hairy, almost naked, prehistoric men standing in front of a cave and trees chiseling on a stone with stone tools. To the right of them are two more men working and a youngster reading. One man is carrying wood and the other one is carving out the insides of a deer that has been slain. Further to the right, there is a Malay Muslim village with Malay traditional homes and a mosque in the background. A Malay boy, girl and male teacher are sitting in front with a small table and some books written in *Jawi script*, Arabic characters. The boy is wearing a black *songkok*, the girl a *tudung*, and the man a white turban wrapped in Arab style. The man is teaching them to write *Jawi* script. A typewriter is to the right of them and on the last panel of this mural there is a Muslim woman wearing a white *tudung* sitting and using a computer. A man dressed in white shirt and black suit and tie is using a computer below her. Behind them looms a large "modern" building and to their right is a sign "Instruments" and below it a list and discussion of several writing tools such as paper, *lontar* leaves[17], ink, pen, and a *rehal*, a stand used to hold the Quran or other highly regarded books. This mural takes us from the prehistoric roots of human literacy to Malays learning to read and write Arabic and culminates with the entrance of Malays into the modern age of technology and computers.

In the room to the right of the entrance is an exhibit with a traditional, Melaka Malay house, the house with stone steps, and two Malay children and a Malay man beneath of sign "Folk Tales." The boy and girl are dressed in Malay-style attire, and the man is on the porch holding a string instrument, a *rebab*, and leather puppets and gongs are behind him inside the house. A plate in the background gives some background on the *rebab* stating that it is an instrument originated from Kurdistan in Northern Iran and played before the time of the holy Prophet Muhammad. To the right of the house is a case with books about folk tales. To the left on the opposite wall there is a "*Sejarah Melayu*" or Malay Annals, and a plate labeled "Mutual Loyalty between People and Ruler" is a discussion of how the Ruler of Palembang, Demang Lebar Daun, coined the expression "Yang Dipertuan" (literally meaning "one who has been made Overlord") to refer to himself and about how local people came to swore a sacred oath before Allah that the ruler must not disgrace the subjects and that the ruler must be upheld and obeyed even if he is corrupt and oppressive. Down the hall, there is a "Society of Malacca, According to the Sejarah Melayu" describing the four-tiered social hierarchy, "royal family, nobility, ordinary freemen, and slaves" as inscribed in the Malay Annals. One of the pictures titled "Malacca 10 August 1511" has a caption that states that "superior European arms and treacherous elements in Malacca helped in the downfall of the Malay empire." Since an earlier part of this caption mentioned "Indian mercenaries that fought on the side of the Portuguese, "treacherous elements" appear to refer to Indians that supported the Portuguese takeover of Melaka.

Further, down the hall, under a sign "Hikayat Hang Tuah" or "The Saga of Hang Tuah" there is a large exhibit that tells the story of this legendary Malay warrior. This exhibit includes more information about the social hierarchy of feudal Melaka society that expands upon the description from the Malay Annals stating the "Raja of Melaka" was "looked upon as God's representative on earth" and "therefore his every wish must be obeyed." In addition, this section stated that there were two types of "lords of the state," ones with fiefs and those without fiefs who lived off of the "kindnesses of the ruler." There were cases of books about Hang Tuah and a picture titled "Amok of Hang Jebat c. 1465" and some of the tale about how Hang Tuah stabbed him and let him die slowly. Before Hang Jebat died, he ran berserk in the streets killing anyone he could catch according to the tale and exhibit. The picture depicted the terror of people running in the streets as he ran "amok." There is also a page of the *Hikayat Hang Tuah* in Jawi script and maps of the period on display, and a large exhibit with a clothed dummy of Hang Tuah that has the title "Ta'kan Melayu Hilang di Dunia" (Never will Malays disappear from this world) located near it. This famous statement, Hang Tuah supposedly made, is a paradigmatic expression of Malay racial pride. The *songket sarong* and head wrap, velvet-looking pants, jacket, shoulder throw, and *keris* positioned in the front of his body, were presented as the "clothing of Hang Tuah."

In the next room titled "manuscript collection" there are several cases of books and displays of letters. Beneath a sign reading "National Malay Cultural Heritage Manuscript" there are some circular plates with *Jawi* script on them representing the "earliest Malay letter, 1521" and the "second earliest Malay letter known, 1522." In one case of books there are seven books written in *Jawi* script and one book written in Chinese characters. Another case has Malay books written in *Jawi* and *Rumi* or Latin script.

The remaining exhibits located in other rooms included a "Laws of Melaka" section with Malay books in both scripts and several pictures depicting the Islamic-based laws of the Melaka Sultanate, a section focusing upon written documentation of Malay political contacts with the outside the world, and a section museum directors devoted to one of the most popular historical figures of "Malay" literature, Munshi Abdullah, born in Kampung Pali, Melaka, in 1796. There is a big sign with his name on it and a plate that tells about his life. It states that "Munshi" was a "British awarded title for someone for someone who taught the customs and traditions of Malays." There is a case with some of his written works and works about him and a case with some other books in *Jawi, Rumi,* and one Chinese text. Around the corner there is a room with paintings of Munshi Abdullah depicting his life as a village boy and a paid instructor of British administrators in Malay written in the *Jawi* script. Some local Indian Muslims find a lot of significance in the claim that Munshi Abdullah was an Indian Muslim or of Indian ancestry.[18] However, there is no mention of any Indian ancestry in this exhibit. This exhibit simply refers to him as Malay, as are most of the other historic and legendary figures depicted in this museum. There were also some other rooms focusing solely upon Malay writers. In the back room upstairs, there are books and maps, and information about the authors of Malay authors in Malaysia. Likewise, the rooms downstairs had lists of works and biographies of Malay writers of prose and poetry. Three Malay women were represented in the "Literature of Melaka" room. In this room there were also pictures of Malay writers and some meetings and association conferences they attended.

This museum, similar to the "gendang nusantara" theme, has a focus upon Malay culture and literary contributions without any significant representations of cultural diversity. There were no Indian or *Melaka Portugis* texts or documents for instance, and the few Chinese texts and documents were not accompanied by any discussion. The only reference to Indians was not favorable and did not present the positive contributions they made to historic or contemporary Melaka. A Chinese man, engaging in trade, did appear in traditional Chinese attire in the section relating to laws during the time of the Melaka Sultanate, but his cultural distinctiveness contributes to the notion of the universality of Islamic law, applying to Chinese traders and the contracts they make with Malays. His distinctiveness did not contribute to the content of the laws. Islamic-based laws and *Jawi* script were an expression of the Malay identity schema embodied in this museum, as central as Islam is to the Malay cultural category. Moreover, the extensive information about the Malay Annals and the Saga of Hang Tuah and the Malay figures and images of history and Malay-dominated society they entail reproduces the Malay identity schema. The use of historical documents and contemporary writers, in this museum, to construct images of the past and to express Malay achievements and capabilities indicate the importance of literature to Malay identity (see David J. Banks 1987). Furthermore, the presentation of information, about Malay authority and social hierarchy in the Melaka Sultanate and the extension of Islamic laws in the old empire, embodies and reproduces the schemata of "Malay privilege."

In contrast to the Museum of Literature, the Museum of History and Ethnography, and the Cultural Museum embody more of a synthesis of the schemata of "Malay privilege" with models and schemata of "Malaysia's diverse society." The Museum of History and Ethnography is located in the former Dutch Town Hall Building, the Studhuys Building. As you enter the museum, there are large versions of the paintings of the "War of Singapore" and the "Covenant between Demang Lebar Daun and Sang Sapurba, Palembang" that also appeared in the Museum of Literature. Down the main corridor, there are some pictures of contemporary Malay political leaders including the current Malaysian Prime Minister. Then there is a small standup folded cardboard display with panels about several legendary characters of Melaka, including a Malay Sultan, some Malay warriors, and "Puteri Li Po," the Chinese princess brought from China for the Sultan of Melaka.

This "ethnography" part of the museum is downstairs and the "history" part is upstairs. In the first room downstairs are exhibits of *Nyonya*, Dutch, Ching, Ming, Japanese, and Thai ceramics in large glass cabinets. On the other side of the room are ceramic fragments found around Melaka and out to sea. In the next room are weapons, including several Malay *kerises*, shields, and swords. Some spears, bow and arrows, lance breakers, and European swords and firearms also are on display. In the back of the room, there is a large stamp and coin collection and some medals given as Melaka State awards. In the next room, there is a Dutch dining room arrangement, some Dutch paintings, and a statue of a Dutch soldier.

Continuing towards the back, there is a full room of exhibits about the "Traditional Melaka Malay Wedding Ceremony." All along the walls in this room are pictures and descriptions of twenty separate stages of a Malay wedding. Yet, none of the roughly ten Malay and Muslim weddings that I have observed even performed half of these stages. In fact, several Malay civil servants in this museum informed me that most Malays do not perform many of these rites nowadays but this room does represent, in their view, Malay past wedding customs, which were more elaborate. An ornate display of a couple seated majestically on their wedding dais with a person fanning them, representing the *"upacara bersanding"* or the "bridal dais rite," is situated in the middle of the back of this room. On one side of the front of the next room is a "Melaka Malay bridal chamber" that is elegantly laid out.

On the other side of the room is a large exhibit of the "Daily Attire of the Melaka Community" or "Melaka Races" with full-size clothed dummies. These clothed dummies have signs that specify the particular cultural category that they represent and these included, "everyday" Tamil, Chinese, *Baba* and *Nyonya, Portugis* descendants, Chitty, and Malay clothing. Malay, *Baba* and *Nyonya,* and Chitty women were depicted as wearing *sarong* and *kebaya.* There were also wedding exhibits of some of these groups. A "Wedding Ceremony of the Chitty Community" exhibit showed a couple standing with stringed flowers, "maleh," around their necks and *bunga manggar* standing in the background. Then there was a "Baba Nyonya Bridal Chamber" with some *Baba* and *Nyonya* furniture and the couple in traditional attire. On the other side is a small exhibit of "Wedding scenery of the Portuguese Descendants" with a couple seated and wearing European style clothing. Each of these wedding exhibits of non-Malay cultural categories was singular displays not nearly as elaborate as the whole room devoted to representing the Malay wedding process. Down from these wedding exhibits, there is a "Melaka Malay House" made of wood on a scale in which people can walk into it and look around. Across the room from the house are some cases of silver, copper, and brass utensils, and some personal ornaments, including some Malay, Chitty and *Nyonya* hairpins. A small adjoining room has some cabinets with several Malay drums and some other instruments used my several local groups, including the accordion, guitar, and tambourine. Then there is a large room with exhibits displaying agricultural and fishing pursuits in the region. This "ethnography" section of the museum has a clear bias towards Malay culture in terms of the extensive wedding display and the traditional house and agricultural and fishing display. In the addition, the Chitty, and *Baba* and *Nyonya* representations express the assimilation of Malay culture and customs just as we have seen in the "cultural heritage" theme of the Melaka Historic Day celebration.

The "history" part of this museum is upstairs beginning with the "Melaka Sultanate Period" across from the director's office. There are various pictures of Malay villages, royalty, Hang Tuah and his warrior friends, and various scenes of battles. Representations of this historical period continue in the next room featuring pictures of the process of Islamization in which foreign Islamic teachers and missionaries are standing in prayer postures before Malay villagers. Malay villages seemed to be in awe of these tall Muslims dressed in white robes. This section focuses upon Malay political and military authority, in all its glory, and the coming of Islam to Melaka, whereas the contributions of Chinese and Indians are confined to a few images of Melaka as a commercial center.

The next room moves on to the "Portuguese Period" displaying Portuguese soldiers, ships, battles, and maps. Likewise, the following room of the "Dutch Period" has photos of Dutch captains, maps, buildings and so on, and the "British Period" is exhibited around the hallway with architectural scenes, lists of British ships, lists of "Colonial Captains" from each period, and scenes of British ships and battles. Museum officials have also posted a replica of a painting of a Chitty Headman in a seated position wearing a *sarong* and Malay-style headdress. Beneath the picture, it states that this Chitty Headman passed away in 1902.

Then there is a section of the "Political Movement" which shows pictures of several Malay organizers and members of organizations, including some Malay youth organizations. A meeting of Malays in Kampung Morten, Malacca, and a meeting of "Muslim and 'Indian Continent' religious leaders in 1948" is depicted as well. Another picture shows the Malacca Chinese Traders Association, headed by Tun Tan Cheng Lock, and the caption states that this group developed into the Melaka MCA.

On the other, "The Emergency" section has pictures of some Communist movement troops, mostly Chinese, and a picture of a building they destroyed, and several pictures of British forces moving in to crush the opposition communists. The "Independence Mission" section comes next and pictures of Tunku Abdul Rahman leading the independence team and leaving for London to negotiate with the British and then there is finally "Independence." In the hallway leading back to the staircase, there is a long exhibit with an array of large pictures of the governors of Melaka. The first governor of Melaka, who was Chinese, wore British Empire military garments, and the rest of the governors were Malay and were dressed in Malaysian official attire. Over this exhibit are flags of the various states of "independent" Malaysia." The "ethnography" and "history" parts of this museum clearly focus upon

Malay culture and historical contributions, while including some representations of non-Malay culture and contributions.

Similarly, the Cultural Museum has some limited representations of non-Malay cultural categories included amidst numerous displays of Malay culture, authority, and past glory. This museum is located at the end of Padang Pahlawan behind of the Independence Memorial just down from the old ruin of Fort A'Famosa. When I arrived at this museum, I asked for one of the Indian civil servants that one of the Malay upper level civil servants, from the Museum Board main offices, recommended I speak to. This Indian civil servant, Mr. Pillai, was just finishing a tour and offered to give me one as well. He took me to the first exhibit boards to the left of the front desk. It was an exhibit with a picture of Parameswara and some of his men in the jungles of this area depicting the story of how Parameswara found Melaka and named it. Mr. Pillai told me that officials opened this museum around twelve years ago and they had it built from 1984 to 1986 as a "replica of the Sultan of Melaka's palace based on historic records, artist sketches, and the Malay Annals." There are "four main posts which hold it up and they did not use nails on most of the structure and instead fit pieces together following the traditional process that did not use nails." Melaka was founded in 1389 according to historical accounts, he informed me. He told me a version of the story of how the Palembang prince, Parameswara found Melaka.

> This Palembang prince fled from Palembang after the fall of Majapahit to Singapore and then fled from Singapore where he was under attack after some intrigue there. He escaped to Muar and went to Bertamhulu, a jungle area in Melaka, and since the "original inhabitants" were hunters and fishermen . . . and so he is depicted as sitting under a tree in the jungle with his men and a bow and arrow and hunting dogs. While he sat under the tree he saw a little white rat kick a large hunting dog into the water and, upon seeing this miraculous event, he asked the name of the tree he was sitting under and they said it was a Melaka tree so he called the area Melaka . . . This is how Melaka was founded and named . . . He was a Hindu when he came to Melaka but was converted to Islam after marrying a princess from Pasai, North Sumatra.[19]

Then there were exhibits of three maps on the wall. One of them depicted the extent of the realm of the Sultanate of Melaka at its high point, which shows that it covered most of the Malay Peninsula and large parts of Northern Sumatra while Siam controlled part of the northern portion of the Malay Peninsula including Kelantan. The other two maps were a Portuguese and a French map drawn during the 18th and 17th century respectively. After the maps there were two color pictures of two kinds of *"Keris."*

Then we came to the "Sultan's Audience Hall" section, a very large and elaborate exhibit at the end of the main level, with lots of dressed dummy figures representing an assembled meeting at the Sultan's court. Mr. Pillai told me that the "most important people are depicted here" but it was really much larger and had at least 148 people in attendance. "There is Sultan Mansur Syah at the front of his throne which has seven steps leading up to where he was sitting; five stairs are for the princes and three for the *rakyat* on the occasion of their marriages." The main reason for the meeting depicted in this display was to deal with business in relation to three Chinese traders who are depicted in the middle. "They are from the Ming Dynasty and are envoys who had weapons with them given by the Sultan," he continued. Behind the Chinese traders were Majapahit envoys from Java and some Indian traders who came from Kalinga or Gua. The color white was used for the Sultan's umbrellas, and yellow ones could be used for the prince and the *rakyat* could use various colored umbrellas. At that time, people used colors to index the ranking of people in the Melaka Sultanate, but nowadays people use various colors in their wedding performances. He went on to describe the important nobles that were present in the exhibit and the roles they played in the court. In the back there was a criminal, he pointed out to me that was found guilty in the court but was brought before the Sultan because it was a murder case and he would be put to death. "The Sultan would free the person if it was someone he liked . . . but nowadays they just get hung except for a few cases in which the *Agong* has pardoned people on his birthday," Mr. Pillai said. To the right of the "Audience Hall" there was a case with various styles of royal headdresses worn by the nine present-day Sultans, and on the opposite were some boards with information on the special colors that were used for the ranked levels of society.

We went upstairs to the "Royal Bedchamber," located on one side of the stairs, and he told me that there were five steps leading to the bed so it was "actually meant for the prince." A dummy of the young Malay prince sat on the side next to some betel nut cases or *tepak sirih*. Mr. Pillai told me that these betel nut cases were antiques and must be at least around one hundred years old. There were several Malay hairpins in this exhibit with flower petal designs, the Malay style of ornamentation.

Some Islamic exhibits were on display in the middle of this large room. A glass case contained two texts: a Quran inscribed in Jordanian-style and a book in *Jawi* script. Museum civil servants posted a large drum on the other wall and he told me that these large drums, *ketuk-ketuk*, were used to wake Muslims up for morning prayers and to announce prayer times. Muslims also used them to announce events during the fasting month.

Museum officials also posted a series of pictures of local mosques of which the oldest stone mosque is Masjid Kampung Hulu and the oldest overall is Masjid Kampung Peringgit, nearby where this museum civil servant lives. Mr. Pillai told me that that they renovated this mosque and they have used bricks on it now. There were some pictures of mosques from other states as well and a large glass case with a model of the recently built Melaka State Mosque, Masjid Al-Azim. "These old mosques in Melaka were done in Chinese-style since the Chinese admiral, Cheng Ho, who led the Chinese envoy here was a Muslim and had built many masjids in China . . . so many masjids were built following Chinese style because Chinese influence was strong." There was also a *mimbar masjid*, or mosque pulpit, with hand carvings and no nails, that Masjid Bacang donated after they built a new one. A *"Kain Tengkolok"* or scarf worn by warriors was on display and not far away from was a *rehal* or Quran stand. This wooden stand is "to show respect for the Quran the Holy Book so that it did not rest on the floor where we walk," he said. There were also some replicas of tombstones and other artifacts, with Arabic writing on them, which indicated the long history of Islam in the region.

In the next area, on the opposite end from the "royal bedchamber," there was a series of glass cabinets exhibiting the dress of people in Melaka and in other areas of Malaysia. The first case had a dressed dummy displaying the "Imam's Dress," a long Islamic robe and a *songkok*. In the case, there were dummies displaying "Indian Dress" and the female wore a sari. "A woman has to know how to wear a sari or she can't put it on unless someone knows how to help her." The sari is wedding attire for Indian brides and the groom wears a *dhoti* or *"westi"* in Tamil on the bottom and a *"jepa"* shirt and a *tunde*, shawl, and the turban-like headdress is called *"telpa."* "This was the type worn at first and then the Indians wore *baju melayu* like what I am wearing now." He told me that he was "born a Hindu" but not a Chitty and his grandparents immigrated to Malaysia. He grew up here in Malaysia and attended Malay schools so he has learned a lot about Malay culture. He was wearing the same colored *baju melayu* that the rest of the museum employees were wearing.

The next cabinet had "Portugis Dress" and he told me that the *Portugis* were fishermen who live near the seaside. "They are less and less now and have married Chinese." The *Baba Nyonya* and Chitty attire, with *sarongs*, were represented in the next cabinets and he told me these groups are "less and less now" too. "The *Baba Nyonya* and Chitty are marrying real Chinese and Indians and have learned Chinese and Tamil and so they are disappearing." The rest of the cabinets in this section contained various kinds of Malay female attire, including "Baju Kurung Johor," "Baju Kedah," "Baju Kurung Cekak Musang," "Baju Pahang," "Baju Negeri Sembilan," "Baju Perak," and "Baju Kebaya Labuh." There was also one of "Kadazan Clothing," representing the female attire during the harvest festival of a group of natives of Sabah.

Most of the Malay female attire looked like versions of the *baju kurung*. Mr. Pillai told me that the *"Baju Kurung Cekak Musang"* was introduced in the 16th century and was worn by the royal family at that time. However "nowadays it is worn by everyone and is a common national culture . . . but many young Malays don't wear *baju kurung* or *kebaya* anymore and choose to wear jeans and T-shirts with *tudung* because they want to be modern." His discourse supports a Malay-based national culture, while depicting the Malays themselves as deviating from it. He went on to say that the *sarong* and *kebaya* were worn by *"Nyonyas* who had intermarried with Malays originally, since Muslims then were not so strict or strong as now and so they married Malays and maintained the Buddhist religion . . . but nowadays you have to become Muslim because Muslims are more strict and stronger." He pointed out how the *Babas* and *Nyonyas* followed Malay customs in reference to the hair ornamentation and broaches used to keep the tops closed since there were no buttons. On the other hand, he also spoke about how the Malay wedding ceremonies follow the Indian style in reference to investigating and inquiring about brides and finger dyeing ceremonies, *berinai,* that Malays have adopted. His statements about Chinese and Indian cultural influence upon Malay culture, expresses a sense of the acculturation process, absent from the museum exhibits and descriptions.

We went back downstairs and he took me to the Hang Tuah and Hang Jebat exhibit. This museum displays images of these legendary Malay warriors armed with curved-bladed swords and locked in fierce combat. He told me a version of their story after which I told him how sad this story is to me. He said he did not know if it was true but it is from the Malay Annals. There was some "old Malay dress" and some "Malay" drums, *geduk, gendang, rebana ubi, kompang,* and other traditional instruments on display back towards the main entrance. He told me that most of these instruments came from India, China, or Europe. He said, *"kompang* are used in India, in the Gujerati area, and I've seen them there before." I signed the museum guest book and thanked him for the tour.

This museum, like most of the others, focused upon Malay culture and history, while representing some cultural diversity at points. The exhibits and array of physical culture embodied and reproduced the dominant synthesis of Malay privilege and cultural diversity. Members of various non-Malay cultural categories have expressed dissatisfaction with the way these museums incorporate and recognize their races and emphasize Malay culture. In the words of one Chinese woman, in these museums, "Chinese are standing behind . . . not standing in the spotlight while Malays are in the spotlight" and Chinese, Indians, and *Portugis* do not get full "recognition." Conventional and personal "mental" representations embedded in such discourse indicate that while non-Malays expect a certain degree of emphasis upon Malay culture, they nevertheless expect more extensive inclusion and recognition than these museums provide. The discourse of the Indian civil servant, Mr. Pillai, suggests that some of the markers of Malay culture represented in these exhibits may be re-interpreted within an acculturative perspective that recognizes the cultural influence of Malays upon other groups and, in turn, the influence of other groups upon Malays. Similarly, Joan, a young Chinese woman of *Baba* and *Melaka Portugis* parentage, told me "Malaysian culture is somehow, like, everyone is adopting everybody's culture." Moreover, Mr. Pillai's comments about Malays eschewing "national attire" in their pursuit of "modernity" and about the current requirement of conversion to Islam before marrying a Malay person may have been shielded criticisms of dominant discourse and Malay privilege. Yet, his explicit statements about Malay dress as common national dress and his donning of *baju Melayu* embodies and reproduces the hegemonic versions of multiculturalism and cultural citizenship.

CONCLUSION

I have demonstrated that the National Day and Melaka Historic Day events and the local government managed museum exhibits are produced through a dominant mode of merging models and schemata of "Malaysia's diverse society" and models and schemata of "Malay privilege." While only one of side of this apparent opposition may be embedded in particular practices, it is their combination that spanned social practice taken more broadly. For instance, the National Day cultural show and the main room of the Art Gallery Museum embodied, reproduced and are directed by models of "Malaysia's diverse society," whereas Gendang Nusantara I, II, and III and the Literature Museum embody, reproduce and are directed by models and schemata of "Malay privilege." On the other hand, most of these events and exhibits when taken as particular practices or in relation to each other are directed by, embody, and reproduce the hegemonic merging of these representations.

Although the form and arrangement these celebrations and exhibits take indicate the institutionalization of dominant models and schemata, it does not mean that local residents in Melaka interpret them in line with these dominant perspectives. In fact, many people express conventional "mental" representations that question or criticize the level and manner of inclusion of non-Malay culture in these cultural shows and museums. While many respondents expect Malay culture to be "made larger" and situated "in the spotlight," their "mental" representations of "Malaysia's diverse society" call for greater incorporation and recognition of non-Malay cultural markers. Some people seek to rectify this lack of overt inclusion through reinterpreting cultural markers conventionally assumed to be Malay attributes within an acculturative perspective in which non-Malay contributions attain greater recognition. Indeed, some personal representations envision cultural shows that elide "Malay privilege" and symbolic advantages through projecting dances, songs, and attire of each race combined in single performances or arrayed on an equal plain in successive performances. Some of these personal representations seem to have become more widespread socially and may therefore be alternative "mental" representations contesting to varying extents the dominant "mental" representations.

Nevertheless, the hegemonic merging of models and schemata produces a form of multiculturalism in which diverse cultural categories and their cultural distinctiveness are represented publicly, included within a framework that emphasizes the Malay element and its culture. Malay cultural attributes are the national ones and the ones that others must assimilate. Non-Malay groups are disciplined by this form of cultural citizenship and must adopt it to fit and to be incorporated within the government-organized celebrations and representations. On the other hand, there are many contexts, outside of direct government control, in which non-Malay groups can produce their own versions of cultural citizenship and contest the dominant one. I will consider some of these events and expressions of cultural citizenship in the next chapter.

Chapter Six

Religious Festivals in Sacred, Public, and Private Places[1]

The Malaysian government has promoted interracial and inter-religious participation in festivals and open house visiting as a means to develop and enhance social solidarity amongst Malaysia's diverse population. Although governmental goals are in accord with Durkheimian functionalist and British structural-functionalist interpretations of such events, many social scientists note that social solidarity is only one of many functions of rituals and festivals (Turner 1974; Comaroff 1985; Kertzer 1988). Festival participants and organizers may use festivals to foster social solidarity and/or to change, resist or subvert power structures and social orders. In this chapter I will explore some of the ways people used festivals and open house visiting to negotiate the position and relationships of groups in Melaka. These negotiations entail reproductions and contestations of mental representations of the social order and are an integral part of processes of cultural citizenship.

In the first section, I will describe and analyze festival activities and inter-group relations in "sacred sites," sites that hold religious meaning to one or more communities. My main aim is to indicate the extent "cognitive convergences" are institutionalized and form a foundation incorporating diverse social groups into a festival cycle that traverses any single community.[2] "Cognitive convergences" are similar to what Aragon (1992, 1996) calls "value equivalences" and "crossroad paradigms" in her analysis of Christian conversion in Sulawesi. Value equivalences involve symbols, core concepts, and cultural premises from new religious currents interpreted as parallel to elements in old religious currents, and crossroad paradigms are multiply interpreted symbols (Aragon 1992:380–390). Here I use "cognitive convergences" as a more general rubric, inclusive of value equivalences and crossroad paradigms that occur within the context of religious conversion, as well as cultural affinities that occur amongst religions in other contexts of interaction.

In the second section, I address festival celebrations in "public sites," sites that do not hold religious meaning to any community and that are shared by various groups. My main aim in this section is to describe the main festivals of the public "festive season" and to interpret the form these public celebrations take in relation to the local social relational system.

In the third section, I will describe and analyze open house visiting in public and personal sites and their significance to the dynamics of social relations and cultural citizenship in Melaka. Overall, I will attempt to highlight negotiations of sacred, public, and personal spaces and the dynamics of social relations. I will argue that the extensive incorporation of cultural categories into the festival cycle embodies models and schemata of "Malaysia's diverse society" and contributes to a sense of cultural citizenship and belonging amongst non-Malays, while the separation of Malays from this cycle reproduces models and schemata of "Malay privilege." In addition, Chinese and Indians vie for social position vis-à-vis the Malay majority in the process of staging festivals in public and private spaces.

FESTIVAL CYCLES IN SACRED SITES: COGNITIVE CONVERGENCES

In Melaka, the annual Amman Festival, held in the Sri Muthu Mariamman Temple under Chitty Hindu management, is an important part of the intercommunal festive cycle. The Amman Festival is centered in the Chitty neighborhood and members of the temple board committee, chaired by an elder male "headman" who is both a religious and political leader of this community, organizes and coordinates this festival each year.[3] This festival is known popularly as "*Sembahyang Dato Chachar*" or "Prayers for the Lord of Chickenpox." "*Dato*" is the shortened colloquial form of "*Datok*" in Malay, meaning Lord or Deity. Local devotees believe Amman or "*Dato Chachar*," the Hindu deity this festival is devoted to, possesses healing powers over smallpox, chickenpox and other ailments.[4] Some Chinese participants brought Chinese elders to the daily prayers of this festival with the *niat* (intent or desire) of having their elder relatives healed by Amman. During the ten main days of prayers of this festival, local Chitty Hindus, Indian Hindus of various ethnic groups, and members of Chinese dialect groups, and *Babas* and *Nyonyas* participate together in prayers and devotional activities.

Chitty organizers made several preparations accommodating the large number of Chinese worshippers they expected as participants. Gigantic incense sticks, like those used in Chinese Buddhist-Taoist[5] temple festivals, were posted in front of the temple, and bronze incense urns used to hold incense were placed inside the temple. Primarily Chinese worshippers, who commonly hold incense in their clasped hands while praying and showing their respect to deities, use these large incense urns. In addition, red candle racks with lit red candles were also posted in front of the temple; these candles are used by Chinese to light incense sticks. On the eighth day of prayers, Indian and Chinese worshippers bought silver effigies of body parts or whole bodies which temple priests present to *Dato Chachar* for them with the *niat* that their sickness be healed by Amman. Chinese worshippers were also amongst those going into trance and performing trance dances during daily prayers.

The climax of the festival is reached on the tenth day when thousands of Hindu and Buddhist-Taoist devotees fulfill their vows, or give thanks, to *Dato Chachar* by carrying silver milk pots and/or metal or wooden frames (*kavadi*) with images of Hindu gods on them. Many devotees, mostly males, also fulfill their vows by having spikes thrust through various parts of their bodies. Indian and Chinese devotees perform these acts with the *niat* to receive benefits or blessings from the *Dato*. These devotees, both Chinese and

Figure 9 Chinese women trance dancing during Mariamman Festival. (Photograph by Timothy P. Daniels)

Indian, usually ask for good health, employment or business benefits, or success in educational endeavors. Many participants perform devotional acts every year to give thanks for prayers answered. Devotees initiate their devotional acts by having *kapoo,* yellow string with turmeric roots attached to them, tied around their wrists, and then they walk from the Mariamman Temple, in the Chitty neighborhood, to the Venayagar Temple, the 18th Century temple located in the middle of town. At this temple, Chinese and Indian set up their personal offerings of coconuts and fruit and incense on banana leaves, and await the temple priest to perform prayers over offerings and to crack their coconuts, thereby extending their prayers to the gods. The white interior of the coconut symbolizes the purity and sincerity of their prayers. After these rites, devotees often go into trance and set out to fulfill their vows by walking back to the Mariamman Temple carrying silver milk pots, margossa leaves, and/or body skewers.

As devotees return to the Mariamman Temple, the grounds of the temple take on a carnival-like atmosphere with large numbers of spectators standing around to watch the devotees come back with body skewers and metal and wooden frames. Local vendors sold drinks, peanuts, and other snacks in front of the temple, along with other products such as tape cassettes and clothes as well. Many local Christians, some of whom enter the Hindu temple to observe the exciting acts of worship, come to watch the activities on the tenth and climactic day of the Amman Festival. Some local Muslims watch the procession of devotees from the roadside as they walk back to the temple, but rarely enter the Chitty neighborhood to watch the festival. Chitties, and other Hindus, often told me that I was the first Muslim to enter the temple, although many Muslims come to the Chitty neighborhood to obtain medicine for chickenpox.

Even though they pray in both Chinese and Indian fashion, Chinese participants in this festival have told me that they pay careful attention to performing these rites as exactly as possible according to local Hindu customs. Many of them have participated in this festival and undertaken vows for several years so that they are very familiar with the procedures and rites. All of the Chinese participants I have spoken to about their participation in the festival have told me that they look at their participation as meaningful religious activities just the same as their activities at Buddhist-Taoist temples and altars. They generally express feelings about the similarity of Hinduism and Buddhism, and the common origins in India; one Chinese woman told me that she feels these religions are basically, "the same religion." She added that *Amman* and *Kwan Yin*[6] are sisters and that *Kwan Yin* was initially a Hindu deity but she crossed over to the Buddhist pantheon, a story, cognitively connecting these faiths, which

Figure. 10 Indian Hindu devotee carrying metal *kavadi*.
(Photograph by Timothy P. Daniels)

many local Chinese and Indians have reported to me. Others have told me that they believe that *Datok Chachar* possesses special powers and that they come before her for particular needs they may have in reference to healing.

The flexibility of moving between various "sacred sites" is definitely the greatest for local Chinese Buddhist-Taoists who do not have the organizational and doctrinal restrictions of local Christians and Muslims providing blocks to such movement. Yet, they see themselves as being "born Buddhists" just as local Hindus, Muslims, and Christians view themselves as inheriting their respective religions from their parents, especially their fathers, and racial backgrounds. However, there appears to be a significant

Figure 11 Chinese devotees in Mariamman Festival procession.
(Photograph by Timothy P. Daniels)

social dimension in their willingness to interpret parallels between the two
faiths and participate in Hindu festivals, and that is their affinity to Indians
as non-Malays and non-*Bumiputera.*

Chap Goh Mei, on the 15th day of the Chinese New Year, is celebrated
with a procession from the Yong Chuan Tian Temple, in Bandar Hilir,
around several streets and back to this temple again.[7] Temple committee
members organize this festival, which several local Chinese businessmen fi-
nancially supported. Five *"Ong Yah"* brothers, high-ranking and titled
Taoist deities or *Dato,* are carried around in palanquin on the shoulders of
Chinese, and a few Indian, youth. *Maleh* or stringed jasmine flowers were
placed around the anthropomorphic images of the *Ong Yah* deities, just as
local Hindus do in worship of their deities. Several *Tang Chi* shamans, all
men in this context, which local devotees believed to be inhabited by Taoist
Dato, walk in the procession with spikes through their faces and arms.
Locals, noting the similarity between these mediums and Hindu devotees,
often call the latter "Indian *Tang Chi."* However, these mediums are generally the only people to have spikes thrust through their bodies in Chinese festivals, whereas in Hindu festivals this practice is left open for the general
population of worshippers. A few Chinese woman who participated in

trance dancing and took spikes through their faces and/or tongues in the Amman Festival, told me that they felt it was easier for women to become *tang chi* shamans in the Indian community than in the Chinese community.[8] According to local respondents, these practices of "self-mortification" developed independently in India and China and Chinese worshippers practiced them in China for several centuries. Chinese immigrants brought these practices as well as syncretic belief systems with them as they settled throughout Southeast Asia. They often merged their traditional beliefs with many elements from other religions in their new places of residence (see Ju Shi Huey 1983; Cecilia Ng Siew Hua 1983; Tan Chee-Beng 1990; Soo Khin Wah 1990; Teresita Ang See and Go Bon Juan 1990).

Hundreds of Chinese Buddhist-Taoists, Indian Hindus, and Christians join in the procession and walk around town following the youth whom race around the streets swinging and tossing the five *Dato* into the air. The *Chap Goh Mei* procession stops in front of several homes and temples along the parade route. Devotees, both Chinese and Indian, stand in front of their homes with tables full of offerings of fruit, cakes, flowers and incense for the deities. They clasp their hands in prayer as the *Dato* carried in the palanquin and in the bodies of *Tang Chi* pass by and/or stop in front of their homes.

Figure 12 *Tang chi* shamans in Chap Goh Mei Festival procession. (Photograph by Timothy P. Daniels)

During the birthday celebration of *Dato* Hian Tian Siong Tay at the Hian Tian Kong Temple in Bandar Hilir, there was also considerable Indian Hindu participation in this three-day festival. On the first day and third day of the deity's birthday celebration, *Tang Chi* shamans went into trance and had spikes thrust through their faces and arms. Chinese and Indian worshippers prayed at the temple altars, and the youth carried *Dato* Siong Tay, a high-ranking deity of the Northern Heavenly Gate, a Taoist deity, on a palanquin around some local city streets and then he was set in the lot behind the temple. Many youth make vows to carry the deity for several years or for every year in return for some blessings, they hope the deity will bestow upon them.

A red bridge was set up behind the temple and Chinese and Indian devotees walked barefoot over the bridge to purify themselves. Red represents luck and good fortune and the bridge is viewed as a sacred path that can improve one's destiny through realigning the Five Elements of traditional Chinese divination, earth, wood, fire, metal and water in one's favor. After crossing the bridge, temple committee members gave participants charms, candy, and a dab of oil in the middle of their foreheads to light their inner lamps. Local Buddhist-Taoists conceive of the life force or energy of a person as being like a lamp; when a person's inner lamp is low or weak, the person is close to death. Many Hindu participants already had some ash and paste in the midst of their foreheads to signify their rising above the ashes of human mortality and the opening of their third eyes. Thus, the placing of substances in the midst of worshipper's foreheads is a sort of "crossroad paradigm" (Aragon 1992) interpreted according to the respective logics of these two religions.

Wesak[9] Festival, the celebration of *Dato* Buddha's birthday, enlightenment, and death is also part of the inter-communal festival cycle of Melaka. This festival often overlaps with the Amman Festival, so Chinese and Indian worshippers often move back and forth between local Buddhist and Hindu temples. The Buddhist Association of Malacca Temple, whose board members organize this festival, is just down the road from the Sri Muthu Mariamman Temple in the Chitty neighborhood. The Chitty headman usually breaks a coconut in front of the main float—an act normally performed by Hindu devotees in front of chariots carrying Hindu deities symbolizing purification of the god's path—in the procession that carries the main "Buddha Image" as it passes in front of the main road leading to the Chitty Hindu neighborhood. In addition, a Tamil priest generally leads a group of Hindus in the Amman procession into the Buddhist temple and leads prayers before the main "Buddha Image." However, this year, 2000, the overlap of

Wesak Festival with the Amman Festival did not allow them to perform these normal observances. To compensate for their later inability to pay respects to *Dato* Buddha, the Chitty headman, a Tamil Hindu temple priest, and many local Chitty and Tamil Hindus attended morning prayers on *Wesak* Eve at the Buddhist Association temple. The Tamil Hindu priest moved some camphor lamps in front of the "Buddha Image" leading the Hindu and Chinese congregation in prayer. Moving camphor lamps in front of deities are a form of Hindu worship believed to bring many benefits and blessings to members of the congregation. Buddhist-Taoist worshippers believe the burning of incense and oil lamps have similar effects. After Buddhists finished chanting for the transference of merits, rites in which a few Hindus participated, Hindus collected flowers from the tables and trays of offerings as blessings from *Dato* Buddha to take to their homes.

Similar to Chinese participants in the Amman Festival, Indian worshippers in Chinese temple activities have told me that they look upon these activities as meaningful religious activity. They have told me that many of the Buddhist-Taoist deities are related to or comparable to Hindu deities. Many local Hindus interpret some of the Buddhist-Taoist deities, Chinese heroes that have become gods, as being similar to Hindu holy men who have reached the high spiritual level of *moksha* in which they attained self-realization and become liberated from the cycle of births and deaths. Local Hindus often pray to such holy men for blessings and favors. Unlike Chinese worshippers who often pray in their customary manner, with incense sticks, in Hindu temples, I have never seen an Indian pray stretched out on the floor before a Chinese temple altar the way they often do in Hindu temples. One young man told me that he feels too shy to pray like this in a Chinese temple so he just joins in and prays the way Chinese do or stands with his hands clasped in prayer without incense. However, some Chinese at the Buddhist Association temple have expressed the excitement they feel when the Indian Hindu contingent enters their temple each year to pray behind their Hindu priest who leads them in prayer in Hindu-style. These sorts of cross-racial experiences during the religious festival cycle embody the representation of Malaysia's diverse cultural categories relating to each other in harmony and mutual respect. They also reinforce and tighten the relationship between the Chinese and Indian communities and enhance a sense of being incorporated in society on a level beyond their own cultural category.

In Melaka, the inter-communal festival cycle also includes Christian religious observance, especially Good Friday services at St. Peter's Church. From 7AM to 10PM, thousands of Chinese Catholics and Buddhist-Taoists, Indian Catholics and Hindus, and Eurasian Catholics line up to pay homage to Jesus Christ, or *Dato Mati* (Dead Lord), as he is popularly referred to by non-Christians, on the occasion of his death a few thousands years ago. Christian and non-Christian worshippers stand in line with long white candles and *bunga rampai,* dried and chopped up fragrant flowers, waiting for their turn to enter the small hall on the side of the church. When they enter the hall, they place white candles in racks in front of kneeling and reclining images of the *Dato Mati,* and kiss and rub dried flowers onto his feet and hands. Worshippers repeat these ritualized acts at a statue of Mother Mary standing in the front of this small hall and with another statue of Jesus Christ lying in a bed in a hall on the opposite side of the church. Christians and non-Christians also burn candles and pray at a few other statues located around the church grounds. Thousands of Buddhist-Taoists and Hindus come to pray before *Dato Mati* with the *niat* to request good health, economic benefits, or other blessings from him.[10]

In the evening, there is a church service and sermon and a candlelight procession, attended by thousands of people, more than half of which are non-Christians according to local church members. Worshippers followed a solemn procession led by a group of *Portugis* Eurasian men carrying the images of *Dato Mati* and Mother Mary around the church grounds. After the procession, some local church members in astonished, and somewhat alarmed tones, told the French priest that there were even more non-Christian devotees than last year. Church members seemed to have mixed feelings about the growing popularity of these rites. On the one hand, they have a positive attitude about Buddhists and Hindus acknowledging the power of Jesus Christ, but on the other hand, they feel that non-Christian worshippers fail to understand the true meaning of Good Friday. Church organizers handed out flyers to non-Christians all day long to explain that Jesus Christ is a "Living Lord" and not a "Dead Lord" and to deliver other messages of Christian doctrine.

Muslim festivals and observances in several "sacred sites" were also an integral part of the inter-communal festival cycle in Melaka, before concerted government efforts to halt Muslim participation in such practices. Chinese Buddhist-Taoists and Indian Hindus would join Malay ritualized feasts and prayers at Malay *keramat,* old Muslim graves held to possess special powers. Locals believed the Muslims inhabiting these graves to have been great Islamic teachers, missionaries, and holy men, and they have come to regard and refer to them as *Dato.*[11] Malays would regularly go to these sites to sacrifice goats and cows and would invite Chinese and Indians to participate in the festivities that used to include communal meals, music, and dancing. Chinese and Indians would also

Figure 13 Christians and non-Christians lining up for worship on Good Friday. (Photograph by Timothy P. Daniels)

sacrifice goats and chickens at Malay *keramat* and other groups would join in the prayers and festivities. During the eighth month of the Chinese calendar, the month of the Mooncake Festival, Chinese, Malays, and Indians would all have large feasts and celebrations at the Malay *keramat* on Pulau Besar, an island lying around five kilometers offshore from the urban area of Melaka. When Chinese Buddhist-Taoists and Indian Hindus held events at *keramat,* they used to invite a Malay Muslim and pay him to officiate at the ancient graves, performing Islamic prayers of supplication and recitation of the Holy Quran.

Malays believe that there are seven brothers buried in the main set of graves at Pulau Besar. Some believe that these seven brothers were warriors who fought for Malaysian independence, but most tend to believe that they were Muslim missionaries whom introduced Islam centuries ago to the local rulers of Melaka and their subjects. For Malays, whom still merge Islamic beliefs with Malay pre-Islamic beliefs in spirits, the *Dato* associated with these ancient graves are spiritual agents, perhaps even *wali* Allah (see Osman 1984:173). The lingering spirits of *wali* Allah, Islamic teachers and holy men sent and blessed by Allah are believed to possess special powers. Chinese Buddhist-Taoist, who are avid worshippers at these sacred sites, believe that there are five brothers buried at

Pulau Besar who were saints and are now lower-ranking *Dato* or deities.[12] Some local Chinese shamans go into trance and have their bodies inhabited by these five brothers and hold birthday celebrations for them. Although local Hindus have not instituted such practices, many do believe that these *Dato* are powerful spirits of holy men that have attained a higher level of existence. Nevertheless, all worshippers, Malay, Chinese, and Hindu agree that these *Dato* are powerful and have the ability to grant one's wishes or *niat*. Both Malay and Chinese shamans serve as hosts for these *Dato* who enter the shamans' bodies and communicate with, and spread blessings to, worshippers.

Figure 14 Chinese men praying at *keramat* in Machap, Melaka.
(Photograph by Timothy P. Daniels)

In addition to worship at Malay *keramat*, the *Mandi Safar* annual festival used to be an integral part of the inter-communal festival cycle. This festival would take place during the beginning of the month of *Safar*, the second month, on the Islamic calendar. According to Malay custom, they believed that any accident during this month could lead to extreme loss or death, so they undertook this festival with the objective of purification and to avoid potential danger and calamity (see Deraman and Mohamad 1995:73). Malays would decorate bullock carts and ride on them, dressed up in fancy clothes, to *Pantai Kundor*, a beach along the coast. They performed prayers and religious rites along the waterside, and feasts and parties would go on for days and nights at the beach. Chinese Buddhist-Taoists, Indian Hindus, and Eurasian Catholics would join in the festivities, dancing and singing and courting for several days. For many Buddhist-Taoists and Hindus, this festival was a time to gain blessings from *datok* associated with water, but for others it was simply a time to join in the carnival atmosphere and to have fun. For instance, Yati, my Malay friend who accompanied me to the 10th Melaka Historic City Day Celebration, told me that she and her young cohorts when they were teenagers, used to follow these activities to just have fun but they were too young to understand what was going on. They did not know that the Department of Islamic Religion did not think that these activities were good at the time. According to Yati, eventually the government stopped it altogether because of the rowdy and un-Islamic activities said to occur during this festival.

Other Malay and Muslim festivals and observances, such as *Hari Raya Aidilfitri, Hari Raya Aidiladha*[13] and *Maulidur Rasul*, were already outside of the inter-communal festival cycle as they took place in and around mosques and prayer halls in which only Muslims were allowed to enter. For the two major Islamic celebrations, *Aidilfitri* and *Aidiladha*, Malays, and other Muslims, mostly wearing colorful *baju melayu* and *baju kurung* or *jubah* (robes) pack into mosques for *takbiran* (chants of praise for Allah) and special prayers conducted on the morning of these celebrations. There are no mass processions or parades organized as part of these celebrations. On the other hand, Muslims generally celebrated *Maulidur Rasul*, the celebration of holy Prophet Muhammad's birthday, with a public parade in Melaka and in other states. On June 15, 2000, in Melaka, thousands of Muslim marchers, comprising over one hundred contingents of government departments, agencies, schools, associations, *kompang* troupes and a marching band marched from Kubu Stadium to Masjid Al-Azim. Most members of each contingent wore the same color *baju melayu* and *baju kurung* or *jubah* and *tudung*. The Indian Muslim League, the group that invited me to march with them, had their own contingent and they wore Malay-style clothing, as did the Chinese, Indians, and Europeans marching in the Department of Islamic Religion contingent. These Chinese, Indians, and Europeans were men and women who converted to Islam in order to marry a Muslim. Many non-Muslims looked on from the roadside as the parade moved through the city streets, but none of these non-Muslims participated in the parade. *Mandi Safar* and Malay worship at *keramat* joined these festivals, following government prohibitions, which Muslims had already kept separate from the inter-communal festival cycle.

Nevertheless, the festival cycle in sacred sites entails the cognitive convergence of aspects of multiple religious systems. Although Hindu, Buddhist-Taoist, Catholic, and Islamic cosmologies are different, each of them has a position for a supernatural being referred to as *Dato* or Lord. In local Hindu cosmology, *Dato*, primarily Shiva, his consort Amman, and their two children, Murukan and Vinayakar, are the highest and most powerful forms of beings that exist. For local Buddhist-Taoists, *Dato* are supernatural beings that fall below the Heavenly Jade Emperor and the Sky God but above the demigods. They also ranked *Dato* according to the titles they have received from the Emperor, and divided them as those on the "Taoist side" and those on the "Buddhist side" of the pantheon. A form of the goddess Kwan Yin is on both the Taoist and Buddhist side, and local Buddhist-Taoists and Hindus believed her to be a sister of the Hindu deity Amman who has crossed over to the Buddhist-Taoist pantheon. In local Catholic cosmology, *Dato* is "God our Father" and "God the Son made man" or Jesus Christ. "God the Father" and "God the Son" together with the "Holy Spirit" completes the "Holy Trinity." Thus, *Dato* is at the pinnacle of Catholic cosmology, above angels, demons, and humans. For local Muslims, *Dato*, the holy men buried in the *keramat* are positioned below Allah and the prophets, but above ordinary humans, angels, and jinn (supernatural beings made of fire). For all local participants in the festival cycle at sacred sites, *Dato* are powerful beings, wherever people positioned them in particular cosmologies, possessing special abilities that command reverence from ordinary mortals.

Furthermore, all of the *Dato*, in these festivals, are associated with sacred objects of worship. Hindu and Buddhist-Taoist *Dato* are believed to inhabit statues and sculpted images generally situated in altars. Some of the *Dato* are bound to these sacred objects and others are unbound and only inhabit them at particular times. Priests must perform rites over these statues or other objects before worshippers can pray at them to assure that the desired *Dato* and not some undesirable, supernatural entity inhabits them. Likewise, statues of Jesus Christ and Mother Mary are the focus of worship and homage on Good Friday and other occasions. Muslim *Dato* are associated with ancient graves scattered around the state of Melaka, other states, and Singapore. Muslim, Christian, Hindu, and Buddhist devotees pour out their devotion onto objects and relics believed to have an intimate relationship with powerful *Dato*. Not only are these formal similarities, moreover, festival participants of various cultural categories and faiths interpret these spiritual entities from each religion as being parallel, in some sense, to spiritual entities in their own religion (cf. Aragon 2000:163–175; Shapiro 1987:128; Hollan 1988:279). In the case of local Buddhist-Taoists and Hindus, these connections are the deepest, as elaborate myths about the relations between deities of each pantheon have developed and spread across these communities.

In addition, there is cognitive convergence in the mutual understanding and interpretation that worshippers of these various religions bring their *niat* before the *Dato* and *bersembahyang* or pray at these sacred objects and sites. Although practitioners of each of these religions have different styles of praying locals interpreted each religion as emphasizing and practicing supplication to a *beneficent* higher power, asking this *beneficent* higher power for favors. This cognitive convergence must not be taken for granted in Malaysia or elsewhere in the world, and must be seen as more than people of various religions simply interpreting the actions of their neighbors. Indeed, even in Melaka, where we find this extensive inter-communal festival cycle, there are many Christians and Muslims interpreting the acts of worship of their neighbors as worship of the Devil, demons, or evil spirits. Furthermore, despite formal similarities between Christianity and Islam, and occasional local Christian references to these similarities, many local Muslims interpret Christian worship of Jesus as *syirik*, making partners with Allah, the worst sin in Islam. In the case of such interpretations, it is a "cognitive divergence" rather than a cognitive convergence that people produce and express. Much of the anthropological literature pertaining to colonial religious encounters exhibits the constraining influence of "cognitive divergences" under these contexts (see Chagnon 1983; Conklin 1995; Kan 1991; Aragon 2000), Christian missionaries and colonial rulers seeking to change religious practices and notions they deem distasteful or offensive. Moreover, many ethnographic cases of "syncretism" also derive from efforts of subordinated peoples to make their religious practices appear more like those of dominant groups (see Slotkin 1956; Wolf 1958; Brown 1987), under conditions shaped by powerful "cognitive divergent" discourse. Thus, it is important to stress that in the case of cognitive convergence, such as the cases I have discussed worshippers of one religious system are interpreting the actions of other religious systems in a positive fashion, as being parallel to their own acts of worship (cf. Lehman 2001; Puttick 1997; Sharp 1994). If it were not for cognitive convergence there would be no shared activities or shared beings for people to make sense of and construe. People, who participate in the inter-communal festival cycle, interpret their fellow worshippers of various faiths as bringing their *niat* to the *Dato,* much as they do themselves, seeking cures, good health, wealth, children, and making offerings and performing devotional acts to win the favor of the Lord.

Not only does the cycle of worship at sacred places entail cognitive convergence, an interpretation of being alike, but it also represents an institutionalization of these cultural affinities. Many Buddhist and Hindu worshippers can reel off the sequence of festivals, spanning several racial and religious groups and incorporating them into a common cycle. For many locals, this festival cycle expressed "true racial and religious harmony" with members of various races and religions worshipping together, embodying models and schemata of 'Malaysia's diverse society.' Not only having the constitutional right to practice their own religions, and receiving permits to stage public processions through the streets, but also the actual participation of other groups in their festivals adds to a sense of being incorporated in the broader society, adds to a sense of cultural citizenship. Only the absence of Malays stands out. Non-Malays often express the feeling and perception that they are only being *tolerated* and not *respected.* During the Mariamman Festival, one Indian doctor criticized Malay leaders for speaking so much about racial and religious harmony and tolerance but they never come to visit Hindu temple festivals. He felt that Malays could at least come and watch and participate in the communal meals on the outside of the temple in order to show their respect for their Hindu friends and their religion.

Inter-communal festivals at Malay *keramat* and the *Mandi Safar* Festival both have met a similar fate. The Department of Islamic Religion and many Malay political and religious leaders in Melaka have restricted these festivities. These festival activities were interpreted as being contradictory to Islamic principles and thus, as "un-Islamic." Believing in lingering spirits, supplicating to intermediary beings rather than seeking help directly from Allah, and mimicking the practices of other religions are some of the main complaints made in reference to Muslim involvement in these activities. The last *Mandi Safar* Festival[14] took place around twenty years ago according to local people who used to participate in them; the last multiracial and inter-religious festival that reportedly took place at the Malay *keramat* occurred around two to three decades ago. Chinese and Indians still pray at the Malay *keramat,* although the government has tried to restrict all worship at these sacred sites, by Muslims and non-Muslims alike (The Sun, 17

May 2000:6). Despite threats of prosecution under state Islamic law for engaging in "un-Islamic" activities many Malays still hold feasts in front of the *keramat* and still bring their *niat* to the sacred graves of *Dato*. However, these feasts and prayers are not open the way they used to be and are not inter-communal any longer.

The separation of Malays from this common festival cycle is part of a more general process of bestowing special status upon them. Malays, as the default Muslims and natives of the country are raised atop the social hierarchy of groups in Melaka. The separation of Malays from the festival cycle in sacred places has sent the message that Malays, as the pure Muslims, should not be diluting their strict adherence to Islam by mixing with other religions. Thus, this separation bestows "symbolic advantages" upon Malays; the official national religion is Islam and Malays must not mix with other religions in ways that are unbecoming of Muslims. This separation has not been lost on other groups involved in the festival cycle. Many interpret it as part of the process of giving special advantages to Malays. One local Straits-born Chinese man, lamenting the changes, told me that, "Malays are jealous of Chinese wealth and want to keep all of the blessings from the *keramat* for themselves." His statement not only expresses the lack of religious barriers from a Chinese point of view, but it also expresses a perception of Malay special rights in the symbolic realm.

PUBLIC CELEBRATIONS OF MAJOR HOLIDAYS

In Melaka, and most of Peninsular Malaysia, *Deepavali, Hari Raya Aidilfitri,* Christmas, and Chinese New Year, are the major public holidays. The period of time spanning these celebrations is generally referred to as the "festive season," roughly from October through February, and is a focal point of pride for many Malaysians as well a prime occasion for national discourse about Malaysia's multiracial society. As such, these festivals are not only celebrated in sacred spaces, but are also presented in public spaces easily accessible to all racial and religious groups. The public spaces in which people celebrated these festivals in Melaka are primarily stages and concourse areas in shopping centers. Promotions department staff, with all key positions occupied by Chinese, formulate the schedule of events for each festival and coordinate the activities.

For *Deepavali* during 1999, one shopping center with a stage had five days of events, which included a *Deepavali* Sari Queen contest, children's fancy dress contest and magic show, dance performances, and speeches given by local Malaysian Indian Congress leaders. The other shopping center with a stage had no *Deepavali* events this year, but mall employees decorated the stages at both malls on the *Deepavali* theme. Consumers and mall visitors of various backgrounds watched Indian cultural shows announced by several Indian masters of ceremonies speaking in Malay, the national language, Tamil, the language of the largest Indian ethnic group, and English. This use of several major languages gave broad appeal to these *Deepavali* events. In addition, municipal employees placed *Deepavali* greetings in overhead archways on major roads around town. Indian political leaders spoke about *Deepavali*, as a "festival of lights," emphasizing universal values of good triumphing over evil, and displaying Indian customs, downplaying the religious nature of the festival.[15] MIC speakers also took the opportunity during this year's events to campaign for the ruling alliance, since the general election was fast approaching. Thus, the Indian leaders used these public *Deepavali* events to negotiate a cultural and political sense of belonging in Malaysian society.

For Christmas and New Year, there was a month of events scheduled at one mall and ten days of events at the other mall. These events included photo sessions with Santa Claus and Garfield, art contests, magic and clown shows, a fancy dress contest, Christmas caroling in Mandarin mostly, Santa Claus candy giveaways, and several game shows. To celebrate the New Year, on the Gregorian calendar, one mall remained open for thirty-six hours straight and had non-stop events featuring a "New Millennium Countdown Bash" with dancing, singing, a brass band performance, a balloon giveaway, and the distribution of 2000 gifts. Participants announced and conducted most of the events on the schedule in Mandarin, but some combined Mandarin and English. Masters of ceremonies in these events spoke very little Malay, or *Bahasa Nasional*. Some Malays and Indians watched the shows, but few participated. Some Europeans and Eurasians participated in a few of the choirs and in other events. Mall employees decorated the stages at the malls on Christmas themes, and municipal overhead arches displayed Christmas greetings.

Local public celebrations of *Hari Raya Aidilfitri* were not as grand. One mall had one event, a children's *kebaya* contest, while the other mall had six day's of events, which included a *ketupat* weaving arrangement contest, two cooking demonstrations by a popular Malay chef, and performances by a Malay troupe, a religious choir, and two Malay musical groups. Mall employees decorated the mall stages with representations of Malay village houses, coconut trees evoking the village environment, and *pelita* (oil lamps) and *ketupat* (woven banana leaf containers), symbols of Malay customs. Except for the religious choir, public celebrations in the malls emphasized the customary character of *Hari Raya Aidilfitri*, rather than its religious meaning, which is about spiritual victory and blessings after a month of fasting and prayer and the distribution of resources to the poor and needy. On the other hand, its religious meaning, unlike other major holidays, was emphasized on nationally televised programs during the fasting month of *Ramadan*. In the malls, in stark contrast, organizers made *Hari Raya Aidilfitri* to represent the Malay race, just as *Deepavali* represented the Indian race. Christmas and New Year customs, unlike other major public holidays, represents Christians, a religious group, rather than any of the major races in Malaysian society. Since the Malay position as the "natives" is secure on top of the political and cultural hierarchy, no political appearances were required or made to negotiate their sense of belonging.

Similar to the Christmas activities, Chinese New Year events were quite extensive. One mall had ten days of Chinese New Year events, while the other mall had twenty-one days of events. These events included several lion and dragon dances, martial arts demonstrations, God of Prosperity appearances and *ang pau* (red envelopes containing candy) distributions, a fancy dress contest, art contests, game shows, a Chinese calligraphy demonstration, and dance and singing performances. Participants announced and conducted most of these events in Mandarin. Other racial groups participated in some of the game show events and watched some of the demonstrations and performances, but most of the audience and participants were Chinese. Besides the extensive schedule, the mall and street decorations were more elaborate than for any of the other festivals. The stages featured three-dimensional dragons in clouds or water. One of the malls used a sea dragon theme and had gigantic sea animals strung from the ceilings in the main concourse area in front of the stage. Mall promotions staff had an exhibit of 2000 golden paper dragons situated just inside of one of the main entrances. Not only were the municipal street arches displaying Chinese New Year greetings, but there were also numerous overhead arches erected on city streets by Chinese businesses and associations that also strung up red lanterns along many of the main roads in town.

Similar to *Deepavali* and *Hari Raya Aidilfitri*, in relation to Indians and Malays, public celebrations of Chinese New Year represent the customs of the Chinese race. The elaborate and extensive form in which mall organizers celebrated Chinese New Year effected a subversion of Malay symbolic advantages. Malays as the "native" majority generally receive the "public and psychological wages" (Du Bois 1935:700) of having the Malay language as the national language, Islam as the official national religion, and Malay customary attire, dance, and music emphasized in public sites. Some Malay shoppers expressed discomfort with the extensive use of Mandarin during the events and told me that all Malaysian groups are "supposed to

Figure 15 Some mall decorations during Chinese New Year events.
(Photograph by Timothy P. Daniels)

use the national language in public events." Some Malay mall employees expressed strong views about the brevity of *Hari Raya Aidilfitri* events and the extensive form Christmas and Chinese New Year celebrations took this year.[16] In these mall events, the Chinese identity schema rather than the Malay identity schema was emphasized and embodied on top of all others. Mandarin rather than Malay, Chinese traditional attire rather than Malay dress, Chinese music and dance rather than Malay music and dance, and Chinese culture rather than Malay culture, took center stage in the public celebrations, thus subverting the symbolic advantages Malays are expected to receive.

OPEN HOUSE PRACTICES

Open house visiting generally accompanied public celebrations of the major holidays. Intra-racial open house visiting is a long-standing tradition in Malaysia, but interracial open house visiting has just been officially encouraged since political independence in 1957 (Armstrong 1988:127–128). Open house visiting has become a "model of" and "model for" (cf. Geertz 1973) Malaysia's multiracial philosophy of tolerance and harmonious relations between the races and religions that compose the country's diverse citizenry. "Open houses" can be grouped into three broad categories: open houses organized by political leaders and parties that take place in official halls or residences; open houses organized by business owners or managers that take place in offices, restaurants, or other public spaces; and open houses organized by individuals and families that take place at their homes. The open houses that occur in official spaces are the most distant and impersonal and the ones that take place in private individual homes tend to be the most intimate and personal; nevertheless, it is the "gastro-politics" (Appadarai 1981:495) of these personal settings that are the most problematic.

In Melaka, Indian political leaders do not hold any official open houses for *Deepavali*. MIC does not have any large political halls, and they are not allotted official spaces by the government or ruling alliance in which to hold large official open houses, a reflection and reproduction of their lower relative status. Party leaders and local Indians primarily hold open houses in their private homes and invite friends from work, school, and the neighborhood. Relatives and friends of all races come to visit Indian homes. Indians generally make special accommodations for Muslim guests by preparing *halal* food that fulfills Islamic requirements. Yet, few Malay visitors will eat food prepared at Indian Hindu homes, and choose to eat *halal* snacks and boxed drinks instead. In contrast, many Indian Muslims accept the hospitality of their Indian Hindu hosts, expressing a sense of respect for and solidarity with the larger segment of their racial community.

Similarly, there are no Christmas open houses held in official halls or residences. Many non-Muslims visit Christian friends' homes, but few Muslims, Malay or Indian, visit Christian homes. If they do visit, local Muslims just eat *halal* snacks or boxed drinks. The low status and marginality of Christians within cultural categories and in Melakan society overall are reflected and reproduced in these open house activities. Christians are not one of the three major races and are not 'core' submaximal groups in any of these three categories: Malays, Chinese, and Indians.

In contrast, Malay officials organize *Hari Raya Aidilfitri* open houses in several official halls and residences, and thousands of people of all races come to partake of the food and drinks. Local Muslims, Malays and Indians hold open houses in their private homes and invite friends and relatives. Malay open houses in public and private spaces generally provide various kinds of meat, including beef, which are set side by side. This often offends Hindu guests who rely on their hosts to respect their food requirements. On the other hand, most Indian Muslims will not have beef on the menu if they expect Hindu guests, or they will offer beef, kept in another area away from the goat and chicken, to Malay guests. This again, reflects the position of Indian Muslims within the "Indian" category and their attempt to forge closer ties with Indian Hindus, especially those who speak the same Indian language.

Chinese officials hold Chinese New Years open houses in several official halls and residences, and thousands of people of all races attend and partake of the food. This indicates the relatively high status of Chinese in the broader society. *Halal* food is prepared to fulfill Muslim food requirements, but no beef is generally served so as not to offend the Hindu visitors. Besides, according to Chinese custom, people are supposed to eat chicken on Chinese New Year, as it is sign of prosperity and good fortune. Some Chinese business owners and managers organize open houses for their multiracial staff, and have *halal* food catered by Muslim cooks. On the other hand, Chinese in Melaka do not hold open houses in their homes, and choose to hold extended family gatherings instead; they extended the family reunion dinner that occurs on the eve of the New Year over the course of several days, and few Chinese forego this custom to invite Muslims to their homes. To accommodate Muslim eating requirements, Chinese would have to provide *halal* food catered from Malay cooks because Malays would generally refuse to eat and drink from Chinese dishes due the perception that Chinese non-Muslims have contaminated them with pork and alcohol. In refusing to meet these requirements, and by not giving Malays the opportunity to reject their hospitality, Chinese in Melaka once again contest and subvert Malay "symbolic advantages."

CONCLUSION

Cognitive convergences, institutionalized in the festival cycle at sacred sites in Melaka, had provided "models of" and "models for" (cf. Geertz 1973) intercommunal relationships and harmony long before the independent Malaysian government decided to use public celebrations and open house visiting to promote similar ideals. Descendants of the diverse populations of peoples that had been involved in trade along the Straits of Melaka have developed deep cultural affinities that transcended their religious differences. These cognitive convergences entail not only formal or abstract similarities but, more importantly, they entail mutual interpretations of parallels in practice and belief. Although similar cognitive convergences have been institutionalized between some of these cultural categories in other places in Malaysia, these affinities have rarely been extended to the level they have been in Melaka (see Daniels 2000). Even in Melaka, the incorporation of Muslims in this cycle was not able to withstand the effects of the Islamic Revival of the 1970s and 1980s. The government has not been successful in stopping Malays and Indian Muslims from worshipping at *keramat* (The Sun, 17 May 2000:6; The Sun,

24 May 2000:14), but they have succeeded in separating Muslims from the festival cycle at sacred sites. This separation has become part of a more general process of singling Malay "natives" out, from amongst other races, to receive special symbolic and material advantages (see Mahathir Mohamad 1970; see Shamsul A.B. 1994).

Nevertheless, non-*Bumiputera* participants forge closer ties amongst themselves in these shared festival activities and enhance a sense of incorporation and belonging in the broader society. Moreover, the cultural citizenship produced in these activities, contrasts with the dominant form of cultural citizenship in which Malays are the definitive race and Malay culture is the foundation of national culture. This cultural citizenship is part of a process of claiming religious and cultural rights and approaching and respecting your own religion and other people's religions as on par with each other and all others.

Indians and Chinese in Melaka have used public celebrations and open houses as one way to negotiate their position in the social hierarchy. Indians, with a relatively large population in Melaka, have formal recognition of *Deepavali* as a public holiday and people considered them to be significant members of the society, though lower in rank than Malays and Chinese. Indians use public celebrations and open houses as a means to reinforce their status and inclusion as one of the three major races in Melaka and Malaysia. On the other hand, Chinese have resisted the clear social and political hierarchy in Melaka by subverting Malay symbolic advantages in public spaces and by not reproducing Malay privilege in private places (cf. Raymond Lee 1986). Chinese have used their economic power to make Christmas and Chinese New Year festivities overshadow other public celebrations.

Part IV

Chapter Seven
Negotiation and Social Relations

There has been a growing awareness, and concern in Malaysia about the nature of social interactions between people of diverse racial and religious backgrounds and the way they contradict popular images. Projecting positive, harmonious, and hopeful interracial relations has become such a major part of public discourse that when some Malaysians are confronted with representations of these social relations that contradict this hopeful image they express a sense of denial. For instance, an academic recently conducted a survey on racial interaction among students at University Malaya and found that the overwhelming majority of Malays, Chinese, and Indians did not interact socially, a condition she and newspaper journalists interpreted as "racial polarisation" (*The Sun* Oct. 14, 1999). Some university officials disputed the validity of her findings and characterized the condition as a "lack of active interaction among students" rather than "racial polarisation" (*The Sun* Oct. 14, 1999; *The Sun* Oct. 16, 1999). Nevertheless, they organized "goodwill speeches" in which students were given the opportunity to speak about the positive attributes of other races and implemented a policy of making students from different races share dormitory rooms. Similarly, a resident of a suburb of Kuala Lumpur wrote a letter to the editor that suggested that the newspaper might have committed a "great injustice to local varsities and students by concluding that polarisation has reached an alarming level" (*The Sun* Oct. 15, 1999). The writer of this letter argued that the academic survey was unrepresentative, and that significant informal interracial interactions do exist and that where they do not exist one must not conclude that there is enmity or tension between the students. It is a "purely individual" choice to stick among your own "'kind.'" In this letter, the writer wrote:

> I am a product of a local university and I am proud to say I had good relations with students of all races and from all states and I cannot be alone in stating this as it has to be reciprocal on the part of my friends. How do you explain students from various ethnic groups having meals together, "hanging out" in each other's [sic] rooms and having group discussions?

On the other hand, an ex-teacher from Melaka wrote a letter to the editor asserting that the academic study merely stated what was obvious to a casual observer who accepted "informal inter-racial interactions as healthy" (ibid). This ex-teacher went on to write:

> Malaysians interact with other races for official matters or for economic activities. Some organized activities like sports do have a semblance of interaction. Otherwise, generally there is a tendency to stay away from others. Many factors have contributed to this, not the least the political culture. Have we ever heard of the UMNO [sic] assembly deliberating the problems faced by the Chinese or the Indians; or the MCA/MIC assemblies discussing the condition of the Malays?

This letter writer also noted that segregated residential and vernacular primary schools and the leadership and behavioral patterns of teachers and principals enhance racial "polarisation."

Both of these opposing points of view have some credence in relation to my observations of interracial social relations, and discussions about such relations, in Melaka. Over the course of nearly two years in Melaka, I have observed numerous informal interactions between members of different "races" and religions although I have observed many more such interactions between members of the same racial and religious categories. I infer patterns of racial segregation *and* integration from my direct observation of and participation in social interactions and activities. As I have discussed in the previous two chapters, there are significant, though problematic, interracial and inter-religious interactions in public celebrations, religious festivals, and open houses. In fact, my original hypothesis prior to conducting this research was that I would find interracial social cliques and voluntary associations in Melaka due to the way regional culture shows and inter-religious open house visiting structure feeling (R. Williams 1977; B. Williams 1988) and contribute to a sense of belonging. I figured that the understandings Melakans derive from multiracial and inclusive festivities and cultural performances would spill over into other realms of social interaction and a general sense of cultural citizenship.

I have found that this hypothesis, at least as I conceived it initially, is only partially accurate. I have found interracial social cliques, voluntary associations, and marriages, and that interpretations people have of public celebrations and cultural shows, religious festivals, and open houses contribute to the growth of these interracial formations. However, as we have noted previously, local interpretations of these activities tend to express inclusive as well as exclusive notions and sentiments, embodying, as these activities do, models and schemata of "Malaysia's diverse society" and "Malay privilege." Local residents tend to use these well-formed and widespread mental representations to explain and comprehend these events and their negotiation of these seemingly contradictory notions contributes to a sense of belonging, a sense of qualitative citizenship. In this chapter, I will demonstrate that the tensions generated by understandings of inclusion and exclusion, belonged-ness and second-class citizenship, foster the growth of informal forms of interracial social organization and their skewing towards non-Malay segments of the population. These understandings of inclusion and exclusion are shaped by processes of subject making and self-making, that is, dominant and alternative forms of cultural citizenship (cf. Aihwa Ong 1999).

INTERMARRIAGE, NEGOTIATION AND BENEFITS

People of various cultural categories that compose Melaka's diverse society still harbor widespread and strong feelings against marrying outside of one's racial and religious group. The idea that one should marry someone of one's own "race" and religion—categories often conflated and taken to be inherently linked if not synonymous—is generally impressed upon the youth as they grow up and acquire knowledge of the culturally significant differences between people and the means of categorization. Even submaximal cultural categories tend to place a high value upon intermarrying within their own categories, although they placed greater stress upon maximal categories. For instance, Gujerati Indians stress intermarriage among fellow Gujerati Indians but a marriage between a Gujerati and Tamil Indian would be more acceptable than one between a Gujerati and a Malay or Chinese person. Moreover, Malaysian Indians still use caste to reckon appropriate marriage partners for their selves and family members (see Ramasamy 1984). Similarly, Chinese submaximal categories, such as dialect groups, tend to marry amongst themselves, although there are considerably more inter-dialect-group marriages than there used to be when ancient animosities and negative stereotypes were stronger amongst Chinese dialect groups. Malays tend to have some reservations about marrying "Minang" or Malays that follow *adat perpatih,* but intermarriage between other submaximal categories of Malays that follow *adat Temenggong* tends to be less restricted. Yet, of course, marrying a "Minang" is much more acceptable than marrying outside of the Malay race or "Muslim race," such as marrying a Chinese or Indian. These sentiments are indicative of the not so distant pluralist past in which, each group lived out its largely separate existence under the auspices of British colonial rule and of the contemporary pattern of communal political and social organization. However, several of my respondents have informed me that these strongly divisive sentiments are beginning to weaken and change and that Malaysians are becoming more "open" to interracial and inter-religious marriages and informal relationships.

Malays and non-Malays alike have expressed their perceptions to me about how racial sentiments are on the decline as more and more Malaysians of various races are becoming more educated and are interacting more frequently with each other in the same primary, secondary, and tertiary schools, work places, and neighborhoods. For instance, Puan Josephine, a seventy-three year old *Portugis* woman, told me that intermarriage between Malays and Chinese is much greater today than in the past because they work together and form friendly relationships on the job. She added, "Now you see a lot of schools all mixed. Last time Muslims they don't go to convent schools. They go to *sekolah kebangsaan*. But now you see Muslims, all, in the convent schools." These processes of social and economic integration are well underway in Melaka. Indeed, more Malays are working and living in town and there has been a gradual increase in Malay enrollment in "convent schools" in the town area over the last few decades. However, most students in these schools are still overwhelmingly Chinese, and Malay families still have reservations about sending their children to these schools where Christian symbols such as statues of Jesus Christ and Mother Mary are still visible to the public. Moreover, these schools are no longer convent schools, except in name; they are now at least partially funded public schools, *sekolah kebangsaan,* administered through the Department of Education. Malay is the language of instruction rather than English and Malays, and other Muslims, receive Islamic religious classes while non-Muslims attend civic moral classes. These former Catholic convent schools are undergoing a process of transition that involves both the inclusion of more Malay students, teachers, and administrators and the replacement of Catholic symbols and values by Malay symbols and Muslim values.

Moreover, local responses to the map survey and my own on-the-ground observations indicate the changing patterns of spatial organization

Figure 16 Muslim schoolgirls at former convent school under statue of Jesus. (Photograph by Timothy P. Daniels)

in Melaka. Although respondents still exhibited strong associations of particular cultural categories with particular spaces—such as links between Malays and *kampungs,* Chinese and towns, Indians and estates, *Melaka Portugis* and the coastal settlement, and Chitty and the Gadjah Berang Street neighborhood—their responses also exhibited perceptions of several "mixed" spaces. Not only did people think several of these spaces as inhabited by "hybrid" categories, like *Babas* and *Nyonyas* and Indian Muslims, but "unmixed" members of Malay, Chinese, and Indian categories, were also thought to inhabit these spaces. For instance, many respondents informed me that a mixture of several categories of people inhabited several areas north and south of the Melaka River, such as Tengkera, Kelebang,

Durian Daun and Ujong Pasir, and areas more centrally located in Melaka Tengah, such as Pengkalan Rama and Banda Hilir. Several respondents also expressed the perception on their maps that the entire inner rim, located between the inner part of the old town and the outlying areas, contains residential neighborhoods where several different groups live together. Many respondents also noted that while the outlying "Malay" *kampungs* in Alor Gajah and Jasin districts are predominantly Malay communities, some Chinese and Indians also reside in these *kampungs*. My observations confirm these perceptions. However, only one respondent mentioned the *taman* or new residential estates that have been built all over Melaka in the last few decades. My observations indicate that these *taman* neighborhoods, typically designated as "high, middle, and low income" housing estates, are increasingly "mixed" places in which people of all cultural categories live in close proximity to each other. Most of the marriages I have data on, interracial or within the same groups, tend to be between people of similar class backgrounds. My interviews with local people indicate that there are widely shared ideas, spanning cultural categories, about marrying someone of the same economic class or higher.

In addition to the changing social structure, several respondents have mentioned that Prime Minister Mahathir, and the Malaysian government under his leadership has in past years advocated interracial marriage as a means of enhancing national unity and to promote greater understanding and respect amongst the diverse groups in Malaysia. This promotion of interracial marriage through the vehicle of state hegemony and its linkage to the dominant models of "Malaysia's diverse society," which are embodied in many public celebrations, festivals and representations, has added some strength to its impact upon the masses. Indeed, occasional pictures and articles of happy interracial Chinese and Malay couples appear in newspapers showing their families celebrating Islamic holidays and hosting open houses. However, these official campaigns and their effects are somewhat muted by seemingly contradictory policies of "positive discrimination" and attempts by local Malay officials to separate Malays from other races and religions. Moreover, these calls for interracial marriage also have to contend with local responses to trends of Malay separatism and special rights, not least of which is non-Malay opposition to the laws and customs that require conversion to Islam upon marriage to a Muslim. A combination of these factors, the changing social structure facilitating more interracial interactions, and hegemonic political campaigns and discourse and local responses, contribute to an "openness" to engage in interracial marriages. Nevertheless, this "openness" varies according to the cultural categories involved; locals generally considered some interracial and inter-religious marriages to be easier to negotiate than other intermarriages depending upon which cultural categories are coming together and combined.

Local people generally considered interracial marriages between Chinese Buddhist-Taoists and Indian Hindus to be the easiest to negotiate due to religious and cultural similarities, including similar food restrictions and allowances. While at the *Chap Goh Mei* procession from the Yong Chuan Tian Temple, I befriended Chai Chin, a young working class Chinese man who is a devotee of Tee Ong Yah, a high-ranking deity of the Taoist pantheon. His elder sister attended the festival with a young dark-skinned child. Chai Chin informed me that his sister married an Indian Hindu. I asked if his brother-in-law has become a Buddhist and he told me that, "he prays to Hindu gods still and prays to Buddhist gods too, they are not so different." Later, when I interviewed him asking about his ideas about Chinese and Indian intermarriages, he expanded on this theme:

> The Hindu and the Chinese temple is almost the same. Also the gods communicate with one another. That, I know-lah. But say, like one story I hear from the elders. They say the girl god, Kwan Yin, last time she was a god from a Hindu temple. After that, I don't know why, the god from that side, throw away Kwan Yin and then our Chinese temple take it in and dress it up and pray to it. She is the god, like the Mother . . . Chinese and Hindu temples cooperate because they both have Kwan Yin. Now the Hindu temples also have Kwan Yin but it is a little different. Ours is much different; it wears the white clothes-lah . . . The Hindu one is a chocolate color. I think because of this the Chinese and Hindus will be like one-lah . . . If we have already married a Hindu, we can still pray to Tee Ong Yah also, the same, and our wife can follow also. Nothing says you can not follow. You can still follow also. Our people can also follow the Hindu gods. The same, nothing is different. We think it is the same god. Sometimes, my mother also goes over to the Hindu temple. Sometimes, if we are sick or something, we go to the Hindu temple also, *bayar niat*[1] or what-lah. Sometimes I enter also. If my heart feels I want to enter I go . . . The difference is the food only. Our eating is different from them. They all want to eat food on the banana leaf. I like it too. If you eat in the banana leaf the smell is much better . . . My sister married a Hindu man . . . But my own brother is very naughty, he say, you have already married a Hindu person, why do you put just a red cup for Chinese New Year. You have to put a banana leaf too (laughter). You have to put both . . . But I think it is not any more different than that . . . I think all the thinking is the same . . .

Chai Chin recognizes the close religious similarities and connections as the main basis for the relative ease in negotiating intermarriages between Chinese and Indians. Their temples are similar and their deities have close connections, communicating with one another and being different forms of the same deity in some cases. Furthermore, there is no conversion required in these marriages and both parties can and do visit each other's temples, worshipping and making vows to the respective deities. The only differences are minor, such as food tastes and offering and prayer styles, and people can easily accommodate these differences from his perspective. He mentioned that Chinese like to pray with incense sticks and make offerings with small red cups to the Sky God for Chinese New Year but the "thinking" behind these actions and comparable Hindu actions are basically the same. On the issue of food restrictions food restrictions, he and his family do not eat beef because they worship Kwan Yin who is a vegetarian goddess but coming from the "Hindu side" she also has a special sensitivity to the cow. Yet, Chai Chin and his family do eat pork.

Rajan, a working class Indian man, also expressed the significance of similar food restrictions and religious similarities tying Chinese and Indians together. Rajan had informed me that Prime Minister Mahathir promoted interracial marriage but that this plan did not work out overall because of religious and cultural differences. When I asked him why, he told me:

> Food-wise-lah. The only thing is food-wise because for Muslims, they will look for *halal* food-lah. So normally they will not go to Chinese restaurants . . . Chinese go to Malay shops. Chinese, some of them eat this cow, some of them. But most of them pray to Kwan Yin, a Chinese goddess, and don't eat cow. Kwan Yin is just like Amman in India . . . Like, among Chinese and Indians, intermarriage works, intermarriage works . . . Malays like to eat their *sambal*. They eat cow . . . Before they became Muslim they did not eat cow. After they became Muslim they eat cow . . . So some Malays eat cow and some Indians eat pork . . . Because Chinese, their culture is more or less like Indian but just in a different way. They pray all this gods. Like we, we have Amman. They got Kwan Yin. So Chinese people can go to a Hindu temple any time they want and Indian people can go to a Chinese temple any time they want. There is no such thing as we can not go there and they can not come here. Buddhist temples also, Hindus can any time they want and Buddhist people can go to Hindu temples because as I said their sacred life is similar. Furthermore, this Malaysia land is very limited. *Bumi* land, Indians are only around two million, so our numbers are very limited. So when they look for a wife, numbers are very limited, so they just look around. Maybe, if they can not get married with an Indian, they get married with a Chinese . . .

Whereas food restrictions divide Chinese Buddhist-Taoists and Indian Hindus from Malay Muslims, food restrictions unite Chinese and Indians in a common bond. Since some Indians eat pork, which is a customary food preference for Chinese and a food taboo for Malays, and some Chinese do not eat "cow," which is a customary food preference for Malays and a food taboo for Indians, Chinese and Indian food habits tend to coincide. Besides, *sambal* or crushed chili pepper paste is an important part of Malay cuisine in contrast to Indian and Chinese cuisine. Furthermore, similar to Chai Chin's views, Rajan recognizes close religious similarities between Chinese and Indians as key reasons for their successful pattern of intermarriage. They have no restrictions when it comes to worshipping in each other's temples, sacred sites that are interpreted as merely variations on a common theme. Rajan also mentions another reason from an Indian perspective; the fact, that the Indian population is relatively small in Malaysia and so they often look to the much larger, and culturally similar, Chinese population for marriage partners in order to expand their limited options. Although same-race marriage within these respective communities is preferred, locals generally considered intermarriage between Chinese Buddhist-Taoists and Indian Hindus as an easily manageable option due to the lack of stress it places upon the continuation of their respective beliefs and customs.

The "openness" to intermarry between the core religious segments of two of the largest racial groups in Malaysia represents a significant move towards racial integration. These groups are clearly mixing *and* combining in sacred and domestic spaces. However, there are no *Bumiputera* benefits at stake in these intermarriages as both partners and their children remain non-*Bumiputera*. Both parents maintain their racial identities although many Chinese brides may receive Hindu names. The official race of the children of these intermarriages, as in all other cases, recorded on the IC (identity cards), birth certificates, and government computerized records, is reported as the same as the race of the father of the intermarriage. This principle of having the race, and conventionally religion, "follow the father," is a continuation of the patrilineal bias institutionalized in the colonial system that resonates with the patriarchal tendencies in the Chinese, Indian, Malay, and *Portugis* communities. The race recorded for the children of a marriage between a Chinese man and an Indian woman would be "Chinese" and between a Chinese woman and an Indian man would be "Indian." In both cases, the children would be non-*Bumiputera,* and therefore no more eligible for special benefits than their parents were. Yet, these intermarriages and the social ties they entail and create foster a sense of non-Malay and non-*Bumiputera* identity and community.

On the other hand, local residents do not recognize intermarriages between Chinese Buddhist-Taoists or Indian Hindus and *Portugis* or

Chinese and Indian Christians as so easily negotiable. Unlike the previous case, these cases involve significant religious differences that have to be resolved. Even within the same maximal categories, as in Chinese Christian/Chinese Buddhist-Taoist or Indian Christian/Indian Hindu marriages, there remains a lot for parties to negotiate in terms of religious conversion, continued observation of religious practices, and the religion of the children. These respective parties, Christians and Buddhist-Taoists or Hindus or Sikhs often attempt to convert the other party to their religion. The couple and their families and religious officials often become involved in working out the details of these marriages. Although Buddhist-Taoist and Hindu marriages also involve the continued observance of both religions, Christians tend to reserve the category "mixed marriages"[2] for marital unions between Christians and non-Christians that do not involve conversion. During a visit to a local Catholic Charismatic prayer meeting, conducted in a private Indian Catholic home, I interviewed several of the group members. Two of the most vocal respondents were Alice, a young middle-aged *Portugis* woman, and Uncle Gomes, an elderly *Portugis* man. There were some Indian Catholics and one Chinese Catholic present as well. Uncle Gomes and Alice describe the process of negotiation in "mixed marriages" from their perspective:

> I: So conversion happens if a *Portugis* marries a Muslim, but what happens when a *Portugis* marries a Hindu or Chinese Buddhist?

> Uncle Gomes: Oh, those marriages are in the church. Then you are in the church. The priest or minister will officiate the wedding, matrimonial. It is a sacrament and a contract; for good, better or worse, sickness or pain . . .

> I: So if the *Portugis* marries a Chinese or a Hindu then what happens. Do they convert to Christianity?

> Uncle Gomes: No. That is what we call a mixed marriage. Mixed marriages are allowed. You go with your religion and I go with my religion. But the children must be Catholic. They come to an agreement first, a contract before you marry. Oh, you want to marry this Chinese, yeah you can, but first you must promise that the children will all be Catholic, right or not.

> Alice: (latching on to the end of uncle's statement) But sometimes, uncle, even though they are Catholics also, they follow the husband, and the children all go and become a Buddhist. It depends on how your faith is-lah.

> Uncle Gomes: Your promise, you can break your promise . . . But you
> can go away from your agreement also. It is up to you. You have
> to face God afterwards.

From a Catholic perspective, they try to bring the other party over to the
church, where they are given the opportunity to convert to Catholicism or
at least make a commitment to have the future children of the marriage be
baptized as Catholics. Yet, as Alice notes, the outcome of these "mixed marriages" is often contrary to stated aims and agreements and is dependent
upon the convictions and values of the parties involved.

Puan Josephine, a seventy-three year old *Portugis* woman, informed
me of her experience negotiating the marriage of her daughter to an
Indian Hindu man. Puan Josephine and her daughters, her husband is de-
ceased, and a Catholic priest negotiated with the Hindu groom and his father and came to the agreement that the groom would not convert to
Catholicism because the father was opposed to it but the children of the
marriage would be Catholics. Puan Josephine describes the process of negotiation from her perspective and experience:

> Puan Josephine: To me mixed marriages is nothing. But only if the boy's
> side and the girl's side can take it-lah. Like what I am saying about
> my son-in-law. Only the father can take it and I can take it, it is OK.
> We are happy. It can not be only one person and the other can not.
> So it can not go together . . . Muslim they can not. To us, Christians,
> can. That is why I am letting you know we do not force the religion.
> We do not force what you are. With Muslims, you have to, no mat-
> ter what religion you are, you know, no matter if you are Christian,
> you are Chinese, you have to convert. But to us, no, to us Christians,
> we do not force. Only the family discusses it and both sides happy. It
> is up to you. Both sides happy. To us Christians it is like that. But we
> must have the voice from that side.

> I: But on the government registration, the government considers the
> child is Indian or Serani?

> Puan Josephine: No, the children have to be a Christian-lah. Children have
> to be a Christian, only the father, if he is a boy, like an Indian boy. But
> if you marry in church, the child has to be a Christian. But once you mix
> marry in church, the child must be Christian, must be baptized.

> I: But if you marry in a Hindu temple?

> R: That one, if the girl goes to the other side, then they go to the other
> side. But to us, we don't mind. We Christians, we don't mind that. It

> is up to them. Muslims only can not. They are very strict . . . To us, we think everyone is human, all the same.
>
> I: Did he get a Christian name or an Indian name?
>
> R: Yes if you want. Like my grandson, his Christian name is "Michael" and then, "Michael Goren." "Goren" is an Indian name. Then "Goren" is the second name. The first name is the Christian name. "Michael Goren" and then the father's name, "Nagamaniam." That is the surname, father's name-lah . . . They are happy. "Michael Goren Nagamaniam."

She stresses the flexibility that Christians have on the issue of religious conversion and the location of the wedding ceremonies, flexibility absent in the case of intermarriage with Muslims. Without the force of the state behind them, they seek to reach a settlement that all sides can live with. On the other hand, just as Uncle Gomes did, she expresses the value Christians place upon the future baptism of the offspring of the marriage. The race of her grandson is officially Indian on government records, following the principle of patrilineal inheritance of racial categorization, and is evident in his name, but his religion is officially Catholic. In the *Portugis* community though, they often identify the children of these "mixed marriages" as "Eurasian" or "Indian Eurasian" in contrast to "*Portugis*" that is reserved for offspring from two *Portugis* parents. Of course, in the case of *Portugis-Portugis* marriages, the children would carry *Portugis* surnames. This distinction is relevant to *Bumiputera* benefits, to some extent, because political officials have awarded *Portugis* "honorary *Bumiputera*" status and thereby making them eligible to put money into high interest savings accounts reserved for *Bumiputera* (see Sarkissian 2000:66, 200). The "Chinese Eurasians" or "Indian Eurasians," like Puan Josephine's grandson, would not be eligible for these benefits because their fathers are Chinese or Indian, but if the father was *Portugis* they would be officially *Portugis*, carrying a *Portugis* surname, and eligible to whatever *Bumiputera* benefits are made available to *Portugis*.

Like Puan Josephine's daughter, Alice also married an Indian Hindu but her negotiations to reach a similar agreement were tenser than what Puan Josephine described and both sides were not happy with the initial outcome. Later in my interview with the Charismatic prayer group, I asked Alice about her personal experiences and she related the following:

> I: So what happened with your marriage (to Alice)? Was your husband an Indian Christian already or a Hindu?

Alice: No, no. He was a Hindu. No for eighteen, nineteen years he was a Hindu and I was Christian. So I think by the way I pray at home and he saw it and the children prayed and every time we had prayers at home. So he got picked up (Uncle Gomes repeats this phrase in the background) and he joined but I never did force my husband. Because our priests, they say we can not force. Don't force them because if they become Christians, then they will not be a good Christian.

I: What was your agreement at marriage? Was it that the children would be Christians?

Alice: No, at that time, uh, the first time he asked me, when we were in love-lah. He asked me to be a Hindu. And he give me an Indian name also. So we were, I think we were, friends for seven years, we knew each other. So he told me I should be a Hindu and the parents gave me a Hindu name. Then I said, 'if it comes to that way and I have to become a Hindu, I think we have to forget the whole thing.' But of course, sadness in my heart-lah, because you know a man for seven years and of course you are in love with that man. It was so much pain. So I put down the phone, sadness I lived with it. Then I thought to myself and my sister said it is written, maybe God wants it that way. So after that he called back again and said, 'OK we can have a mixed marriage.' I will be a Hindu and you will be a Catholic. At that time I quickly spoke about the children-lah. And then he said we would see about it. So when the children was born, I remember that time, I said, 'I think it is time for my children to be baptized.' He had tears in his eyes, so much tears, because he knew that his children were going to be Catholic. He was very unhappy about it. So after that, but he had no choice (swallowed this word). Since I talked to him and slowly he, but he did not like being a Christian-lah, so much of problems. He would send me to church of course he would not go into church. We had a mixed marriage-lah. And he would not even kneel down. I said, 'I cannot force you.' Your God is your God and my God is my God. After that I came in here and had prayers in my own home, with the children, and I did not force him. And after that, I think, seventeen or eighteen years. I did not force him but he decided to become a Christian.

Alice also expresses the idea of flexibility and not forcing the conversion of the spouse while on the issue of the religion of the offspring she is not so flexible. She was firm on the matter of not converting to Hinduism and on the baptism of her children as Catholics. Alice and her husband have two daughters and they both are Catholic girls who attend a public "convent school." However, after getting married, she and her husband did not openly display religious pictures or altars in their home, a sensitive issue in many such marriages. Her husband had a room in which he kept his altar and deities and he worshipped them privately in this room. Alice's husband converted to Catholicism after around eighteen years of a "mixed marriage." After many tense years, she and his family are on good terms.

As Alice noted, contrary to the negotiated outcome of Puan Josephine's daughter's case, these "mixed marriages" between Christians and non-Christians are open to lots of possibilities and are contingent upon the convictions and values of the parties involved. Sumitra, a Malayali Hindu professional woman, described the "mixed marriage" of two of her fellow office workers, the groom was an Indian Christian and the bride was an Indian Hindu, in which the whole process was fraught with tension and the mixture of both side's religious practices. In the engagement ceremonies, they had Hindu lamps and coconut offerings and chants as well as readings from the Holy Bible, and in the "church" wedding, the couple wore *maleh* (flowered garland) as in Hindu temple weddings but no *pottu* (paste dots in the midst of the forehead). Sumitra described the couple as being "caught between two in-laws that would not budge," both sides wanted proceedings to follow their religious practices and would not accept the practices of the other party. The children from this marriage are "born Christians" officially but what will happen in the future was not settled according to Sumitra.

Similarly, in many cases of "mixed marriages" between Chinese Buddhist-Taoists and Chinese Christians or *Portugis* Catholics, the outcomes are quite variable. In some cases, all of the children follow the religion of the Christian parent, but in many others, the children are split religiously, with the sons following the Buddhist-Taoist father and the girls following the Christian mother. Sons are of a special category in Chinese families, they are the ones that must carry on the clan name, and so Chinese fathers often send them to Chinese vernacular schools viewing them as the key perpetuators of Chinese culture. Chai Chin, perplexed with the way a Chinese Christian girl rejected his advances, expressed his unwillingness to negotiate the religion of his sons.

> One thing I don't understand-lah, this is different from Hindu, it is Christian-lah. Last time, before I met my girlfriend in Singapore, I met one here who told me she was Christian. I told her I liked her and wanted to move (get involved) with her. She told me she was Christian and that she could not move with me. I asked her why. She said because our race is different. She is Chinese but Christian. Because she is Christian and I am Buddhist, she said she could not. I did not know the reason . . . I think it is nothing. All the god is the same god. If you love the person why can't you move with them . . . I would not say you can not go to the church if that is your wish. If you want to go you go. I know in my house I will put the Tee Ong Yah, or what, all, if you think

you want to pray you can pray. Why not, the same god. If you don't want and you want to go to the church, than it is your wish. I know after that, all my sons will actually follow me, what. Then it is your wish. I will not force you and say you can not go to church . . . Until now I can not understand her reason . . .

I: Some Christians want people to convert or to have the children be Christian . . . But you want your sons to follow you.

R: If she had already told me that, I would have thought about it-lah. If you want that, see, the girls you can get it, they can be Christian, but the boys, no, they have to follow me. The boys are actually mine, or what.

In contrast to his recognition of the similarities and lack of barriers between Hinduism and Buddhist-Taoism, he could not comprehend the barriers erected between him and a Chinese Christian girl. Chai Chin understood that they were of different "races" but could not understand why it should matter because from his perspective all of the gods, from whatever religion, are all the same. He expressed flexibility on the issue of religious worship, she could worship the gods he will have in the home or go to church, and the female children can follow their mother but the sons, are in a special class, and must follow him. In fact, this is what I have observed in many cases of this sort, the sons "follow the father" and become Chinese Buddhist-Taoists and Confucian ancestor worshippers whereas the daughters "follow the mother" and become Christians.

However, as we have noted in cases of Buddhist-Taoist and Hindu marriages, Christians point out their similarity to and solidarity with other non-Malays and non-*Bumiputera* in "mixed marriages" in contrast to the distance that exists in cases of interracial marriages with Muslims. As we have seen, local Christians and other non-Malays often criticize the fact that conversion is only mandatory when anyone, man or woman, is marrying a Muslim. Many assert that if people were only applying the principle of "women-following-men" in all cases, it would not be so strongly opposed. After all, non-Malays often point out that in the cases of Chitty and *Babas* and *Nyonyas*—hybrid cultural categories—"local" Malay women followed their Indian Hindu and Chinese Buddhist-Taoist husbands and the children followed their fathers in terms of religion and race. It is the fact that women *and* men, and the offspring have to follow their Malay partners regardless of gender that appears to be most perturbing to non-Malays.[3] On an episode of the nationally televised program, *Global*, entitled "National Unity: The Key to Development," which was aired during March 2000, a prominent

Indian *Datuk* amidst a diverse panel of discussants argued that the requirement of conversion should be eliminated so that the assimilation of ethnic
minorities can be facilitated by intermarriage. He asserted that a "relaxation
of religion" would remove this major obstacle to national unity. A Malay
man who called at the end of the program found his comments insulting and
outrageous, as did several of my Malay friends. In addition, Christians and
other non-Malays often criticize the "strictness" of Islamic rules that leads,
in their view, to the separation of their converted family members from their
families. Puan Josephine expressed it in this fashion:

> Yes, because uh, you know if a Chinese becomes a Christian or an
> Indian becomes a Christian, because especially the *makan* (food), you
> know, all the same. Only to a Muslim, it is different-lah. So if they con-
> vert to Christian they can sit in one table with the parents. But when
> they become a Muslim they can not sit together at one table. See like my
> friend's sons, both, I told you, marry a Muslim. Christmas only they
> come, but they don't eat. They just take only cold drinks. You see the
> difference. You see the divide. But if they were Chinese, then they could
> eat together. That is the big difference, with *makan*, that is the big dif-
> ference-lah. Then like my friend also, she can not ask the daughter-in-
> law to eat because you know the eating is not the same. So, if she eats
> and she doesn't know also, we create the sin, you know. Because she is
> innocent, she does not know anything. So we create the sin. So we can
> not do that, we can not do that. Things only we can give, we give.
> Things what we can not, we don't.

Similar to Chai Chin and Rajan, Puan Josephine points out the distance that
food restrictions produce between Muslims and non-Muslims whereas the
lack of divisive food taboos among non-Muslims facilitates social solidarity
and intimacy. Moreover, Muslim food taboos place a moral onus on the
non-Christian family members which makes the distance seem insurmount-
able because there is no way they can disregard Muslim food taboos and
serve something *haram* (forbidden), this sin would be theirs and not the
Muslim who eats the food unwittingly. To the contrary, Christians just like
other non-Muslim and non-*Bumiputera* parties to "mixed marriages" can
reinforce intimate relations through sitting down at the same table and sharing food together with their relatives. While commensality and hospitality,
key means of constituting and enacting consanguineal, affinal, neighborly,
and friendship ties within and across diverse communities of Melaka, are
problematic in relations with Malays, they foster ties amongst non-Malays.
These kinship relationships, crossing racial and religious categories, become
part of the growth of non-Malay and non-*Bumiputera* identity and commu-

nity and part of the process of incorporation into the broader society. Their "openness" to these intermarriages and their interpretations and feelings that these non-Malay groups are all "one-lah" and "all the same" expresses a sense of belonging and a sense of cultural citizenship in contrast to the dominant sense of cultural citizenship that sets Malays apart from other groups. Moreover, this sense of cultural citizenship contrasts with, and sometimes contests, the dominant, hierarchical sense of cultural citizenship that sets Malays apart from other groups as the "natives" or "original inhabitants" who most fully belong (cf. Hefner 2001:29).

Intermarriages between any non-Muslims, from any non-Malay cultural category, and Malays or other Muslims, are generally considered to be the most difficult to negotiate and, from Malay and non-Malay perspectives, the most undesirable. Non-Malay cultural categories, as indicated in much of the discourse presented above, point to cultural differences, such as food choices, and their divisive ramifications, and the fact that religious conversion is mandatory to demonstrate the undesirability of marriage to Malays. In contrast to all cases of non-Muslim marriages, which are under the jurisdiction of civil law, all Muslim marriages fall under Islamic personal law, administered on the state level, and must adhere to local interpretations of Islamic law. Local non-Muslims know that conversion to Islam is mandatory before a non-Muslim can marry a Muslim and they highly resent this practice. They generally turn to, or the Department of Islamic Religion directs them to, the Malaysian Muslim Welfare Organization (Perkim— Pertubuhan Kebajikan Islam Malaysia) for assistance with the process of converting to Islam before marrying a Muslim. Puan Fariza, a Perkim employee, told me that about 90% of all converts to Islam in Melaka enter the Islamic faith for marriage, and around 10% convert after getting information from their friends and studying about the religion. She estimated that from 120 to 150 people convert annually, with the highest percentage Chinese, followed by Indians, other *Bumiputera* groups, and foreigners.

There is a widespread notion that when people from non-Malay races convert to Islam, these people are becoming Malay. Many people use the popular phrase *masuk Melayu* or "becoming Malay" to refer to conversion to Islam, expressing the intimate association between Islam and Malay categorization. Despite some Muslim activists' attempts to dissociate Islam from Malay identity, separating *agama* (religion) from *bangsa* (race in this context), religion and race remain intertwined in the popular mindset. When I confronted Wong, a Chinese woman who works in a shopping center, with the fact that many Muslims in Malaysia and around the world are from racial backgrounds other than Malay—like me for instance, an African

American—and that therefore being Malay and being Muslim are two different things, she told me that,

> For us here they are the same, Malay and Muslim is the same. Almost 98 to 99% of Malays are Muslims, so it is the same . . . We do not know much about or pay attention to Muslims elsewhere in the world . . . Being Malay and being Muslim is the same for us . . .

Furthermore, this wedding of the Malay category with Islam and the perception that non-Malays who convert to Islam are "becoming Malay" indicates the conventional distance between being "Indian" or "Chinese" or "*Portugis*" and being a Muslim. People of non-Malay cultural categories tend to look at the process of converting to Islam for marriage as a process of losing their own identity and heritage. They perceive the changes that their family members or friends undergo in the process of conversion to Islam for marriage as so thoroughgoing and complete that they feel that their relatives are opting for another "race" over their own (see Raymond Lee 1987:73). In response to this state-mandated conversion, many local non-Muslims erect and tighten their group boundaries against the perceived threats that intermarriage to Muslims holds for them. Several Indians and Chinese have informed me that their parents and other family members have told them they will disown them if they marry a Muslim. Gita and Chandra, two Indian nursing students, informed me that their parents told them that they can marry any of the diverse groups in Malaysia they like, except for Muslims, and that if they broke this rule by marrying a Muslim they would be disowned. When I asked Chai Chin if many Chinese marry Malays, he told me that they do not and continued:

> Occasionally someone may fall in love and want to marry a Malay, but it is not good for Chinese men to marry Malays, they are in a special category . . . since they will carry on the clan name. If they marry a Malay then they will not be able to carry on the clan name and it will be very bad, especially if they are the only son. If there are more sons then it is not so bad. Many Chinese parents disown and disinherit their children if they marry Malays, but that is sort of old-fashioned (he looked for my response).

> I: What would you do if your son married a Malay woman?

> Chai Chin: I would disown my son if he was the only son I had and give the money to an orphan home where it would be put to better use since my son would not even carry on his father's and grandfather's name.

The pressure on Chinese sons, especially only-sons, to not marry Muslim women and convert to Islam, is heavier than the pressure on Chinese daughters due to the high value placed upon males carrying on clan names. Even if Chinese daughters married Chinese men, their children will carry on the clan name of their husbands. Many Chinese converts cope with this intense familial pressure by keeping their conversion a secret.

Ibrahim, a Chinese office clerk, has kept his conversion to Islam and plans to marry a Malay woman a secret from his family because his relatives have threatened him with grievous consequences were he to commit such acts. His mother has threatened to kill herself and other relatives have threatened to disown him even though he has several other brothers and is not the only son. Ibrahim converted to Islam by stating his declaration of faith[4] in front of witnesses at Department of Islamic Religion offices in the state mosque almost two years ago as of the time I left the field. Officials of the religious department filed documents verifying his conversion and changed information on his government registration identifying him as a Chinese Muslim. He fell in love[5] with a Malay woman who he has worked with for over seven years and some of his Malay friends have taken him to their village to teach him some rudimentary knowledge about Islam. He also attended classes organized by the Muslim Welfare Association, a non-governmental organization that works closely with the government to service converts to Islam and to invite non-Muslims to Islam. Ibrahim informed me that he plans to let his family know he has converted to Islam after he gets married and moves out of their house. He hopes to be able to go back to visit his family for Chinese New Years and to sit down at the same table with them for the customary family reunion dinner but he plans to bring *halal* food for him and his future wife to eat. According to Cik Mat Goh, a local Chinese professional who converted to Islam around two decades ago and is familiar with many Chinese converts, these sorts of cases and pattern of secrecy are not rare amongst Chinese.

> Cik Mat Goh: After already converting to Islam little by little I even looked for a way to support myself.
>
> I: Did your family already know?
>
> Cik Mat Goh: At that time my family did not know because it is also the culture of Chinese converts to Islam to like to keep it secret in Malaysia. From my experience, Chinese converts do not like to let their families know. Because we can say that 80% of their families will be angry and will threaten them and they want to be left alone by their family.
>
> I: I have a Chinese friend who says his mother threatened to kill herself. His family still does not know.

> Cik Mat Goh: Yes, that is the culture of those who enter Islam, keeping
> it a secret. I was also just like that. For me, after two years only-lah.
> They found out when I was already in Muar (town bordering Melaka
> in neighboring state of Johor). (my translation)

Cik Mat Goh, as a young man, kept his own conversion to Islam a secret from
his family for over two years. Ibrahim has also kept this secret from his Chinese
co-workers and friends. When I called him on his job, I used his former
"Chinese" name and not his "Muslim" name so as not to tip off his Chinese
co-workers about his conversion. Ibrahim would attend Friday congregational
prayers in one of the local mosques during his lunch break. I often saw Ibrahim
at Friday prayers with his Malay co-workers. However, when he came alone, I
noticed that none of the Malay Muslims would talk to him or befriend him.
Oftentimes, Chinese converts are isolated from their families and isolated
within the predominantly Malay, Muslim community. This isolation, within
the Muslim community, is not as drastic for Indian converts because there is a
sizable Indian Muslim segment that has a long history in Malaysia.

On the other hand, Malays generally consider marriages to non-
Malay, Muslim converts to be undesirable as well. The non-Malay and non-
Muslim backgrounds of the converts is frowned upon and viewed as a
potential problem. Zalidah, a young Malay professional, informed me that
it is not so bad if you are of a different "race" but have an Islamic background but if you are of a different "race" and of a non-Islamic background
than that is very bad. There is the fear that the person may not embrace
Islam wholeheartedly and may turn back towards their old ways. Yati and
Liza, two married Malay women, discussing one of their younger, unmar-
ried co-workers, expressed these concerns and reservations about marriage
to non-Malays.

> Yati: This Wati, I do not like her attitude at all. She said she does not
> want to marry a Malay man. They always lie . . . she says. . . . So she
> wants to marry a Chinese man and she has lots of Chinese friends. . . .
> I told her she should marry within her race and should not give up
> on Malay men. A Chinese man would have to convert to Islam but it
> is different for a Malay man marrying a Chinese woman. He is the
> man and can lead the women along the right path but she is a woman
> and cannot lead her husband . . . They may both become *murtad*[6] . . .
> She should marry in the Muslim race.

> Liza: It is better to marry someone brought up in Islam because if they
> stray it will not be too far. They still have their moral upbringing to
> keep them from going to far. . . . but converts may go back to their
> old ways . . . they have no foundation to fall back upon . . .

> Yati: Yes, that is true. I tell my daughter to marry in the Muslim race but it is his family and religious background which is most important. He does not have to be wealthy . . . and my husband agrees with me . . .

Their concerns are gendered values, as they are more prohibitive of a Malay woman marrying a convert than they are of a Malay man because they assume a man is able to exert greater leadership and influence over his spouse. From this perspective, if a Malay woman marries a convert she may not be able to keep her non-Malay husband on the path of practicing Islam, whereas a Malay man would be able to lead his non-Malay wife to an Islamic way of life. Wati is a young Malay woman who usually does not wear a *tudung* and wears tight pants and blouses rather than *baju kurung*, flouting local Islamic dress codes. Yati does not like Wati's attitude and behavior and feels that she is a "free thinker" in need of coaching and discipline so that she will uphold Malay traditions and customs rather than "modern" ideas and practices. Zalidah also informed me that although Malay families do not want their children, male or female, to marry other races and religions, the pressure is stronger on Malay daughters and sisters to marry within the "Muslim race" than it is for Malay sons and brothers. This contrasting sense of compulsion reflects and reproduces gender constructions of men and women in Malay communities (see Banks 1983:68, 92–101; Ong 1987:87; cf. Carsten 1997:22). The convergence of Malay values upon daughters and Chinese values upon sons, no doubt accounts for the much higher frequency of Malay male-Chinese female intermarriages that I have observed and been informed about.

In addition to strong attitudes about the undesirability of such unions, non-Malays and Malays have negative perceptions of the non-Malay, converting party, in these intermarriages. There are widespread notions that the non-Malay person is marrying a Malay person in order to get access to *Bumiputera* benefits such a business, employment, house buying, and educational privileges and priorities (see Raymond Lee 1987:73). Wong and Sumitra both told me that Chinese businessmen marry Malays to obtain access to favorable contracts and some of the high percentage of business deals set aside for Malays. Similarly, Rajan told me that some Indians marry Malays because of the incentives of land and money promised to them by the Malay government. Some local Chinese and Malays have even told me that some wealthy Chinese men convert to Islam in order to practice polygamy legitimately like their Malay counterparts. These popular conceptions tend to coincide with other negative perceptions of non-Malay converts; in particular, non-Malay assertions that they are "becoming Malay" and Malay suspicions about how they are not sincerely embracing Islam.

However, contrary to popular conceptions, *Bumiputera* benefits are not so easily accessible by means of intermarriage to Malay Muslims. Although non-Malay persons in these intermarriages convert to Islam and people often perceives them as "becoming Malay," they generally do not identify themselves as Malay and their official registration still identifies them as Chinese or Indian. After conversion, they become "Chinese Muslims" or "Indian Muslims" officially and so they remain non-*Bumiputera* and not entitled to special benefits. In some cases, as Muslim converts or *mualaf,* they may receive *zakat mualaf,* or alms to poor Muslims if they qualify economically. I knew of one case in which a middle aged Chinese widow, her Malay husband has passed away, who received financial assistance from the government but it was not *Bumiputera* benefits. Similarly, the children of many non-Malay and Malay intermarriages are not officially *Bumiputera* although non-Malay respondents have often expressed the view that they were. A few, more highly informed respondents, Sumitra, for instance, told me that only the second generation of offspring from these non-Malay and Malay intermarriages become *Bumiputera* and then only if they intermarry with Malays. This is only true in some cases, because according to the conventional patrilineal rule of "following the father," this depends on the race of the father. If he is Malay then the children will also be officially Malay and *Bumiputera* but if the father is an Indian or Chinese convert to Islam then the children will be Indian or Chinese Muslims and not *Bumiputera*. However, even the children of Indian and Chinese male converts, generally identify themselves as "Malay" in public and are perceived as "Malay" in public, and are identified as such by others. Yet, government officials, who have the power to decide whether they are qualified for *Bumi* benefits, have access to other legal and computerized records that identify them as "Chinese Muslims" or "Indian Muslims" and their fathers as "Chinese" or "Indian." The converted parents appear on these records with the *bin Abdullah* (son of Abdullah) or *binti Abdullah* (daughter of Abdullah) at the end of their new Muslim names marking them as non-Malay and *non-Bumiputera* converts. Nowadays, civil servants also record the original "non-Muslim" names of converts in the government documents. Moreover, personal identity cards (IC), computer records, and birth certificates identify this first generation of offspring according to the race of their father. On the other hand, even this first descendant generation, if their father is Malay, is entitled to *Bumi* benefits and special privileges.

Cik Mat Goh, who is married to a Malay woman, describes how things work from his experience in contrast to popular opinion:

So this is their culture in Malaysia, especially if a Chinese person is entering Islam; it is a sort of negative thinking-lah. If people are entering Islam, they say it is to raise their status, to raise some profits, *Bumiputera* benefits. Because *Bumiputera* in Malaysia get benefits if they buy a house, whatever-lah . . .

I: Special privileges.

Cik Mat Goh: There are privileges. We do not get them. We are not considered *Bumiputera*. Converted people are not considered *Bumiputera*.

I: You are not Malay?

Cik Mat Goh: Always Chinese. There are no special privileges.

I: You don't get any of them? How about the *amanah saham* (shares in high interest savings accounts)?

R: There are none. Those *amanah saham,* there are some who can receive them but it has to go through a process. They consider the application for a long time. I don't know much about it so I have been slow to ask.

I: But there are no other benefits?

R: Because we all know here, *Bumiputera,* they have an easier life. *Bumiputera* are Malays, pure Malays. Those who are Malay descendants are called *Bumiputera*. Like *Bumiputera* in Sabah, Sarawak, Malays are *Bumiputera* . . .

I: But your and other convert's children get *Bumiputera* status?

R: All of my children are Chinese Muslims; they are not considered *Bumiputera*.

I: Because their father is Chinese. They have 'of Chinese descent' on their IC?

R: But this does not really follow the Constitution; I feel that it does not mention this sort of thing. It is just the government that sometimes likes to push this because I have already come across this sort of problem . . . A Chinese person who has entered Islam gets results that are very good. He asks for a scholarship to go to a university, but he can't get it, because he is not *Bumiputera*.

I: But he was rich or a normal person?

R: Oh here, he was a normal person.

I: A normal person, why was he not able to get it?

R: Because they said just for *Bumiputera*. There are departments, like doctors, medical-lah. Medical always have a quota. This is for *Bumiputera* in Malaysia. These people, if they go to study they get assistance. But if you are Chinese, Muslim-lah, or converted, you can not get it.

I: Chinese Muslims can not get it?

R: Even if we buy a house also, we don't have any privileges.

After pointing out that people, including his Chinese relatives, have a negative attitude about Muslim converts in Malaysia, he explains that converts do not receive any *Bumiputera* benefits, except for shares in high interest savings accounts but this is not automatic and requires an uncertain application process. *Portugis* "honorary *Bumiputera*" reportedly receive more, definite access to these savings accounts as the main benefit of their unofficially declared special status. As is the case with *Portugis,* according to Cik Mat Goh, Muslim converts and the children of non-Malay, *male* converts, do not receive any of the other special privileges reserved for *Bumiputera.* He expresses the opinion that reserving these special rights for Malays, whereas the state excludes Chinese Muslims, is not consistent with the Malaysian constitution and is only the whim of government. Moreover, he is critical of the fact that non-Muslim *Bumiputera* in Sabah and Sarawak receive special privileges, just like Malay *Bumiputera,* while the government denies Muslim converts such support. For Cik Mat Goh, this is not consistent with Islamic principles that dictate that all Muslims be treated equally.[7] In the next segment of the same interview with Cik Mat Goh, he clarifies how the patrilineal principle works to deny eligibility of *Bumiputera* benefits to the children of non-Malay male converts.

I: But I spoke with a Malay man who married a *Nyonya,* she just entered Islam and all their children get scholarships, all are *Bumiputera.*

R: Because it follows the father.

I: But this is normal?

R: It is normal because it follows the father but on the other hand if it is a Malay woman married to a man who is a Chinese Muslim, he does not get *Bumiputera.* Like my marriage, my children can not get it because my children follow me, follow the father.

I: But is this official, because I have met a woman who wears a *tudung,* she has a Muslim name, is it possible that she can get it or not? What is your experience? When I spoke to her she told me that her father was Chinese, her mother is Malay, and she considers herself Malay, perhaps she can get a scholarship, I don't know yet, but what is your experience like? People can negotiate, you know, and possibly get it for their child?

R: OK, like my new identity card (he pulls it out and shows me) in Malaysia, a youngster who has already reached the age of twelve years, I think in America there is also the same thing, he has to get an IC. On this IC, they write, they place *"keturunan"* (descent). *Keturunan* here, later they will look at this listing, oh your father is Chinese Muslim, his children are also Chinese Muslim. They can not get *Bumiputera* . . . They can not get special rights because their background is in the computer . . . and on the birth certificate . . . This is the actual situation. Because many people figure that we who converted, especially in Malaysia, can get all sorts of privileges but this really does not happen.

I related the case of Encik Yunos, a Malay man, long married to a *Nyonya,* who has three children from this marriage and they are all considered Malay and *Bumiputera.* Encik Yunos proudly informed me that all of his children, now professionals, attained a high degree of education due to government support and scholarships. As Cik Mat Goh explains, the children of Malay fathers and non-Malay women are eligible for benefits because the children inherit Malay classification and *Bumiputera* entitlement from their father. Then I described the case of Norhayati, a young "Malay" woman, born of a *Baba* father and Malay mother, who tried to negotiate *Bumiputera* educational benefits in order to be able to attend a local college. Norhayati, like most of the other children of these intermarriages I was familiar with, chose to identify herself as Malay contrary to official identification as Chinese Muslim, and tried to negotiate *Bumiputera* status and benefits. According to Cik Mat Goh, civil servants and administrators generally decide these cases by the racial descent of the person on official documentation. However, Norhayati's case demonstrates that these situations are not so cut and dry and that they are in fact open to negotiation. She was able to qualify for *Bumiputera* financial aid, but only after her father wrote a letter to the program administrators explaining how he converted to Islam to marry her mother and so forth. Indeed, the children of non-Malay male converts are not automatically entitled to benefits due the conventional application of the patrilineal principle and their official categorization, but possibilities for negotiating qualification are still open given the satisfactory fulfillment of additional criteria.

Now we can see why Sumitra's comment about the second generation of descendants for these intermarriages attaining *Bumiputera* status is only partially true. Once again, it would depend on the gender of the Malay party to this marriage. For instance, if Cik Mat Goh's daughter, a "Chinese Muslim," marries a Malay man, the children of this marriage would become Malay and *Bumiputera,* but if Cik Mat Goh's son marries a Malay woman, the children of this marriage would remain Chinese Muslim and non-*Bumiputera* like their father and grandfather. However, the offspring of this generation would not be as marked as non-Malay and non-*Bumi* as the previous generation because their fathers would not necessarily have the *bin Abdullah* or original "Chinese" names as their grandfathers did. Nevertheless, official Malay classification and *Bumiputera* status, legal categories inscribed in the Constitution and NEP, are inherited through the male line and are only attainable with the infusion of the "blood" of a Malay father (cf. Shamsul A.B. 1994:107; cf. Boulanger 2000:61–62).

Not only are the non-Malay perceptions of and responses to these intermarriages and the official modes of classification and entitlement embedded with "Malay privilege," so is the Malay and non-Malay intermarriage process, from conversion to everyday domestic life. Although conversion

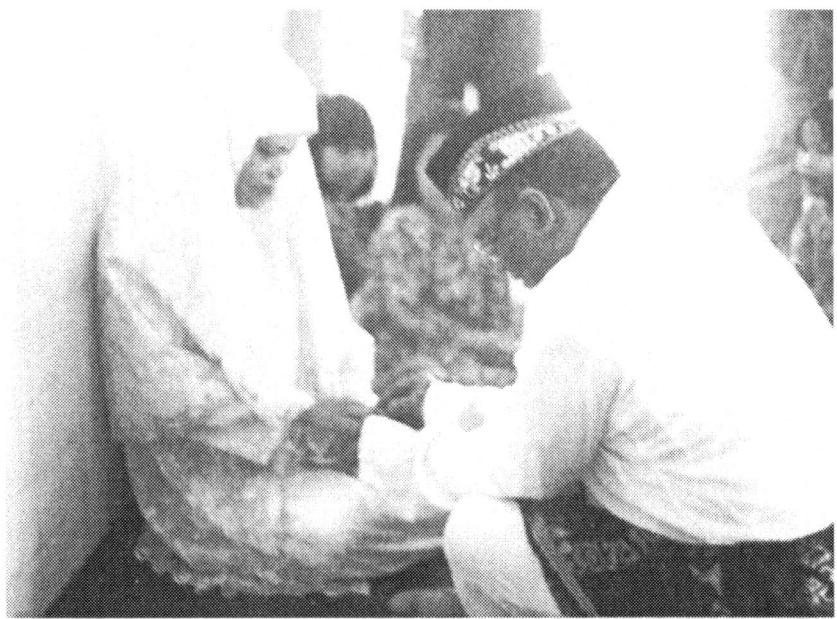

Figure 17 *Melaka Portugis* groom placing ring on finger of Malay bride in local mosque. (Photograph by Timothy P. Daniels)

does not generally entail the shift of identity from non-Malay to Malay, it does involve a drastic shift in the personhood of the individual. The convert undergoes a sort of rite of passage, of being separated from his or her family, educated about Islamic beliefs and practices, and then re-aggregated into society with a new name and religious identity (see Van Gennep 1960[1909]; see Victor Turner 1969). The separation from one's family, and racial community, often continues long after the phase of re-aggregation occurs, and is a major criticism of such marriages from a non-Malay perspective. However, Malays often see this separation as a necessary condition to the successful perpetuation of the marriage as the former non-Muslim must be separated from his former non-Muslim background to make sure that he or she has made a full break from a non-Islamic way of life. The Department of Islamic Religion and Islamic enforcement are important and useful institutions for the disciplining of these new converts and their families. Muslim officials in these government departments often have to deal with angry non-Muslim family members who are opposed to their children marrying a Muslim. In some cases, they have to argue with angry non-Muslim parents who feel that the state is allowing their children to convert without their permission and intervene to keep non-Muslim parents from forcibly stopping the marriage process. In addition, government officials often organize the actual wedding ceremonies that are performed in accordance with local Malay Muslim customs. Following the wedding, the couple lives with the Malay family or at least in a Malay neighborhood, and any contact with the non-Muslim family members is a sensitive matter because of the *haram* behavior assumed to go on in the non-Malay household. How can the new Muslim and spouse eat, drink and pray in a place made "unclean" by the presence of pork, alcohol, idols, and perhaps even dogs?

The Department of Islamic Religion holds a series of classes and symposia for new Muslims and their spouses and continually seeks to involve them in activities in the state mosque and monitor these new families. When problems arise in these new families, the Malay husband or wife often looks to the Department of Islamic Religion and its civil servants for counseling and support. Oftentimes, the non-Malay party requires discipline in order to keep an acceptable distance from his non-Malay family members and to fit into the traditional Malay Muslim style of life. If their attempts to salvage difficult marriages are unsuccessful, then assistance is there for the Malay party to dissolve the marriage through the Islamic courts. Many couples try to stay away from the government officers and view them as a constant nuisance. However, after conversion, they fall forever under the jurisdiction of Islamic personal law and the watchful eye of the Department of Islamic enforcement that arrests and punishes Muslims that break Islamic laws. Their "new" re-aggregated status literally follows them to the grave. Many local non-Muslims have informed me of several cases of converts who lived in the Chinese or *Portugis* communities, living the way other non-Muslims of these communities live, some even eating pork and drinking alcohol. Nevertheless, when they pass away Muslim officials come, in a group, to pick up the converts' bodies to give them a proper Muslim burial in a Muslim cemetery. Non-Muslim family members often fight a losing battle to reclaim their converted relatives and to give them proper Chinese or *Portugis* funerals. But in the end, after the imposition of state power, they must learn to live with the legal fact that whatever un-Islamic behavior their relatives may have committed in their lives that made them "bad Muslims" did not make them "non-Muslims" before the law (see Ahmad Ibrahim 1997:283–287).

Non-Malays, Chinese Buddhist-Taoists and Chinese Christians, and Indian Hindus and Christians, and *Portugis* Catholics, seek to avoid the negative effects they feel intermarriages with Muslims will have upon their families and communities through the erection of boundaries and the prohibition of such marriages. They often feel that these intermarriages are an expression of Malay privilege, as only for these marriages is conversion state-mandated and compulsory, and entail a detrimental impact on the perpetuation of their culture and heritage. Although intermarriages between Christians and Buddhist-Taoists, Hindus, or Sikhs are often opposed by parties involved as well, they are generally seen as more open to negotiation and the perpetuation of one's culture and heritage than marriage to Muslims. Furthermore, intermarriages with Christians are frequently included with Buddhist-Taoist and Hindu intermarriages, ones viewed as the easiest to manage and negotiate, in contrast to intermarriages with Muslims, as optional marriages were one to marry outside of one's own racial and religious categories.

INTERRACIAL VOLUNTARY ASSOCIATIONS

Many voluntary associations of particular maximal and submaximal cultural categories exist that are consistent with and constitutive of the dominant trend of separate social organization. There are dialect group and clan associations in the Chinese community composed of Chinese members. These dialect associations work together to support and support the interests of Chinese that speak particular Chinese dialects, while the clan associations are composed of Chinese of various dialect groups that share the same clan name and assumed patrilineal ancient ancestry. *Babas* and *Nyonyas* also have a separate Peranakan Association with connections to *Babas* and *Nyonyas* in Penang and Singapore. Similarly, in the Indian community, several associations such as the

Melaka Indian Association exist that engages in various kinds of social activities for its Indian membership. There are also associations of members of particular Indian languages, such as Tamil and Malayali associations. Tamil-speaking and Malayali-speaking Muslims have separate associations that tend to interrelate with each other as well as with Hindus of their respective language groups. Chitty and *Melaka Portugis* also have their own social organizations that reproduce and express solidarity amongst members of these communities. Malays also organized themselves into various organizations in local communities, centering mostly in the mosques and prayer halls. Some Indian Muslims are also involved in these local Muslim councils.

However, even as locals perpetuated this communal pattern, there has been the growth of interracial and inter-religious voluntary associations that constitute a significant resource for "civil society" (see Hefner 2001). Again, similar to intermarriage, the changing social structure and ideological campaigns appear to have had a strong influence on the emergence of these voluntary associations. In this case, the government has also promoted a "caring society" in which non-governmental organizations take up some of the responsibility for providing services and humanitarian support to Malaysians in need. Members organized some of the associations or branches in an earlier period, but they founded most of them in the 1980s and 1990s during a time at which structural changes have reached an intense level of development. In particular, the Rotary Club had one branch organized in Melaka in the 1930s and the Lions Club had a branch organized in 1966, but organizers formed the rest of the local branches of these clubs in the 1980s and 1990s in Melaka. Likewise, organizers formed the Kiwanis Club and Melaka branches of the Diabetes and Thalassaemia associations in the 1980s and 1990s. Earlier organizers formed the local branch of the Young Women's Christian Association (YWCA) in 1921 but the current multiracial and multi-religions membership joined the association in the 1980s and 1990s. The growth of these benevolent voluntary associations during these decades reflects changing social structures and ideologies as well as the negotiation of tensions between being included and excluded in Malaysian society at-large.

The Lions Clubs and Rotary Clubs, both with international headquarters in the U.S., have largely reproduced the communal pattern of organization although some local branches exhibit a limited degree of integration. For instance, the eldest branch of the Rotary Club in Melaka is composed of mostly Indian professionals and business people and local members of various voluntary associations referred to it as an "Indian club." On the other hand, local club members considered two of the most recent branches formed "Chinese clubs," one English-speaking and one Mandarin-speaking. Yet, the club formed in the mid-1980s is a multiracial club consisting of mostly Chinese and Indian professionals and entrepreneurs, but some Malay professionals and civic leaders have joined this club as well. Similarly, local club members considered the oldest Lions Club in Melaka an English-speaking "Chinese club" but a few prominent Indians have joined this club. Three of the other four Lions Clubs formed in the 80s and 90s are all "Chinese clubs," while the most recent club formed in 1998 is an all "Indian club." An Indian doctor in the oldest Lions Club who has been awarded the title *Datuk* was instrumental in forming this latter all Indian club, the first of its kind in Malaysia.

These local Lions and Rotary clubs, like the rest of the benevolent associations in Melaka, perform a variety of humanitarian service activities directed towards people of all racial and religious categories, but they also focus on the needs of particular non-Malay communities. For instance, the local Rotary clubs organized blood donation campaigns, vocational training programs, and visits to elderly people who live in homes for the aged. In addition, the multiracial Rotary Club of Kota Melaka organized an education fair at a local hotel for young students of all races who were able to acquire information about various colleges and universities across Malaysia. Similarly, local Lions clubs organized fundraising activities, such as cycling events, to purchase an "Eye Bus" that would be equipped with eye testing equipment in an attempt to prevent blindness and the loss of sight. They also have campaigns to provide wheelchairs to disabled people in need and to donate film for optical cameras used to detect retinal disorders. On the other hand, unlike the other benevolent associations considered here, these largely communal-based Lions and Rotary clubs also perform service activities aimed at the needs or concerns of their particular communities. For instance, some Chinese Rotary clubs collected donations to send food and other forms of assistance to flood victims in China, and the recently formed Tamil-speaking Lions Club raised funds to build a school on an agricultural plantation outside of town where many Indian laborers reside. When I have asked several Chinese and Indian members of these clubs, why there are so few Malays in these voluntary associations in contrast to Chinese and Indians, they have expressed the view that as non-*Bumiputera* and non-Malays, Chinese and Indians have to provide needed services for their own communities. One Chinese member of a Lions Club chapter, told me that,

> Malays get help from the government when they have problems; the
> government helps them. But for other groups, we have to help ourselves,

since we do not get help from the government . . . They are *Bumiputera* . . . It is political . . . As you see there are lots of Chinese and Indians here doing service work; we have to because if we do not do it our communities will not get these services.

The experience and perception of being excluded from government programs helps to motivate Chinese and Indian participation in these clubs and contributes to the communal form they take. This Chinese club member also informed me that performing these community services is nothing new for Chinese-based organizations because Chinese clan organizations did some of the same things to support poor Chinese immigrants upon their arrival in Malaysia.

In contrast, the local Kiwanis Club does not reproduce the communal form of organization exhibited by most Lions and Rotary clubs, and its members often referred to Malaysia's multiracial philosophy in order to explain its diverse composition. Formed in 1986, the Kiwanis Club of Melaka, is a multiracial and multi-religious voluntary associations, consisting of Indian Muslim, Indian Hindu, Chinese Buddhist-Taoist, Chinese Christian, and Malay professionals and business owners and their spouses and friends. One of the main projects of this voluntary association for the last few years has been to provide health and material resources to residents of a *Temuan, orang asli*, village located outside of town in the district of Alor Gadjah. I visited this village with several members of the association on a few occasions and participated in their service activities. They passed out packages of vitamin C and bicycles to young children and clothing to the adults. Puan Hamidah, an Indian Muslim, cautioned me not to criticize the government for the poverty in the *orang asli* village, explaining that the government has provided some help for residents of this village but it was not enough in many cases. Besides, the government had a program to bus them to school in the past but they stopped going and did not want to be involved in this education program, she explained. The government also put in a small road, wide enough for one-way traffic leading to the village, several small cement homes, and electrical lines. Members of this club were proud of the fact that these *orang asli* villagers were wearing the clothes they had given to them and were no longer practically naked, the way they were when they first began to visit them. In the future, they plan to provide medicine for the worms that inflicted many of the children and to counsel residents of this village on cleanliness and hygiene. The Kiwanis Club also organizes fundraising activities to support local service projects for disabled children and have recently opened a Downs Syndrome Clinic and School in Melaka. Unlike the

Lions and Rotary clubs, the Kiwanis Club does not engage in communally oriented projects, directed towards servicing one of the major racial groups, Indians, Chinese, and Malays. Its work amongst *orang asli* appears to be motivated by the aim of incorporating these marginal *Bumiputera* more fully into Malaysia's diverse society.

However, similar to the Lions and Rotary clubs, the Kiwanis Club does not consist of *orang sederhana,* people who are just able to fulfill the necessities of life, or even *orang biasa,* people who have a "normal" car, house or apartment, and monthly income. These voluntary associations primarily consist of middle and upper class people, referred to in local terms as *orang kaya,* rich people who often own several cars, including luxury cars, and houses and other real estate, and have an above average income. Many of these wealthy (*orang kaya*) association members are professionals, doctors, lawyers, accountants, who have attained tertiary education, but many are business people who have only graduated from high school. Some members are of the middle classes, such as nurses and office clerks, who often have a more modest income but are upwardly mobile and seek to achieve higher social status through associating with *orang kaya.* Moreover, *orang kaya* in these voluntary associations often use their involvement in these groups, and the public recognition they attain through them, as a basis to enhance their business contacts, achieve higher social status, such as royal titles, as well as launch political careers.

Figure 18 Diverse members of local Kiwanis Club.
(Photograph by Timothy P. Daniels)

The core group of organizers and board members of the local YWCA and Diabetes and Thalassaemia associations are also primarily *orang kaya,* middle and upper class people, although they do not achieve the same level of recognition and notoriety for working in these organizations. Many *orang sederhana* and *orang biasa,* working class people, have joined these associations and benefit from their humanitarian services. Similar to the Kiwanis Club, the local YWCA is highly multiracial, and multi-religious despite the obvious association with Christianity. It consists of *Portugis,* Indian, and Chinese Christians, and Indian Hindus and Chinese Buddhist-Taoists. A Malay Muslim woman, active in the leadership of the Thalassaemia Association, was said to have joined the YWCA for networking purposes but I never observed her participating in YWCA activities. To the contrary, many of the ladies of the YWCA supported the campaigns of the Thalassaemia Association. Several non-Christian women were board and committee members but Christian women had to hold the positions of President and Treasury.

The YWCA organizes vocational training for women of all "races" and religions, and tries to raise public consciousness about violence towards women. Local members also informed me that they have worked for the passing of the Spouse Abuse Act and have successfully lobbied the government for the opening of a Women's Shelter that their members help to operate. In addition, they hold prayer meetings and talks on a variety of topics of interest to its members and Christian and non-Christian women participate in these activities. For instance, I attended a prayer session at the local YWCA office in which Chinese Buddhist-Taoists and Indian Hindus actively participated in prayers and sang Christian songs. They used publications from the World YWCA headquarters in Geneva that combined statements about the abuse of women in Pakistan and Mali and about creating solidarity to eliminate violence towards women with several prayers and verses from the Holy Bible. At the end of the prayer and study session, we all ate some rice porridge prepared by a middle-aged Indian Hindu woman who lives just down the road from the YWCA office. Although group members conducted these prayer sessions within a Christian framework, there was no pressure for anyone to convert to Christianity and the general philosophy and outlook stressed the empowerment of women, a secular concern that all these women were in support of regardless of religion. Many of the Indian and Chinese husbands of these ladies participated in the lectures and other activities, indicating a non-*Bumiputera* and non-Malay consciousness and identity. Furthermore, this group also expressed a sense of a qualitative citizenship of the women of all races as they argue and strive for more just and equal inclusion within Malaysian society.

The Diabetes and Thalassaemia associations focus upon providing services to people, and their families, who are afflicted with these diseases. They strive to raise funds so that they can donate medical resources or at least reduce the expenses for people with these diseases. Some Chinese and Indian doctors and nurses organized the Diabetes Association and serve as advisors on the predominantly Chinese board. There are many Malay members of the association but only one Malay Muslim serves on the board and is active within the core group of organizers. In contrast to Diabetes, which afflicts all races in Malaysia, Thalassaemia is a hereditary disease that mostly afflicts the Malay and *orang asli* communities. Some local Malays, primarily people that have children afflicted with Thalassaemia, organized a local chapter of this association initially, but before long many Chinese joined the association offering their support. A Chinese businesswoman has recently been elected to the position of President and has been active raising funds within the Chinese community to assist the mostly *orang sederhana* Malay families that are afflicted with this chronic illness. Some group members have informed me that due to intermarriage with Malays or *orang asli,* there are a few cases of Chinese children inheriting this disease. Practically half of the group members are Malays who for the most part have family members afflicted with this disease and around half are Chinese who have joined as supporters or sponsors. There are no Indian or *Portugis* members of the Thalassaemia Association, so unlike the YWCA and Lions and Rotary clubs, Chinese involvement in the Diabetes and Thalassaemia associations does not seem to express a non-*Bumiputera* and non-Malay identity or consciousness. Yet, like the mostly Chinese and Indian participation in all of these associations, the mostly Chinese participation in these disease-related benevolent associations express a "caring society" philosophy and a sense of being included within the broader society. Chinese contribute to the welfare of the poor and afflicted segment of the Malay community, providing much needed help to Malays in a way that the government cannot afford to help. Just as the Kiwanis Club helps *orang asli* who receive insufficient support from the government, these Chinese participants in the Thalassaemia Association support Malays who in this case are beyond the bounds of full government support. Except for the Thalassaemia Association, Malay participation in these associations is rather sparse. Malay Muslim charity work does not usually venture far beyond the confines of communal organization closely tied to local mosques and prayer halls.

INTERRACIAL AND INTER-RELIGIOUS CLIQUES

Patterns of interracial and inter-religious affiliation in social cliques are similar to patterns of intermarriage and patterns of association in benevolent service organizations. Most social cliques I observed or acquired information about through interviews were composed of members of the same cultural category. Friends of the same "race" and religion regularly visit each other's homes and enjoy various forms of home entertainment. I frequently observed Chinese in the apartment complex in which I lived playing cards and gambling for long hours throughout the evening. Although many Chinese and Indians visit Malay homes for festive open house activities, they rarely form social cliques with them and visit them on other occasions or go out to engage in various forms of entertainment or leisurely activity. Cliques of Malay young men often play *sepak takraw,* kicking a rattan ball over a net, on courts located next to apartment buildings where many Malays live in town. At times Malay youth stand in a circle in the parking lots of apartment buildings and kick the rattan ball to each other. Similarly, Chinese youth often play badminton or lift weights with other Chinese youth, and Indian youth often go out to play soccer with fellow Indians. Although there are some organized sporting activities in which these groups participate together, on a daily basis they interact in small groups composed of friends of their same cultural categories.

These groups generally go out to eat with family and friends of the same cultural category at restaurants that cater to their particular food tastes and/or taboos. Chinese often frequent the large restaurants in Bandar Hilir, Melaka Raya, and Bunga Raya, areas with a large concentration of Chinese businesses and residents. Indians restaurants located near the small Indian business area on Temenggong Street are often full of small Indian cliques. Malay restaurants and food stalls, located near Padang Merdeka, and not far from Malay neighborhoods are frequented by small Malay cliques. Occasionally there are small groups of Indians eating in Chinese restaurants or Chinese eating in Indian restaurants, but Malays generally go out to eat with their friends in Malay restaurants and food stalls.

The malls and shopping centers are some of the most popular places for social cliques to go for food and entertainment. Large groups of Malay young men often stand or sit in front of the malls or inside where there are sitting areas or areas overlooking the mall concourse. Chinese and Indian youth rarely interact with Malay youth in these spaces. Chinese and Indian young men often frequent the malls in separate small and large groups as well, visiting the video game arcade, watching movies in the theater, and eating in the food courts or fast food restaurants. Malay, Chinese, and Indian women often frequent the malls in small groups of women from their cultural categories, engaging in some of the same activities as the young men.

Occasionally, these social cliques, in the malls and other venues, involved interracial mixing, exhibiting the new "openness" many of my informants spoke of and embodying the models and schemata of 'Malaysia's diverse society.' In fact, people appeared to form many of these social cliques around an interracial marriage, including as they did the couple, their children and other family members, and friends of either or both races. Most often, as noted earlier, these cliques were formed around intermarrying non-Malay couples but sometimes they were formed around intermarried couples that included Malay men or women. Similarly, small interracial cliques of high school and college students would often visit the mall to eat together or to just walk around and look at things in the stores. These cliques were most often composed of Chinese and Indian or Chinese and *Portugis* youth, but sometimes, much less frequently, they included some Malay youth. Of the cliques that included Malays, most of them consisted of Malays and Indians, rather than Malays and Chinese or *Portugis*.

Most of my respondents, even those that attended segregated primary schools, told me that they had friends of various racial and religious backgrounds, but they began to grow apart as they got older. As children or young high school students, they interacted with their fellow students and race and religion held little significance for these interactions most of the time. However as they grew older, their respective distinctiveness, stressed by their families, friends, and school officials became more relevant to their interaction and a gulf began to grow. This gulf appears to grow to be the largest between Malays and non-Malays as it is Malays, which social institutions often singled out from the rest. Non-Malay youth often complain about the special institutional treatment for Malays, in relation to separate *halal* food, separate *"agama"* (Islamic religion in this context) classes versus civic moral classes. Many non-Malay young women have expressed the feeling that they grow apart from their Malay friends when the Malay young women begin to wear *tudung* as part of their school uniforms. From their perspective, the *tudung* creates a large distinction between them and they begin to grow more distant. Many non-Malay people and their families, develop a great deal of animosity towards Malays, and the privileges they receive, when it comes to the matter of post-high school graduation matters. Whereas non-Malays have to attend "Form Six" (a grade in high school) which entails two additional years in high schools, Malays are able to leave high school after "Form Five" and attend "matriculation" programs that prepare them for college and university education. In addition, non-Malays complain about the racial quota system that allows Malays to enter colleges and universities with lower grades than non-Malays.

On the other hand, Malay respondents have told me that non-Malay students often ridicule them because they wear *tudung* or Malay-style hats and make fun of them when they do not know the material taught in class. They have expressed more animosity towards Chinese students who they say feel that they are superior to them and often express it by speaking English rather than Malay or by using English names. They express less animosity towards Indians, who, as the smallest of the three major races, often seek to be friends with everyone. Nevertheless, as non-Malays and non-*Bumiputera,* Indians tend to share sentiments and solidarity with Chinese, especially in relation to Malay special privileges and feelings of exclusion.

Moreover, as children grow older and become young adults, their parents become more concerned about the people they are interacting with, after all these friendships may lead to marital relations. Parents, non-Malay and Malay, as we noted earlier have strong feelings about interracial and inter-religious marriages and they begin to impress these values upon their teen-age children in a stronger way then they did when they were younger. For instance, Elaine, a young *Nyonya* woman, informed me that she grew up in a predominantly Malay village and her friends were mostly Malays, but as she grew older her father moved them out of the Malay village because he was concerned about her marrying a Malay man. As the proscription against marrying outside of one's race is strongest in relation to Malays, it tends to drive a wedge between Malays and non-Malays more than it does between non-Malay cultural categories. Chinese, Indians, and *Portugis* are freer to interact with each other than they are with Malays. As their children become older, Malay parents also become more concerned about their interactions with non-Muslims as these interactions may bring their children in contact with non-Islamic activities and behavior. At puberty, Muslim youth are responsible, and disciplined to, meet their religious obligations of prayer and fasting. Moreover, they impress the value of marrying within the Malay or "Muslim race" in order to uphold the Islamic faith.

CONCLUSION

The patterns of interracial informal social organization, intermarriages, voluntary associations and cliques, are not simply directed by understandings of inclusion or understandings of exclusion, but rather a combination of the two. Negotiations and tensions between understandings of inclusion and exclusion contribute to the growth of these multiracial formations. Moreover, the predominance of non-Malays in these multiracial and multi-religious social relationships and groups and the less frequent appearance of Malays in such unions indicate that combinations of these understandings are at work. For it is people in non-Malay cultural categories that seek to connect with other groups out of feelings of exclusion and second-class citizenship, out of feelings and experiences of being barred from Malay privileges. Furthermore, some of their deepest aspirations are that Malaysians of all races and religions work and live together in harmony and peace and that they will eventually enjoy the same rights of citizenship. Feelings of inclusion and the perception that they are able to negotiate as equals, contributes to the lowering of restrictions in regard to intermarriage with fellow non-Malays. On the other hand, feelings of exclusion and inequality and the fear that cultural identity and heritage will be forfeited, contributes to the tightening of restrictions in relation to intermarriage with Malays or other Muslims.

Local residents and religious and government officials interpret and ascribe different meanings to intersections of race, religion, and gender along the spectrum of intermarriages. Local residents tend to interpret the principle of "following the father," present in all communities, in cases of Chinese Buddhist-Taoist and Indian Hindu intermarriages as an openly flexible principle negotiated between social equals. Both spouses are expected to maintain their respective religions, perceived as closely related, and their children are expected to "follow their fathers" in terms of race and religion. This principle applies regardless of the race or religion of the father; if he is Chinese Buddhist-Taoist or Indian Hindu, it applies equally, although Chinese tend to lay greater stress on sons than daughters following fathers. Government officials recognize the race of the children of these intermarriages as "following the father," non-*Bumiputera* in either case, and their religion remains non-Muslim and so they are officially under the jurisdiction of civil personal law.

In both cases of Chinese Buddhist-Taoists and Indian Hindus intermarrying with Christians and Muslims, people violate the principle of "following the father" in some respect. Church officials and Catholic family members strive to have the non-Christian spouse convert to Christianity or at least have the children of the marriage follow the Catholic parent, in terms of religion, regardless of gender. In these cases, locals tend to dissociate race and religion; the children follow the father's race but the Catholic parent's religion. Government officials, as in the above cases, recognize the race of the children as "following the father" and their religion as non-Muslims. Similarly, in cases of intermarriage with Malays, people violate the principle of "following the father" since the non-Muslim spouse is required to convert to Islam and they recognize the offspring of these marriages as Muslims regardless of the race or "original" religion of the parents. Yet, in contrast to the Christian case, religious institutions *and* the state are involved in policing "conversion" as an ongoing process (see Aragon 2000). Once again, within these marriage processes, officials and some others dissociate race and religion interpreting that children inherit the race of their fathers, while their religion is Islam.

Only when their fathers are Malay and *Bumiputera* do their children inherit eligibility to *Bumiputera* rights and special privileges. The negative attitudes and evaluation non-Malays often express about non-Malays who intermarry with Malays indicate their negotiations with notions of Malay privilege. People routinely depict these intermarrying non-Malays as "becoming Malay" or as opportunists seeking access to *Bumiputera* benefits, in either case opting for Malays over their own races. Nevertheless, these benefits are not as easy to acquire through intermarrying with Malays as often thought, because eligibility to official Malay *Bumiputera* status and benefits is gendered, flowing through Malay *fathers* and not Malay *mothers*.[4] Despite violations of the principle of "following the father" in relation to religion, government officials apply this principle in *all* cases to reckon the racial identity of the offspring of intermarriages.

On the other hand, the children of intermarriages between Malays and non-Malays tend to self-identify as "Malay," and are generally recognized as such by the general public, regardless of whether their fathers are Malay or not, and thusly, regardless of their official ascription on government documents. These children of "mixed" parentage identify with the "definitive" and "preferred" cultural category in Malaysia, "Malays," and thereby accumulate symbolic capital (Bourdieu 1984; Urciuoli 1996), prestige and potential access to material benefits. Nevertheless, there remains an important obstacle to their becoming "Malay" (see Nagata 1993:519; see also Winzeler 1988:94). Non-Malay maximal categories in Malaysia are constrained from becoming "Malay" through the institutionalization of the principle of "following the father" and the formalized delineation of cultural attributes from matters of the "blood." Even young women of "mixed" Malay/non-Malay parentage that publicly don Islamic-style garb, speak Malay, and practice customs associated with Malays, are not necessarily recognized as *legally* Malay. State-mandated and administered religious conversion, converted spouses coming under the jurisdiction of Islamic personal law, and the bestowing of full *Bumiputera* status and benefits through official application of "following the father," contributes to local perceptions that intermarriages with Malays are substantially different from other intermarriages.

Similar, in some respects, to their involvement in intermarriages, non-Malays participate in voluntary associations in large numbers to provide services to their communities or segments of all communities who will not receive sufficient assistance from the government. The notion that they are non-*Bumiputera*, ineligible for the privileges Malays receive, offers some motivation for their involvement in these voluntary associations, especially ones with a communal base from which to provide services to their own communities. In addition, participation in these groups links them with other groups in the broader society and provides an avenue for their acquisition of status and higher ranking. Members of these benevolent associations, supporting the government's call for a more "caring society" and the involvement of non-governmental organizations in the providing of services to people in need, earns them public recognition and social capital. Public onlookers have the opportunity of viewing them as expressing loyalty and practicing sacrifice for the country and the welfare of its citizens.

Non-Malays also intermingle in social cliques more often with other non-Malays than they do with Malays. This stems from the fact that more non-Malays than Malays intermarry and associate with each other in benevolent organizations since people formed some of these social cliques around these bases. Moreover, non-Malays and Malays grow apart as they advance through high school years and racial and religious differences take on greater significance in the schools and in their homes. In school, they begin to experience the institutionalization of Malay privilege, in terms of food, dress, religious classes versus civics classes, and in connection with post-graduation prospects. At home, partially in response to Malay privileges, and partially as an expression of their own racial and religious sentiments, their parents tighten social boundaries between them and their Malay friends. Shared experiences and a growing consciousness of being non-Malay and non-*Bumiputera* as well as widespread multicultural notions contribute to the proliferation of informal social cliques composed of people of various non-Malay cultural categories.

In contrast, Malays seek Malay or Muslim organizations, rather than multiracial and multi-religious social formations when they feel left out of the broader society, as these feelings of exclusion are usually aimed at "non-Malays" and "immigrants" who are often viewed as taking advantage of "Malay natives" in their own country. Malays with these sentiments are apt to turn to Islamic organizations and political parties, such as Tabligh, PAS, and a variety of other religious and cultural organizations, in which they can voice their aspirations for a more Islamic or Malay-dominated society. Although there are strong feelings in the Malay community against marrying Muslim converts, some Malays are not opposed to such intermarriages as long as the marriage candidate embraces Islam and some aspects of Malay Muslim culture. Some feel that intermarriage with non-Malays is a good way to enhance interracial understanding and sensitivity, but the prerequisite of conversion to Islam is not negotiable. Malays not only view this prerequisite as a religious stipulation but it is also an important expression of the fact that Malaysia is officially a Muslim country. It is a powerful public institutionalization of Malay special rights and symbolic advantage.

Similarly, Malays do not generally involve themselves in multiracial and multi-religious voluntary associations and cliques. Most Malays tend to concentrate their efforts to assist the needy to activities in the mosques, prayer halls, and with government agencies. After all, the Malays dominate other groups in government, which has made a commitment to redistribute resources for Malays as the "natives" or "first settlers" of the Malay Peninsula. The small number of Malays in the voluntary associations, I examined above, were Malays with a "moderate" perspective on multiculturalism, the dominant government model, or Malays looking to network with other groups and professionals. Only the Thalassaemia Association, a group servicing mostly Malay victims of thalassaemia, this chronic and expensive disease to provide long-term care for, has a large Malay membership. Malays generally follow the dominant trend separating them from non-Malays on grounds of religious and cultural differences, and do not have strong motives to combine with non-Malays.

Clearly, it is the tension between and negotiation of feelings and understandings of inclusion and exclusion that direct the emergence of multiracial and multi-religious forms of informal organization. The models and schemata of "Malaysia's diverse society" and of "Malay privilege" and the motives they entail in combination and complex interrelation contribute to the formation of the patterns described in this chapter. In the next chapter, I will further explore the influence of experience upon the resolution of the apparent contradiction between these models and schemata of equality and inequality, of horizontal and vertical relations, and of full and qualified citizenship.

Chapter Eight
Cognitive Resolution and Experience

Over the course of the last several chapters, I have demonstrated how models and schemata of "Malaysia's diverse society" and "Malay privilege" are often in conflict and combination as they are directive of, and embodied in, social practices. Now, I will turn to the matter of the apparent contradictions between these representations and whether (or not) and how, they are resolved or integrated. I must consider the diverse ways in which local Melakans of various cultural categories make sense of these seemingly dissonant representations. As we have seen, they use them to interpret public celebrations, museum exhibitions, religious festivals, and social relations and their experiences in educational, economic, and voluntary institutions. Their interpretations of these aesthetic and social realms routinely stem from models and schemata of "Malaysia's diverse society" and "Malay privilege," and at times, they even interpreted one particular event through the prism of both of these representations. For instance, when speaking about the National Day Celebrations or many other government organized public celebrations and cultural shows, several local people have noted both how all the diverse groups of Malaysian society are included and how Malay culture is emphasized. Some have even gone further to imply that all Malaysians are equal citizens but that Malay *Bumiputeras* have special rights. These sorts of "knowledge elements" require a process of cognitive re-organization in order to reduce the cognitive dissonance (Festinger 1957).

Festinger (ibid:3) argued that "the existence of dissonance, being psychologically uncomfortable, will motivate the person to try to reduce the dissonance and achieve consonance." More particularly, he proposes that his theory of cognitive dissonance apply to "elements of cognition," things people know about themselves, their behavior, and their surroundings, that do not fit together and are relevant to each other. People can try to reduce cognitive dissonance by changing their behavior or environment or adding new cognitive elements (ibid:18–24). I will apply the core of Festinger's theory (see Beauvois and Joule 1996) to the elements of cognition expressed or implied in several tape-recorded conversations I had with local people in Melaka and attempt to discern the dynamics of dissonance reduction.

Yet, it is necessary for us to make a distinction between "elements of cognition" and "clusters of cognition," a distinction that Festinger did not see the need to make due to his emphasis on the measurement of dissonance (see Festinger 1957:10–11). In particular, models and schemata of "Malaysia's diverse society" and "Malay privilege" are bundles or clusters of elements, whereas "elements of cognition" are constituents of, and cognition that stems from, models and schemata. With this distinction, we can consider and infer how processes of dissonance reduction, in respect to elements of cognition, impact the organization and connections between models and schemata, as these representations change over time. Although there is a wide range of possible ways to reduce dissonance between relevant cognitive elements, I will try to demonstrate some broad patterns of reconciling cognition that stem from these representations. I will argue that these broad patterns of adding cognition to lower cognitive dissonance are indicative of the different positions and experiences that Malays and non-Malays have in Malaysian society.

NON-MALAY COGNITIVE DYNAMICS

Non-Malay youth and adults generally combine cognitive elements that stem from representations of "Malaysia's diverse society" and "Malay privilege" in such a fashion expressing qualitative citizenship, in this case, a sense of "second class citizenship." I made this observation in passing in chapter four as I discussed a segment of Flora Goh's discourse that I will now further analyze. The cognitive element, "we are citizens," clearly stems from the schema of "Malaysia's diverse society," whereas the cognitive element, "they have every right to protect these *Bumi* people," stems from the schema of "Malay privilege." A combination of these notions produces the ranks of "first class"—for the original or *Bumi* people of Malaysia—and "second class" for Chinese immigrants who are only residing in Malaysia on a temporary basis. The addition of ranks constitutes a reinterpretation of the notion of citizenship and reduces the dissonance between the two cognitive elements. Thus, the element "we are all citizens" makes more sense in relation to the element of "the Malay government making special provisions for Malays" when you add the idea that some citizens come first and others come second. Moreover, the cognition "we are only *tompang*" supports the distinction between *Bumi* and non-*Bumi*, first class and second class, and justifies *Bumis* in power extending special privileges to Malay *Bumis*. It is also important to note that Flora informs us that the government does not explicitly specify their second-class citizenship, but this is how Chinese feel about and perceive their status in Malaysia. Indeed, as we have noted, the dominant ideological formulations emphasize equality and harmony amongst the diverse groups of citizens that compose Malaysian society, rather than inequality and discrimination.

Mr. Krishnan, an elderly Gujerati businessman, situates these sorts of ideological formulations after combining cognitive elements, much as Flora Goh did, to express a sense of qualitative citizenship.

> Mr. Krishnan: *Bumiputeras* are the Malays, they are the Malays. They are the real natives of this country. It was their country. The Indians and the Chinese came from elsewhere. So there is two citizenships, one is *Bumiputera* citizenship, and one is non-*Bumiputera* citizenship. Their citizenship is, of course, I should say, more powerful.
>
> I: In what way is it more powerful?
>
> Mr. Krishnan: Because they have so many rights which we don't have. Like there are some lands that are called *Bumiputera* reservation lands, I can not buy it. Mr. Salim[1] can not buy it. We are both citizens. Only the *Bumiputera* citizen can buy it. There are lots of lands, lots of things, scholarships for example. There are so many things which only a *Bumiputera* has got the right, we don't have, and, uh, I think it is perfectly OK. I am not jealous, as far as I am concerned. Many times they will condemn, you know, but it is their country, naturally they have the rights, they will have more rights than us. Like in Singapore, they talk very big, oh, 'all citizens are equal.' Bullshit! But when you really come to the point, first they will give to a Chinese, and then only to a Malay or an Indian. So where the hell is the same status. Talk only, because it is a Chinese country. In India, same thing, Mr. Salim, if you and I were to go and apply for a job, I would get it first. Mr. Salim will also get it but later, after me, not before me. If we both go to the interview, that fellow will choose me first. Neither of us is an Indian citizen. I am a Malaysian citizen and you are an American citizen. But I am an Indian, my ancestors came from there, so they will give me the job first. It is everywhere. So, uh, I am not jealous. But the Malays, I think, without any reasonable doubt, the Malays are the best people in the earth. They are very honest, very sincere, very religious, very simple, very easy to get along with them. The Malays, best people in the world . . .

Mr. Krishnan combines the cognitive elements of citizenship with Malay privileges producing the cognition of "two citizenships," *Bumiputera* and non-*Bumiputera*, a form of qualified citizenship in which the *Bumiputera* citizens have more power and rights. In addition to this re-interpretation of the notion of citizenship, he reduces cognitive dissonance by adding several cognitive elements such as "rhetoric about equality is only big talk." In Malaysia, as in Singapore and elsewhere, ideological formulations about equality and the like, is just rhetoric and is not, at all, the way things actually work. This knowledge element qualifies notions of equal citizenship and lessens its dissonance with cognition about the realities of Malay special rights. We should note that non-Malays do not have the power to change the institutionalization of Malay privileges, so they can only reduce dissonance by changing their own behavior and thought. Mr. Krishnan also adds the thought that "the dominant majority or original people of every country discriminates in favor of their people," thereby buttressing the practice of Malay special rights. From this perspective, it is natural for Malays, the majority in Malaysia, to discriminate in favor of their own people. Mr. Krishnan implies that many non-Malays are upset and "jealous" about the special benefits that Malays receive; their behavior, in this case, being dissonant with the fact of Malay privilege. To the contrary, his behavior, and the cognition about his behavior of not being "jealous about Malay special benefits" that he promotes in his community reduces dissonance and is consonant with the realities of Malay special rights. Furthermore, the cognitive element, "the Malays are the best people on the earth," also serves to reconcile his attachment to Malaysia with the realities of inequality. Mr. Krishnan is an active worshipper at ancient Muslim graves, Malay *keramat,* and frequently interrelates with Malays, paying them to make Islamic prayers at the graves and sponsoring feasts at mosques in fulfillment of his vows when *keramat* answer his prayers.

Despite his strong awareness of non-*Bumiputera* or second-class citizenship, he expresses a strong sense of belonging to Malaysia.

I: So how do you feel you belong in Malaysia?

Mr. Krishnan: I feel this is my country, Mr. Salim. I am born here; I am going to die here. I love this country. Supposing there is a war between India and Malaysia, without a shadow of a doubt, I will raise guns against India, not against Malaysia. Supposing there is a war between India and Malaysia, I will take a bloody machine gun and go around shooting those guys there in India. My mother country is Malaysia. I have nothing to do with India. I am a patriot. I love this country. In fact, I have never been to India for the past twenty-five years, neither feel like going . . .

I: How do you feel your belonging is recognized by the society?

Mr. Krishnan: I don't care whether they recognize or not, as you said, your heart or soul, even if I did not have a citizenship paper, uh, I don't care, as far as I know, this is my mother land.

Mr. Krishnan tries to reduce the cognitive dissonance between the thought of belonging in Malaysia with the thought of being a non-*Bumiputera* citizen by adding thoughts about his strong sentiments and sense of attachment and commitment to Malaysia.

Similarly, Katherine, a thirty-six year old Indian Christian, adds several cognitive elements reducing the dissonance between second-class citizenship and belonging to Malaysia.

I: How do you feel, overall, in terms of belonging, as an Indian Christian, in Melaka and Malaysian society?

Katherine: Because I was born and brought up here, I do not think of India as my, my motherland, or anything like that, you know. So, I think that, I was born and brought up here, everything's, Malaysia is for me. So, I don't think I would like to go back to India also, to stay there, but for a visit, of course, I would.

I: You feel attached to Malaysia. But how do you feel that your attachment is being recognized in this society overall?

Katherine: Since I was born and brought up down here in Malaysia, I've not thought about any other place in the world where I would want to be other than this. I'd like my last breath to off and set down here, in Malaysia.

I: How do you feel that Malaysia is satisfying those feelings? Do you feel they are recognizing your belonging?

Katherine: Because until now they have not segregated, Hindus one side and Malays one side, because they are still living as one whole family, you see, so I am not facing any other problems, other than that. So, I think, this is the best place. But in time to come, if they have to ask us to go out. That is a big question mark. I do not know where I would like to go. I've not made a choice of another state.

I: Would you go back to India?

Katherine: No, not India, no, because I have heard a lot about India . . . But I would not like to . . . Staying in Malaysia also, we have to give most of our rights to Malays. Even though you are in the right, you also have to just say, yes, I am in the wrong. You have to give your ways to them, because we are staying in their land (almost swallowed this last phrase) and now they are always telling you, 'just *tompang* only, you are just here on a temporary basis.' So, this is some sort of, telling us we don't belong down here. But then who are they to say that, because I've got a very good prime minister, Datuk Seri Dr. Mahathir. Well, he is still behind Indians. He is giving a lot of job opportunities, a lot of things, which he is also for our Indians, but then, still Malays, they still want their place to be FIRST. So, I don't think so, that I would like to go and fight about it, with the Malay. If worst comes to worst, then I have to be a Muslim.

The lack of fit between the thoughts of non-Malays being "second" and of belonging to Malaysia, as an Indian Christian, is reduced by adding the thoughts of "being born and brought up in Malaysia" and of "being familiar with Malaysia." In addition, Katherine tries to reduce dissonance by adding the thoughts that "Indians have not been forcibly segregated from Malays" and that they "still live as a whole family." This last phrase appears to stem from the dominant model of "Malaysia's diverse society" that no doubt gives non-Malays a measure of comfort with its hopeful images of all Malaysians living in peace and harmony.

Yet, strong feelings of exclusion from first-class, full, citizenship bring Katherine, like Flora Goh, to consider what she would do if the dominant majority group forced Indians to leave Malaysia. From this perspective and subjectivity, their second-class citizenship is just a temporary pass that can be revoked at any time according to the wishes of their hosts, the Malay *Bumiputeras*. Again, similar to Flora Goh, Katherine uses the term *tompang* to mark the position of non-*Bumiputeras* in Malaysia. However, Katherine informs us, this is a term Malays often use to remind non-Malays of their contingent and secondary status in the country. She expresses how sensitive these matters are to non-Malays and how much it pains her to be excluded from full citizenship in the country of her birth as she almost swallows the phrase, "because we are staying in their land." She decreases the dissonance between thoughts of equality and belonging with thoughts of Malay privilege and secondary non-Malay status by adding the thoughts "who are they to say non-Malays only *tompang*" and "the Malaysian Prime Minister is behind Indians" and "he is giving us jobs and other opportunities." Common Malays may make these statements but the Malays in political power are more "moderate" and striving to include Indians in the broader society. On the other hand, her thoughts about her behavior are brought in line with the realities of Malay dominance and special rights by adding the cognitive elements "I would not go and fight Malays about it" and "I would even become a Muslim if worst came to worst." That is to say, she would even convert to Islam if she had to in order to stay in Malaysia and to live in peace and harmony with Malays.

Sumitra, a Malayali Hindu woman, relates her thoughts about the discrepancies between equality and Malay privilege and about her experiences with institutionalized bias in favor of Malays.

> I: I am trying to understand what it means in terms of a multiracial society where everyone is sharing but at the same time there are some differences that are made for different groups.

> Sumitra: OK, in those terms, to me, uh, I think it is a challenge. There are things that I cannot change, OK, and there are things that I can change. So this is what I would like to teach to my children . . . I think if we go to any country, any small group, there are sure to be some kind of prejudice, some kind of bias, yeah, and we as individuals must be able to fit that, accept it, and be able to take it to our advantage . . .

> I: But it is not just for individuals. There are certain things that are done for *Bumiputeras* as a group and then non-*Bumiputeras* do not get.

> Sumitra: Yeah, true, true, but the way I see it is that if the government doesn't give to me then there is always the private sector (laughter). There is always somebody, I don't have to depend on somebody to give it to me. I can always do it on my own . . . As a group, it is a challenge . . . To me it is more with education. I had problems, uh, to enter the college, and I tell you this, it was because of the government biases and I felt so much anger. They say it is only to INTAKE, you know. But even if you go to the local U (university) you can see, even with the lecturers, and mainly people of their own ethnic group, you know. And it becomes frustrating, because to find an Indian professor, an Indian lecturer, in the universities, is very difficult. Even to find a Chinese is difficult. So it is difficult for you to get, um, how to say, to get better guidance or support. For your project, you need advice. It is very difficult to explain it to them. I was very frustrated, like I told you. I didn't accept the fact that why should there be these biases. Why couldn't it be fair? I question it, you know. So, when I do go out, of course, because of that situation, I strive more myself. I learn extra. I mean, I do extra. I do this. I do that. I expose myself and when I do come out and I face the world, I am able to take these challenges. And people who is at my same level. Academically, they did not excel. I don't want to condemn them but to myself, I think I have done quite well . . . I am assistant manager . . . I am able to take challenges. I can accept it. If people are not being fair, fine, I can accept it and I can get on . . . If you ask yourself sometimes, we all tend to be unfair to other people . . . So we have preferences. We all have them. Everyone has them. I think it is something natural. If it deals

with us, OK, and the other person, it is not minor, may be angry, and
if that person loses control of his anger, then he will probably lose
everything . . . But I don't feel that this person is being fair to me, I
just think, why is this person not being fair. How can I get this position . . . If it takes me to work an extra one hour to be in the same
position, then that is what I do. And in the end, I find that over the
long term, I fair far better than they do, in terms of, to me, myself, I
feel I develop better . . .

Sumitra informs us that she feels Malays discriminated against her when
she went to college and it was very difficult for her to deal with it. This discrimination was not just in relation to "intake" or admissions quotas, but
she also found that most of the staff and faculty was Malay and it was difficult for her to get adequate support and understanding from them. Yet,
she reduces the dissonance between her thoughts of equality and fairness
with thoughts about the realities of institutionalized biases and Malay privilege by adding the thought that "there are sure to be biases, prejudice, and
preferences in any country or small group." Similar to Mr. Krishnan,
Sumitra reconciles her thoughts with the social facts by looking at Malay
privilege as something natural that occurs everywhere in some form. Since
non-Malays do not have the power to change it, it is best for them to bring
their behaviors in consonance with it by "accepting it, adapting to it, and
taking advantage of it."

This dissonance reducing thought of "taking Malay privilege and bias
as a challenge" is a major theme of her discourse. She asserts that this is the
idea that she teaches to her children, that they have to take it as a challenge,
and "work harder" and "strive more." In addition, she adds the thought
that in the end, after trying harder and working harder than Malays to get
to the same position, non-Malays are "better off because of the challenges"
and they "excel over Malays" because they were under more pressure. She
thinks that she is better off and has excelled pass some of her fellow Malay
students to become an assistant manager in a private sector corporation.
Also, the thoughts that non-Malays can "depend on themselves" and "look
for employment in the private sector" reduces dissonance because, although
Malays are dominant in the government sector, non-Malays, especially
Chinese and foreigners, are dominant in the private sector.

Sumitra continues with these themes in the following segment of the
same interview in which she also expresses her thoughts of equality and
notes how they contrast with the biases she sees in economic institutions, biases distributed in society-at-large that come into play when people strive to
satisfy their "self-interest."

I: Do you think that in Malaysia there will be a sort of multiracial society in which everyone is equal and there is no discrimination?

Sumitra: We are not satisfied. Most of the time we are not satisfied, with all of these biases. That is not to say that we are upset, that is not to say that we are angry about it. We are not upset about it but we are not satisfied . . . But we get by, we get by . . . You know the story of Animal Farm . . . No matter who you put up there, they are bound to be biased. Politicians, that's how they live. I don't see it in my children. I don't see it in myself, that I am better than you or vice versa. I see equality. But when it comes to work. I come to work, I see, when it comes to promotion, I see biases. When it comes to giving equal jobs, I see biases. But within myself I don't see it and I don't see it in my children either. It's the people. It is the politicians. It's the people's self-interest who are dividing us. So as long as I know these people won't move me, not because of the color of my skin, not because of who I am, nor because I am not capable, but because he is too ignorant to admit that his prejudice, his prejudice, is, um, influencing his decision. So I shouldn't be angry.

I: But do you think it will change?

Sumitra: I believe it will change. Have you met those Sarawakian and Sabahan people? They are very nice people. They are very, how to say, they are also, Indians are, some Indians are, because we are small, you know, when you become small, we learn to accept it. We learn to accept it, and it doesn't bother us, and to us, it is better for us. Because people like them (Malays), because they are so used to receiving, once it has stopped, for them, it is a problem. For me, I have never received in the beginning, so if you stop giving, so I wouldn't know . . . So, I think it is better for my children not to receive, so that if they stop giving, they don't feel the pain. I think it is more of a disadvantage to get it than actually an advantage for them. They get used to it. They are pampered, being pampered is the word, being pampered . . . At one point in time maybe the government just will not be able to pamper them, then there will be a problem.

I: I have seen Indians and Chinese excel . . . on their own . . .

Sumitra: They did it all on their own and they are becoming better for it . . . because the experience has taught them. That is the answer, they're becoming, that is the answer. Even with a lower grade, these people can go in, and how are these people going to diagnose sickness (laughter) when even at a lower level they cannot, they can't go . . . So that, themselves, once you cannot, when you come out, you can't perform your duties as a doctor or engineer. But the government will not accept you, whether that person can make the same grade

> with you, but came from a different group, but if they cannot per-
> form, they just can't perform . . .

Once again, Sumitra brings her thoughts about her behaviors in consonance with realities of Malay dominance and special rights by adding the cognitive elements, "we are not satisfied but not upset or angry" and "we get by." As she noted in the previous segment, it is counterproductive to "get angry and lose control" because you will "probably lose everything." In this segment, she further explains that, "Indians are a small population in Malaysia," similar to the non-Malay *Bumiputeras* of Sabah and Sarawak, and have "learned to accept it" and "not to let it bother us." These thoughts serve to reduce dissonance as does the thoughts that it is "better for non-Malays not to receive benefits" and "it is a disadvantage rather than an advantage for Malays to receive benefits." Moreover, the dissonance reducing thoughts that "Malays are pampered by special privileges" and are worst off and less qualified, unable to "perform their duties as doctors and engineers," are widespread thoughts that I often encountered in discussions with non-Malays.

On the other hand, Sumitra reduces the dissonance between the thoughts about her behavior of "seeing equality" with "seeing biases in employment and promotions" by once again adding the thought that whoever you put up there in positions of power "they will be biased and prejudiced." Furthermore, these politicians or others in positions of administrative authority who discriminate are responsible for their unjust actions. If they do not hire or promote her, or other non-Malays, it is due to their being "too ignorant to admit that it is their prejudice influencing their decision" and not due to anything about her or other non-Malays. With this cognitive element, she preserves her vision and outlook of equality, for inequality and bias is rooted in the "ignorant" person making discriminatory decisions and not in any characteristic of the victim of such prejudice. Moreover, Sumitra buttresses her ideals of equality with the cognitive element, "I believe it will change," keeping her hopes alive for what *can be* in Malaysia, although present reality does not fit her outlook.

Similarly, Hong, a twenty-six year old Chinese marketing executive, who studied abroad in Australia, expresses a sense of idealism as she criticizes biased admissions standards, according to many, one of the more flagrantly unfair aspects of how Malay privilege is institutionalized.

> I: How do you place your educational experience within the larger
>   Malaysian educational system?
>
> Hong: Well, I think, um, maybe, the quota system to a certain extent is
>   fair. But I think the grades that you get that require you to go into the

different kinds of fields should be dropped. You get what I mean. It's like for Chinese to get into a medicine faculty, you have to be at least five As, minimum is five As so you cannot do anything worse than that and that is the best already, that is the highest you can get . . . So if you make a requirement for Chinese to have five As to be in the medical faculty then I think the Malays should also get five As, and the Indians should also get five As, because the intelligence levels that you are talking about, is not whether, oh, you are Malay, also, I give you three As also you can enter but you are going to be, you know, not as good as the other medic students or what, you know, if you want then the Chinese should also have three As and they can qualify to go into medic school. It's like you spoil the profession and all, it's like, oh, Malay doctor, you are not trustworthy because you are obviously not as smart as the Chinese doctor (laughter). So, it does happen, sometimes we are biased in the sense that we tend to feel that they are not as good as Chinese so we are afraid. And the Indians, I am not sure about their requirements . . . Like I said they are not up to the standards, you know, so how can you compete with who is, it is very difficult. Chinese, basically, they are doing better academically. Just like in accounting, there are more Chinese students in accounting then the Malay students, and that is also they dropped the standards for accounting for Malays to get in . . . If you were to check out the papers, right, how many Malays scoring five A's and how many Chinese scoring five A's you will see. But the quota system is fine because if you think that, you know, your Malays are the majority, the Malays are the biggest group, right, so maybe you should do that so that they have more space in the universities . . . I think it is their culture. Their emphasis is very different. Probably they are more family, I don't know, different, they (Malays) are more, like, quite contented with what they have and things like that so they are not so competitive. Chinese are very competitive. You can tell and, I am not so sure, it is probably their standard of living, I don't know. Because you can tell the numbers of Malay students that go to tuition (tutored) classes, do additional classes, most of them are Chinese. They do additional classes. They go. Their parents send them, 'go and learn piano lessons, art classes, art lessons, painting.' But you don't see Malays doing that. I don't know if it is that they can't afford or I am not sure . . .

Hong sustains her commitment to equality, despite its contradiction with the prevailing realities of Malay privilege, by adding the cognitive elements, "I think the grades specific groups have to attain to get into the different fields be dropped" and "the grade requirements to enter particular fields should be the same for all groups, regardless of race."[2] This indicates that although these ideas of equality are not models of how things are or conducive to reducing dissonance, they are still models of how many non-Malay people think things should be. They are also still motives for change. These cognitive elements or private opinions survive the general trend towards greater consonance and are highly resistant to the impact of forced compliance (see Festinger 1957:120).

Nevertheless, people incorporated them within a broader framework that serves to reduce cognitive dissonance with the realities of institutionalized Malay privilege. In particular, although Hong criticizes a particular aspect of the quota system, she adds the thoughts that the quota system is "fair to a certain extent" and is "fine because Malays are the majority" and "maybe you should have quotas to give them more space in the universities." These cognitive elements bring her divergent thoughts into a closer fit with the quota system that non-Malays have been forced to comply with publicly. In addition, she lowers dissonance, as Sumitra did, by adding the thoughts that "you spoil the profession of medicine with Malay doctors who are unqualified," and "not trustworthy" and "obviously not as smart as Chinese doctors." She admits that Chinese harbor biased feelings towards Malay professionals and are afraid of going to them for services, because they suspect their capabilities given the lower academic standards applied to them. The addition of such thoughts to knowledge about Malay special rights reduces dissonance, again turning Malay advantages into disadvantages because Chinese will go to the Chinese doctor who had to endure the highest standards. Hong adds several other cognitive elements that are consonant with these attitudes and opinions, such as "Chinese are doing better academically" and "mostly Chinese are the ones scoring straight A's" and "Chinese are more competitive than Malays" and "large numbers of Chinese attend additional classes." Of course, Chinese will out perform Malays, even if Malays have special rights, because Chinese are "smarter, more competitive, and driven to excel" while Malays are "family-oriented, content with what they have, and not so competitive." These stereotypes express her thoughts of Chinese superiority and reduce the cognitive dissonance fraught by Malay privilege.

In the following segment of the same interview with Hong, she reflects on the perceptions of Malays in the private sector and the significance of overseas education and English standards.

I: So what has your experience been like after college?

Hong: I think if you are in private sector, well, um, there are some companies that actually prefer students if you come back from overseas rather than the local universities. I think they may be afraid that probably, that, because in the local universities they are still using very much of the BM, the Malay language. Many of them do use English and Malay, but I think when they answer the essays most of them are still in Malay. I am not sure why some companies prefer students that come back from overseas. Probably, it is because they feel that, you know, they have been here, they are more open to different things. I am not sure . . . In the government sector there are lots of Malays. And you will find, if you go and ask, I think if you ask those Chinese in the government sector and the Malays, they will probably tell you, even the way you work is different. Chinese and Malay, the way they work is different. I think, for, even for Malays right, most of them, those, I am not sure, only, for Malays who come back from overseas, who have been overseas for a few years or something, then they will probably get some good position in some quite good private companies. Other than that I don't think so. I don't think they think very highly of like MARA students, or things like that. Unless, oh, you have like been overseas for a few years and your grades are good, then they will probably take you in. That is, I think, the cream of them, and their thinking is more Westernized. They are not those *kampung*-thinking Malays . . . I think they should change the standard of English. They should increase the standard. The syllabus for the English here is very low. It is very, very simple. For Chinese to score A in English is no problem, right, but when you go over to the *kampung* schools, they already have problems doing this sort of simple English, you know. That is why they have to lower down the standard because they cannot cope. They cannot push it too high and then they realize, oops, all of them will fail English.

Here again, Malay institutionalized benefits are re-interpreted as disadvantages in the private sector. Hong notes that some companies in the private sector "prefer students who studied overseas rather than in local universities" because in local universities "they are using a lot of Malay language" and the "English standards are too low." In addition, they tend to perceive Malays who studied overseas as being more "open minded" and "more Westernized" and not as being "*kampung*-thinking Malays." They may also be more likely to perform their jobs like Chinese in the private sector than like Malays in the government sector. In any event, these Malays who studied abroad are considered the "cream of them" and are much more likely to be looked upon favorably and hired in the private sector than Malays who stayed in Malaysia and benefited from Malay-medium education in MARA (*Majlis Amanah Rakyat*) institutions. MARA educational institutions are government-funded schools set up for Malays as part of the policies of Malay special rights. These perceptions tend to indicate the futility of special programs aimed at uplifting Malays, bringing them on par with other races, given the negative perception of Malays passing through such institutions. In any event, these thoughts about the perceptions of Malays in the private sector reduces the cognitive dissonance presented by the realities of Malay benefits and are consonant with the thoughts that Chinese are more qualified, hard-working and intelligent.

Similar to Hong and Sumitra, Tariq bin Abdullah, a forty-five year old Muslim convert, from a Malayali Hindu background, combines cognitive elements stemming from models and schemata of "Malaysia's diverse society" and 'Malay privilege,' maintaining his commitment to ideals of equality and justice within a larger dissonance reducing framework. However, in contrast to the earlier discourse segments, Tariq's discourse indicates more clearly, how the processes of cognitive dissonance unfolded in relation to his personal experiences. He begins his narrative with a description of his typical interactions in primary school with children of different backgrounds, a description that indicates that representations of "Malaysia's diverse society" are embodied in, and directive of, social practice.

> Tariq: Now of course, when we went to (primary) school, we started mixing with, you know, non-Hindu kids, that is, the Chinese and the Malay children. And then, of course, there is very little, very little, interaction as far as religion is concerned, in the school environment, in the primary schools. We don't have, you know, interaction in the sense that we do not discuss about religion. Everybody accepts and acknowledges one another's religion and it is never raised as an issue, as far as the primary school is concerned. We just learn to accept them as friends and live with each other and even go to the extent of, um, celebrating each other's festivals by patronizing, you know, on their religious festival days. That is what we were basically accustomed to, you know.

The children of various cultural categories were accustomed to interacting with each other as friends and as equal, though somewhat different, members of society. "We started mixing with" Chinese and Malay children, and we all "accepted and acknowledged" each other's religions and "learned to accept children from different backgrounds as friends and lived together," even "celebrating each other's religious festivals days." This series of cognitive elements stem from representations of "Malaysia's diverse society," depicting a situation of peaceful, harmonious, and friendly relations between members of diverse cultural categories. Such relations were made possible, in a sense, by the fact that they did not "discuss about religion" and religion was "never raised as an issue." Not discussing religion made it easier for them to maintain "tolerance" and "acceptance" of religious differences. As we noted in the case of religious festivals and public celebrations, as long as people could represent and look at non-Islamic religions as simply customs, markers of racial difference, authorities could permit them in the public sphere. It was only when they became clearly religious that they were problematic. Avoiding discussions of these matters made it easier to keep them in the acceptable range of customary differences, differences that everyone could acknowledge as representations of their diverse society. Moreover, the fact that these differences were "never raised as an issue" indicates a sense of inclusion and an absence of discrimination based on religious, racial, and cultural differences.

This was to change with Tariq's "bitter experience" in secondary school when he came to learn of the realities of Malay special rights.

> Tariq: The real, I would say, issue of realizing the differences of race, of culture, and of religion came about when we were in the secondary schools. As for me, it came about when I was sixteen years old, sixteen years old. I had a very bitter experience, a very bitter experience. The bitter experience that I had was that when I received my, or should I say, when I received the results of the lower certificate of education examination. I was qualified to enter the science stream, but unfortunately six of my Malay friends who did not get the same results as me, whose results were very much below mine, were given admission into the science stream but I was denied admission into the science stream and I was admitted into the arts stream. Now, this really made me wonder, why was there such discrimination? That was the first taste of discrimination that I felt. Because I was better qualified than my own friends but I was denied admission. So I decided to go to the Education Department in Melaka to see the officials there. I had a chance to talk to the chief education officer himself and the chief education officer told me that there's nothing he can do because the streaming was done by the ministry and the list was issued by the ministry and this was their policy to promote and allow *Bumiputeras,* that is Malays, indigenous Malays, to go into the science streams, so as to encourage greater Malay participation in the science education and so on. But I still felt why should an eligible person be deprived of his right so that this right can be given to another race? That was something that I could not accept and I could not understand. At that time, you know, being only about sixteen years old. In any case, although I continued with my education in that same school . . . in the art stream, I still pursued the matter by asking the principal of the school to make an appeal. The principal told me that his hands are tied; he can not do very much about it. So I had to settle and accept the fact that there is no recourse for me and just to accept that I had to study in the art stream although at that time my ambition was to either be a veterinary surgeon or to pursue some field which involved science. Well, that was the greatest, and I would

say, most painful experience I had to go through in the secondary
school, and this was when I began to realize that there was a distinction in being a Malay and a non-Malay. And this is the first time I
started to realize that there was such a thing as discrimination and
this is the first time I started to realize that there was special rights
and privileges for the Malays which the non-Malays did not have
and this was the first time I started to realize that there is such a
thing as injustice.

In high schools in Malaysia, teachers and administrators give students a
lower certificate of education examination and the results are used to
"stream" or divide them into different curricula; administrators direct students with higher grades to the science curriculum while they direct students
with lower grades to the arts curriculum. Tariq had earned grades high
enough to enter science stream, which he very much wanted to enter, but
they denied him entrance into this stream, whereas they allowed several of
his Malay friends to enter. This bitter experience was his first experience
with discrimination and Malay special rights and it caused a high degree of
cognitive dissonance for him, as it contradicted his notions of equality, fairness, and togetherness that he had experienced during his primary school
years. His thoughts about his behaviors after finding out they would not
admit him to the science stream were consonant with these notions and dissonant with the realities of institutionalized Malay privilege. For instance,
he "wondered why there was such discrimination" and "decided to go to
Department of Education" and "met with the chief officer" and when that
failed to attain a reversal of the discriminatory decision he "pursued the
matter by asking the principal to appeal the decision." The public officials
and administrators upheld the decision and explained the rationale behind
"Malay privilege" to Tariq, but he could not understand why the goals of
"promoting and encouraging greater Malay *Bumiputera* participation in the
sciences" could not be advanced without "depriving the rights of other
races." In fact, the dissonance he experiences with these two cognitive elements continues into the present, although he has added several cognitive elements to reduce the lack of fit.

   After authorities forced Tariq to comply with the administrative decision, his experiences brought his thoughts about his behaviors into line with
the realities of Malay privilege. Similar to Katherine and Sumitra, Tariq
began to reduce cognitive dissonance by adding the thoughts "so I just had
to settle and accept the fact that I had to study in the art stream" and "I
began to realize there was such a thing as discrimination, injustice, and
Malay special rights and privileges." He and other non-Malays, forced to

comply with institutionalized "positive discrimination," changed their private opinions and attitudes, to varying extents, towards consonance with these political realities. In the following segment of the same narrative, Tariq informs us of how his ideas have changed over the years.

> Tariq: Now, but I, cannot blame my Malay friends, for the simple reason that I realized they had nothing to do with the system, they had nothing to do with the policy. They were still my friends. I was still close to them. We acted the same way we did in the primary school . . . and we continued, you know, living the same way was we were, although, you know, it still pains me to think why they did that to me. Although now that I am already forty-five years old, when I reflect back, it is still painful to me, because I feel that one can, provide opportunities for the less fortunate ones, such as the Malays, indigenous Malays, without depriving the rights of others, by creating opportunities, and by expanding opportunities. And this is what I feel now, you know, that it should be done that way and not depriving or denying someone else's rights. This is the greatest problem, you know, that I had when I was in the secondary school. And it also became quite apparent, when were growing up, especially when we were in the secondary school that most of us took cognizance in our religions, and also in our, you know, racial backgrounds, and the differences in our languages, although, you know, we were in the English medium of instruction at that time. *Bahasa* (Malay) was being introduced very strongly to be the main medium of instruction but we were not, but of course, we were not required to adopt the *Bahasa* as the main medium during our time. English was still the main medium but *Bahasa* was made compulsory and many of my Chinese friends failed the *Bahasa Malaysia* examination and as a result they failed the entire examination because they could not get a Grade One certificate. Because it was a compulsory paper that they should pass *Bahasa Malaysia* if they want to get a Grade One or a Division One in the Malaysian Certificate of Education, which is called the M.C.E.

Now, the differences that I mentioned, in race, in culture, in language, and in religion, having become apparent at that period of time, then we realized that as we grow up that we have to face these things and these things are going to be the major hurdles that we have to overcome or we have to cope with or live with and we accepted it, that there's nothing we can do at that point in time about overcoming this. But as a human being, I had my own vision. My vision was that, some day, all Malaysians should live on an equal footing without any special privileges being granted to any race, but only on merit. But although that was what my vision was, I had to admit that my vision and viewpoint at that particular time was absolutely wrong because I did not realize the prevailing situations in the country at that time which were faced by the majority of Malays. The Malays were backward. They did not enjoy the wealth of the nation as they should. There was unequal distribution of wealth where the wealth of the nation was enjoyed more by the Chinese and by the elites than by the general population of the country, and this brought me into the realization, that the bitter experience, or the painful experience, which I went through when I was in secondary school, being deprived of my place in the science stream had a lot to do with the disparity between the Malays and the non-Malays in the country. But still, although I acknowledge the fact of disparity, I still feel strongly that there should not be discrimination in trying to work out this problem but there should be some form of positive discrimination, or some form of measures, taken to overcome this problem rather than denying other races their rights.

As Tariq and his non-Malay cohorts, moved through high school, they became more and aware of Malay special rights and "how they would be major hurdles for them to overcome" and to "cope with, live with, and accept." They began to realize that "there was nothing within their power they could do" to change these realities at the present point in time. These sorts of thoughts served to reduce cognitive dissonance, however he continued to blame those in administrative power and "the system" for the perpetuation of these policies and he preserved "his vision of equality and justice." His vision, as a teenager and young man, was still strongly dissonant with the realities of Malay privilege despite the addition of several cognitive elements noted above. His dissonance reducing thoughts, at this early stage, were directed towards coping with the realities of discrimination but they did not add any cognitive elements that justified them. He still did not understand, in a deeper sense, why Malays had to have special rights, while policies accorded other Malaysians second-class treatment. He had a vision of all Malaysians "being equal" and "being distributed benefits and resources" according to "merit" and not according to cultural differentiation.

Later in his life, after converting to Islam as a young man, and interacting with Malays of various social classes, he became more sensitive to the structural need for the institutionalization of "positive discrimination" for Malays, not just to keep the peace and harmony, but also to rectify socio-economic inequality. He brought his thoughts into greater consonance with Malay privilege by adding the cognitive elements that "Malays were backward" and "they did not enjoy the national wealth as they should" because "there was an unequal distribution of wealth." Tariq began to add more cognitive elements that acknowledged the "prevailing conditions experienced by Malays" and "the disparity between Malays and non-Malays in the country." This deeper understanding of the rationale behind institutionalized

Malay privilege is often rejected by non-Malays that express the opinion that these policies directed towards helping out Malays are no longer necessary. However, Tariq, perhaps due to his experiences of interacting more closely with Malays, fellow Muslims, and being involved in Muslim organizations has developed this understanding. On the other hand, the pattern of thoughts consonant with his values of equality and justice, are continued, albeit incorporated within the framework of refining the implementation of "Malay privilege." That is, he still thinks that officials can implement special programs to help Malays without "negative discrimination" and "denying and depriving other groups of their rights," by "expanding and creating new opportunities." His ideals of justice and equality are still strong motives for change, partially directing his involvement in political movements.

MALAY COGNITIVE DYNAMICS

Similar to non-Malays, Malay youth and adults combine cognitive elements that stem from schemata of "Malaysia's diverse society" and "Malay privilege" so as to construct a distinct sense of citizenship for themselves, as "natives" of Malaya or Malaysia, and for other groups that are "originally" from somewhere else. However, in contrast to non-Malay re-interpretations of notions of citizenship, as exemplified by notions of "first class" or "*Bumiputera* citizens" and "second class" or "*Bumiputera* citizens," Malay re-interpretations and combinations of these notions tend to add greater emphasis upon the conditional and contingent position of non-*Bumiputera* "citizens." For instance, Mohamad Mahathir (1970:126) clearly expresses this widespread pattern of re-interpretation in the Malay community.

> There are other areas in Southeast Asia where the Chinese have been for as long as they have been in Malaya. But nowhere have they claimed to be or have they been accepted as indigenous peoples of these areas. The burden of my argument is that the Malays are the rightful owners of Malaya, and that if citizenship is conferred on races other than the Malays, it is because the Malays consent to this. That consent is conditional.

The cognitive dissonance between the thoughts that "Malays are the rightful owners of Malaya," and that "citizenship is conferred on races other than Malays" is reduced by adding the cognitive elements "because Malays consent to this" and "this consent is conditional." From this perspective, *Bumiputera* and non-*Bumiputera* citizens are not only graded and accorded differential access to power and resources, but non-*Bumiputera* citizens are also *supposed* to fulfill the terms of citizenship *Bumiputera* citizens impose upon them. Mahathir Mohamad goes on to add the thoughts that in Malaysia, just as in Australia and the U.S., immigrants of various races must be "made to assimilate the language, customs, norms and other cultural attributes" of the "definitive race" whose attributes "should be perpetuated as the distinctive national characteristics" (ibid:122–153). Moreover, "the rights of the citizens of immigrant origins concerning the control and perpetuation of their own distinctive characteristics are limited" and these "new citizens" have a duty to "submit to and insist upon those policies with regard to language, immigration, education, and culture which are calculated to create and preserve the distinctive national characteristics" (ibid:135–142). These sorts of cognitive elements, emphasizing the conditional and qualified nature of non-*Bumiputera* citizenship, serve to increase consonance with thoughts of the special status of Malays as the "original owners" and "true belongers" of Malaysia.

Mohamad Suhaimi, a young Malay professional, expresses this value of assimilating non-Malay citizens while noting that this is not how things have been actually working in contemporary Malaysian society. We had been discussing local open house practices, when he stated:

> But Chinese usually don't have many Malay friends because they do not speak Malay well and they prefer to speak English at work and Chinese at home . . . and they eat pork and drink alcohol and like to gamble . . . So Malays don't want to come around this environment . . . The talk about how we all relate and participate is just a lot of rhetoric . . . Chinese are more of the immigrant mentality . . . We are not working to form an integrated Malaysia or a melting pot anymore, like we were before. Ever since around 1986, when Semangat 46 was strong, and the courts ruled that UMNO was illegal, the government was in effect not valid, so Mahathir relied upon the MCA and MIC to appoint him as the leader or else they would have been the legal leaders, especially MCA . . . Since then, they have been allowed to follow their own course and to develop their own cultures and communities and we only get together for economic development, but they speak more and more Chinese and are demanding more Chinese and Tamil schools now . . . Each of these groups are following their own separate course now, and the Chinese speak more Mandarin than Malay now . . . But they are supposed to speak Malay. What happened when the Chinese got control of Hong Kong back? They cleared out all the English and implemented the Chinese language instead . . . But the Chinese want to have their own here. They came here when they were very poor, leaving China with only the shirt and trousers because they were the poor Chinese and were oppressed by the rich ones . . . and now they come here and owns things and want to claim it for themselves . . . Like the Chinese man at my apartment complex, they put their names on parking spots and so on to

claim them for their own. They want to claim that they belong here . . . like the claims they are making about Laksamana Cheng Ho[3] . . . They have control of China and now they want to say that they belong here too . . . and Malaysia can be an extension of the 'Greater China' . . . Indonesian Chinese have Indonesian names and speak Indonesian and so there is a distance between them and Chinese here in Malaysia who speak Chinese and have Chinese surnames and stay in their own communities very close to each other.

Mohamad Suhaimi reduces the dissonance between cognitive elements stemming from dominant models of "Malaysia's diverse society" and his thoughts about how things actually work by adding the thought that all the talk of "friendly and harmonious relations between Malaysians of diverse backgrounds" is "just a lot of rhetoric." In particular, these thoughts often bantered around in public, in almost cliché form, about how "Malaysians of all backgrounds relate with each other" and "participate in each other's festivals," and his personal opinions about "Chinese usually not having Malay friends" and "Malays not wanting to be around Chinese who engage in behaviors prohibited by Islamic teachings" are brought into a closer fit when he re-interprets dominant ideological formulations as "mere rhetoric." From his perspective, thoughts that stem from models of "Malaysia's diverse society" do not adequately describe the *real* state of interaction between Malays and Chinese.

Moreover, it is important for us to note, the dissonance reducing thoughts for Malays in regard to non-Malay immigrants adhering to Malay terms of citizenship and assimilating Malay attributes, are contradicted by his thoughts about how Chinese and Indians are perpetuating their own distinctive characteristics. His thoughts about how "Chinese are *supposed* to speak Malay in Malaysia" and "Indonesian Chinese have Indonesian names and speak Indonesian" and "Chinese implemented the Chinese language in Hong Kong after regaining control" and "they *should* work to form an integrated Malaysia or a melting pot" express his ideal of having the non-Malay immigrant groups assimilate "definitive" Malay attributes. However, these cognitive elements do not fit with his thoughts about the course things have taken in contemporary Malaysian society. In particular, his thoughts about "Chinese speaking English at work and Chinese at home in Malaysia" and "Chinese speaking more and more Chinese instead of Malay" and "Chinese and Indians demanding more Chinese and Tamil schools" and how "these groups are following their own separate courses of developing their own distinctive cultures and communities" do not fit. These thoughts produce a great deal of cognitive dissonance for him. He moves to reduce this dissonance with the explanation that this turn away from integrating diverse groups into the "definitive national culture" or melting pot took place when UMNO, declared as an illegal organization, was made to rely upon the other major constituent National Alliance parties, MCA and MIC, making concessions to them in order to remain in power.[4] Before this political incident, after the riots of 1969 at least, Chinese and Indians were undergoing a process of assimilation and were acting less centered in their own distinctiveness. On the other hand, following this incident, things are not going the way they are *supposed* to because Malays, at a point of political weakness, loss some power and ground to non-Malays, after which, non-Malays were allowed to follow their own distinctive cultures rather than assimilating to Malay culture.

In the absence of the cognitive reducing thoughts of non-*Bumiputera* assimilation, thoughts of Malay special rights and status are dissonant with the ways things are going, taken to be a sort of erosion of the special position of Malays and a move towards a state of equality or mutual belonging. Mohamad Suhaimi expresses this dissonance between his thoughts of how things *should* be and how they are by referring both to Chinese immigrant status and to his perceptions of their present behavior of laying claim to *belonging*. His thoughts about "Chinese leaving China in the past and coming here when they were very poor" recognizes their position as non-*Bumiputera* who have a rightful claim of belonging to another country, China, but not *Tanah Melayu*. However, his thoughts about their behavior are not consonant with this status, as "Chinese want to have their own here in Malaysia" and "now they come here and own things and want to claim it for themselves" and "they want to claim that they *belong* here too." Chinese not only have control of their own land, China, but they want to have a claim to *belonging* and thus to power in the "lands of Malays as well," perhaps even making Malaysia come under the influence of a "Greater China" empire or sphere of influence. These highly dissonant thoughts of equating equality with Chinese domination and of Chinese seizing political power in Malaysia are powerful cognitive elements that we will encounter in several other discourses below.

On another occasion, around the time of the last general election in late 1999, Mohamad Suhaimi again expresses this discrepancy between his ideals of Malay special rights and status and the realities of public expressions of Chinese and Indian cultural distinctiveness and of increasing minority political influence.

> I: A Chitty man told me the other day that Chitty and many Indians are friendly and open like Malays in contrast to most Chinese.

> Mohamad Suhaimi: The problem with Chinese is that they have too much freedom and rights here and now the Indians are demanding the same thing. They used to just have a few shows on and some Western movies during Deepavali but now they are demanding the same rights as Chinese and this year they had a long list of Hindustani movies, for hours and hours they were on television . . . Now the Chinese are the key factor in the elections. Mahathir has gone over to seek support for them and they have made a list of demands and we Malays felt that this was insulting, so they said they are just things that they want to give their political support to BN . . . and one of the things they want is more support for the vernacular schools . . . and Mahathir has allowed them to have it. Now they do not have to pay for the land the schools are on, no fees at all, and before they had to pay maybe 300,000 *ringgit* depending on the size of the land they were . . . Chinese have the most schools, there are only around 300 vernacular Tamil schools and *sekolah rakyat,* Muslim schools, are fewer than the Chinese schools so the Chinese benefited the most from this and now they use this money to further their own cultural programs in their community, developing their people.

His thoughts of the pattern of assimilation represented by the Chitty community strongly contrast with his thoughts about "Chinese having too much freedom and rights in Malaysia" and "Indians making the same demands as Chinese." Mohamad Suhaimi and many Malays prefer the period immediately following the 1969 riots in which there were restrictions on public displays of Chinese and Indian cultural distinctiveness. Things were closer to the way they are *supposed* to be at that time. He laments how there has been a steady increase in Chinese language television programming and advertising, many of the programs nowadays even present Chinese wearing dynastic attire that was formerly restricted. This year around the time of the main, public recognized Hindu festival, *Deepavali,* there was numerous television broadcasts of Indian-language movies, and Mohamad Suhaimi interpreted this as an indication that "Indians are demanding the same rights as Chinese." These demands for more public recognition of their cultural distinctiveness contradict his thoughts about how non-*Bumiputera* immigrants *should* be behaving in *Tanah Melayu.*

Moreover, he is alarmed at the increase in Chinese political influence and the "special" benefits they are able to garner in return for their agreement to support *Barisan Nasional,* the ruling alliance party. Mohamad Suhaimi's thoughts of Malay political supremacy are dissonant with his thoughts of "Chinese being the key factor in the elections" and "Prime Minister Mahathir going over to seek Chinese support" and being "confronted with a list of demands." This public expression of Chinese political influence was so highly dissonant with Malay expectations of political control that they took it as an "insult." Once again, caught in a position of weakness, given the political split in the Malay community, UMNO leaders were forced to make concessions to the Chinese community. One of their demands, Mohamad Suhaimi thinks, was "more government support for vernacular schools" which was announced before the general election "benefiting Chinese more than it does Indians or Malays." Such government support, he thinks, will "allow Chinese to fund more of their separate cultural programs for their community," fostering "greater cultural distinctive" rather than "assimilation to the dominant host culture." The trend of Malay thought represented in this discourse is dissonant with thoughts of Malay special rights and status, whereas they are consonant with thoughts of "equality" and "power-sharing amongst citizens."

Thus, the question remains as to how Mohamad Suhaimi tries to reduce dissonance between his thoughts of ideal Malay advantages and the realities of things "gone astray" from the proper economic and political order. His explanation given above in reference to the crucial, shift in power politics when UMNO was declared illegal, and his depiction of UMNO leaders becoming beholden to non-Malay political parties, especially to MCA, are good indications of the direction we should look. He thinks that the Malay political leadership has been "broken" and must be "fixed" in order to set things straight again. His thoughts about "his plans for political action inside and outside of Malay political parties" and about "his efforts to foster greater unity in the Muslim community" in order to "fix the system of intergroup relations" and to "re-establish proper Malay special rights and standing" tend to reduce dissonance.

Norijah, a twenty-four year old Malay woman, who recently returned from the U.S. after completing an engineering degree, expresses a strong sense of pride in the quality of Islamic practice in Malaysia in comparison to many other "Islamic countries." She argues that an extension of Islamic criminal law to Muslims does not contradict the existence of a diverse society in Malaysia, implying that this would be a positive change for Malaysian society because Muslims are *supposed* to be under the jurisdiction of Islamic law.

> I: How do you work out this emphasis on *Al Islam* (Islam) in Malaysia with the fact that there is a multiracial, multi-religious society in Malaysia?

> Norijah: I think we can still put the Islamic law in Malaysia where it only, basically, applies to the Muslim society. But you don't enforce it to the other cultures. It can happen. I talk about it with my family,

and we believe that it can be done . . . But here in Malaysia you have two types of courts, Islamic courts and civil courts.

I: But it is the civil court that is dominant throughout society right?

Norijah: Yes, but something to do with Islamic things, people should take to the religious court, the Islamic court. Like, if you are doing a kind of *khalwat* (close proximity between men and women who are not married to one another) or you are doing, whatever, but not like if you *rasuah* (commit acts of corruption), or something else . . . But for me, like that, can change. If you are Islamic people, you are suppose to be under *Syar'ia* (Islamic law), *agama Syar'ia* (religious law), and if you are not Muslim than you are flexible . . .

I: That would be more of an Islamic state. Plus in an Islamic state, according to some *ulamas* (Islamic scholars), it would be fine to have a multiracial, multiethnic, multi-religious society, but the non-Muslims would become *dhimmi*[5], they would have a contract with the Islamic state and through that contract they would have all the rights equal with all of the Muslims in the society. That is something that may be in contradiction to some of the policies, of like the NEP, and some of the advantages that some of the Malays have.

Norijah: Yes, yes, but that is really for just the Malays here. Our condition is very important so . . . But if you are talking to a Malay person, they will usually say that it is very important. So we would rather to have the law now than having it the same, all equal . . . It is just because if the Chinese take over, Malays are gone, Islamic state is gone, and that is what scares us a lot. And when they take over the economics, the Malay will go down, down, and this Malaysia will not be Malaysia right now. So we cannot take this chance. I can't imagine if the, because I have a few experiences, seeing if Chinese is in control, it's going to be very difficult.

I: But when you have Chinese having a contract as *dhimmi,* as non-Muslims, they have a contract of equality, it doesn't mean they are equal in terms of the power. It is still an Islamic state . . . So, here the Malays would be in power, but non-Malays would have equal rights to education, resources, jobs, land, all those kinds of things, economic things, they would have equal rights. There wouldn't be any favoritism, if anything there would be a policy to help all of the poor people regardless of what race or religion they are.

Norijah: But if they are in control, all of the big jobs would go to them, rather than to us, because believe it or not, they are better than us (Malays).

I: What do you mean?

Norijah: The Chinese, they are more self-survival than us, so they are very strong, so, if we take that chance when they are on top, with equal rights and equal opportunities, basically, the top part will be them. We wouldn't be on top. They may be in power instead of us.

I: But even under the policy now, I have visited at least two major industrial parks, and seventy-five percent of the lower level are Malays and the top executives are all Chinese.

Norijah: And they are not, they don't have equal rights, right. They have not yet got their equal rights yet. Just imagine if they have their equal rights.

Norijah's thoughts about the "highly Islamic nature" of Malaysian society are consonant with her thoughts about "Malay special rights and privileges" because the Islamic attribute of Malay social identity is highly significant to her. She asserted, earlier in the conversation, that "Malays are the best Muslims in the world," qualifying this statement with recognition that there are several Islamic schools of thought. Furthermore, the "highly Islamic nature of Malaysian society," given the abundance of mosques and prayer halls and the widespread observance of Islamic prayers and fasting and other practices, can be improved even further by "extending Islamic law more completely to all Muslims." The government has already institutionalized Islamic personal law for marriages, divorces, and funerals and for prohibited behavior, such as drinking alcohol and engaging in close proximity with members of the opposite sex on the state level. Norijah and her family think that Islamic criminal law, which would pertain to criminal cases, such as theft, murder, and corruption, could and should be implemented in Malaysian society without disrupting relations between Muslims and non-Muslims. Islamic law would only apply to Muslims, whereas non-Muslims would still fall under the jurisdiction of civil law.

However, her enthusiasm for Islamic principles does not include Islamic notions for equality amongst "citizens" of a diverse society under Muslim political leadership. When posed with the contradiction between equality, even under an Islamic state, and the preservation of Malay special rights, Norijah chose the "continuation of present laws and policies that provide special privileges to Malays," a cognitive element consonant with her thoughts that stem from the schema of "Malay privilege."[6] In fact, she asserts that, "Malays in general would rather have the law the way it is now than to have things be the same for everyone, all equal." In addition, Norijah adds several cognitive elements such as "the special benefits are really just for Malays" and "our condition is very important to us" that reduces dissonance between equality and Malay privilege. She also tends to equate a system of equality amongst all of the "citizens" of Malaysia with a condition in which the Chinese have taken over and achieved total domination, a thought that makes the notion of equality highly distasteful. In particular, her thoughts that "if things are equal then the Chinese will takeover" and "attain total economic control" and "Malays and the Islamic state would be gone" and "Malays would go down" and "all Chinese would be on top." If things were equal for all groups, Chinese would gain control and then "Malaysia would be very different" and "things would be very difficult under Chinese control."

These thoughts are consonant with her thoughts about "perpetuating Malay special rights" and find further support in her thoughts of experiences of working under Chinese authority in the past. She has had several experiences of Chinese, who generally occupy management positions in the private sector, discriminating against her. In fact, she was having problems finding employment in the private sector, despite her overseas degree in electrical engineering. Several Malays have reported experiences of discrimination in the private sector corporations. For instance, Mohamad Suhaimi informed me that when he worked for a foreign firm Chinese managers and coworkers told the foreign white executives that he was "lazy, unqualified and not a good worker because he was Malay." They also told the white executives that he would take lots of time away from work in order to make his Islamic prayers, even though he used his lunch break to make his afternoon prayer.

Aishah, another young Malay university graduate, informed me that she realized that there was a pattern of discrimination against the Malay employees in a stock trading company she used to work for. This company did not treat any of the Malay employees well, she said. Company managers promised year-end bonuses to all employees based upon their production but only the Chinese got good bonuses despite the fact that many Malay employees had earned them as well. Aishah did not wait to see what her bonus would look like quitting before the end of the year. She wrote a letter to the company, after she quit, reprimanding the Chinese management for the way they treat Malay employees. Nevertheless, she later gave her Malay friend moral support because Chinese co-workers, at the same company, had been harassing her. After leaving this stock company, Aishah soon found a job as personnel manager in a large Chinese-owned manufacturing corporation. They hired her to supervise the predominantly Malay assembly line workers and she was the lowest paid person in management, which she did not feel was fair.

In any case, Norijah's thoughts about her experiences of being discriminated against and maltreated by Chinese, experiences shared by many Malays, are consonant with her thoughts about the need to perpetuate the policies of Malay special rights and privileges. These thoughts are further supported with the cognitive elements that "if the Chinese were in control all of the jobs would go to them" and "believe or not, Chinese are better than Malays." The latter statement of Malay inferiority was explained as meaning that "Chinese are stronger and more oriented towards self-survival" than Malays. Whereas Chinese express a sense of superiority to reduce cognitive dissonance with the realities of institutionalized Malay privilege, Malays express a sense of inferiority, at least in terms of certain characteristics, to reduce cognitive dissonance with the need to perpetuate Malay privilege. Therefore, with the added cognition of Malay inferiority, one could assume that "if Malays took a chance with equality" then "Chinese would be on top," and "all of the top part would consist of them" and "Malays would not even be on top politically" because "Chinese would assume the positions of power instead of Malays." The risk of removing all institutionalized Malay privileges is too high, because it would leave Malays with no protection against the "stronger" and more "survival-oriented" Chinese. Indeed, the fact that Chinese are already dominant in the economic sphere even though they have not yet been bestowed equal rights supports her thought "that things would be even worse for Malays" if they did have equal rights. Norijah's thoughts about the realities of Chinese domination in the economic sphere are highly consonant with her thoughts about the need to maintain Malay special rights.

In the following discussion segment, Nurul Izzah, a twenty-seven year old Malay optometrist, supports the notion of Malay special rights with historical representations and relates some of her experiences with education and employment that add further support for the perpetuation of Malay special rights.

> I: Well along with, or part of, the idea of the Malaysian multiracial society there is also the idea of *hak-hak istimewa Melayu* (Malay special rights). How is that related to multi-
>
> Nurul: (interrupting) Because in history, this is my opinion-lah, uh, in history, this *Tanah Melayu,* we call it *Tanah Melayu,* it is opened by a Malay-lah, I mean, Parameswara, he came from Temisir, last time . . . Uh, Indonesia, so Indonesia, is a Malay-lah, right. So, uh, from history last time, this *Tanah Melayu* is for Malays, that is why we call it *Tanah Melayu*-lah. And then when *perang* (war), when wars happened, some Chinese or Indians came from China or from

India. So these, uh, that's why I think we still need these *hak-hak Melayu*-lah because this is our own country. There, now that we are having all Chinese or all Indians, we can still work together, still can live together, but for *hak-hak Tanah Melayu*, we still *kekalkan* (make permanent).

I: How does it relate to your experiences, going to school, and now, as a professional?

Nurul: When I was working here, my Chinese mates who did not graduate like me, always ask me, 'maybe because of your, you Malays are having *hak-hak istimewa Melayu*, you *sampai* (arrive) at this stage-lah, you graduate. Maybe if you like us also, you don't graduate like us-lah.' When I first started working I heard this sentence-lah from my clique also. They said, 'maybe if I, uh, *Melayu* don't have this *hak-hak Melayu*, maybe all *anak Melayu* (Malay youth) also like, uh, not graduate, only work as like contract workers-lah.

I: So what is your view about that?

Nurul: From my part, I say, I worked hard because of, because of me, not because of these *hak-hak Melayu*-lah. Because, sincerely, I tell you that I worked hard because of my family-lah. My family is not, um, is not well enough. I mean, my mother and my father, um, I do not like to stay at home because I always heard their problems. From there, I too, I tell my mother I have to work hard, I want to live in that hostel, so that I can forget about them, I mean, forget about their problems-lah. But now it is OK-lah.

I: Did you get any special benefits when you went to school?

Nurul: Special benefits, because I am *kampung*, yes, when I came to secondary (school) because I came from *kampung*, my father used to work for FELDA (Federal Land Development Authority), you know, doing construction work, so I get some help from government-lah. We call it *biasiswa, biasiswa*, it is a scholarship. Then when I pass my secondary, I go for matriks (matriculation classes), and I, I, *minta* (politely request) from MARA-lah. First it is a loan, then when I already finished my, my degree, I *lulus* (pass), them they turned it into a scholarship. If they *tak lulus* (don't pass) so they have to *bayar*-lah (pay-lah), have to return the money-lah. But mine is *lulus*, so I don't have to pay-lah . . .

At the beginning of this segment, Nurul Izzah reconciles the discrepancy between Malay special rights and equality by adding thoughts, such as "this land was opened up by Malays" and "from history this land is for Malays"

and "this is our country," that stem directly from schemata of "Malay privilege." Similarly, her thoughts of "Chinese and Indians as immigrants coming to Malaysia for refuge" and as "people who have their own countries,
China and India," add support to her thoughts that "Malays still need special rights because Malaysia is their country." Mohamad Suhaimi also expresses these fundamental thoughts that constitute a primary justification
for the existence and perpetuation of Malay special rights: "This is our
country, we have nowhere to go; Chinese have China, Singapore and
Taiwan . . . and Indians have India, this is our country."

In response to several statements, containing thoughts that are dissonant and tend to undermine Malay special rights, made by her Chinese
coworkers and schoolmates, Nurul Izzah adds several cognitive elements to
reduce dissonance. Thoughts such as "you only made it to this position because you got special benefits as a Malay" and "if you were non-Malay like
us you would not have made it" are indicative of a non-*Bumi* critique of institutionalized Malay privilege, one that we have seen instances of above.
Nurul rebuffs these claims and reduces dissonance with Malay privilege by
adding the thoughts "I worked hard because my family is poor" and "I have
to work hard" and "I moved out and lived in the dormitories in order to
focus on education." These thoughts argue that she arrived at her present
position as an optometrist because she was motivated and worked hard to
advance herself. Her background of poverty motivated her to work hard.
She goes on to add more support with her thoughts "I received special benefits because I came from a poor village background" and "my father was a
government construction worker." Her father, a FELDA, government
works, construction worker did not have a high salary and her family always
had many problems at home. Nurul's thoughts, that these "special programs
for Malays, such as MARA, helped her out" and "gave her an opportunity
to excel" are consonant with her thoughts that these special benefits *should*
be made permanent.

In the next segment, taken from the same conversation, Nurul relates
her experience and the experience of some of her friends, of working in a line
of business traditionally, and still, dominated by Chinese enterprises.

> I: So how do you relate these ideas of Malaysia's multiracial society and
> *hak-hak istimewa* and think about them?

> Nurul: Sometimes, when I have a problem with, uh, my work here, some-
> times, uh, when I have a problem with a Chinese, sometimes I call
> them (old friends from school), I call them, sometimes, I say *sebab*
> (because), when I first work, I quite sad, because maybe none of them

don't trust me, to check their eyes also. Sometimes I call my clique, my Chinese clique, and ask why this thing happened, Chinese *tak suka Melayu ke* (don't like Malays or) or what-lah. So, normally, they said, uh, because in optical line most of the opticians is a Chinese. Seldom we saw a Malay shop-lah, they say. Only because when UKM (University Kebangsaan Malaysia) start this, um, UKM start this optometrist (program), then some more optometrists start-lah, some are Malay. Because in this Malaysia, for a long, long time ago, this optical line is, uh, dominated by the Chinese . . . Only when UKM start this course, then a Malay got, a Malay students take part. So from there only, um, because they said opticians is Chinese, opticians is Chinese. Because in *kampung, mana-mana kampung pun* (even, all over, in Malay neighborhoods), uh, to make glasses, they go to a, only other optical shops are Chinese optical shops, so no Malays or Indians. I think more Indians go into legal groups, not into optical shops . . . I think their *pikiran* (thinking) is still biased against Malays . . . But I think now that more Malays open up their optical shops, so I hope they can, uh, although it is a Malay optical shop, but a Chinese or an Indian still can, uh, try, because, um, my clique said that they opened a shop. I asked them how is your customers, is it mostly Malay? They said, yeah, in the beginning most of them is a Malay, Malay customers, for a Malay optical shop, you know. But then when they tried and they know the optometrist is good, so then Chinese and also Indians, uh, but not so much compared to Chinese optical shops, all Malays, Indians, or Chinese go there. But for a Malay optical shop, only, normally-lah, most of them is only a Malay. I think this is a bad thing. So I hope, uh, maybe, because we have an association, maybe they can do something with this, so that, uh, their minds is more opened, uh, they go to this one . . . So I hope they can do something . . . Especially because in Malaysia, I thought that Malays still, um, we have Chinese, Indians, and Malays, and others, *Bumiputeras,* that one is not *Bumi.* Among others, in education or in business, Chinese is the number one-lah. OK. Malays in the second, but Indians in the third one. But not all-lah, this is the *acara perata* (average pattern). I thought this *hak-hak keistimewaan Melayu* must be *teruskan* (continued), because, um, in Malaysia, most of the Malays is the *petani* (farmer), *golongan rendah* (lower class), *petani, orang kampung* (rural people), so there is not enough money for them to support their children's study. Like mine, myself, my family is not so, so, when I have this opportunity, I can get until my college and then finish with college, and, so I hope this *hak-hak* can help, especially Malays in *golongan rendah* because although Malaysia *sekarang membangun* (is developing), but still have, if you heard about, *orang miskin miskin* (very poor people), some of them do not have a *rumah* (house) and just put up a *pondok* (shack), so we must help these people-lah . . . Because, maybe because, we are Malay here, because, uh, *yang buka* (ones who opened) this land is a Malay people-lah. So, when the Chinese have a problem, they come here (from China), to do business, to *perdagang* (trade) here, so, um, because in some countries they do not allow others to, to, but, but now we are, we are here together, so, I think, but the Malays are the *tuan rumah* (the hosts) here-lah, yeah, although I know, although now, we are more open, but the *hak-hak istimewaan* must be continued.

Nurul and her Malay friends have experienced what she interprets as a "lack of trust" from Chinese customers who "give her problems" and "do not trust Malays to provide for their optical needs." As young Malay professionals, they are experiencing the biases Sumitra and Hong spoke of earlier, biases clearly related to the undermining thoughts of Malays only being in professional positions because of Malay special rights. This critique often continues to include thoughts that "Malays are not qualified to be in these positions." Once again, Nurul rebuffs these dissonant thoughts with cognitive elements that try to reduce the lack of fit between her thoughts of these behaviors and her thoughts of Malay special rights. She begins in this direction with her thoughts questioning Chinese behavior, "why does this happen" and "why don't they trust us," and thoughts of her behavior of asking her friends for an explanation. Her friends add the consonant thoughts that "all of the shops are Chinese" and "this line of business has been dominated by Chinese for a long time," and Nurul thinks that Chinese behavior towards her indicates that "their thinking is still biased against Malays" and that "this is a bad thing." In addition to these thoughts that suggest a need for Malay special rights, she adds the thoughts "only when UKM started this program do you see Malays in this profession" and "maybe our association can do something to change the bias against Malay optometrists" to enhance consonance with thoughts of "bringing Malays on par with immigrant races."

Similar to Norijah, Nurul refers to Chinese superiority in education and business, "Chinese are number one and on top in these areas," and to the structural disadvantage of Malays economically, "most Malays are from the lower rungs of society," to reinforce the need for Malay special rights. She uses her personal background as an example, coming "from a poor Malay family," Malay special rights "provided an opportunity for her to attend college" and "to move up in society." She ends this segment by returning to the primary justification for Malay special rights, reiterating several thoughts that stem from schemata of "Malay privilege": "Malays opened this land" and "Chinese are immigrants" and "other countries don't allow immigrants to take over" and "Malays are the hosts in Malaysia." She combines these thoughts that stem from representations of "Malay privilege" with thoughts that stem from representations of

"Malaysia's diverse society," such as "we are all here together," in order to reduce dissonance, projecting Malays as the "preferred hosts"[7] on top of a "diverse society in which all groups work and live together."

Although these hopeful images of diverse Malaysians living and working together in harmony hold some degree of credence for Nurul, Abdul, a young Malay factory worker, considers these ideas to be "mere rhetoric" as Mohamad Suhaimi did above. Abdul works as a skilled technician testing and grading products. In this conversation segment, Abdul describes the inter-group relations in the factory and the restriction placed upon Muslim employees in reference to their attendance at Friday congregational prayers.

I: How many people work on the line?

Abdul: There are a lot of workers on the line. You can say there is around 120 people within one line.

I: How many Malays, Muslims?

Abdul: Ninety percent are Muslim, not one hundred percent . . . Indians are not a large percentage, Chinese five percent, and there are lots of Malays . . . The upper section are mostly Chinese . . . There are two Malay engineers and six Chinese . . . There are two Malay engineers and six Chinese . . . The situation in most factories is almost the same . . .

I: Are Muslims allowed to pray?

Abdul: Except for Fridays, if you have a shift, for those who don't have a shift they can go out on Fridays and pray in congregational prayers, but for those who have a shift they can not go out.

I: Is there a letter of permission?

Abdul: There is a letter. You still are not allowed to go out. For praying Zohor (early afternoon obligatory prayer), we are allowed to pray in the factory prayer hall, but to pray Friday congregational prayers, for us workers who have a shift, we are not allowed to join in.

I: Why?

Abdul: I don't know but it is possibly from the business side. There are those who request-lah, that time there was some who requested permission, went to the Department of Agama (Religion) of Melaka, informed them, and it still did not happen. It is the company that has made this continue.

I: But I thought there was a law that a Muslim could not miss three Friday prayers in a row.

Abdul: This is definitely the case . . . He will become a *murtad*.

I: But how can people not be allowed to go?

Abdul: . . . We are forced to follow the government-lah. What else can we do?

I: They have already been notified?

Abdul: We already informed them but we have not gotten permission, even the Department of Agama couldn't, it is difficult.

I: How about the Department of Labor?

Abdul: Yeah, they follow them-lah, follow the company management. If management does not give it; it can't be granted . . .

I: Is there a union?

Abdul: Here, there is a union . . . The union here can't say anything, when actually there is a union here, but they can't say anything, and it is caused by the attitude of Muslims too. At first we were allowed to pray Friday congregational prayers, even if you had a shift. Because several individuals who did not want to pray went outside, when it was time for people to go out to pray on Friday, they went to other places. They had to be pulled back-lah. Now it is not allowed . . . We used to get a letter, one, something like a pass, a pass that granted permission-lah . . . At first there was but now there are none . . .

I: When did this start?

Abdul: Around two years ago . . . because several individuals took advantage, it is finished-lah . . . Because of people like this-lah: One drop of indigo ruins the whole pot of milk . . . Because it is said, one drop of blood entered the milk, all-lah of the milk turned red; it won't be white. Even though there are people who are good, they are all considered bad. This is the case with it not being allowed, if not, before this it was all OK, everyone could pray. This person that was allowed to go freely to pray went to karaoke-lah, singing-lah, later they entered the factory like normal, ruining-lah the name of Islam . . .

Similar to the case with Norijah and Nurul, Abdul's thoughts of Malay special rights and status are in contradiction to his thoughts about the reality of low Malay socio-economic status in most companies in the private sector of the economy.[8] He informs us Malay employees "predominate in the lower status positions in the company" and the "Chinese predominate in the higher status positions" and this is "the situation in most factories." Moreover, his thought that "all Muslim employees who work shifts Friday afternoons are restricted from leaving the factory to attend Friday prayers," is highly dissonant with his notions of Malaysia as a Muslim country and as a country where Malay Muslims are dominant. It is all right to perform other prayers in the factory prayer hall, but Friday congregational prayers, interpreted as obligatory for men in Malaysia, must be performed in a mosque. In Malaysia, if Muslim men miss three Friday congregational prayers in a row, they are legally *murtad,* considered outside of the Islamic faith. Thus, his thought about Muslim men being restricted from fulfilling their religious obligations "in their own country" is highly dissonant for Abdul.

His thoughts about Muslim employees' attempts to regain their rights to leave the factory for Friday prayers tend to reduce dissonance but these attempts were unsuccessful. The dissonance of Abdul's thoughts about how things *should* be and the way they *really* are, is increased by the addition of thoughts about how the "Department of Religion" and the "Department of Labor upheld the factory's position of denying Muslims the right to leave work for prayers." His thoughts of these Malay-dominated government institutions "following the company management" are dissonant with his thoughts of "Malay political supremacy." Although some Malays misrepresented Islam and "gave Islam a bad name" with their irresponsible and dishonest actions, he thinks that it is "unfair to look at all Muslim employees as bad" and "to punish all of them for the actions of only a few." In the following, segment of this conversation, Abdul continues to express his dissonant thoughts and shows us how he strives to reduce his high degree of dissonance.

I: What do you think about the situation in this company, the upper level people are mostly Chinese and the lower level people are mostly Malays?

Abdul: But from the perspective of worker's oppression, this is definitely the case. Worker's oppression is really caused by people following their racism. Like white people with Negroes-lah, there is racism. There always is . . . We take the approach that this situation is normal . . . Some people suffer the consequences of speaking out, voicing their opinions freely. But in the opinion of most people this is not accepted as a problem. This is not just a problem of Chinese management. The problem is that German managers, themselves, do not want to accept the views of the workers . . . There is a manager, managing director is German-lah . . . The assistant manager is Chinese. And the HR (Human Relations) section only, a Malay person holds that position. . . . Yeah, a Malay person has it, not allowed to hold any other (management) position . . . Because within the state, within the Malaysian government, Malays are wherever there is a human relations section. Malays definitely have this position; it is allowed . . .

I: Why do *Bumiputera* hold this position?

Abdul: Because it is easy for them when they want to play a role, easy to ask for holidays, easy, except for one thing, yeah, even though that is easy, Friday prayers we can't get. Those people who have a voice won't accept it . . . We are pushed to the side . . . They are on that high level, but they don't change the situation. It is like, even though we are already free, yet we are still colonized. From the perspective of labor and thought even, we are still colonized-lah.

I: And what do you think should be done about this colonialism?

Abdul: Lift up the level of Islam, Islam for lifting up religion, but the problem is that when we speak up about religion, most of us are pushed to the side. It is different from American, speaking out about religion is embraced-lah. Here it is troublesome. We will inform them and later they say, 'You are smart, I am not.' It is over. If we have an opinion why is it not accepted? Ah, that is the problem. Sometimes we are frank and speak out for all and not just for ourselves, right, for all Muslims. But these people are, 'dead but not buried.'

I: Why is it still the situation that Chinese dominate in the economy although Muslims dominate politics? I don't understand.

Abdul: Perhaps, it is that many people make it this way. For example, it is like this here, that many laws in use in Malaysia are laws from the British. If people use Islamic laws, this would not happen. That-lah is the truth . . . If he uses small pieces of Islamic rule, how can you bring in Islamic law, like in Saudi Arabia, Iran, just recently, wonderful! But what the people voice is not accepted-lah. It doesn't mean that the people are ignoring the problem but the upper level people are not concerned. This prime minister . . .

I: What is the situation, for Malays, in other factories in this area?

Abdul: Their fate is the same-lah as the fate that we receive.

I: But there are factories owned by other people from other countries? Usually who owns these corporations?

> Abdul: The ones who own (this company) . . . are Germans-lah, the company next to mine is Japanese . . . United States . . . Taiwan . . . Korea . . . The fate of most of the workers is the same, technicians, operators, their fate of not having their liberty is actually the same . . . Most of the citizens are mistreated. As for the approach of diversity, it really can't be seen, but when you really are uncover things and look deeply for what is really going on, there is, you really are oppressed . . . There are only Chinese who have (companies), but there are no Malays. It is difficult to find Malays . . . Chinese . . . This economy is dominated by the Chinese race . . .

Abdul reduces the cognitive dissonance between his thoughts about structural inequality of low status Malay workers vis-à-vis high status Chinese supervisors and managers, and his thoughts of how things *should* be. He does this through adding the following thoughts: "there is always racism," "we take it as normal," "worker's oppression is caused by people following their racism," and "Malay structural inequality vis-à-vis Chinese is like Negro inequality vis-à-vis whites in the U.S." Similarly, his thoughts about the repercussions for speaking out against the prevailing structural conditions, "some people suffer the consequences of voicing their opinions openly" are consonant with the approach of taking these things as a normal part of life. His dissonance reducing thoughts in this regard are similar to non-Malay thoughts of "coping and learning to accept" the prevailing realities of institutionalized Malay privilege. In this case, economic and political elites force Malays to comply with the prevailing structures of inequality in the private sector.

Moreover, Abdul reduces the cognitive dissonance through his explanations of what kind of system they have in Malaysia and with his prescriptions for changing things in the right direction. In particular, he continues to depict the lack of power of local Malay officials and petty managers, such as the human relations' manager, "who are able to get time off for holidays but not for Friday prayers." When their efforts contradict the position of the European and Chinese managers, they are powerless. The "foreign and local Chinese bosses are the ones in control" and "they are the ones that won't accept what the workers say" and "they are the high ones that have a voice" and "the lack of liberty of workers is the same in most companies" and "most citizens are maltreated." He sums up current structures of inequality as "still being colonized although they have political independence" and "from our perspectives as workers, we are still *colonized*." All of the talk of diversity is "mere talk," if you "look below the surface you will see that the workers are truly oppressed." This thought of "still being colonized" reduces dissonance between ideals and reality by explaining, in a succinct fashion, why things are not in the proper order. He continues to reduce dissonance, in a more satisfying way, by adding the thoughts that "lifting up the level of Islam" and "implementing Islamic rather than British civil laws" will solve the present "colonial" problems and organize society the way it is *supposed* to be.

CONCLUSION

The application of the core of Festinger's theory of cognitive dissonance to non-Malay and Malay discourse I have recorded in Malaysia demonstrates that there is divergence in processes of cognitive re-organization which is connected to differing positions and experiences these groups have in Malaysian society. Non-Malays, experiencing inequality and discrimination in the "public sector," tend to reduce cognitive dissonance between ideals of equality and the reality of Malay privilege by adding cognitive elements about coping with and accepting Malay privilege and viewing it as natural and universal. In addition, they tend to take institutionalized Malay privilege as a challenge, a better way to improve, and to make themselves more qualified in their respective professions and vocations. Chinese, and perhaps Indians to a lesser extent, also reduce dissonance with thoughts of superiority over Malays. Moreover, non-Malays think of, and value, the "private sector," given Malay economic disadvantage, as a corrective and counterbalance to Malay advantage in the "public sector."

On the other hand, Malays tend to reduce cognitive dissonance between thoughts of equality and Malay privilege by adding cognitive elements that directly stem from and are constitutive of schemata of "Malay privilege." They draw upon thoughts of Malays as the original and earliest inhabitants to control the Malay Peninsula to justify their special rights and status. In addition, Malays tend to interpret the introduction of policies of equality—the eradication of Malay special rights in the "public sphere"—in a negative light, often equating it with, or assuming it will lead to, total Chinese domination. Malays tend to reduce dissonance with thoughts of their inferiority and disadvantage vis-à-vis Chinese, be it educational, economic, or "cultural" inferiority. Moreover, thoughts about their structural disadvantage and experiences of discrimination in the "private sector" of the economy tend to reduce dissonance with thoughts of the need for Malay special rights. Malays often experience cognitive dissonance with respect to the discrepancy between how things *should* go according to the ideal implementation of Malay special rights and the realities of things going contrary to these ideals. They try to reduce this dissonance with explanations of the state of things in Malaysian society, explanations such as the change in course after a Malay loss of power or the continuation of the system of colonialism despite formal political independence. Furthermore, thoughts about "fixing the system" somehow, perhaps through the establishment of an Islamic state or through a change in direction of the Malay political leadership, produced more, significant moves towards reducing dissonance.

Furthermore, non-Malay and Malay experiences tend to effect re-organizations of representations of "Malaysia's diverse society" and "Malay privilege." Many Malays and non-Malays integrate and re-interpret dominant models of "Malaysia's diverse society" and schemata of "Malay privilege" so as to consider ideological formulations stemming from dominant models of "Malaysia's diverse society" as "mere rhetoric" or "just talk" and not as indicative of how things really are or work in Malaysian society. However, non-Malays tend to refer to the realities of institutionalized Malay privilege as evidence of these models lack of fit with reality, whereas Malays tend to refer to the lack of inter-group interactions and the preservation of non-Malay cultural attributes as evidence of the inapplicability of these models to the way things really are. Nevertheless, some non-Malays and Malays still use these models to interpret some aspects of Malaysian society, such as public festival activities, open houses, and general recognition and acceptance, though limited, of group differences. Indeed, many non-Malay people maintain commitment to these ideological formulations as, at least, a sense of hope that they will continue to be accepted as part of Malaysian society and that their differences will continue to be tolerated.

In addition, non-Malays and Malays preserve some personal opinions that manage to survive the pressures of forced compliance. In particular, many non-Malay people maintain a strong attachment and commitment to ideals of equality and justice, although they do not fit the realities of institutionalized Malay privilege. Similarly, Malays preserve a strong commitment to ideals of establishing Islam more completely in Malaysian society and freeing themselves from Chinese and foreign domination in the private sector of the economy. In both cases, these ideals are dissonant with the current structural conditions in Malaysian society and are opposed to the dominant policies of the Malaysian government.

Finally, the differing positions and experiences of Malays and non-Malays in the persisting arrangements of Malaysian society tend to influence patterns of combining models and schemata of "Malaysia's diverse society" and "Malay privilege" and sense of qualitative citizenship. Non-Malays tend to combine these representations in such a fashion producing a graded citizenship of *Bumiputera* full belongers and non-*Bumiputera* second-class belongers. This widespread combination of these representations tends to produce a sense of being excluded, and of being "outsiders" and "temporary" guests in the land of Malays. On the other hand, although Malays also tend to combine these representations in a graded fashion, they tend to include greater emphasis on their prerogatives as "natives" of the region and the conditional quality of non-*Bumiputera* citizenship that often leads to a different sense of qualitative citizenship. Malay combinations of these representations in conjunction with thoughts of how present realities in Malaysia diverge from the ways they think they *should* be leads to a sense of qualified citizenship in which they feel they are "at a disadvantage in their own country."

Chapter Nine
Conclusions

REPRESENTATIONS AND NEGOTIATING CULTURAL CITIZENSHIP

A look below the surface of nationalist rhetoric and displays, and expressions of hopeful togetherness, reveals Malaysians of diverse backgrounds interpreting social events, their positions in the broader society and experiences with each other. Their often heated views vary across social groups and the sites of events, whether these events are government-organized or community-based and whether on public stages, religious institutions, or in private homes. Although many Malaysians make interpretations of their positions and experiences that express seething tensions between groups, competition over jobs, entrance and desired tracks in schools, and status and influence, they also tend to take seriously surface pronouncements of national unity and togetherness. Indeed, there is a fire below the surface, incinerating strains between notions and realities of equality and inequality, and yet, the sanguine surface resonates with some everyday experiences and deeper yearnings of many Malaysians.

My study suggests that representations of diverse social groups and their horizontal inter-relations as equal citizen-members and representations of Malay privilege and special status on top of vertical re-arrangements of diverse social groups are closely related to dominant and alternative senses of cultural citizenship. Such representations have been intertwined in processes of legal and cultural citizenship during, and even prior to processes of forging Malaysian nationality. Malays had viewed themselves as the only true belongers as they were the "citizen-subjects" of Malay Rulers who inherited their sovereignty from a "blood" line that flows back to the original and initial settlers of the Malay Peninsula. It was these sorts of notions that stemmed from representations of Malay privilege that were involved in Malay rejection

of the Malayan Union plan that liquidated Malay special rights and Malay negotiation for a Federation of Malaya or Malaysia and a Federal Constitution
that perpetuated their privilege. On the other hand, Chinese and Indians, new
arrivals and long-term residents, welcomed the Malayan Union plan with its
termination of Malay special rights and its calls for an equal citizenship for all,
Malay and non-Malay alike. However, it was not to be, and their commitment
to notions of equality and equal citizenship was expressed in their involvement
in the Communist-led insurgency, especially for Chinese, and in their negotiations for a broad extension of citizenship based on the principle of soil, of
being *born in Malaysia.*

A combination and integration of representations of "Malaysia's diverse society" and "Malay privilege" was inscribed and embodied in the
Federal Constitution and the legal nationality and citizenship it entailed.
Legal citizenship, through an application of principles of "blood" and
"soil," was extended to include practically all Malays and a majority of resident Chinese and Indians. Malaysian citizens of all cultural categories were
accorded certain restricted civil rights and special rights were reserved for
Malays and other *Bumiputeras.* Legal citizenship was constructed combining notions of equality and inequality in such a fashion so as to create realms
in which all Malaysians were formal equal citizen-members and realms in
which Malays, especially Malay *husbands* and *fathers,* were the default or
generic Malaysians, the only *real* citizens or full belongers. This legal citizenship, with its combination of inclusive and exclusive qualities, constitutes a
hegemonic form of cultural citizenship that was institutionalized by the
Malay-dominated government and civic organizations.

Moreover, the social contract or compromise between Malay
Bumiputeras and the *new citizens* of immigrant "races," that formed the
basis of the Federal Constitution and dominant forms of cultural citizenship, was, and still is, a flexible and hotly contested agreement. It is flexible in the sense that what is encompassed within the parameters of
equality, citizenship, and freedom on the one hand, and within the parameters of Malay special rights and status on the other are left open to interpretation and on-going negotiation. In any event, non-Malays were not
satisfied with all of the rights and privileges they forfeited to Malays in
order to produce this social contract and their political agitation reached
a climax with opposition parties' victories and tragic violence of 1969
May 13. These predominantly Chinese opposition parties' victories called
into question Malay representations of special rights, expectations of political domination, and prerogatives of *Bumiputera* citizenship and only a
change in the manner of interpreting and implementing the social contract

with Malaysia's *new citizens* could reconcile these contradictions (cf. Loh and Kahn 1992:9–15). New Malay leaders rose to the occasion and extended the parameters of Malay special rights to incorporate a broad array of New Economic Policy programs and benefits designed specifically to distribute resources and opportunities to the Malay community. They also limited the parameters of equality, civil rights, and freedom for members of non-Malay cultural categories, although gradually these parameters were extended once again under the rubric of top-down multiculturalism, often used in the tourism industry, and the accompanying models or ideological formulations of "Malaysia's diverse society."

My research in Melaka shows that the manner of integrating representations of "Malaysia's diverse society" and "Malay privilege" and the sense of cultural citizenship it embeds are still contested in Malaysian society. In the government, organized cultural shows, public celebrations, and museum exhibitions, Malay civil servants reproduce the dominant form of combining these representations in which diverse groups are included within a framework in which Malay culture and identity are emphasized. Such events express a sense of cultural citizenship in which Malays are the default full belongers, the definitive national group, and non-Malays are second-class citizens who should assimilate many aspects of the definitive Malay, written as national, culture. In fact, in many of these events, as Sarkissian (1998:98) also noted, it is the *Babas* and *Nyonyas,* Chitties, and *Portugis* Eurasians, the more assimilated "hybrid" groups and segments of the Chinese and Indian communities, who are most prominently represented. Although the Chinese and Indian *Peranakan* submaximal identities are not "core" belongers, possessing a "graded membership" within the "Chinese" or "Indian" categories, they are accorded a greater sense of cultural citizenship within the dominant framework due to their adoption of many aspects of the "definitive" national culture. This is an instance of the disciplining influence of the dominant form of cultural citizenship, part of the process of making citizens (see Ong 1999).

On the other hand, this dominant form of integrating representations of Malaysian society and of producing cultural citizenship, are contested in the broadly inclusive religious festival cycle, in public celebrations in the mall, and in some open house practices. In the religious festival activities, Chinese and Indians, intermingling with each other and to a lesser extent with Christians and Muslims, and at times expressing a philosophy of religious universalism (see Ackerman and Lee 1988:117–118), embody a sense of cultural citizenship in which all Malaysians are equal citizen-members inhabiting the same horizontal plane. Similarly, Indians try to negotiate their inclusion and incorporation in the broader society, on the same level with the two main races, through staging their public celebrations in more central and public venues. Moreover, Chinese, who control large public stages in shopping centers, subvert the dominant mode of combining these representations and produce a sense of cultural citizenship in which all groups are included to some extent within a framework in which Chinese culture and identity are emphasized instead of Malay culture and identity. In addition, official Chinese open houses that take place in government venues often observe the food prohibitions of both Muslims and Hindus embodying a horizontal sense of equality and mutual respect. However, Chinese in Melaka, in contrast to Malays and Indians, rarely hold open houses in their homes, thereby rejecting Malay symbolic advantages and dominant forms of cultural citizenship as they choose to continue their distinctive customs of holding family gatherings over following the government promoted pattern of extending open house hospitality to members of other cultural categories. In this form of gastro-politics (Appadurai 1981), it is the extension of hospitality and having it accepted or the rejection of the hospitality of others that serves to enhance social prestige.

Furthermore, I also suggest that Malaysians of non-Malay cultural categories produce a more inclusive sense of cultural citizenship through participating more frequently in interracial and inter-religious voluntary associations and cliques and through their increasing openness to intermarry with fellow non-Malays. Non-Malays use these informal forms of social organization as a way to enhance their incorporation within the broader society. It offers them an opportunity to openly participate in the government call for non-governmental organizations to help create a more "caring society" and to participate in the dominant communal framework of politicking and rallying together in separate social segments. Furthermore, for non-Malays who experience discrimination in the public sector, participation in these groups gives them an opportunity to reduce cognitive dissonance between their thoughts of equality and the realities of institutionalized Malay privilege.

To the contrary, Malays seldom join and participate in the activities of interracial cliques and voluntary associations, choosing to do their charity work in Malay or Muslim institutions and agencies. Malays generally do not contest the dominant merging of representations of "Malaysia's diverse society" and "Malay privilege," as they have come to accept the presence of, and the prospects of living with, *new citizens* in their land. Besides, the dominant form of cultural citizenship singles them out as the main *Bumiputera* citizens, the first-class citizens. However, many Malays feel marginalized by government policies that they perceive as being beneficial for a select group of Malays and for "immigrant races" and foreigners and by the perceived increase in Chinese and Indian political influence. These perceptions tend to contribute to a sense of cultural citizenship, a "marginalized first-class citizenship," in which Malays perceive themselves as being treated as less than they should be "in their own country." Malays often try to reduce the cognitive dissonance brought about by this perception of things through participating in activities to set things straight, returning them to a state in which Malay special rights are accorded their proper place in the workings of society.

ISSUES OF MALAYSIAN ETHNOGRAPHY AND BEYOND

The fragmentation and contestation of social identities has been a major concern of Malaysianists, as it has been for researchers elsewhere. Many of these researchers (see Loh and Kahn 1992; Kahn 1998; Z. Ibrahim 1998) combine constructionist and interpretive perspectives in a manner that suggests that constructed social identities are in a state of total flux, constantly being re-interpreted, and re-constituted with new knowledge. Loh and Kahn (1992:10) even suggest that we approach social identity as an "idiom" that is continually changing and being re-interpreted. While it is true that the meanings of social identities such as "Malay," "Chinese," and "Indian," are not fixed and given by simple linguistic definitions, it is also true that many aspects of the underlying knowledge that constitutes them are reproduced in changing social and cultural contexts. Indeed, an approach that highlights both the continuity and transformation of underlying knowledge is best equipped to analyze the significance of social identities in changing and multiple contexts. My use of a cognitive approach for describing and analyzing social identities has allowed us to pinpoint specific aspects of social identities—categories, attributes, expectations, and evaluations—being given new meanings and those that are being reproduced in social processes. Moreover, it is generally specific elements of social identities that are being contested and appropriated in processes of fragmentation and not all of the underlying knowledge that constitutes social identities.

In addition, this cognitive approach to social identity has allowed us to discern how various cultural categories or subgroups are tied into overarching cultural categories. That goes to say that, although specific attributes include members within the categories, "Eurasian," "Malay," "Chinese," and "Indian," not all of these members are included in the same way or to the same extent. There is a form of "graded membership" in these maximal categories, which constructs some subgroups as "core" and others as more or less peripheral. This approach also allows us to note and compare cross-culturally how people embed so-called "hybrid" persons and categories within or assign membership to particular social identities and how these conventionalized practices relate to processes of social stratification. For instance, in Melaka, persons classified as "Chitty," "*Baba* or *Nyonya*," "*Portugis*," or "Mamak," are assigned membership in these categories based upon the categorization of their fathers; for instance, children born to a Chinese man and a Malay woman are officially considered Chinese and non-*Bumiputera*, whereas the children of a Malay man and Chinese woman are considered Malay and *Bumiputera*. However, some of the children of the former union may try to "pass" or have others recognize them, as Malay and *Bumiputera* in order to obtain the special privileges of the preferred category. In contrast, in the U.S., persons classified as "Blacks" or "Whites" are assigned membership in these categories based upon the presence or absence of a parent or ancestor of any gender categorized as "Black." If both parents and all ancestors are categorized as "White" then the child is categorized as "White," but if either parent or any ancestors are categorized as "Black" then the child is categorized as "Black." As in the Malaysian case, some children with "White" and "Black" parentage or ancestry try to "pass" as "White" in order to obtain the special privileges of the preferred category. Although the principles of assigning group membership contrast in these two societies, the role underlying, moral evaluations play is crucial in both cases. Clearly, the American "one-drop of Black blood" principle of group assignment is conducive to a more rigid form of social hierarchy. Nevertheless, the cognitive approach allows us to pinpoint the fact that it is the *underlying elements of evaluation,* in both cases, that serve to reproduce the prevailing patterns of social hierarchy rather than the principle of assignment alone. The underlying elements of evaluation, at least, provide the rationale while the principle of ascription provides the vehicle for constructing social inequality.

Most Malaysianists, and researchers in other regions, move directly from discussions of social identities into considerations of nationality, nationalism, and citizenship, occasionally with mediating discussions of the political economy or social structure. My work in Malaysia suggests that it may be fruitful to first consider the ways in which social identities are incorporated within other forms of knowledge that pertain to the ways these social identities are interrelated and arranged in connection to each other. In Malaysia, I have demonstrated that people routinely speak and think of constructions of diverse social identities and several concepts together, indicating the bunching together of this knowledge into representations I have distinguished as either models or schemata. These models and schemata and their combinations, integration, and negotiation have a lot to do with the other major concern of many Malaysianists: the issue of *bangsa Malaysia,* of national identity.

Although Loh and Kahn (1992:12) share the assessment with many pluralist and political-economic theorists that 1969 was a critical historical juncture that marked a breakdown in the "liberal consensus" of the Malaysian political leaders, they disagree in regard to explaining this political and cultural phenomenon. They criticize pluralist and political-economic explanations that refer to "an eruption of mass cultural particularism into the politics of the elite" and an erosion of an ideology that maintains the domination of the ruling class and deludes the working classes of all cultural categories. My research findings in reference to the dynamics of social identities, inter-group social and religious ties, and the significance of social group (maximal and submaximal) consciousness are in agreement with Loh and Kahn's critique that these pluralist and political-economic perspectives are overly static and narrow. However, I think that Loh and Kahn's treatment of what they consider "liberal consensus" requires further analysis. They describe this "liberal consensus," that broke down after 1969, as a commitment that the Malaysian elite and to some extent the masses had to a "variant of western liberalism." My work suggests that an analysis of this "liberal consensus" or "social contract" as I characterized it above, in terms of how it combines universalizing and particularizing discourses can elucidate processes of negotiation between citizen-members of liberal nations. In the case of Malaysia's "variant of western liberalism" I have demonstrated that there has been an ongoing negotiation and contestation over how horizontal representations of equal citizen-members are integrated and combined with vertical representations of graded citizen-members, default citizens and qualified citizens (cf. Anderson 1983). Struggles over the "liberal consensus," embodied in the Federal Constitution, the dominant merging of these representations and discourses, led to its breakdown and recombination in the aftermath of 1969. Furthermore, we need to look at how dominant combinations of these notions entail stipulations, perhaps unwritten and implicit, as to how the definitive members are accorded special rights and non-definitive members are accorded contingent rights. Negotiations and contestations over such combinations and re-combinations of horizontal and vertical representations of citizen-members are an integral part of ongoing processes in other Southeast Asian countries and beyond.

For instance, in Indonesia, *pribumi* (natives) are on the top of vertically arrayed representations of the nation and are the generic full citizens. Various *pribumi* maximal categories, such as Javanese, Sundanese, Malays, Bataks and Dayaks compete and negotiate for ranking and relative prestige in particular cities and regions of Indonesia (see Bruner 1974 and Cunningham 1989). Furthermore, with control of the Indonesian "center," in Jakarta, Javanese have been able to project themselves, and their "glorious history" and culture, as the preeminent *pribumi* maximal category (see Daniels 1999:47; Lian Kwen Fee 2001:872). This contrasts with Malaysia where the distinction amongst "natives" is largely between Malay *Bumiputera* and non-Malay *Bumiputera* with a broad range of submaximal identities being tied into an overarching Malay identity. Nevertheless, the darker-skinned indigenous peoples, for instance the "Negritos" of Malaysia and "Papuans" of Irian Jaya, Indonesia are stigmatized and marginalized in both of these societies. Chinese, Indians, Arabs and other cultural categories are qualified members of Indonesian society, especially those who have not openly assimilated attributes of the *pribumi* populations. While all of these non-*pribumi* groups have been marginalized to varying extents, the Chinese have often been the target of intense animosity due largely to their disproportionate control of wealth, their relatively higher-class position than *pribumi*. Many Chinese after several generations of living in Indonesia still have "foreigner" or "citizen of a foreign nation" marked on their passports and other forms of legal documentation. Even when Chinese have obtained legal citizenship, *keturunan* (descent) and *agama* (religion), which are recorded on official documents, continues to qualify their inclusion and acceptance within the broader society. However, some of the official policies restricting the public expression of Chinese culture, such as use of Mandarin and lion and dragon dances, are being changed under the influence of the *Reformasi* Movement.

In Thailand and the Philippines, native Thai and Filipinos are imagined to be on top of vertical representations of these nations. Many upland indigenous groups are marginal members of the nation just as they are in Malaysia and Indonesia. The Thai Theravada Buddhist and Filipino Catholic cultures are the "definitive" cultures of these two nations that *new citizens* have had to contend with in processes of social and cultural incorporation. Chinese and other cultural categories are qualified members of these societies even when they manage to attain legal citizenship and assimilate native cultural attributes as in Malaysia. However, Chinese in Thailand and the Philippines have become more assimilated and integrated into these societies than their counterparts have in Malaysia and Indonesia. This is due, in part, to the construction of more flexible and less politicized cultural categories in political-economic contexts in which there were substantial numbers of upper and middle class native Filipinos alongside wealthy Chinese (see Blanc 1997) and politically independent and culturally aggressive Thais formulating policies (see Skinner 1960). Another contributing factor has been the way in which Chinese immigrants have been able to synthesize their religious beliefs, and thereby social identities, with Theravada Buddhism and Filipino Catholicism, which they were not able to accomplish on a large scale with Islam in Malaysia and Indonesia (see Tan Chee-Beng 1990). "Malay" Muslims, *Pattanis* in southern Thailand and *Moros* in southern Philippines, are highly marginalized and lowly ranked citizen-members of these nations like Muslims minorities in Burma, Cambodia, and Vietnam. In contrast to Malaysia, Indonesia, Thailand, and the Philippines, Chinese in Singapore are the default citizen-members imagined to be on top of vertical representations of the nation. Malays, Indians, Eurasians and other cultural categories are second-class citizens in Singapore, and are forced to comply with the hegemonic rule of the Chinese majority. In each of these nations, people combine these sorts of vertical arrangements of groups, which I have only been able to sketch here, with horizontal arrangements of citizen-members of imagined national communities. Further research is required to explicate the particular character of these vertical and horizontal representations and their varied and complex manner of combination and re-combination in changing historical contexts.

My description and analysis of representations of Malaysian society supports the claims Loh and Kahn (1992:12–14) and Kahn (1998:17–27) make about the inapplicability of some "post-modernist" and "post-nationalist" perspectives to Malaysian society. In particular, many "critical" views that explain contemporary cultural fragmentation, social identity de-territorialization, and the proliferation of competing visions as tendencies of late capitalism and the decline of nationalism are contrary to ethnographic research in Malaysia and Southeast Asia. Loh and Kahn (1992:13–14) demonstrates that the Malaysian government has explicitly devised and implemented a National Culture Policy that strives to restrict cultural particularism and promotes shared values and visions of a Malaysian nation based upon *Bumiputera* culture and Islam. Similarly, Kahn (1998:25) argues that, "appeals of blood, territory, and race continue to characterize cultural conflicts at all levels in Southeast Asia and beyond." My work in Malaysia, and similar work in the U.S., Canada, and British Virgin Islands, directed towards explicating processes of cultural citizenship, exemplifies this point (see Renato Rosaldo 1994a, 1994b, 1997; Ong 1993, 1999; Chavez 1998[1992]; Flores and Benmayor 1997; Bill Maurer 1997; Mitchell 1997).

Loh and Kahn (1992), in contrast to pluralist, political-economic, and post-modernist perspectives, argue that the post-1969 period, following the breakdown in "liberal consensus," is characterized by elite and middle class fragments that have competing political and cultural visions. The elite and middle class fractions "can no longer be controlled and hence brought under the shared consociational vision of the years before 1969" (ibid:14–16). Surely, this inter-group and intra-group fragmentation is a characteristic of post-1969 Malaysian society. But we must not assume that it is a wholly new phenomenon and instead consider how much of this fragmentation is a continuation of diverging visions in early historical periods and how these visions are integral to processes of economic growth and social differentiation. As Shamsul A.B. (1998b:26) points out, there has been inter-group and intra-group fragmentation in terms of "nations-of-intent," ideas of the form of a nation and national identity, for some time before 1969. He describes how the present context is characterized by several competing "nations-of intent," including several within *Bumiputera* communities such as the hegemonic "Malay-dominated plural society" nation and the contesting "Islamic nation" and "Kadazan nation" and "Iban nation." In addition, my findings are in concert with his suggestion that much of the debate over "national culture" is framed in terms of divergent nations-of-intent such as the dominant "Malay-dominated plural society nation" and the "pluralized nation," advocated by non-*Bumiputeras,* in which "the culture of each ethnic group in Malaysia is accorded a position equal to that of the *Bumiputera*" (ibid:24).

Moreover, many researchers have begun to investigate the expanding middle classes in Malaysia (see Robison and Goodman 1996; Kahn 1996; Abdul 1998) brought about by recent periods of rapid economic growth. Abdul (1998) finds that many new members of the Malay middle class are paying for their own educational expenses rather than receiving support from the government and they are choosing to seek employment in the private sector rather than the public sector. However, my work suggests these fragments of the Malay middle class still have to negotiate negative perceptions of them by their Chinese and Indian counterparts who assume that they have only become educated professionals due to government support. These expanding middle classes and their experiences in a changing Malaysian social and economic structure are bringing about new visions and new commitments to older visions as they seek to reconcile their thoughts of Malay special rights to the realities of Malaysian society. On the other hand, much of the focus on the emerging middle classes tends to overlook the expanding Malay working class which inhabits the lowest rungs in the rapidly growing industrial sector. Aihwa Ong (1987) observed symbolic resistance amongst Malay female factory workers, but few researchers have given lower class Malays serious consideration. Shamsul A.B. (1998b) implies that this is part of "ethnicised knowledge" that focuses upon criticizing the NEP and the special rights of Malays but tend to overlook the ways Chinese have benefited from the NEP by setting up businesses with *Bumiputera* partners. He suggests that researchers should take a middle ground thereby helping

Malaysians to find less polarized terrain rather than taking ideologically biased positions toward a particular segment of Malaysian society. My research has sought to seriously consider the narratives, perspectives and experiences of non-*Bumiputera* as well as *Bumiputera,* considering the disadvantages they both experience and seek to cope with in the public and private sectors, as they negotiate cultural citizenship in contemporary Malaysian society.

Upon further reflection, much of the literature about divergent visions and nations-of-intent, and fragmented and contested identities may be searching for evidence of the emergence of *Bangsa Malaysia,* Malaysian national identity, in the wrong directions. Many of these writers and commentators are looking to substantiate the existence of *Bangsa Malaysia* in shared cultural perspectives, values, and visions, whereas *Bangsa Malaysia* may be emerging through the sharing of common institutions. Common experiences of growing up in Malaysia, and attending schools, workplaces, public celebrations and festivals, voluntary association activities, and even market places appear to be contributing to a sense of belonging to *Bangsa Malaysia.* As one of my Indian respondents expressed, everything in Malaysia fits with them and has become a normal part of their everyday lives. Even though their structures of feeling (see R. Williams 1977 and B. Williams 1988), manner of reducing cognitive dissonance and interpretations are divergent, they share an abstract unity on what the models and schemata of Malaysian society are and what the issues are that stem from their combinations and re-combinations. This abstract sharing of matters to disagree about and to interpret from divergent perspectives—such as the position of and meanings of "natives" and "new citizens"—is an integral part of processes of national formation and imagination, and not contrary to them, for nations are always unfinished projects, projects-in-the-making.

COGNITIVE ANTHROPOLOGY, NATION-MAKING, AND SUBJECT-MAKING

In this study, I was able to demonstrate that this abstract sharing of knowledge occurred across the Malay and English languages pointing out the importance of making a systematic distinction between surface linguistic structures and underlying cognition (see Lehman 1995). However, Benjamin Lee Whorf's suggestion that language structures thought is still confused with the notion that cognition is inseparable from and dependent upon language. Although language use contributes to the acquisition of cognitive structures and surface linguistic structures are often cues for the existence of underlying cognition, it is not safe to assume that the use of a particular language carries with it a particular worldview or set of values. Yet, researchers often assume that when people switch from language to language that they are "code switching," not only in terms of the grammatical rules that govern the particular language use, but also in terms of the underlying cognition and outlook on the world. When analysts take this sort of linguistic relativism to the extreme, they view meanings, as so intimately connected to a particular language that translation is not even possible. My findings, among speakers of different languages, and other research on miscommunication among speakers of the same language supports the view that language and thought are closely intertwined but separable. Indeed, people speaking the same language often experience miscommunication due to variation in underlying "codes." In this study, across speakers of English and Malay and with people shifting between these languages, "codes," in the form of conventional representations, were embedded in spoken discourse and practice. In the future, I would like to test these findings in Tamil and Mandarin or Hokkien.

In addition, a cognitive anthropological perspective that views culture as particulate, consisting of multiple representations and knowledge structures at higher levels of organization, and instituted in public practices as well as internalized in individual minds has allowed me to situate these conventional representations within their social and cultural contexts. Moreover, I have contributed through providing a detailed study of the close and dynamic connections between representations. I show how people negotiated and integrated these representations on public and personal levels and their significance for interpretations of equality, hierarchy, and inclusion of persons and groups in society. Furthermore, I extend upon the insight that these representations are "twice born" in publicly instituted forms and in individual minds (Bradd Shore 1996) through examining their connection and negotiation in a variety of social contexts. It becomes evident as we move through malls, government squares, and temples that individuals and groups institute, internalize, and integrate these conventional representations in quite different ways in these contexts.

Indeed, it is important to consider context together with knowledge and practice in a unified theory of practice. Alternatives to the dominant synthesis of representations emerged as we moved from government squares to mall stages, and temples and churches under the control of segments of politically subordinate communities. The manner in which conventional representations were re-interpreted and transformed in these contexts indicate that they are "re-born" as "mental" representations in a manner that often puts the hegemonic perspective at risk. Moreover, despite the institutionalization of dominant representations in government squares and museums, people still attempt to re-interpret these exhibitions from different perspectives destabilizing processes of cultural reproduction. Although power is an important dimension of social relations, these findings reflect the irreducibility of human cultural creativity and caution us to avoid all too popular modes of turning to power to explain almost everything, reducing culture to power. My study suggests that it is also important to consider personal models in contrast to dominant instituted models. In the future, I want to follow some of these personal models and the processes through which they become more widespread and perhaps even instituted in a variety of contexts. I also want to consider how the intervention of the state and businesses in the name of tourism, for instance, transforms these sites and constrains the ways in which people negotiate and connect representations to each other.

In addition, in future research, I would like to examine situated knowledge in relation to social practice more than I have in this study. I have laid a useful foundation for looking at the dynamic connections between people's social identities and overarching categories and representations of society more broadly. I also have begun to examine the negotiation of these representations on a personal level in relation to their individual experiences and commitment to ideological formulations and cognitive structures. I want to extend this work by looking further in a more focused fashion at how different individuals negotiate, transform, and produce ideology and knowledge over time. Similar to Holland and Eisenhardt (1990), I would like to follow the life histories of several individuals, for instance intermarried couples and their children, and consider the ways in which they manipulate representations of social identity, community, and nation over time. This can give us a highly textured account of negotiations of "double consciousness" (Du Bois 1989[1903]) within maximal social identities as well as within the national community from individual to individual and over time. Moreover, such a focus on situated knowledge in connection with social practice over time and life histories can provide us with a view of emergence for not only are nations projects-in-the-making, but citizen-subjects are also projects-in-the-making.

REFLECTIONS OF THE ETHNOGRAPHER

I have been hesitant to make recommendations, based on my research and experiences, for Malaysians to use in their continuing efforts to improve Malaysian society, and I venture upon this charged terrain, with a fair amount of trepidation, at the request of several Malaysian friends and colleagues. My acute awareness that "western" anthropologists have too often taken a judgmental stance towards "other" societies, while turning a deaf ear to problems in their "own" societies, has tempered my hesitance. It has become a mode of anthropological discourse to criticize and ridicule other societies, holding them up to the ideals of "western" societies, ideals too often not realized in our practices and patterns of social relations. Indeed, I venture to make several recommendations to assist Malaysians on their path of refining their "civil society," despite my realization that, in many respects, Malaysia already has much from which the United States and other societies can learn and take to heart. For instance, we in the United States can learn from the model of multicultural practice in Malaysian society that formally recognizes several minority religions by making some of their religious festivals national and state holidays. In contrast, in the United States, Christianity dominates the public sphere and minority religions such as Islam, Hinduism, and Buddhism are not given the recognition and inclusion of minority religions in Malaysia. Moreover, Malaysians are not only aware of the diversity of their society, but they also have a widespread and instituted philosophy of multiculturalism, a philosophy of how groups should interact with each other. In the United States, we are still struggling to acknowledge the diversity of our society and trying to come to some shared meanings, a "common will," about its significance.

Furthermore, for the last several decades, there has been a synergy between the Malaysian state and many non-governmental organizations on issues of multiculturalism, inclusion of minorities, and structural transformation, and Malaysia has made much progress in the short period since *Merdeka*. On the other hand, there have been few periods in the United States during which such synergy existed between the state and non-governmental organizations struggling around similar issues, given the much longer time since political independence. A few notable exceptions are the periods of the "New Deal" in the 1930s and the "Great Society" in the 1960s, when significant forces coalesced and converged in the national government and in local communities to strive for progressive structural changes in society. On the other hand, there have been long periods of conservative backlash in the United States such as the demise of Reconstruction and the erection of legalized racial segregation, "Jim Crow," American-style Apartheid, and the last three decades of conservative reaction to civil rights movements. Clearly, "Americans" have much to learn from Malaysia to continue our efforts towards creating a more "civil society" (cf. Hefner 2001).

Nevertheless, I will try to utilize insights from my research and experiences as a Black man in the United States, to make several helpful recommendations for Malaysians of diverse backgrounds. Hopefully, the peculiar position of Black people in the United States, as a minority striving for full inclusion and a structurally disadvantaged segment, will assist me in trying to find a "middle ground" where I can productively relate to Malaysian minorities striving for less graded cultural citizenship and to Malays striving to rectify structural disadvantages inherited from a colonial past. First, I think Malaysians should look for ways to extend upon and refine the synergy between the state and non-governmental organizations. I have come across some of the most insightful, unconventional, progressive-thinking people in non-governmental organizations that can contribute new ideas to processes of forging national unity, sustainable development, and novel mixes of conceptions of Malaysian society. Secondly, Malaysians can use this extension of synergy to incorporate more bottom-up forms of multiculturalism in government programs and policies. Several alternative and personal models and schemata of Malaysian society and frames of interaction and interpretation hold immense possibilities to enhance inclusion and national unity. I have at times been puzzled by the intense emotions Malaysians of diverse backgrounds expressed when members of other cultural categories appeared in public in attire associated with people of their category. Chinese in "Malay" attire and Malays in "Chinese" attire, on public stages has brought some of the most enthusiastic responses from audiences. These sorts of creative mixtures, destabilizing and blurring conventional boundaries, can be a way to build upon the spirit of

Figure 19 Malay victor of Chinese New Year fancy dress contest. (Photograph by Timothy P. Daniels)

friendly relations and the "openness" to venture beyond group boundaries to form ties with others of different backgrounds. Malaysians can create "national" attire drawing upon the customary dress of a variety of social groups; it can be a sort of *"pakaian rojak"* or "clothing salad."

Thirdly, a bottom-up oriented synergy, should also look to the Islamic morality of the common, everyday Malay (see Banks 1983, 1987, 1990; Scott 1976, 1985, 1990, 1992). The focus in dominant national and international discourse on changing the common, *kampung* Malay puzzles me, when it appears that *kampung* Malays have contributed so much to the national patterns of hospitality, friendliness, loyalty, and neighborliness. Many *kampung* Malays I have met and interacted with ensconce these modes of behavior in references to the Quran and Sunnah, statements and practices of holy Prophet Muhammad, and the etiquette of the companions of the Prophet. Early Black migrants to northern cities often ridiculed recent migrants to urban areas, citing their rural mentalities and behavior patterns (see DuBois 1973[1899]; Drake 1940; Drake and Cayton 1993[1945]). However, contemporary Blacks and others are beginning to realize that it is the rural-based culture of Blacks kept alive in northern and southern cities that provides a powerful resource for community formation, self-help institutions, and progressive change in an increasingly postmodern context in which people lack depth to social relationships and places to call "home" (see Stack 1996; Gregory 1999). Similarly, Yoshihiro (2001:256–7) finds in conclusion of his thirty-year study of Malay community life that Malay rural culture provides an important resource for Malays in urban areas living under changed ecological conditions. I am convinced that there is great potential in *kampung* Malay culture and in the Islamic morality and values of the common Muslim for moving beyond rifts in the Malay community and healing the wounds between Malays and other social groups. To the contrary, the top-down approach of elites using Islam for ideological and political motives, whether wrapped in secular or theocratic clothing, has deepened the crises in Malaysian society.

Finally, in relation to Malay special privileges, I think that a new economic policy needs to be devised continuing efforts at producing structural transformation and achieving economic equality. Similar to the new strategy of struggling for economic justice for Blacks and other minorities Doctor Reverend Martin Luther King, Jr. was developing before he was assassinated, I think Malaysia's new economic policy can strive to rectify patterns of economic inequality for a broad range of peoples in Malaysian society. It can reach out to assist *orang susah, miskin, sederhana* (poor and working class) people of all cultural categories, Malays, Indians, Dayaks and so on, citizens and immigrant workers alike. I have been truly appalled at the way many Indonesian and Bangladeshi workers are abused and oppressed by Malaysian employers, law enforcement officers, and street gangs. Shared human values of people across the world, expressed in the Declaration and Programme of Action of the World Conference against Racism, Racial Discrimination, Xenophobia and Related Intolerance (2001), and the Islamic morality of the common Muslim requires that we treat poor people and workers better no matter their background or place of origin.

I offer these broad recommendations for Malaysians, extending state-NGO synergy, incorporating more bottom-up and common Muslim perspectives, and devising a new, more inclusive, economic policy, even as I hope that "American" citizens and other "westerners" benefit from the epistemological distance of looking at people and groups struggling in the cauldron of belonging in Malaysian society.

Notes

NOTES TO THE PREFACE

1. All of the names used for respondents in this study are pseudonyms in order to protect the privacy and safety of individuals. I use the real names of public officials whose public speeches or statements I use as data, but if these officials gave me information in private contexts, I use pseudonyms as well.

2. Furnivall uses the notion of "race" as if it were a biological or scientific category. I do not subscribe to this notion of "race" but I do use the words "race" and "racial" occasionally throughout this text, hereafter often without quotation marks, as an expression of the point of view of others. Malaysians have acquired a usage of the notion of "race" from the British that refers to distinct segments of humanity that are viewed as a mix of biological and cultural attributes. The character of this mix has changed over time with the late nineteenth and twentieth century conceptions laying a greater stress upon biological attributes, than the early nineteenth century conceptions (see Milner 1998). Seeing that these distinct segments do not actually exist in nature, I adopt a constructionist perspective, detailed in chapter three, that views biological and cultural attributes as underlying knowledge, often intertwined, that constitutes cultural categorization. Malaysians have given new meanings to "race" and "racial" categories over time (ibid; see also Shamsul A.B. 1998).

NOTES TO CHAPTER TWO

1. See Anthony Reid (2001:297–301) for a discussion of the early Chinese, Egyptian, Arab, Japanese, and Portuguese uses of the category *Melayu*.

2. Anthony Reid (2001:304) notes that dating the Malay term "tanah Melayu" is difficult but that its application solely to the Malay Peninsular appears to have English colonial origins. The only Malay pre-modern text, *Hikayat Hang Tuah*, Reid cites as having used the term applied it to the Peninsula as well as other areas in the region with Malay kings. See also Leonard Y. Andaya (2001) for a discussion of the historical negotiations of "Melayu origins" in the archipelago and peninsula.

3. See James T. Collins (2001) for a discussion of the relationship of cultural and sociolinguistic phenomena to Malay identity. He cautions us not to assume an inherent tie between Malay language, culture, and identity, an error many nineteenth century European intellectuals committed in their analysis of Europe and elsewhere (see Reid 2001:303).

4. Lian Kwen Fee (2001) discusses constructions and negotiations of Malay identity in Riau-Lingga-Johor following the fall of Melaka.

5. See Reid (2001:299) for a discussion of some early Portuguese and British interpretations of "Jawi" as mixtures or crosses of anything such as people of different categories, and cultural traits such as languages, dress, and patterns of behavior and organization.

6. The post-war animosity between Malays and Chinese was variable across different parts of Malaysia. Oral histories in Melaka often telling of Chinese families sending their children to Malay families who took them in and cared for them tends to indicate that in Melaka these animosities may have not been so intense. Chinese families often sought to protect their children from potential Japanese persecution in this fashion. After all, close relations and acculturation between Malay and Chinese communities has a much longer history in Melaka than in other areas of Peninsular Malaysia.

7. These are some of the Arabic terms that are part of Muslim religious language in Malaysia and in most other Muslim societies or communities. *Ibadah* means to serve and worship; *salat* means prayer, as in the five obligatory Muslim prayers made daily; *Rasul* means messenger and *Nabi* means prophet; *Imam* refers to an Islamic religious leader, for instance the one who leads prayer. *Dakwah* refers to acts of calling people to the religion of Islam. *Assalamualaikum* is an Islamic greeting that means peace be unto you, *Alhamdulillah* means all praise is due to Allah, *Allahu Akbar* means Allah is the Greatest, and *Subhanallah* means all glory be to Allah.

NOTES FOR CHAPTER THREE

1. I am referring here to a general theory of cultural categories and social identities considered in local terms to be "mixed" or a combination of other categories and identities, and not to the sort of theory of "hybridity" of popular forms of behavior proposed by David M. Guss (2000: 4, 130). Guss, and many other scholars, are working towards a theory of "hybridity" that reconceptualizes state interventions in the production of cultural performances. Both of these approaches to theorizing "hybidity" undermine the tendency to impose "outside" interpretations of authenticity and essential origins, though in different respects.

2. These forms of dress are key markers of Malay culture and identity. *Sarong* is an article of clothing wrapped around the lower part of the body and tied or folded over at the waist. Men and women wear sarong, but women often wear them with a special style of blouse called a *kebaya*. *Baju kurung* is a two-piece female garment composed of a long skirt and matching tunic. *Baju melayu* literally means "Malay dress" but it is used to refer to a form of male attire composed of matching pajama-like slacks and shirt. In the

Malay community, these forms of dress are generally thought to be a reflection of Islamic modesty in the way they are supposed to cover the male and female body. According to local interpretations of Islamic principles of decent dress, Muslim men generally cover their bodies from below the knee to their shoulders and Muslim women generally cover their bodies from their ankles to their shoulders. In recent decades, as a result of resurgent Islam or *Dakwah* movements, the interpretation that Muslim women must also cover their heads in keeping with Islamic precepts of decency has become more widespread. Most but not all of the Malay women I saw in public wore *kerudung* or scarves over their heads. When non-Malays wear *sarong kebaya*, baju kurung, or *baju melayu*, Malays tend to interpret it as a sign of their assimilation of Malay and Malaysian culture and evaluate it positively. Yet they often note that the style of *kebaya* worn by the non-Muslim "assimilated" groups such as the Chitty and *Babas* and *Nyonyas* are shorter and more revealing than the Muslim styles.

3. "Daugher of" is also written as *binte* and abbreviated as *bte.*

4. *Dakwah* comes from the Arabic da'wah and refers to the process of calling people to Islam and struggling against ideas and practices deemed contrary to Islamic principles. In Malaysia, *Dakwah* organizations have focused upon striving to bring Muslims closer to Islamic teachings and principles rather than calling non-Muslims to the Islamic faith. For some historical perspectives of some of these *Dakwah* organizations, see Judith Nagata (1980, 1993) and David Banks (1990). Many of these *Dakwah* organizations such as *Tabligh* and *Darul Arqam* have come under intense repression from the Malay-dominated government. In the contemporary context, many Malay *silat* (martial arts) organizations have become centers of Malay discontent with the current political and economic order. Some of these *silat* organizations combine the study of martial arts with the study of spiritual and mystical paths to power and Islamic-based millenarian notions. One such *silat* organization, Al Ma'unah, was implicated in the July 2, 2000 arms heist and hostage episode that left two government officers dead and sent a shock wave through the country (see *The Sun,* Friday, July 7, 2000).

5. Khoo Kay Kim (1993:278–280) suggests that Malays have negative attitudes about dark skin tones associated with the majority of Indians in Malaysia, South Indians, whereas they have more positive feelings and evaluations about the more "Caucasian-looking" and lighter skinned North Indians they see in Hindi movies. On several occasions I have observed Indians comment upon the light complexion of a young woman or child, interpreting this to be a sign of "beauty." This indicates, to some extent, that members of the Indian category also internalize these skin color evaluations, negative for darker skin and positive for lighter skin.

6. In 1984, the Malaysian federal government opened the Amanah Saham Nasional (ASN), a national savings bond scheme previously reserved only for Malays and other *Bumiputeras*, to Eurasians of Portuguese descent (see Goh Beng Lan 1998:189; see also Sarkissian 2000:66, 200).

7. Judith Nagata (1993) describes the long history of assimilation of Indian Muslims in the Malay world. She notes that under contemporary post-colonial

conditions some Indian Muslims manage to be recognized as Malay through adopting Malay style dress, behavior, and the use of *bin/binti* on their identification cards and are able to acquire special benefits reserved for Malays. However, despite adopting markers of Malayness and self-identifying as Malay, some Indian Muslims are still rejected when it comes to receiving special economic and educational benefits (ibid:526–527). I explore these negotiations in greater detail in chapter seven.

8. Lian Kwen Fee (2001:877) notes that although Malay intellectuals have often criticized *kerajaan* (Malay kingdoms) as an impediment to racial progress, it has remained an "important pillar of ethnic identity." The local, and national, significance of *adat temenggong* to core Malay identity underscores this fact as well as the way a broadened concept of royal descent, as "Malay" heritage, has been combined with Islamic principles and values.

9. Lian Kwen Fee (2001) argues that the concept of *bangsa Melayu,* of Malays as a single community, sharing a common identity and collective destiny, emerged in a colonial context in the early 20th century when Malay intellectuals began to view and write about "Malays" as competing economically with growing numbers of Chinese and Indian immigrants. I think it is important to note that in the past as well as in the current context the "Malay" cultural category has incorporated numerous sub-racial categories and that, from the basis of my ethnographic work late in the 20th century, similar social conditions in the post-colonial context continue to fuel the absorptive power of overarching Malay identity in Malaysia.

NOTES FOR CHAPTER FOUR

1. Margaret Sarkissian (2000:12) notes that these images of "happy multicultural coexistence" are directed at outsiders, visiting dignitaries, businessmen, and tourists, and at insiders as representations of "established reality." She questions whether these images are mere "glittering illusions" and observes that cultural troupes are generally organized along "ethnic" lines and very little interaction occurs between groups of different cultural categories that share stages and dressing rooms (ibid:177).

2. Malaysian and Indonesian political tensions and close identity relations have a long complicated history. Some local Malays still couch their distrust of Indonesians, especially Javanese, in pre-colonial histories of war and intrigue between Malay and Javanese empires. However, it is in the de-colonizing and early post-colonial era where we find the key roots to current political weariness on the part of Malaysia towards Indonesia. During the last days of the Japanese Occupation of Southeast Asia, many Indonesian and Malaysian nationalists agreed upon plans for a post-colonial merger of their two territories into a single nation, a Greater Indonesia or *Indonesia Raya* (Gullick 1981:106, 202; see also Shamsul A.B. 1998:30). These plans were not to come into fruition. Although some of the Indonesian parties to these plans, including Sukarno, the first Indonesian president, came to power, their Malayan counterparts, members of the Malay left, were not to come to assume national positions of power. The Malay leaders of UMNO

who did come into power after independence sought to form a united Malaysia incorporating Singapore and several territories on the island of Borneo. Political leaders in Indonesia and Philippines were vehemently opposed to these plans. President Sukarno proposed an alternative scheme that involved the formation of a regional organization of the three nations but Malaysian leaders had no interest in becoming submerged into political units in which their much larger neighbor, Indonesia, would be the dominant party. Malaysia forged ahead with its plans and formed a united Malaysia including Peninsular Malaya, Singapore temporarily, and Sabah and Sarawak. Brunei opted out of the plan to uphold the position of its own Sultan. In response Indonesia and Philippines took hostile measures against Malaysia. Indonesia waged an undeclared war or *Konfrontasi* (Confrontation) against Malaysia, from 1963 through 1965, engaging in a trade embargo and a series of internal and external sabotage activities (see Gullick 1981:200). Sukarno, a dynamic leader of the non-aligned movement, was critical of the fact that there were still British military bases in Malaysia. He and other Indonesian leaders looked at the newly independent Malaysia as a "neocolonial" puppet of Western imperialists in contrast to the more "revolutionary" Indonesia. From their point of view, Indonesians had fought a bloody war of national liberation against the Dutch, while Malaysia collaborated with the British to put down the Communist insurgency and peacefully negotiated political independence, remaining pawns of Western interests. Malaysians, for their part, having inherited an economically strong country saw Indonesian leaders as overly rash and politically unstable. They saw Indonesia as still being saturated in the sort of Communist nonsense that Malaysia had successful gotten rid of during the "Emergency." After the military coup and mass disturbances in 1965, General Suharto came to power in Indonesia and signed an agreement with Malaysian leaders ending the Confrontation in 1966. Yet the tensions between identities and visions that span both countries and the dominant nationalism within each country was to continue. The majority populations of both countries imagine themselves to share a common racial identity as the *Bumiputera* or *Pribumi* of the region, the indigenous peoples of the region. Historical origins, language, artistic genres and customs tie the majority populations of Malaysia and Indonesia together. As noted in chapter four, when "Indon" Muslim migrants become legal citizens in Malaysia, they automatically acquire rights to all of the special benefits of the "Malay" majority. Moreover, the majority populations of Malaysia and Indonesia share a common religious identity as Muslims and many Islamic organizations, such as Tabligh and Darul Arqam, have spanned both countries. This shared racial and religious identity is an active current for the flow of ideas across the current colonial-based boundaries dividing the countries. Given these trans-national connections and the deep commonality they entail, the nationalist leaders of both countries have been at great odds to blow up small differences in order to support the construction and reproduction of separate national identities. Even though, Malaysian and Indonesian languages are, basically, different dialects of the same language, nationalists of both nations have stressed minor differences like transcription styles and pronunciation and word choice to buttress claims to national distinctiveness. In addition, Malaysian leaders have created an image of Malaysians as peaceful, easy-going and moderate in contrast to the aggressive, extremist and emotional nature of Indonesians. Thus, they use contrasting representations of their national personalities. Such images and contrasts are evident in the discourses I have cited, as Malaysian leaders try to check the flow of ideas, like *reformasi* and *keadilan* and the political activism they encourage, from Indonesian popular movements into Malaysian society.

3. I analyzed this speech and other discourse that occurred in the Malay language, such as *Harakah* newspaper articles, some interviews and other speeches, in Malay first before translation and presentation in English. In Malay, as is evident in English, I noted a pattern of bunching of certain propositions and terms indicating common underlying cognition embedded in the discourse of both languages. Moreover, the fact that this pattern of bunching occurs across Malay and English languages and across the discourse of people of various cultural categories suggests that the underlying representations are somewhat conventional representations.

4. It is significant that Datuk Gan spoke the "Malaysian language" before a mixed audience on the occasion of this public Hari Raya event, whereas during Chinese public events in the mall he rarely spoke Malay, choosing to speak Mandarin instead. Datuk Gan and Datuk Raghovan, whose speech is presented later in this chapter, both began their speeches in the typical style of this genre.

5. "lah" is a particle added to the end of emphatic words in a sentence. Its usage originated in the Malay language but it is used in both Malay and Malaysian English. It appears in my Malay translations and Malaysian English transcriptions.

6. Sue Lin, as was the case with many Chinese, Indians, and *Melaka Portugis,* chose to speak in English rather than Malay, a language in which she teaches and has a high level of competence. In choosing to speak English, many local people express a sense of "modernity" and sophistication as English is associated with the industrialized and technologically developed countries that are dominant in the global economy. On occasion, people of these non-Malay cultural categories have stopped me when I was speaking in Malay, and requested that I speak in English with them instead, expressing their preference for speaking in English rather than Malay.

7. Unlike many other *Melaka Portugis,* Puan Josephine chose to speak in Malay and was quite comfortable speaking Malay. She spoke a variety of colloquial Malay commonly spoken in Malay neighborhoods in Melaka. Puan Josephine grew up interacting with Malays in Banda Hilir and spent much of her adult life living in predominantly Malay villages and neighborhoods. Most of the initial part of this interview was conducted in Malay and some of the latter portion was conducted in English and Malay, with us both combining these languages. This segment was analyzed in Malay prior to translation and presentation in English.

8. Haji Rashid seemed to be almost equally comfortable speaking English as Malay. He attended an English-language school in Melaka as a teenager, and lived and worked in Singapore for several years as an adult. I often noticed him switching from Malay to English when he was speaking with Indians and Chinese who spoke English, whereas he spoke Malay in his home while socializing with Malay friends and neighbors. Speaking English may be an expression of his "modern" Malay perspective and identification.

9. KeADILan (Justice) or *Partai Keadilan Nasional* (National Justice Party), DAP or *Partai Tindakan Demokratik* (Democratic Action Party), PRM or *Parti Rakyat Malaysia* (Malaysian People's Party), and PAS issued a joint manifesto detailing their alliance political platform prior to the 1999 election.

10. It is significant to note that these lexical items, *tompang* and *Bumi*, were used within an otherwise English language discourse. These terms are associated with complex underlying notions that are partially constitutive of conventional schemata and are often used as a shorthand index of this knowledge and the social relationships they entail.

11. A phrase partially in Malay, "*orang Melayu* is the *banyak sekali,*" intrudes into an otherwise English context. Yet, we must note how this concept is repeated later in English in almost identical fashion. This suggests that the same or similar notions were being expressed in both languages.

12. *Tanah Melayu* and *hak-hak istimewa* are readily translatable into English and occasionally are but these terms are often maintained in Malay in an otherwise English language context. They are also similar to *Bumi* and *tompang* in the way they index and are closely connected with underlying schemata.

13. Haji Rashid draws upon a cliché in Malay expressing the traditional Malay sense of courtesy, self-restraint, and giving way (see Mahathir Mohamad 1970:115–120)—often interpreted as the easy-going "nature" of Malays—and then situates it within the Malay Muslim's religious world view and relationship of submission to the Divine Will.

14. Khoo Kay Kim (1993:272) shows that many Indians in Malaya during the 1930s were pressing for "equal rights" and criticizing the British administration for "pampering certain communities." In 1937, after the British High Commissioner announced his decision to admit non-Malays into "responsible posts in the technical services," many Malays publicly voiced their opposition to this decision and expressed their anger at Indians who they perceived to be lowering the positions of Malays in the government service. One Malay man wrote in an excerpt of his letter to the press: "Again, I am not in favour of unqualified preference for Malays while considering applications for employment in the Clerical Services. Other things being equal, the Malays should, of course, be given preference in view of the fact that they are the true sons of the soil of Malaya, which is essentially the country of the Malays" (ibid:272). The schemata of "Malay privilege" encompassed entitlement to preference in filling civil service positions under British rule just as it does nowadays. However, in 1937 this knowledge was being called upon to keep more Indians from gaining access to higher level civil service positions, a problem Malays are rarely concerned about today under post-colonial conditions of Malay political hegemony.

NOTES FOR CHAPTER FIVE

1. Race is a term used in Malaysia to describe collectivities or classes of persons. Its usage has been shaped, in many ways, through the colonial experience and through the history of interrelations between locals and successive waves of immigration. Local meanings of race have changed over time, both in colonial and post-colonial times. Contemporary sensibilities in Melaka tend to view race as a category that includes both biological and cultural attributes, in contrast to the typical usage in the U.S., which makes a distinction between "race" and "ethnicity," with the latter entailing cultural differences and the former biological differences. In Melaka, and perhaps in Malaysia overall, nowadays, biological and religious attributes are highly stressed and viewed as intimately intertwined as discussed in chapter three. Nevertheless, despite strong religious associations with particular cultural categories, people still think of *agama* (religion) as separate from *bangsa* (race or some sort of collectivity of persons) in some contexts.

2. See Sarkissian (2000:79) for some biographical information on Joe Lazaroo and other *Melaka Portugis* bandleaders.

3. *Hindustani* is a local label used for Indian language movies, mostly Hindi and Tamil.

4. "Cik" is a colloquial Malay form of the respectful term of address *Encik* used for adult males and "*Mat*" is a popular abbreviated form for the common Malay Muslim name Mohamad. Thus, "Cik Mat" is a popular way of saying Encik Mohamad or Mister Mohamad. "Puan" is a formal term of address in Malay for a married woman or woman of higher social status than the speaker.

5. *Congkak* is game played on a wooden board with holes in it. Players compete in moving cowries or marbles around the wooden board, from hole to hole.

6. For further discussion of the *mandi safar* festival and how its termination relates to inter-group relations see chapter seven.

7. *Dondang sayang* is a Malay genre of song in which men and women engage in a call and response, *jual* and *beli,* sequence of four-line *pantun* (poems) that generally have several levels of meaning (see Sarkissian 2000:194). Sarkissian describes the structural similarity of *dondang sayang* to a *Melaka Portugis* male-female song duel genre called *mata kantiga* and notes that *dondang sayang* is "widely held to be of Portuguese origin" (ibid:63). However, most local Malays consider *dondang sayang* to be a traditional genre created by Malays and interpret the performance of this genre by Chinese and Indian *Peranakan* and *Serani* as evidence of their having assimilated many aspects of Malay culture.

8. *Songket* is cloth embroidered with bits of gold and silver thread and *tanjuk* is a head wrap that stands erect on ones head.

9. *Sirih junjung* is the Malay custom of offering betel in small wooden or metal cases to honored guests as a show of respect and hospitality.

10. *Bunga manggar* literal means the "flower of the coconut palm" but in this context it refers to sections of banana tree trunks, or other materials, stuck on the top of a small stick or pole with numerous decorated thin spikes stuck

into it. The thin spikes stuck into the banana tree trucks from all directions have shiny paper of various bright colors hanging from them. *Bunga mang-gar* are usually posted or carried in parades or opening ceremonies when Malays engage in festive activities.

11. *Sanggung lentang* are multiple-layered headdresses worn customarily by Malay brides in wedding ceremonies. If families want to have these made for weddings nowadays, they must go to specialists that still have the knowledge on how to construct them. Most of the Malay or Indian Muslim weddings I have attended, the brides chose not to wear them. Some women complain that they are heavy to wear for any protracted time.

12. Dataran Sejarah is a plaza and amphitheater recently built in Ayer Keroh, Melaka, an area to the northwest of the Melaka town area that has become a focus of government development, including governmental office buildings, factories, and tourist sites.

13. *Dikir* comes from the Arabic *zikir* that refers to an Islamic form of worshipping Allah by recitation of praises and Divine attributes or names.

14. The *kulintang* and *angklung* are traditional musical instruments that originated from Northern Sulawesi and Western Java respectively.

15. Anthony Reid (2001), Leonard Y. Andaya (2001), and Lian (2001) explore the history of Malay "origins" and identity, noting the variety of constructions of, and contests over, Malayness in different historical contexts. Andaya underscores historical contests over claims of being the "center" or "origin" of Melayu on both sides of the Straits of Melaka, and how the peninsula, Malaysia, eventually won this political struggle, although these claims are still disputed in other parts of the "Malayo-Indonesian" world (see also Daniels 1999).

16. The other museums not described in this section are The Royal Malaysian Navy Museum, The Maritime Museum, The Kite Museum, and The Museum of Beauty that focuses upon various societies around the world.

17. *Lontar* leaves are palmyra palm leaves used in the past for writing in many areas of Southeast Asia.

18. Khoo Kay Kim (1993:266–268) suggests that Munshi Abdullah was a prominent example of the union of Indian Muslims and Malays in the pre-nineteenth century period when large numbers of Indians were traders, Islamic teachers, and literary figures. Khoo also suggests that many Indian Muslims who contributed to Malay literature in the twentieth century were a continuation of this trend from the times of Munshi Abdullah.

19. In most other versions of this story I have heard, people called the small miraculous animal a *kancil* or deer instead of a rat. Many local Hindus emphasize the Hindu religious background of the founder of Melaka in their re-tellings of this story. However, detailed historical research tends to suggest that Parameswara and the rulers of the Kingdom of Sriwijaya were Buddhists (Wolters 1970). On the other hand, Buddhism and Hinduism in that period were much more alike than they are today. In contrast, Malay re-tellings of this story tend to emphasize his "Malay" racial background while de-emphasizing his non-Muslim religious background.

NOTES TO CHAPTER SIX

1. Some of the ethnographic materials in this chapter have been used for a comparison with Kuching published in my paper, "Cognitive Covergence and Symbolic Advantage in Melaka and Kuching," In Borneo 2000: Ethnicity, Culture & Society, pp. 166–194, Kuching: University Malaysian Sarawak, pp. 166–194.

2. This discussion only includes a small sample of such festivals at sacred sites.

3. The municipal and state government of Melaka recognizes the Chitty "headman" who serves as a power broker between the local Chitty community and the local government. Malay government officials and civil servants have been trying to get the Chitty community to hold more "cultural" events that lack religious meaning and take place outside of temple contexts in which Malays could also participate. Although this festival appears on the government tourist listings, it does not fit the bill of a "cultural" festival according to government officials and does not receive governmental financial support.

4. Fresh "vellapai" (margossa) leaves, known locally for their medicinal properties for the treatment of chickenpox, are hung in the middle of the temple on the first day of this festival and are carried by devotees as they perform acts of devotion on the tenth, and climactic, day of the festival. In Melaka, in the past, when smallpox was more of a threat, and in other Hindu communities, Amman was more strongly associated with smallpox and was believed to possess the power to ward off this disease (see Dumont 1959:79). Nowadays, in the Melaka Hindu community, Amman is primarily viewed as the goddess that has the power to cure smallpox, chickenpox, and other diseases that involve skin eruptions (see Mearns 1995:163).

5. Ju Shi Huey (1983) and Tan Chee-Beng (1990) use the label "Chinese religion" and "Chinese Religion" with a capital "R" respectively for referring to the complex, syncretic belief system of many Chinese in Southeast Asia, Taiwan, and Hong Kong. I think that this label implies that a particular rubric of beliefs and religious themes are essentially Chinese, unduly wedding these beliefs and practices to the Chinese cultural category. Although many locals do make these associations, as I have noted in chapter four, I see no need to assume these behavioral expectations within my descriptive labels. Many Chinese in mainland China would argue that they have no religion and many Chinese in Southeast Asia try to practice Christianity and Islam without mixing in "traditional" elements of the syncretic religious systems of their ancestors. I choose to use the label "Buddhist-Taoist" for this syncretic religious system in which entities from Buddhist and Taoist cosmologies are merged with Confucian philosophy and elements from other religions. The "Buddhist-Taoist" label acknowledges the complex syncretic character of this religious system without implying that it is inherently "Chinese" in any way.

6. Kwan Yin is the female aspect of the Mahayanist Bodhisattva Avalokitesvara. In many local Buddhist-Taoist temples, she appears in two forms: one form is a vegetarian deity considered to be on the Buddhist side

of the pantheon, and one is a meat-eating deity considered to be on the Taoist side of the pantheon.

7. Chap Goh Mei, the first full moon of the Chinese year, is the climax of the New Year Celebration and is a universal time of celebration and ancestor worship for Chinese of all dialect groups. Several different customs have developed in particular parts of Malaysia. In Melaka, the procession described in this section has become an annual event and part of the inter-communal festival cycle.

8. Margery Wolf (1990) examines the experience of a woman in a village in Taiwan who appeared to fulfill all of the local criteria for becoming a shaman except her gender. Wolf argues that gender constructions in Taiwanese families and ideology in combination with other structural means of ranking people in these village contexts militated against this woman becoming a shaman, a status very few other Taiwanese women have been able to achieve. In the Chinese community in Melaka, I have observed a few women serve as shamans at the end of temple festivals when participants surround shamans looking for healing and other forms of assistance. However, during festival processions when shamans perform several feats displaying the power of the deities inhabiting their bodies, I have not observed any woman shamans.

9. *Wesak* is the Hindu and Indian Buddhist month, April-May, and is often taken as defining the spring season.

10. Ju Shi Huey (1983:39) found that a branch of a Chinese spirit-medium "sect" in Singapore had installed and worshipped images of the Virgin Mother Mary and Letchmi, the goddess of wealth in the Hindu pantheon. Worshippers believed that these deities would help to bring them wealth. Similarly, Teresita Ang See and Go Bon Juan (1990:54) found that many Chinese Filipinos display and worship images of Jesus Christ and Blessed Mother Mary together with Buddhist and Taoist images on the same altars in temples, homes, and businesses. Many Buddhist-Taoists and Hindus in Melaka also travel to Bukit Mertajam, Penang, like thousands of other pilgrims all over Malaysia and Singapore, for the annual St. Anne's festival and make vows and offer candles and flowers to St. Anne, the grandmother of Jesus. In Melaka, Good Friday is the main occasion for large-scale non-Christian involvement in Christian observances, but many non-Christians also go to annual prayers in an old church, St. Cruz, located north of the town area. Non-Christians go to this church to gain some blessings from an old cross that is believed to have miraculous powers.

11. The veneration of Muslim saints has a long history in Muslim societies the world over. See Zohra Khatoon (1990) for a discussion of the history of Sufi and Shia saints in India and Christopher S. Taylor (1999) for a discussion of the worship of Muslim saints in late medieval Egypt. The early immigration and acculturation of Indian Muslims no doubt influenced the growth of these practices in the Malayo-Indonesian world.

12. Cecilia Ng Siew Hua (1983) found that two Malay *datuk, Datuk Bakul* and *Datuk Puloh Besar,* were displayed and worshipped along with several Buddhist-Taoist deities at a predominantly Straits-born Chinese temple in

Singapore. A few Indians and many dialect-speaking Chinese also worshipped at this temple. *Datuk Bakul* is a deity attached to a basket made to
appear human-like and *Datuk Puloh Besar* is a deity believed to be attached
to the island lying off the coast of Melaka. *"Puloh"* is the local way of saying *"Pulau,"* the Malay word for island. Similarly, Tan Chee-Beng (1990)
found that Chinese Buddhist-Taoists in Bukit Rambai, Melaka and in a village in Kelantan worship a earth spirit, Na Tok (derived from *Datok*) Kong,
alongside deities of the Taoist pantheon. Offerings, such as yellow rice (*kun-
yit),* raw coconuts, fruits and other foods and substances deemed suitable
for a spirit of the Malay cultural category were presented at these altars in
Singapore, Melaka, and Kelantan. No pork was offered to Malay *keramat.*
In Singapore, Hua (1983) reports that Chinese worshippers have Malay
Muslims prepare the yellow rice and chicken to assure that the offerings fulfilled Muslim food requirements.

13. *Hari Raya Aidiladha* is the Muslim celebration that takes place during the
climax of the Muslim pilgrimage to Mecca. This celebration is also called
Hari Raya Haji and *Hari Raya Korban* because of its association with the
Hajj season and because it is customary to sacrifice (*korban*) animals as acts
of obedience to Allah during this celebration. In local areas all over
Malaysia, cows and sheep are slaughtered at mosques and prayer halls and
the meat distributed to members of the community.

14. The Malaysian King, Minister of Culture, Arts, and Tourism, and the Chief
Minister of Melaka launched the National Water Festival at Pantai Kundor,
Melaka on the 1st day of Safar, May 5th 2000.

15. For Hindus from South India it pertains to the victory of Sri Krishna over
the demon Narakasura, while for Hindus from North India it relates to the
triumphant return of Sri Rama to Ayodhya. It is also a day for the worship
of Laxmi or Letchmi, a female deity in many local Hindu homes, as lighted
lamps are associated with her (see Noor et al. 1985:16). Hindus perform
several rites at home and attend prayers at local temples for Deepavali.

16. The former year's festive season events also laid greater emphasis upon
Chinese New Year and Christmas events, but there were more *Deepavali*
and *Hari Raya Aidilfitri* events than this year. There were roughly eight days
of *Deepavali* events featuring a Saree Queen contest and cultural shows
staged at both malls with stages. *Hari Raya Aidilfitri* events were staged for
around two weeks with a single event each day. The P. Ramlee and Saloma
impersonation contest, dance shows, and a young girl's beauty contest were
featured events and other day's cultural shows, fashion shows, and religious
choir events took place on the mall stages. Chinese New Year events last
year lasted for a little over two weeks and had numerous events staged on
several days on the schedule and the stage and concourse decorations were
the most elaborate of all the mall events. Chinese cultural shows, dance and
music programs, and lion dances were among the featured activities.
Christmas activities lasted for almost a full month featuring church-organ-
ized Christmas caroling, and Christian religious dramas and musical programs. There were also several Santa Claus candy giveaways and game
show events on the Christmas schedule. Thus, the public mall celebrations

of the 1998–1999 festive season, also affected a subversion of the dominant government trend of emphasizing Malay culture and identity, but they included Malay and Indian representations more than the following year. Similar to the "cultural heritage" theme of the Melaka Historic Day events, the 1998–1999 mall events combined models of "Malaysia's diverse society" with an emphasis of a particular cultural category, in this case Chinese rather than Malay.

NOTES TO CHAPTER SEVEN

1. "Bayar niat" refers to the practice of paying back the deity for the blessings you have received, a way of giving thanks. For instance, if one made a vow to make certain types of offerings to the deity every year if one were healed of an illness, "bayar niat" would be to make these offerings in fulfillment of the vow. This idea traverses all of the religious communities in Melaka.

2. Sarkissian (2000:26) notes that contemporary *Portugis* use the phrase "mixed marriage" to refer to the union of two people from different religious backgrounds rather than two different ethnic or racial backgrounds. She suggests that this linguistic usage is a continuation of the sixteenth-century royal edicts that promoted assimilation into a community defined primarily through its adoption of the Catholic faith.

3. There are a few well-publicized cases of Malay women marrying non-Muslims without their husbands converting to Islam. These cases were highly controversial and elicited strong opposition from large segments of the Malay population, including Islamic religious officials. While people spoke to me about these past cases, I did not encounter, or hear about, any recent cases of Muslim/non-Muslim intermarriage that did not involve conversion of the non-Muslim party to Islam before the performance of wedding rites. Although there are stringent social and legal pressures militating against such unions, they still may occur secretly, outside of public scrutiny.

4. The statement that there is no God but Allah and that Prophet Muhammad is His Messenger.

5. Ibrahim and many others employed the notion/emotion of "love" in explanations of the process of forming ties with a marriage candidate or spouse and in justifications of acting in contradiction to the wishes and expectations of relatives and onlookers. In fact, all of the youth I discussed such issues with, expressed their intentions to "fall in love" with their future spouse before marriage.

6. A *murtad* is a person who was formerly a Muslim that has moved outside of Islam and become an apostate. Many states of Malaysia, including Melaka, have laws and programs to discipline and to re-educate *murtad*.

7. Tabitha Frith (2000:128) suggests that Malays suffer a high degree of "ontological insecurity" in their negotiations of religious and ethnic identity, given the way these are deeply intertwined, when confronted with the "not so 'other' Chinese Muslim."

8. These social dynamics of intermarrying with and becoming, at least through one's offspring, the "preferred" or "definitive" racial category in Malaysia

can be compared to other regions, including the United States. In contrast to Malaysia, European "ethnics"—Irish, Italians, French, Poles, and so forth— who immediately began to intermarry with "native" whites upon arriving in the U.S., were able to initiate their process of becoming "white" themselves, gradually decreasing the cultural "stuff" to be assimilated through successive intermarriages (Sanjek 1994). A major distinction is made in the identity placement of the offspring of intermarriages along the axes of an "ethnic" or "racial" model; in the latter case, there is only identity inheritance from one parent, the non-white one, whereas in the former case the "ethnicity" of both parents is recognized. "A white person may be Croatian-Irish, but not Croatian-Irish-African American. In the eyes of white Americans, at least up to now, such a person is black, and race overrides ethnicity" (ibid:108). The "ethnic" model has been the route to inclusion as first class citizens in the U.S. (see Sanjek 1994; see also Urciuoli 1996), while the "racial" model has been a way to perpetuate racial hierarchies and the second-class citizenship of blacks and other minorities. In the Malaysian case, children inherit their race from their fathers in *all* cases but only in the case of "Malay fatherhood" can the children inherit immediate access to the privileges of the "definitive" race. "Malays" of official *Bumiputera* status can be of Malay-Chinese, Malay-Indian, Malay-*Portugis*, or Malay-Chinese-Indian parentage, but their male parent must be Malay.

NOTES TO CHAPTER EIGHT

1. Salim is my "Muslim name" that I am called by my family and friends in the U.S. and that I was known by locally in Melaka in both Muslim and non-Muslim communities.

2. The Democratic Action Party (DAP), a predominantly Chinese opposition party with some local Indian and *Portugis* members, has kept the "Malaysian Malaysia" concept and political slogan alive, but not without controversy. The "Malaysian Malaysia" concept was a key part of the platform of DAP's predecessor, the People's Action Party (PAP), prior to the separation of Singapore from the Federation of Malaysia in 1965. PAP leaders were arguing for a "Malaysian Malaya," in which all races and ethnic groups would enjoy equal political and cultural rights, instead of a "Malay Malaysia" which they claimed was being imposed by the Malay-dominated Alliance government (Andaya and Andaya 1982:276; Heng Pek Koon 1998:64). The reconstituted Malaysian-based party, DAP carried on this slogan and its underlying principles as part of the foundation of its political platform. One of the areas in which DAP has agitated for complete equality and an end of Malay special rights has been in education. Prior to the last election, Lim Kit Siang, the secretary-general of DAP, declared the "second Malaysian-Malaysia" notion that he said was "to fight for the people's right to fairness-for-all irrespective of race and religion so that all will be able to appreciate justice, freedom and democracy (The Sun, May 14, 1999). A public controversy in which UMNO and DAP leaders exchanged words was reported in the newspapers for several days. Prime Minister Datuk Seri Dr

Mahathir Mohamad reportedly said that the "Malaysian Malaysia" idea "promotes meritocracy, which only benefits the rich . . . there will be communal tension if the DAP continues to call for the implementation of 'Malaysian Malaysia' concept . . . even though the term says 'Malaysian Malaysia,' the concept only favours one particular race" (The Sun, May 14, 1999). This article went on to report the Prime Minister's threats to bring charges of sedition against DAP if their statements lead to "hatred among the various races." A few days later, the newspaper printed an article in which Lim Kit Siang reportedly threatened to file sedition charges against UMNO leaders for accusing DAP of wanting to abolish Malay special rights (The Sun, May 16, 1999). The DAP is highly popular amongst the urban-dwelling Chinese of Melaka who often speak of their votes for DAP as "protest votes" against the domination of UMNO on a state wide level. DAP wins many elections for urban-based districts in which Chinese are the majority.

3. Laksamana Cheng Ho is the Chinese admiral who led the fleet of ships from China that stopped in Melaka in the early fifteenth century. Mohamad Suhaimi is referring to an exhibit about the travels of Cheng Ho displayed at Mahkota Parade Shopping Center in Melaka. A Chinese Buddhist association arranged and coordinated this exhibit. The exhibit made the claim that Cheng Ho was a Muslim. Suhaimi interpreted this claim along with representations of an early Chinese presence in Melaka as an attempt to assert belonging in this region.

4. Suhaimi is referring to the 1987 internal contest for top positions in UMNO between two factions, one led by Razaleigh and one by Mahathir, the incumbent UMNO president. Mahathir won the election by 761 to 718 votes, but the legality of the election was challenged on the grounds thirty unregistered branches had been allowed to participate in the divisional elections. The High Court declared UMNO an unlawful society in 1988 (Goh Cheng Teik 1989:42). The Mahathir-led faction organized a new UMNO that was recognized by the court and other ruling alliance parties.

5. *Dhimmi* was a concept of a non-Muslim citizen in a society with an Islamic state that I have seen written about in the Islamic alternative newspaper, Harakah. It was not written about often in the Harakah newspaper and even supporters of the party I have spoken to about it were not aware that the Islamic party embraced ideas that were opposed to bestowing special rights upon Muslim citizens in a multi-racial, multi-religious society with an Islamic state. The few articles I have seen in Harakah newspaper about *dhimmi* referred to their position in early Muslim societies in which they were given equal economic and cultural rights with Muslim citizens. These articles also stated that *dhimmi* paid special taxes to the Islamic state in return for military protection.

6. Tabitha Frith (2000) argues that Malays resolve the tensions posed by contradictions between Malay ethnicity and Islam by subsuming Islam within Malay ethnicity and forging Islam into a tool for the demands of their ethnic group and ethnic nationalism. She discusses instances, similar to the one here, of Malays privileging their Malay or *Bumiputera* identity over their

Islamic identity when they are opposed in particular contexts. From the cognitive perspective adopted in this study, Malay ethnic and religious identities are not viewed as distinct, but rather Islam is considered an attribute, albeit, a major attribute, of Malay maximal identity. Thus for Muslim identity to become the maximal identity and Malayness to be subsumed within it as an attribute or liquidated altogether would require a radical cognitive transformation, and given the social and political uses of Malay maximal identity this sort of transformation is unlikely in the near future.

7. Nurul and I often spoke in Malay, so when she felt that she needed to pull words from Malay she knew that it was no problem because I would understand her. Many of the words she uses in Malay here are of this practical sort, used when she could not think of the word in English. However, some of the Malay words are the same ones used in other discourses, cited in earlier chapters, which are indices and closely related to underlying representations. One such term not discussed earlier that I would like to point out here is the term "*tuan rumah*" which appears to me to be closely related to two other key terms, *tompang* and *asli*. When viewed in contrast to these other terms, one can note that "*tuan rumah*" are the "hosts" or "early settlers" and not the "aborigines" or "temporary sojourners." Whether or not the "hosts" have the "original claim" to the land, they are the ones managing it and have a stronger claim to this position than the "immigrants" who arrived later.

8. As was the case with other discourse in Malay discussed earlier, I analyzed this interview in Malay first before translating and presenting it in English.

Bibliography

A. Aziz Deraman, and Wan Ramli Wan Mohamad
1995 *Perayaan Orang Melayu*/Malay Festivals. Shah Alam: Penerbit Fajar Bakti Sdn. Bhd.

Abdul Rahman Embong
1998 Social Transformation, the State and the Middle Classes in Post-Independence Malaysia. *In* Cultural Contestations: Mediating Identities in a Changing Malaysian Society. Zawawi Ibrahim, ed. Pp. 83–116. London: ASEAN Academic Press.
2001 The Culture and Practice of Pluralism in Postcolonial Malaysia. *In* The Politics of Multiculturalism: Pluralism and Citizenship in Malaysia, Singapore, and Indonesia. Robert W. Hefner, ed. Pp. 59–85. Honolulu: University of Hawaii Press.

Ackerman, Susan E., and Raymond L. M. Lee
1988 Heaven in Transition: Non-Muslim Religious Innovation and Ethnic Identity in Malaysia. Honolulu: University of Hawaii Press.

Agar, Michael
1980 Stories, Background Knowledge and Themes: Problems in the Analysis of Life History Narrative. American Ethnologist 7(2):223–240.

Agar, Michael, and Jerry R. Hobbs
1985 How to Grow Schemata out of Interviews. *In* Directions in Cognitive Anthropology. Janet W. D. Dougherty (Keller), ed. Pp. 413–431. Urbana: University of Illinois Press.

Ahmad Ibrahim
1992 The Malaysian Constitutional System. *In* Constitutional Systems in Late Twentieth Century Asia. Lawrence W. Beer, ed. Pp. 507–528. Seattle: University of Washington Press.
1997 Family Law in Malaysia. Third Edition. Kuala Lumpur: Malayan Law Journal Sdn. Bhd.

Andaya, Barbara Watson, and Leonard Y. Andaya
1982 A History of Malaysia. London: Macmillan.

Andaya, Leondard Y.
2001 The Search for the 'Origins' of Melayu. *In* Journal of Southeast Asian Studies 32(3):315–330.

Anderson, Benedict
1983 Imagined Communities: Reflections on the Origin and Spread of Nationalism. New York: Verso.

Ang See, Teresita, and Go Bon Juan
1990 Religious Syncretism among the Chinese in the Philippines. *In* Contributions to Southeast Asian Ethnography. Tan Chee-Beng, ed. Number 9 (December): 53–65. The Preservation and Adaptation of Tradition: Studies of Chinese Religious Expression in Southeast Asia. Singapore: The Editors, Contributions to Southeast Asian Ethnography.

Anzaldua, Gloria
1987 Borderlands/La Frontera. San Francisco: Spinsters/Aunt Lute.

Appadurai, Arjun
1981 Gastro-Politics in Hindu South Asia. American Ethnologist (3):494–511 (Special Issue: Symbolism and Cognition, N. Whitten, ed.)

Aragon, Lorraine V.
1989 Divine Justice: Cosmology, Ritual, and Prostestant Missionization in Central Sulawesi, Indonesia. Ph.D. dissertation, UIUC.
1996 Twisting the Gift: Translating Precolonial into Colonial Exchanges in Central Sulawesi, Indonesia. American Ethnologist 23(1):43–60.
2000 Fields of the Lord: Animism, Christian Minorities, and State Development in Indonesia. Honolulu: University of Hawaii Press.

Armstrong, M. Jocelyn
1988 Festival Open Houses: Settings for Interethnic Communication in Urban Malaysia. Human Organization 47(2):127–137.

Bachtiar, Harsja W.
1993 Indians in Indonesia: A Component of Indonesian National Integration. *In* Indian Communities in Southeast Asia. K.S. Sandhu and A. Mani, eds. Pp. 131–150. Singapore: Times Academic Press.

Banks, David J.
1983 Malay Kinship. Philadelphia: Institute for the Study of Human Issues.
1987 From Class to Culture: Social Conscience in Malay Novels Since Independence. Monograph Series 29. New Haven: Yale University Southeast Asia Studies.
1990 Resurgent Islam and Malay rural culture: Malay novelists and the invention of culture. American Ethnologist 17(3):531–548.

Banton, Michael
1983 Racial and ethnic competition. Cambridge: Cambridge University Press.

Barth, Fredrik, ed.
1969 Ethnic groups and boundaries: the social organization of cultural difference. London: George Allen and Unwin.

Beauvois, Jean-Leon, and Robert-Vincent Joule
1996 A Radical Dissonance Theory. London: Taylor & Francis Ltd.

Bennett, David
1998 Introduction. *In* Multicultural States: Rethinking difference and identity. David Bennett, ed. Pp. 1–25. New York: Routledge.

Bhabha, Homi K.
1994 The location of culture. London: Routledge.

Blanc, Cristina Szanton
1997 The Thoroughly Modern "Asian": Capital, Culture, and Nation in Thailand and the Philippines. *In* Ungrounded Empires: The Cultural Politics of Modern Chinese Transnationalism. Aihwa Ong and Donald M. Nonini, eds. Pp. 261–286. New York: Routledge.

Boulanger, Clare L.
2000 On Dayak, Orang Ulu, Bidayuh and other Imperfect Ethnic Categories in Sarawak. *In* Borneo 2000: Ethnicity, Culture and Society. Proceedings of the Sixth Biennial Borneo Research Conference. Michael Leigh, ed. Pp. 44–63. Kuching: Universiti Malaysia Sarawak.

Bourdieu, Pierre
1977 Outline of a Theory of Practice. Richard Nice, trans. Cambridge: Cambridge University Press.
1984 Distinction: A Social Critique of the Judgement of Taste. Richard Nice, trans. Cambridge: Harvard University Press.
1990 The Logic of Practice. Richard Nice, trans. Stanford: Stanford University Press.

Boxer, Major C. R.
1947 The Topasses of Timor. *Mededeling* No. LXXIII *Afdeling Volkenkunde* No. 24. Amsterdam: Uitgave Van Het Indisch Instituut.

Brown, Karen McCarthy
1987 "Voodoo." *In* The Encyclopedia of Religion, Vol. 15, Mircae Eliade, ed. Pp. 296–301. New York: Macmillan.

Bruner, Edward M.
1974 Urban Ethnicity. London: Tavistock Publications.

Carsten, Janet
1997 The Heat of the Hearth: The Process of Kinship in a Malay Fishing Community. New York: Oxford University Press.

Chagnon, Napoleon A.
1983 My Adventures with *Ebene:* A Religious Experience. *In* Yanomamo: The Fierce People. Fort Worth: Holt, Rinehart, and Winston.

Chandra Muzaffar
1993 Political Marginalization in Malaysia. *In* Indian Communities in Southeast Asia. K.S. Sandhu and A. Mani, eds. Pp. 211–236. Singapore: Times Academic Press.

Chavez, Leo R.
1998 [1992] Shadowed Lives: Undocumented Immigrants in American Society. Fort Worth, Texas: Holt, Rinehart and Winston.

Clammer, John R.
1986 Ethnic Processes in Urban Melaka. *In* Ethnicity and Ethnic Relations in Malaysia. Raymond Lee, ed. Pp. 47–72. DeKalb, Illinois: Center for Southeast Asian Studies, Northern Illinois University.

Colby, Benjamin N., James W. Fernandez, and David B. Kronenfield
1981 Toward a convergence of cognitive and symbolic anthropology. Symbolism and Cognition. Special Issue. American Ethnologist 8(3):422–450.

Collins, James T.
2001 Contesting Straits-Malayness: The Fact of Borneo. *In* Journal of Southeast Asian Studies 32(3):385–395.

Comaroff, Jean
1985 Body of Power, Spirit of Resistance. Chicago: University of Chicago Press.
Conklin, Beth A.
1995 "Thus are our Bodies, Thus was our Custom": Mortuary Cannibalism in an Amazonian Society. *In* American Ethnologist 22:75–101.
Conklin, Harold
1969 Lexicographical Treatment of Folk Taxonomies. *In* Cognitive Anthropology. Stephen Tyler, ed. New York: Holt, Rinehart and Winston.
Cunningham, Clark
1989 Celebrating a Toba Batak National Hero: An Indonesian Rite of Identity. *In* Changing Lives, Changing Rites: Ritual and Social Dynamics in Philippine and Indonesian Uplands. Susan D. Russell and Clark E. Cunningham, eds. Pp. 167–200. University of Michigan: Michigan Studies of South and Southeast Asia, No. 1.
D'Andrade, Roy
1995 The Development of Cognitive Anthropology. Cambridge: Cambridge University Press.
D'Andrade, Roy, and Claudia Strauss, eds.
1992 Human Motives and Cultural Models. Cambridge: Cambridge University Press.
Daniels, Timothy P.
1999 Imagining Selves and Inventing Festival Sriwijaya. Journal of Southeast Asian Studies 30(1):38–53.
2000a From Margin to Center, Anthropology's Pioneers: Ruminations on Du Bois, Davis, and Drake. Transforming Anthropology 9(1):30–43.
2000b Cognitive Convergence and Symbolic Advantage in Melaka and Kuching. *In* Borneo 2000: Ethnicity, Culture and Society. Proceedings of the Sixth Biennial Borneo Research Conference. Michael Leigh, ed. Pp. 166–194. Kuching: Universiti Malaysia Sarawak.
Davis, Allison, Burleigh Gardner, and Mary Gardner
1988 [1941] Deep South. Los Angeles: University of California. Department of Statistics, Malaysia
2002 Press Statement. Population Distribution and Basic Demographic Characteristics Report. Population and Housing Census 2000. http://www.statistics.gov.my.
Dominguez, Virginia R.
1989 People as Subject, People as Object: Selfhood and Peoplehood in Contemporary Israel. Madison: University of Wisconsin Press.
Dougherty (Keller), Janet W. D.,ed.
1985 Introduction. *In* Directions in Cognitive Anthropology. Pp. 3–14. Urbana: University of Illinois Press.
Drake, St. Clair
1940 Churches and Voluntary Association in the Chicago Negro Community. Chicago: Work Projects Administration District 3.
1963 Hide My Face? On Pan-Africanism and Negritude. *In* Soon, One Morning. Herbert Hill, ed. Pp. 78–105. New York: Alfred A. Knopf.

Drake, St. Clair, and Horace R. Cayton
1993 [1945] Black Metropolis: A Study of Negro Life in a Northern City. Chicago: University of Chicago Press.
Du Bois, W.E.B.
1935 Black Reconstruction. Millford: Kraus-Thomson Org. Ltd.
1973 [1899] The Philadelphia Negro. Philadelphia: University of Pennsylvania Press.
1989 [1903] The Souls of Black Folk. New York: Penguin Books.
Dumont, L.
1959 A structural definition of a folk deity of Tamil Nadu: Aiyanur, the Lord. Contributions to Indian Sociology, 3.
Festinger, Leon
1957 A Theory of Cognitive Dissonance. Stanford: Stanford University Press.
Flores, William V.
1997 Citizens and Citizenry: Undocumented Immigrants and Latino Cultural Citizenship. *In* Latino Cultural Citizenship: Claiming Identity, Space, and Rights. William V. Flores and Rina Benmayor, eds. Pp. 255–277. Boston: Beacon Press.
Flores, William V., and Rina Benmayor
1997 Introduction: Constructing Cultural Citizenship. *In* Latino Cultural Citizenship: Claiming Identity, Space, and Rights. William V. Flores and Rina Benmayor, eds. Pp. 1–23. Boston: Beacon Press.
Frith, Tabitha
2000 Ethno-Religious Identity and Urban Malays in Malaysia. Asian Ethnicity 1(2), September 2000, pp. 117–130.
Furnivall, J. S.
1956 [1948] Colonial Policy and Practice: A Comparative Study of Burma and Netherlands India. New York: New York University Press.
Geertz, Clifford
1960 Religion of Java. New York: Free Press.
1973 The Interpretation of Cultures. New York: Basic Books.
Gilroy, Paul
1991 [1987] 'There Ain't No Black in the Union Jack': The Cultural Politics of Race and Nation. Chicago: University of Chicago Press.
Goh Beng Lan
1998 Modern Dreams: An Enquiry into Power, Cityscape Transformations and Cultural Difference in Contemporary Malaysia. *In* Southeast Asian Identities. Joel S. Kahn, ed. Pp. 169–202. Singapore: Institute of Southeast Asian Studies.
Goh Cheng Teik
1989 Racial Politics in Malaysia. Kuala Lumpur: Syarikat Percetakan Lian Hup.
Goodenough, Ward H.
1951 Property, Kin and Community on Truk. New Haven: Yale University Publications in Anthropology No. 46.
1970 Description and Comparison in Cultural Anthropology. Chicago: Aldine.
1981 Culture, Language, and Society. Second Edition. Menlo Park, California: The Benjamin/Cummings Publishing Company, Inc.

Gramsci, Antonio
1971 Selections from the Prison Notebooks. Q. Hoare and G.N. Smith, eds and trans. London: Lawrence and Wishart (Notebooks).

Gregory, Steven
1999 Black Corona: Race and Politics of Place in an Urban Community. Princeton: Princeton University Press.

Gullick, J. M.
1963 Malaya. New York: Frederick A. Praeger, Inc.
1981 Malaysia: Economic Expansion and National Unity. London: Ernest Benn Ltd.

Gunn, Geoffrey C.
1999 Timor *Loro Sae:* 500 Years. Macau: Livros Do Oriente.

Guss, David M.
2000 The Festive State: Race, Ethnicity, and Nationalism as Cultural Performance. Berkeley: University of California Press.

Hack, Karl
1999 "Iron Claws on Malaya": The Historiography of the Malayan Emergency. Journal of Southeast Asian Studies 30(1):99–125.

Harakah
1999 *Pelajar Melayu semakin tersepit*/Malay secondary school students increasingly squeezed. 4 October, p. 7.
1999 *Cina Kelantan puji Nik Aziz*/Kelantan Chinese praise Nik Aziz. 4 October, p. 37. By Salman Husin.
2000 *Beri peluang usahawan Bumiputera majukan Primula Beach Resort*/Give Malay entrepreneurs the opportunity to develop Primula Beach Resort. 11 February, p. 28.

Harrison, Faye V.
1995 The Persistent Power of "Race" in the Cultural and Political Economy of Racism. Annual Review of Anthropology 24:47–74.

Hefner, Robert W.
2001 Introduction: Multiculturalism and Citizenship in Malaysia, Singapore, and Indonesia. *In* The Politics of Multiculturalism: Pluralism and Citizenship in Malaysia, Singapore, and Indonesia. Robert W. Hefner, ed. Pp. 1–58. Honolulu: University of Hawaii Press.

Heng Peck Koon
1998 Chinese Responses to Malay Hegemony in Peninsular Malaysia (1957–1996). *In* Cultural Contestations: Mediating Identities in a Changing Malaysian Society. Zawawi Ibrahim, ed. Pp. 51–82. London: ASEAN Academic Press.

Hollan, Douglas
1988 Pockets Full of Mistakes: The Personal Consequences of Religious Change in a Toraja Village. *In* Oceania 58(3):275–289.

Holland, Dorothy, and Margaret Eisenhart
1990 Educated in Romance: Women, Achievement and College Culture. Chicago: University of Chicago Press.

Holland, Dorothy, and Naomi Quinn, eds.
1987 Cultural Models in Language and Thought. Cambridge: Cambridge University Press.

Hoyt, Sarniah Hayes
1993 Old Malacca. Kuala Lumpur: Oxford University Press.
Hutchins, Edwin
1980 Culture and Inference. Cambridge: Harvard University Press.
Ifekwunigwe, Jayne O.
1999 Scattered Belongings: Cultural Paradoxes of "Race," Nation and Gender. London: Routledge.
Jackendoff, Ray
1993 Languages of the Mind: Essays on Mental Representations. Cambridge, Massachusetts: The MIT Press.
Jackson, Peter, and Jan Penrose, eds.
1993 Introduction: placing "race" and nation. *In* Constructions of Race, Place and Nation. Pp. 1–23. London: UCL Press.
Jacobs, Michelle
2000 Coming Full Circle: The African-American Struggle for Full Citizenship under Color of Law. Transforming Anthropology 9(1):44–46.
Jain, M. P.
1992 Fundamental Rights in Malaysia. *In* Constitutional Systems in Late Twentieth Century Asia. Lawrence W. Beer, ed. Pp. 528–570. Seattle: University of Washington Press.
Jesudson, James V.
1989 Ethnicity and the Economy: The State, Chinese Business, and Multinationals in Malaysia. Singapore: Oxford University Press.
Ju Shi Huey
1983 Chinese Spirit Mediums in Singapore: An Ethnographic Study. *In* Contributions to Southeast Asian Ethnography. Number 2 (August):3–48. Studies in Chinese Folk Religion in Singapore and Malaysia. Singapore: The Board of Editors, Contributions to Southeast Asian Ethnography.
Kahn, Joel S., ed.
1996 Growth, economic transformation, culture and the middle classes in Malaysia. *In* The New Rich in Asia: Mobile phones, McDonald's and middle-class revolution. Richard Robison and David S. G. Goodman, eds. Pp. 40–78. London: Routledge.
1998 Introduction. *In* Southeast Asian Identities. Pp. 1–27. Singapore: Institute of Southeast Asian Studies.
Keesing, Roger M.
1970 Toward a Model of Role Analysis. *In* A Handbook of Method in Cultural Anthropology. Raoul Naroll and Ronald Cohen, eds. Pp. 423–453. Garden City, New York: The Natural History Press.
Keller, Charles M., and Janet Dixon Keller
1996 Cognition and tool use: The blacksmith at work. Cambridge: Cambridge University Press.
Kertzer, David
1988 Ritual, Politics, and Power. New Haven: Yale University Press.
Khatoon, Zohra
1990 Muslim Saints and Their Shrines. Jammu, India: Jay Kay Book House.

Khoo Kay Kim
1993 Malay Attitudes towards Indians. *In* Indian Communities in Southeast Asia. K.S. Sandhu and A. Mani, eds. Pp. 266–287. Singapore: Times Academic Press.
1996 The Melaka Sultanate: Internal Administration and Control of Its Empire. Sejarah: Jurnal Jabatan Sejarah Universiti Malaya. No. 4. Pp. 37–47.

Kijang Puteh
1972 Harvest Drums. NST Annual 1972. Kuala Lumpur: TST Press (Malaya) Berhad.

Kuper, Adam
1999 Culture: The Anthropologists' Account. Cambridge: Harvard University Press.

Lave, Jean, and Etienne Wenger
1991 Situated Learning: Legitimate peripheral participation. Cambridge: Cambridge University Press.

Lee, Raymond L. M.
1986 Symbols of Separatism: Ethnicity and Status Politics in Contemporary Malaysia. *In* Ethnicity and Ethnic Relations in Malaysia. Raymond Lee, ed. Pp. 28–46. DeKalb, Illinois: Center for Southeast Asian Studies, Northern Illinois University.
1987 Amulets and Anthropology: A Paranormal Encounter with Malay Magic. *In* Anthropology and Humanism Quarterly 12(3–4):69–74.

Lehman, F.K.
1967 Ethnic Categories in Burma and the Theory of Social Systems. *In* Southeast Asian Tribes, Minorities, and Nations. Peter Kundstadter, ed. Pp. 93–124. Princeton: Princeton University Press.
1995 Cognitive Science Research Notes (14). Notes on Logical Form in an Intensionalist Semantics. Unpublished paper.
1996 Can God Be Coerced? Structural Correlates of Merit and Blessing in Some Southeast Asian Religions. *In* Merit and Blessing in Mainland Southeast Asia in Comparative Perspective. Cornelia Ann Kammerer and Nicola Tannenbaum, eds. New Haven, Connecticut: Yale University Southeast Asia Studies.
1997 Cognitive Science Research Notes. Unpublished papers.
2000 Cultural Models (and Schemata) and Generative Knowledge Domains: How Are They Related? Paper for the panel on Cultural Models and Schema Theory, American Anthropological Association Annual Meeting. Unpublished paper.

Lehmann, Arthur C.
2001 Eyes of the *Ngangas:* Ethnomedicine and Power in Central African Republican. *In* Magic, Witchcraft, and Religion: An Anthropological Study of the Supernatural. Mountain View: Mayfield Publishing Company.

Lian, Kwen Fee
2001 The Construction of Malay Identity across Nations, Malaysia, Singapore, and Indonesia. *In* Bijdragen tot de Taal-, Land en Volkenkunde 157(4):861–879.

Lim, Linda Y. C.
1983 Chinese Economic Activity in Southeast Asia: An Introductory Review. *In* The Chinese in Southeast Asia, Volume 1: Ethnicity and Economic Activity. Linda Y. C. Lim and L. A. Peter Gosling, eds. Pp. 1–29. Singapore: Maruzen Asia.

Loh Kok Wah, Francis, and Joel S. Kahn
1992 Introduction: Fragmented Visions. *In* Fragmented Visions: Culture and Politics in Contemporary Malaysia. Joel S. Kahn and Francis Loh Kok Wah, eds. Pp. 1–17. Honolulu: University of Hawaii Press.

Lounsbury, Floyd
1964 A Formal Account of the Crow- and Omaha-Type Kinship Terminologies. *In* Explorations in Cultural Anthropology. W. H. Goodenough, ed. New York: McGraw-Hill.

Mahathir Mohamad
1970 The Malay Dilemma. Singapore: Times Books International.
1999 A New Deal for Asia. Subang Jaya: Pelanduk Publications (M) Sdn. Bhd.

Mandal, Sumit K.
2001 Boundaries and Beyond: Whither the Cultural Bases of Political Community in Malayasia? *In* The Politics of Multiculturalism: Pluralism and Citizenship in Malaysia, Singapore, and Indonesia. Robert W. Hefner, ed. Pp. 141–164. Honolulu: University of Hawaii Press.

Mani, A.
1993a Indians in North Sumatra. *In* Indian Communities in Southeast Asia. K.S. Sandhu and A. Mani, eds. Pp. 46–97. Singapore: Times Academic Press.
1993b Indians in Jakarta. *In* Indian Communities in Southeast Asia. K.S. Sandhu and A. Mani, eds. Pp. 98–130. Singapore: Times Academic Press.

Manzo, Kathryn A.
1996 Creating Boundaries: The Politics of Race and Nation. Boulder, Colorado: Lynne Rienner Publishers.

Mauer, Bill
1997 Recharting the Caribbean. Ann Arbor: University of Michigan Press.

Mearns, David James
1995 Shiva's Other Children: Religion and Social Identity amongst Overseas Indians. New Delhi: Sage Publications.

Milner, Anthony
1998 Ideological Work in Constructing Malay Majority. *In* Making Majorities: Constituting the Nation in Japan, Korea, China, Malaysia, Fiji, Turkey, and the United States. Dru C. Gladney ed. Pp. 151–169. Stanford, California: Stanford University Press.

Mitchell, Katharyne
1997 Transnational Subjects: Constituting the Cultural Citizen in the Era of Pacific Rim Capital. *In* Ungrounded Empires: The Cultural Politics of Modern Chinese Transnationalism. Aihwa Ong and Donald M. Nonini, eds. Pp. 228–256. New York: Routledge.

Mohd. Taib Osman
1984 Bunga Rampai: Aspects of Malay Culture. Kuala Lumpur: Dewan Bahasa dan Pustaka, Kementerian Pendidikan Malaysia.

Murdock, George P.
1949 Social Structure. New York: Macmillan.

Nagata, Judith
1980 Religious Ideology and Social Change: The Islamic Revival in Malaysia. Pacific Affairs 53:405–439.

1993 Religious and Ethnicity among the Indian Muslims of Malaysia. *In* Indian Communities in Southeast Asia. K.S. Sandhu and A. Mani, eds. Pp. 513–540. Singapore: Times Academic Press.

Ng Siew Hua, Cecilia
1983 The Sam Poh Neo Neo Keramat: A Study of a Baba Chinese Temple. *In* Contributions to Southeast Asian Ethnography. Number 2 (August):98–131. Studies in Chinese Folk Religion in Singapore and Malaysia. Singapore: The Board of Editors, Contributions to Southeast Asian Ethnography.

Nonini, Donald M.
1997 Shifting Identities, Positioned Imaginaries: Transnational Traversals and Reversals by Malaysian Chinese. *In* Ungrounded Empires: The Cultural Politics of Modern Chinese Transnationalism. Aihwa Ong and Donald M. Nonini, eds. Pp. 203–227. New York: Routledge.

Ong, Aihwa
1987 Spirits of Resistance and Capitalist Discipline: Factory Women in Malaysia. Albany: State University of New York Press.
1993 On the edges of empires: Flexible citizenship among cosmopolitan Chinese. Positions 1:745–778.
1999 Cultural Citizenship as Subject Making: Immigrants Negotiate Racial and Cultural Boundaries in the United States. *In* Race, Identity, and Citizenship: A Reader. Rodolfo D. Torres, Louis F. Miron, and Jonathan Xavier Inda, eds. Pp. 262–293. Malden, Massachusetts: Blackwell Publishers.

Ong, Aihwa, and Donald M. Nonini
1997 Introduction: Chinese Transnationalism as an Alternative Modernity. *In* Ungrounded Empires: The Cultural Politics of Modern Chinese Transnationalism. Aihwa Ong and Donald M. Nonini, eds. Pp. 2–33. New York: Routledge.

Ortner, Sherry B.
1984 Theory in Anthropology since the Sixties. Comparative Studies in Society and History 26(1):126–166.

Puttick, Elizabeth
1997 Women in New Religions: In Search of Community, Sexuality, and Spiritual Power. New York: St. Martin's Press.

Quinn, Naomi
1984 Commitment in American Marriage. *In* Directions in Cognitive Anthropology. Janet W. D. Dougherty (Keller), ed. Pp. 291–320. Urbana: University of Illinois Press.
1987 Convergent Evidence for a Cultural Model of American Marriage. *In* Cultural Models in Language and Thought. D. Holland and N. Quinn, eds. Cambridge: Cambridge University Press.

Radcliffe-Brown, A. R.
1958 Social Structure. *In* Method in Social Anthropology, Selected Essays by A. R. Radcliffe-Brown. M. N. Srinivas, ed. Pp. 166–177. Chicago: University of Chicago Press.

Reid, Anthony
2001 Understanding Melayu (Malay) as a Source of Diverse Modern Identities. *In* Journal of Southeast Asian Studies 32(3):295–313.

Rex, John
1996 Ethnic Minorities in the Modern Nation State. New York: St. Martin's Press.
Robison, Richard, and David S. G. Goodman, eds.
1996 The new rich in Asia: economic development, social status and political consciousness. *In* The New Rich in Asia: Mobile phones, McDonald's and middle-class revolution. Pp. 1–18. London: Routledge.
Rosald, Renato
1994a Cultural Citizenship in San Jose, California. Polar 17:57–63.
1994b Cultural Citizenship and Educational Democracy. Cultural Anthropology 9(3):402–411.
1997 Cultural Citizenship, Inequality, and Multiculturalism. *In* Latino Cultural Citizenship: Claiming Identity, Space, and Rights. William V. Flores and Rina Benmayor, eds. Pp. 27–38. Boston: Beacon Press.
Sahlins, Marshall
1981 Historical Metaphors and Mythical Realities: Structure in the Early History of the Sandwich Islands Kingdom. Ann Arbor: The University of Michigan Press.
Sands, Robert R., and F.K. Lehman
1995 The Nature of Social Identity and Identity Relationships. Unpublished paper.
Sanjek, Roger
1994 Intermarriage and the Future of Races in the United States. *In* Race. Steven Gregory and Roger Sanjek, eds. Pp. 101–130. New Brunswick, NJ: Rutgers University Press.
Schulte Nordholt, H. G.
1971 The Political System of the Atoni of Timor. *Verhandelingen Van Het Koninklijk Instituut Voor Taal-, Land- En Volkenkunde.* The Hague: Martinuus Nijhoff.
Sergei, Kan
1991 Shamanism and Christianity: Modern-Day Tlingit Elders Look at the Past. *In* Ethnohistory 38(4):363–387.
Shapiro, Judith
1987 From Tupa to the Land Without Evil: The Christianization of Tupi-Guarani Cosmology. *In* American Ethnologist 14(1):126–139.
Sharp, Lesley A.
1994 Exorcists, Psychiatrists, and the Problems of Possession in Northwest Madagascar. *In* Social Science Medicine 38(4):525–542.
Sta. Maria, Bernard
1982 My People, My Country: The Story of the Malacca Portuguese Community. Malacca: The Malacca Portuguese Development Centre.
Sta. Maria, Joseph
1994 *Undi Nos By Di Aki?* [Where Do We Go from Here?]. Malacca: Joseph Sta. Maria.
Sarkissian, Margaret
1997 Cultural Chameleons: Portuguese Eurasian Strategies for Survival in Postcolonial Malaysia. Journal of Southeast Asian Studies 28(2):249–262.
1998 Tradition, Tourism, and the Cultural Show: Malaysia's Diversity on Display. Journal of Musicological Research 17:87–112.
2000 D'Albuquerque's Children: Performing Tradition in Malaysia's Portuguese Settlement. Chicago: University of Chicago Press.

Schlesinger, Arthur M., Jr.
1992 [1991] The Disuniting of America. New York: W.W. Norton & Company.
Scott, James
1976 The Moral Economy of the Peasant: Subsistence and Rebellion in Southeast Asia. New Haven: Yale University Press.
1985 Weapons of the Weak: Everyday Forms of Peasant Resistance. New Haven: Yale University Press.
1990 Everyday Forms of Peasant Resistance. *In* Customs in Conflict. Manning and Philibert, eds. Pp. 413–448. Petersborough: broadview press.
1992 Domination, Acting, and Fantasy. *In* The Paths to Domination, Resistance, and Terror. Nordstrom and Martin, eds. Pp. 55–84. Berkeley: University of California Press.
Shaari Mohd. Noor, Jamaliah Kamis, David Fong Chong Sin, and Lim Kar Keng, eds.
1985 Festivals and Religious Occasions In Malaysia (First Series). Kuala Lumpur: National Unity Department.
Shamsul A.B.
1994 Religion and Ethnic Politics in Malaysia: The Significance of the Islamic Resurgence Phenomenon. *In* Asian Visions of Authority: Religion and the Modern States of East and Southeast Asia. Charles F. Keyes, Laurel Kendall, and Helen Hardcare, eds. Pp. 99–116. Honolulu: University of Hawaii Press.
1998a Bureacratic Management of Identity in a Modern State: "Malayness" in Postwar Malaysia. *In* Making Majorities: Constituting the Nation in Japan, Korea, China, Malaysia, Fiji, Turkey, and the United States. Dru C. Gladney, ed. Pp. 135–150. Stanford, California: Stanford University Press.
1998b Debating about Identity in Malaysia: A Discourse Analysis. *In* Cultural Contestations: Mediating Identities in a Changing Malaysian Society. Zawawi Ibrahim, ed. Pp. 17–50. London: ASEAN Academic Press.
Siddique, Sharon
2001 Corporate Pluralism: Singapore Inc. and the Association of Muslim Professionals. *In* The Politics of Multiculturalism: Pluralism and Citizenship in Malaysia, Singapore, and Indonesia. Robert W. Hefner, ed. Pp. 165–182. Honolulu: University of Hawaii Press.
Shore, Bradd
1996 Culture in Mind: Cognition, Culture, and the Problem of Meaning. New York: Oxford University Press.
Skinner, William G.
1957 Chinese Society in Thailand: An Analytic History. Ithaca: Cornell University Press.
1960 Change and Persistence in Chinese Culture Overseas. Journal of the South Sea Society 16:86–100.
Slotkin, J.S.
1956 The Peyote Way. *In* Tomorrow 4(3):64–70, (1955–1956).
Smith, M. G.
1965 The Plural Society in the British West Indies. Berkeley: University of California Press.

Smitherman, Geneva
1977 Talkin and Testifyin: The Language of Black America. Detroit: Wayne State University Press.

Soo Khin Wah
1990 The Cult of Mazu in Peninsular Malaysia. *In* Contributions to Southeast Asian Ethnography. Tan Chee-Beng, ed. Number 9 (December):29–51. The Preservation and Adaptation of Tradition: Studies of Chinese Religious Expression in Southeast Asia. Singapore: The Editors, Contributions to Southeast Asian Ethnography.

Stack, Carol
1996 Call to home: African Americans Reclaim the Rural South. New York: BasicBooks.

Strauss, Claudia
1992a Models and Motives. *In* Human Motives and Cultural Models. Roy D'Andrade and Claudia Strauss, eds. Pp. 1–20. Cambridge: Cambridge University Press.
1992b What makes Tony run? Schemas as motives reconsidered. *In* Human Motives and Cultural Models. Roy D'Andrade and Claudia Strauss, eds. Pp. 197–224. Cambridge: Cambridge University Press.

Tan Chee-Beng, ed.
1990a Editor's Introduction. *In* Contributions to Southeast Asian Ethnography. Number 9 (December):1–4. The Preservation and Adaptation of Tradition: Studies of Chinese Religious Expression in Southeast Asia. Singapore: The Editors, Contributions to Southeast Asian Ethnography.
1990b Chinese Religion and Local Chinese Communities in Malaysia. *In* Contributions to Southeast Asian Ethnography. Number 9 (December):5–27. Singapore: The Editors, Contributions to Southeast Asian Ethnography.

Tan Sooi Beng
1992 Counterpoints in the Performing Arts of Malaysia. *In* Fragmented Visions: Culture and Politics in Contemporary Malaysia. Joel S. Kahn and Francis Loh Kok Wah, eds. Pp. 282–302. Honolulu: University of Hawaii Press.

Taylor, Christopher S.
1999 In the Vicinity of the Righteous: Ziyara and the Veneration of Muslim Saints in Late Medieval Egypt. Leiden: Brill.

The New Straits Times
1998 Malaysians celebrate Deepavali in unity. 20 October, p.14.
1999 Fair share for everyone. Dr M: Not proper for any one race to demand everything for itself. 5 November, p.1. By Carolyn Hong.

The Sun
1998 Real cause for joy. 25 December, p. 1.
1999 'Malaysian Malaysia' favours only one race. 14 May, p.2.
1999 MYC (Malaysian Youth Council) derides Malaysian-Malaysia concept. 14 May.
1999 DAP wants UMNO to stop sensitive claims. 16 May.
1999 Racial polarisation among students is real. Comment & Letters. 14 October, p. 16. By Susie, Klang.

1999 We see segregation as the norm. Comment & Letters. 15 October, p. 19. By Ex-teacher, Malacca.

1999 Paper does injustice to varsities and students. 15 October, p. 19. By S. Lakshmi, Petaling Jaya.

1999 UM making effort to increase racial interaction. 16 October. By Hizreen Kamal.

1999 22 taken to undisclosed destination. 7 July, p. 2.

2000 PM: Don't be ungrateful. 8 January, p. 2.

2000 State acts to curb grave worshipping. 17 May, p. 6. By Geetha Renganathan.

2000 Pulau Besar faces a grave situation. 24 May, p. 14. By Geetha Renganathan.

Torres, Rodolfo D., Louis F. Miron, and Jonathan Xavier Inda, eds.

1999 Introduction. *In* Race, Identity, and Citizenship: A Reader. Pp. 1–16. Malden, Massachusetts: Blackwell Publishers.

Turner, Victor

1969 The Ritual Process. Ithaca: Cornell University Press.

1974 Dramas, Fields, and Metaphors: Symbolic Action in Human Society. Ithaca, NY: Cornell University Press.

Urciuoli, Bonnie

1995 Exposing Prejudice: Puerto Rican Experiences of Language, Race, and Class. Boulder: Westview Press.

U.S. Government (Central Intelligence Agency)

2003 Map of Malaysia. *In* CIA World Factbook. New York: Bartleby.com.

Van Gennep, A.

1960 [1909] The Rites of Passage. London: Routledge and Kegan Paul Ltd.

Wallerstein, I.

1974 The Modern World-System: Capitalist Agriculture and the Origins of the European World-Economy in the Sixteenth Century. New York: Academic Press, Inc.

Wan Hashim

1983 Race Relations in Malaysia. Kuala Lumpur: Heinemann Educational Books (Asia) Ltd.

Williams, Brett

1988 Upscaling Downtown. Ithaca: Cornell University Press.

Williams, Raymond

1977 Marxism and Literature. Oxford: Oxford University Press.

Wilson, R. A., and F. Keil, eds.

1999 The MIT Encyclopedia of the Cognitive Sciences. Cambridge, MA: MIT Press/A Bradford Book.

Winzeler, Robert L.

1987 Ethnic Groups and the Control of Natural Resources in Kelantan, Malaysia. *In* Ethnic Diversity and the Control of Natural Resources in Southeast Asia. A. Terry Rambo, Kathleen Gillogly, and Karl L. Hutterer, eds. Pp. 83–98. Ann Arbor: University of Michigan Press.

Witherspoon, Gary

1977 Language and art in the Navajo universe. Ann Arbor: University of Michigan Press.

Wolf, Eric R.
1958 The Virgin of Guadalupe: A Mexican National Symbol. *In* Journal of American Folklore 71:279–284.

World Conference against Racism, Racial Discrimination, Xenophobia and Related Intolerance
2001 Declaration and Programme for Action.

Yelvington, Kevin A.
1995 Producing Power: Ethnicity, Gender, and Class in a Caribbean Workplace. Philadelphia: Temple University Press.

Yoshihiro, Tsubouchi
2001 One Malay Village: A Thirty-Year Community Study. Kyoto: Kyoto University Press.

Yuval-Davis, Nira
1991 The Citizenship Debate: Women, Ethnic Processes and the State. Feminist Review 39:58–68.

Zawawi Ibrahim
1998 Introduction: Mediating Identities in a Changing Malaysian Society. *In* Cultural Contestations: Mediating Identities in a Changing Malaysian Society. Zawawi Ibrahim, ed. Pp. 11–15. London: ASEAN Academic Press Ltd.

Index

A

Adat (customary principles and practices) *perpatih* 72; *temenggong* 72
Administration of Muslim Law Enactment of 1959, 49
affirmative action 97, 99, 239
ancient Muslim graves 50, 164, 166, 170, 176, 226
Anglo-Dutch Treaty 28
Anwar Ibrahim
  arrest and imprisonment *xxii*
  background and protests 83
  comparison to Hang Jebat 21
  in museum exhibit 140
Alternative Front 93

B

Baba and *Nyonya* (Straits-born Chinese)
  attire in exhibit 151
  social identity 68
Benjamin Lee Whorf 273
Benedict Anderson 5
British colonists 28
Buddhist Association of Malacca Temple 162
Bumiputera
  benefits 192, 201–2, 216, 234–9, 252, 272
  census *xv*
  honorary 26, 192, 204–5
  in discourse 98
  special rights *xix*, 40

C

Catholic Charismatic movement 66, 190
census figures *xv*
Cheng Ho 19, 142, 151
Chap Goh Mei celebration 160
Chinese
  associations 208
  census *xv*
  clan names 63
  Chingay group 126, 129
  European nicknames 63
  in Mariamman Festival 157
  lion dance group 120
  maximal identity 61
  pre-colonial presence 23
  religion 61, 159, 161
  submaximal categories 73
  subvert Malay hegemony 174, 176–7, 266
  superiority 33, 217, 249–50, 254, 260
  suppression of *xix*
Chinese New Year 173, 176
Chitty (Straits-born Indians)
  attire in exhibit 151
  social identity 69
Christmas 82, 172, 175
citizenship
  and cultural show 123
  and gender 35–6, 39
  cultural 7, 42–3, 153, 170, 177, 183, 197, 225, 261, 264–5
  inherent contradictions 5
  in liberal nations 4
  legal 7, 35, 38–9, 42, 264, 270
  schemata of 94
civil society
  and British colonialism 32
  and voluntary associations 209
  path of refinement 276
class